W9-BYC-458

contents

Introduction

Working with a natural material such as wood is both a rewarding and satisfying pastime. Wood has a special quality that is like no other material—it is a pleasure to touch and a delight to look at.

Above: Much of the joy of working with wood is derived from the fact that it is a natural living product.

Opposite: This dining chair (see pages 375–83) combines elegant design and functionality while displaying a high degree of skill in woodworking.

Every piece of lumber is unique, with a diversity of color, texture, and strength. Its versatility and unique qualities are a source of constant inspiration to the creative woodworker. It is an appreciation of these qualities, combined with good function and design, that will give you many years of enjoyment in fine furniture making.

To gain the most pleasure from your woodworking experience, it is important to give yourself a firm skill base that will allow your interest and enthusiasm to develop fully. To help you achieve this, this book has been divided into four sections.

The opening chapter, "Wood and other materials," gives general information on the foundations of woodworking, including an introduction to the natural resource of timber

and its unique qualities and challenges. This will help you to make the right choices when you come to choose, buy, and store wood for yourself.

The second chapter, "Design and construction," concentrates on the importance of design and shows how every piece that you make needs to be both functional and aesthetically pleasing. There are useful tips that will help you to achieve a harmonious balance between the two.

The third chapter, "Tools and techniques," moves onto the practicalities of woodworking. It opens with advice about workshop design, and the accessories and tools that you will need to begin your woodworking experience. All the basic skills needed to produce fine woodwork are clearly and succinctly explained

Project rating

Basic
Simple woodworking exercises that are suitable for beginners.

Intermediate
Moderately difficult projects for those woodworkers who have some previous experience.

Advanced
Complex, challenging projects for more advanced woodworkers.

Right: Coming to grips with basic woodworking skills is a fundamental part of your woodworking adventure.

Far right: Make sure that you have all the necessary tools that you need for each project before you start.

with illustrations and photographs to help wherever relevant. From straightforward common processes, such as sawing and planing, and to more specialized aspects of woodworking, such as carving and turning, this section will enable you to master and develop your skills.

The fourth chapter features stylish projects that will enable you to put your skills into practice. Divided into basic, intermediate, and advanced, you will be able to go straight to a project that is suitable for your level of expertise. From a simple letter rack, to a challenging

workbench, to a complex linen chest, these pieces will make stunning additions to your home.

Each project contains a materials list, a tools list, and step-by-step instructions. Illustrations and photographs are included to help you complete each project, and drawings show the sizes of components and how they fit together. Measurements are given both in imperial—feet, inches, and fractions of an inch—and metric—meters and millmeters. It is important to choose one method or the other as the measurements are not direct conversions. Do not use

a mixture of the two as the project may not work out exactly. When beginning the projects, do not cut all the lumber to the size given in the materials list. Work through the steps and always check measurements as you progress.

This book provides a sound foundation for the acquisition and development of your woodworking knowledge and skills. It also provides you with the opportunity to develop your skills through a wide range of interesting, creative, and useful projects. The importance of precision and accuracy are emphasized, as is the need to develop a sense of appreciation, and an ability to produce quality work. Producing quality work requires much effort and skill, but the sense of achievement and the pleasure of working with the unique natural resource of wood are what makes woodworking such a popular and rewarding experience.

Right: An elegant linen chest—just one of the challenging projects that lies ahead in this book.

Wood
and other
materials

A natural resource

Timber is a natural product, unlike so many of the materials we use for everyday living. So the woodworker could be said to renew the essential bond between man and nature that has, to some extent, been lost in our modern world.

The beauty of a growing tree contributes to the pleasure of woodwork.

The range of different timber species—both hardwoods and softwoods—offers an extremely wide choice of materials. Each species has its own properties and characteristics. Even when using the same species of timber, each piece will present different challenges. They will also differ in appearance, giving variations in color, pattern, texture, and finish.

In order to gain the best results from working with timber, it is important to be aware of some basic facts about the material—for example, how trees grow, how they are converted for use, and how we can utilize these characteristics.

ECOLOGICAL CONCERNS

The issue of ecological matters is an important concern, and it has rightly become difficult to source endangered species. It is now recognized that forests must be maintained to ensure a continuous supply of quality trees. In a well-run forest, mature timber is extracted with care and new planting is constantly taking place. The science of forestry has greatly improved in the developed world and pressure is also being put on developing countries to ensure forests are carefully managed so that the disastrous effects of deforestation are avoided in the future. Many nations are also seeking to help sustain their economies by not exporting the logs they produce, but carrying out conversion nearer the source.

HOW A TREE GROWS

To appreciate the various properties of timber, it is useful to understand how a tree grows and to learn about its structure. A tree is an extremely efficient organism. The trunk is the main conduit for transferring water and minerals, which are absorbed from the soil through the roots. The leaves of the tree take in carbon dioxide, give off oxygen, and harness the energy of light, which, through the process of photosynthesis, produces all the nutrients that the tree requires to thrive.

Tree structure

The trunk's structure consists of tubular cells, which are held together with a chemical known as lignin. The direction of these cells determines the nature of the timber's grain. The cells tend to be long and thin, running lengthwise along the trunk and branches.

Food storage and the sap circulation take place through the cells of a tree. In a softwood tree the cells have a simple structure of hollow, spindle-like cells, while hardwood trees have long and needle-like cells. This difference in cell structure is what distinguishes a softwood from a hardwood.

A section through the tree's trunk shows the pith at the center. This is formed from the original sapling, is often weak and can suffer from fungal attack. The heartwood, which surrounds the pith, is the mature timber that forms the structure of the tree as well as providing some food transference. Sapwood surrounds the heartwood, and is where most of the transference and storage of nutrients takes place. Sapwood from most timbers is not used for furniture making since it offers little resistance to fungal and insect attack.

A tree trunk has medullary rays, or ray cells, which conduct nutrients through the sapwood. These medullary rays

A cross-section of this tree trunk shows the various layers of growth.

are usually quite visible in hardwoods, but can be difficult to see in softwoods.

Growth rings

Each year, the tree grows because the living cells in the cambium layer, which lies immediately behind the bark, sub-divide. As the tree grows, the cells in the cambium layer develop into specialized sapwood cells, and a new sapwood ring is formed around the growth from the previous year. At the same time, the oldest sapwood converts into heartwood. This means that, with each period of annual growth, the heartwood becomes larger, while the size of the sapwood does not vary much during the life of a tree.

This annual growth is seen in concentric rings, or growth rings, through the timber and can be used to determine a tree's age. Each growth ring contains large earlywood and smaller latewood cells. Early-wood is the part of the annual growth rings that grows at the start of the season. Latewood is produced toward the end of the season, and is usually denser and darker.

The growth rings in hardwood timber are either ring porous or diffuse porous. Ring-porous timber shows a difference in cellular structure between timber laid down in the different growth periods—open cells when the tree is growing in spring and summer, and tighter grouped cells when growth slows in fall and winter. Diffuse-porous timber is found in trees where there are no marked seasonal changes and the cells are regular in size. This more even distribution and regularity of fibers make diffuse-porous hardwoods, such as beech, easier to plane and sand than ring-porous ones, such as ash or oak.

latewood | earlywood

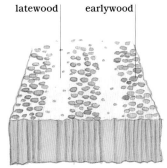

Earlywood and latewood

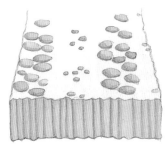

Ring-porous timber

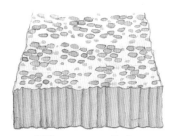

Diffuse-porous timber

Hardwoods and softwoods

The terms "hardwood" and "softwood" do not refer to the hardness or softness of a specific tree species. They are biological divisions into which trees are grouped and not a description of the wood's durability.

Even though most hardwoods are hard and most softwoods are soft, hardness cannot be used to classify different woods. Balsa is a hardwood and some softwoods can be very hard.

Hardwoods grow in most parts of the world, and are generally preferred by furniture makers. Although they are often more expensive than softwoods, they are usually more durable and come in a larger range of colors with widely varying characteristics. They can, however, be difficult to obtain and a few of the more expensive, exotic hardwoods are cut into veneer sheets to make better use of the lumber. Most countries have indigenous species, even though fashion has, in the past, led to the importation of particular types for specific uses, such as teak for outdoor furniture and boats and mahogany for fine furniture.

Softwoods are usually light in color, ranging from off-white to mid-brown. They can be easily identified from the growth rings where the contrasting grain pattern of the earlywood and latewood is found—these differ in color and density. Softwoods often have a more open grain, are easier to work, and are generally used for building and carpentry work. Fashion has intervened, however, and there is a strong market in many countries for pine furniture.

Below left: Hardwood trees growing in their natural habitat.

Below: Some softwood trees growing in their natural habitat.

Species of hardwood

The term "hardwood" generally refers to trees that have broad leaves. Hardwoods are found in both temperate and tropical climates and can be either deciduous or evergreen. They are generally preferred by furniture makers because they have a wider range of colors and textures.

Ash trees produce lumber particularly suited to laminating and bending.

Pericopsis elata **AFRORMOSIA**
Origin: West Africa
Characteristics: Durable type of wood, with a grain that varies from straight to interlocked. Yellow-brown in color, which darkens over time when exposed to light. It is similar to teak but is less oily and often used as a teak substitute in furniture making (as is iroko, see page 18).

Fraxinus spp. **ASH**
Origin: Europe (right), North America (left)
Characteristics: Heartwood and sapwood of similar color in pink, gray, and cream. Prominent growth rings best highlighted using back-cut of live-sawn board with a tangential cut. Quarter-sawn boards produce straight grain. Suitable for laminating and steam-bending. Sands and finishes well.

Fagus spp. **BEECH**
Origin: All over Europe, best from Baltic regions
Characteristics: This type of wood is whitish in color with little variation between sapwood and heartwood. Growth rings visible with distinctive fleck produced by medullary rays. Easily worked and commonly used in furniture for bent wood pieces. Cracking and warping can occur if seasoning is not carefully controlled.

Buxus sempervirens
BOXWOOD
Origin: Southern Europe and parts of West Asia
Characteristics: Boxwood is a fine and even-textured wood; straight grain and dense. Often found as a hedgerow tree and therefore seldom available to buy in lumber form. It is most commonly used for making small items of furniture, such as those produced by turning or carving.

Liriodendron tulipifera
AMERICAN TULIP TREE
Origin: Central and South America
Characteristics: Dense and fairly hard. Texture can vary but it usually has irregular grain. The wood has very attractive color, ranging from pink to red stripes over a yellow base. Difficult to work and, due to limited availability, it is used for smaller items or veneering.

Toona Australis
AUSTRALIAN CEDAR
Origin: East coast of Australia
Characteristics: Rich red color in heartwood; sapwood pale cream to pink. Medium-density with tendency to be a little soft—requires careful handling. Good grain pattern in back-cut boards; quarter-sawn boards produce straight, even grain. Scarce and expensive in large section sizes. Sands and polishes to mirror finish.

Acacia melanoxylon **BLACKWOOD**
Origin: Tasmania and east coast of Australia
Characteristics: Medium-weight hardwood. Sometimes called Tasmanian blackwood, the resins can stain your hands black. Fairly straight grain, but can have fiddleback appearance. Pink-yellow to mud-brown tones with dark-brown growth rings. Works well with sharp tools. Sands to a high polish.

Guilbourtia demensei **BUBINGA**
Also known as African rosewood
Origin: West Africa
Characteristics: Coarse but even-textured wood; grain varies from straight to interlocked and irregular; relatively durable. Bubinga is red-brown in color with a purple hue. It can be used in fine furniture making when crafted and finished.

Cedrela **CEDRELA**
Origin: Brazil and Mexico
Characteristics: Cedrela is a prized wood from Brazil that is used extensively in furniture manufacturing throughout Europe. White-colored sapwood, tending to pink; heartwood pinkish brown with purplish highlights. Works particularly well and has a fine texture, allowing you to achieve a high-quality finish with minimal effort. Sands, glues, and polishes well.

Ceratopetalum apetalem
COACHWOOD
Also known as satinwood
Origin: Australian east-coast rainforests
Characteristics: Pink to light brown color with good grain pattern when tangentially cut and straight grain when quarter-sawn. Easily machined with distinctive odor when cut or sanded. Finishes well with hand tools, sands well, and accepts most polishes. Becoming hard to get and relatively expensive.

Ulmus spp. **ELM**
Also known as nave or red elm
Origin: Central and Southern Europe, Scandinavia and North America
Characteristics: Sapwood yellow to white, contrasting with brownish red heartwood. Medullary rays are not prominent and pores are fine, giving a fine texture. Used in carpentry and cabinetmaking. Difficult to achieve fine finish.

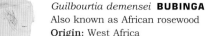

Cherry wood is particularly good for cabinetmaking.

Milicia spp. **IROKO**
Origin: West Africa
Characteristics: Medium yellow-brown in color and can be difficult to work because of occasional stone deposits. It has an interlocked grain and is strong and durable. Like afrormosia (see page 16) it is used as a teak substitute because it is very durable but less oily. It is good for outdoor use as well as for indoor furniture.

Dyera costulata **JELUTONG**
Origin: Malaysia and Indonesia
Characteristics: Classified as hardwood though soft in texture. Exercise care in handling. Close, even grain in a pale color range. Grain has tendency to crush when chiseling, so sharp tools are important. Easily workable by machine and used extensively for pattern making. Sands and polishes well.

Prunus spp. **CHERRY**
Origin: Europe (left), Asia Minor and the United States (right)
Characteristics: Open grain with dark, open pores and pink-to-brown heartwood; often used as decorative veneer. Susceptible to insect attack and shrinkage. Can be machined easily, but warps badly if not seasoned properly. Sands well and holds a finish very well—it is particularly good to use for cabinetmaking.

Diospyros spp. **EBONY**
Origin: Parts of Africa and India
Characteristics: Very dark to black heartwood with black grain structure. Sapwood lightish pink. Extremely hard but works well with sharp tools. Available in very small sizes and quantities, hence used only as inlays and on musical instruments. Density means it can be difficult to polish. Sanding dust can stain pale lumber.

Astronium fraxinifolium
GONÇALO ALVES
Also known as tiger wood (USA) or zebrawood (UK)
Origin: South America
Characteristics: Difficult to work because of its irregular grain, which varies in hardness; medium-textured and durable. Its character is given by its dark streaks and it can be very attractive when used in furniture either as solid or veneer.

Eucalyptus marginata **JARRAH**
Origin: South-western Australia
Characteristics: Hard, heavy wood. Heartwood varies from pink to dark red. Fairly coarse texture and generally straight grain. Back-cut boards can show pleasant grain pattern, but gum veins and pockets sometimes spoil finish. Can be difficult to work as hard. Sands well, finishes to a high polish.

Dalbergia cearensis **KINGWOOD**
Also known as violet wood and violetta (USA)
Origin: South America
Characteristics: Lustrous and even-textured wood, with very attractive coloring; fairly good to work. Kingwood is usually straight-grained and durable. Due to its limited availability, it is often used as veneer, inlay, or in marquetry. Also used in turning.

Guaiacum officinale **LIGNUM VITAE**
Origin: West Indies
Characteristics: Known as the
heaviest of all hardwoods. Even grain
and texture, with greasy feel. Brown
coloring with a green tinge. Density
and oil content makes it very durable.
Mainly used as decorative trim pieces
in fine furniture. Density makes it
hard to work and gluing is difficult
because of high oil content.

Swietenia spp. **MAHOGANY**
Origin: Honduras, the Caribbean
islands and Mexico
Characteristics: Medium-weight of
varying density. Yellow sapwood and
pink to reddish- brown heartwood.
Revered cabinet lumber for several
centuries now. Grain pattern can
range from plain to magnificent.
Works very easily and stain highlights
the grain patterns tremendously.

Quercus spp. **OAK**
Origin: Europe (right), North
Africa, North America (left) and
Asia
Characteristics: This type of wood
is strong and durable with pronounced pores. Can be extremely
heavy. European variety generally
yellow and North American pink
to reddish. Commonly used in
furniture, boatbuilding, and
kitchen cabinet work.

Platanus spp. **PLANE**
Also known as lacewood
Origin: Europe, except far north, and
Asia Minor
Characteristics: Yellowish sapwood and
copper-colored heartwood. Strong,
close-linked medullary rays. Used in
wood turning, fine cabinetmaking, and
inlay work. Sands well but can be
difficult to finish.

Gonystylus spp. **RAMIN**
Origin: Borneo, Indonesia and the
Philippines
Characteristics: Medium-density
tropical rain-forest wood prone to
infestation of insects and fungi. Pale
yellow to white in both sapwood and
heartwood. Straight, even grain, making
it easy to work in all directions. Glues
well and can be easily polished.

Tilia vulgaris **LIME**
Origin: Europe
Characteristics: Straight-grained wood
with uniform texture. Fairly soft and
light in color, which darkens to light
brown with exposure—it is best to
treat it with a preservative. Lime is
good to work and is often used in
carving, turning, and for making
some musical instruments.

Shorea spp. **MERANTI**
Also known as Pacific maple and lauan
Origin: Malaysia, Indonesia and the
Philippines
Characteristics: Color ranges from
pale brown to pink and dark red.
Susceptible to insect attack. Weight
and density varies greatly. Plain grain
pattern with occasional interlocking
grain. Not ideal for outdoor work. Best
used as base product for veneering
over, or it can be easily stained.

Pterocarpus spp. **PADAUK**
Also known as African coralwood and
Andaman redwood
Origin: Africa and South-East Asia
Characteristics: Medium density with
striking red colour—ideal highlight or
contrast wood in marquetry or inlay
work. Straight grain and even texture;
can have fiddleback feature.
Unfortunately the very strong color
on recently worked wood darkens
with time.

Peltogyne spp. **PURPLEHEART**
Also known as amaranth (USA)
Origin: Central and South America
Characteristics: Fine- to medium-textured wood, which is strong and durable. Generally straight-grained and attractive purple color when freshly worked but darkens over time. Is commonly used for furniture making, veneer work, and turning.

Dalbergia spp. **ROSEWOOD**
Origin: Brazil, India, Honduras
Characteristics: These trees are short so sawn lumber is often not of great length or width. Very dense and hard to work. Sapwood off-white and heartwood yellow to pale pink, with dark brown to purplish veins. Best suited for small decorative projects such as jewelry boxes and inlays.

Castanea sativa **SWEET CHESTNUT**
Also known as European chestnut and Spanish chestnut
Origin: Mediterranean, Switzerland and Germany
Characteristics: Similar appearance to oak. Sapwood is much whiter than heartwood. Used for handles, shutters, in wood turning, and for kitchen-cupboard door making, rather than actual cabinetmaking. Sands and polishes well. Slight acidity can corrode metals and stain wood.

Tectonais grandis **TEAK**
Origin: India, Burma and South-East Asia
Characteristics: Whitish sapwood and heartwood brown to ocher with dark growth rings. Oily and waxy to touch. Natural oils make it durable; resists water and fungus. Sands well; gluing may be a problem. Ideal for outdoor furniture. Machines well. Finish with teak oil. Expensive and hard to find.

Millettia laurentii **WENGE**
Origin: Central and East Africa
Characteristics: Very hard and heavy timber. Difficult to work and be aware of painful splinters when working. However, wenge has a superb black color with either fine grain or an elaborate figure. It can be used to make interesting furniture and is also used in turning. When finishing, use black wax.

Acer pseudoplatnus **SYCAMORE**
Origin: Europe and West Europe
Characteristics: Sycamore has a fine texture, often straight-grained but boards with quarter-sawn fiddleback grain are very sought after for some musical instruments; is one of the whitest woods but its grain darkens over time. Good to work and makes attractive, light-colored furniture.

Juglans spp. **WALNUT**
Origin: Eastern United States (right) and Canada, and mild regions of Europe (left)
Characteristics: Dark brown with occasional purplish tinge. Used for high-quality cabinetmaking. Mostly straight grained but can exhibit fiddleback grain. Walnut is a generic term often applied to many species of dark brown wood.

Microberlinia brazzavillensis
ZEBRANO
Also known as zingana and sometimes zebrawood (not to be confused with gonçalo alves, see page 18)
Origin: West Africa
Characteristics: Coarse and open-textured wood, which is light in color with interlocking grain. Expensive to buy and so generally used as veneer or inlay, though it is sometimes used in fine furniture or cabinetmaking.

Species of softwood

"Softwood" refers to types of trees that grow in cold regions, primarily in the northern hemisphere. Softwoods tend to have needles instead of leaves and are usually evergreen.

Pseudotsuga menziesii
DOUGLAS FIR
Origin: North America, Canada and Europe
Characteristics: Straight, pronounced grain; clear definition between earlywood and latewood. Yellow with prominent orange growth rings. Tough and water resistant. Used as building lumber, but prone to splitting so should be coated with preservative to improve external durability. Nails tend to follow grain direction.

Tsuga spp.
HEMLOCK
Origin: North America, Himalayas to North Burma, West Vietnam, China and Japan
Characteristics: Pale yellow with distinctive growth rings. Even textured with good, straight grain. Easy to work, but predrill for nailing near end sections. Poor seasoning can cause surface checking. Not very durable for exposed work and does not accept preservative treatment well.

Larix spp. LARCH
Origin: All over Europe and North America
Characteristics: Straight-grained, uniform texture tougher than many other softwoods. Heartwood pale to rich red. Dries fairly rapidly, which can result in shrinkage and distortion; knots can fall out. Not very durable and resists preserving treatments. Slightly difficult to work and should be predrilled for nailing and screwing.

Araucaria angustifolia
PINE, PARANA
Origin: South America
Characteristics: Mid-weight and straight-grained with an even texture, its growth rings are not very conspicuous. Heartwood light brown with occasional red streaks. Can distort during the seasoning process and end splits are conspicuous. Treat with preservative when using externally. Tendency to twist and jam on blade when sawed.

Pinus strobus
PINE, YELLOW
Origin: North America and Canada
Characteristics: Quite soft, but with straight grain and mild texture. Pale yellow to brown; can show resin-duct marks. Easily dented so protect when being worked. External use not recommended; treat with preservative. Works easily but blades must be sharp to avoid furry finish. Nails well; screws can strip thread if inserted with a screw gun.

Picea abies
SPRUCE, EUROPEAN
Origin: All over Europe
Characteristics: The "Christmas tree." Pale with little color difference between sapwood and heartwood. Straight-grained, even-textured and visible growth rings. Can be very knotty. Not a durable wood so treatment with preservatives is recommended for outdoor use. Easily worked and glues quite well, but staining can be patchy.

Scots pine is often grown in plantations although resins can be a problem in the timber.

Thuja plicata
WESTERN RED CEDAR
Origin: North America
Characteristics: This wood is used outdoors because it is very durable. Light pink to reddish-brown, changing on exposure to silver/gray. Extremely light and not particularly strong; avoid structural use. Larger sections suffer from collapse during seasoning, but can be reconditioned. Works well, glues easily, and accepts all finishes.

Pinus sylvestris **PINE, HARD**
Also known as Scots pine
Origin: Western Europe and Great Britain
Characteristics: Tall tree up to 130 ft. (40 m); plantation planted in many countries. Light yellow to reddish-brown color and can have much resin present, particularly in sapwood. Distinct figure and matures to beautiful color over time. Can suffer distortion and resins may bleed through a finish.

Pinus ponderosa **PINE, PONDEROSA**
Also known as British Columbia soft pine (Canada), western yellow pine and California white pine (USA)
Origin: Western USA and Canada
Characteristics: The sapwood is soft and even-textured, while the heartwood is darker, striped and resinous. Used in furniture making and carpentry.

Sequoia sempervirens **SEQUOIA**
Origin: North America
Characteristics: Texture can vary but generally straight-grained, colored reddish brown with a contrast between earlywood and latewood. Generally nonresinous. Owing to its properties, it can be used for exterior work such as shingles, exterior sidings, and posts, but it can also be used effectively for interior carpentry.

Picea sitchensis **SPRUCE, SITKA**
Also known as Menzies spruce and western spruce
Origin: North-western United States
Characteristics: Grows to 245 ft. (75 m). Straight-grained with even texture, nonresinous and creamy white with occasional pink tone. Treat with preservative for outdoor use. Works well with sharp tools, but knots can bleed resin. High strength-to-weight property.

Taxus baccata **YEW**
Also known as common, Irish or European yew
Origin: Europe, North Africa, Middle East, India
Characteristics: Tough and very hard. Heartwood orange-red to purple-brown; sapwood light. Decorative interlocked grain patterns. Durable but can be difficult to work. Gluing difficult due to oily nature. Stains well and finishes to a high-quality polish. Burr pieces often used in veneers.

Lumber milling and seasoning

Once the tree has been felled the wood is converted into workable pieces of lumber, which are then dried out or "seasoned" in the open air or in kilns.

MILLING THE LOGS

Felled trees are cut into logs, which are then sent to sawmills to be converted into planks or boards on large bandsaws or circular-saw machines.

Usually only the trunks or very major limbs are milled. Branches help to support the foliage, hence wood from branches has a high degree of movement and contains reaction wood that is prone to splitting, making it economically unviable for use in a piece. Instead it is used for chipping in certain manufactured boards.

METHODS OF MILLING

When timber dries it shrinks When lumber dries it shrinks and, because this shrinkage can cause distortion, the annual growth rings always try to straighten out. Therefore, wood cut from different parts of the trunk will move in different ways—for example, planks cut horizontally across the top of the trunk will be more prone to distortion than those cut across the center.

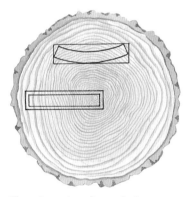

The orientation of growth rings determines the degree of distortion.

Through-and-through sawing

Lumber is very often milled "through and through," which means the log is sawed into planks in a series of slices. As a result, planks cut from the edge have different properties to those cut across the center.

This is also known as plain-sawing, and although it produces lumber at its widest, it is prone to uneven shrinkage and distortion. These boards can show a highly figured grain pattern because they are cut across the growth rings.

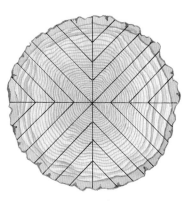

Quarter-sawn lumber.

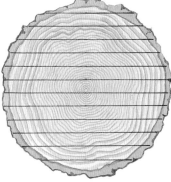

Through-and-through sawn lumber.

Through-and-through sawn lumber at the sawmill.

Quarter-sawing

Where minimum timber movement is required, the log can be quarter-sawn. True quarter-sawing would mean the boards were tapered, but this is uneconomic and less wasteful methods of sawing are used. Quarter-sawn lumber shrinks more evenly than through-and-through lumber and produces a more stable plank because a smaller amount of growth ring is available to shrink. Quarter-sawn boards have much straighter grain patterns.

METHODS OF SEASONING

All newly cut lumber contains a high percentage of water, which must be removed by a process of drying out called "seasoning." This water is present either as free water or as moisture, the latter being present in the cell walls. The first stage of seasoning is to remove the free water and then, as seasoning continues and moisture is lost from the cell walls, movement and shrinkage will start to occur within the lumber. If, however, seasoning takes place too quickly, stresses are created within the lumber. The whole process therefore needs to be very carefully controlled.

There are two main methods of seasoning lumber—air drying and kiln drying.

An industrial kiln for drying large quantities of lumber.

Air drying lumber

Planks that are seasoned by air-drying are stacked on spacer battens at least 18 in. (450 mm) apart—the air spaces between each plank are essential to avoid mold and fungal attack. The stack is built in a dry, sheltered spot and protected from rain and direct sunlight. It takes approximately one year to dry every 1 in. (25 mm) of board thickness for hardwoods and slightly less for drying softwoods. With this method, lumber can only dry to the ambient humidity—the humidity of the atmosphere it is drying in—which is generally about 15 percent. If the lumber is meant for interior use, the humidity needs to be reduced in a kiln where the extraction of moisture is carefully controlled.

Kiln drying lumber

A kiln for drying lumber is like a large oven in which temperature and humidity can be carefully controlled, so that moisture content is reduced to 8 percent or less. Planks are fed into the kiln on racks, a mixture of hot air and steam is introduced, then the humidity is slowly reduced to the required moisture content. Kiln-dried lumber needs to be stored in a controlled environment. If it is dried to below the air's moisture level and then placed outside, it will take up moisture again.

Lumber drying naturally in the open air, with spacer battens in between the planks.

Properties and defects of lumber

When choosing a lumber for woodwork our choices are often influenced by the look of the grain, figure, and texture, and whether the wood is free of any defects.

PROPERTIES OF LUMBER

Since lumber comes from a living tree, the characteristics and properties of each species will vary greatly. Different characteristics can also occur within a species or even within an individual tree. Some lumbers will be easy to work, others less so; some will be strong, others weaker. The color and appearance of the grain, the figure, and the texture of the wood will also vary from tree to tree. All of these characteristics are determined by cell structure.

Grain

In lumber where growth has been even and the cell structure is in line with the main axis of the tree, the wood will be straight-grained and easy to work. However, in some trees growth will not be even and so the grain may not be straight. This is called interlocked grain, wavy grain, and curvy grain. A fiddleback grain is wavy with regular light and dark streaks and is used to make violin backs. Irregular grained woods are often difficult to work, but can look attractive. The term "grain" is also used to describe the way wood is worked. Sawing and planing can be done with the grain—in the direction of the wood fibers. Sometimes sawing, chiseling, and planing are done across the grain—at right angles to the grain. Where the grain is random, planing may have to be done both against and across the grain.

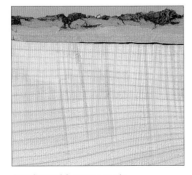

Lumber with wavy grain.

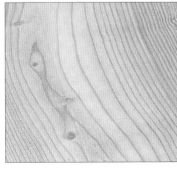

Lumber with interlocked grain.

Figure

Figure is another term for grain pattern. Figure can be caused by grain direction, but also marked differences between earlywood and latewood, size of the growth rings, method of milling, and color distribution. "Imperfections" also contribute to the figure. These might include curls—which occur at the fork between a branch and the trunk—and burls, which are abnormal growths of some sort, usually as the result of an injury the tree has sustained.

Texture

Fine-textured woods have densely spaced cells, while coarse-textured woods have large, open-spaced cells.

Even-textured lumber has only a slight variation between early and latewood. Uneven-textured lumber, as the name suggests has much greater contrast between the seasonal growth rings.

COMMON LUMBER DEFECTS

Some lumber defects can arise from felling, some from careless kilning and some from incorrect storage. For example, if lumber has not been dried correctly, stresses are introduced, which make the wood hard to work. If the lumber has not been dried sufficiently, shrinkage, warping, and splitting can occur. Defects such as these will be marked at a good lumberyard and are best avoided because they are harder to work with.

Shakes

Shakes are splits in the wood that are caused by poor felling or stresses that incurred during shrinkages.

Honeycombing

The problem of honeycombing occurs in a board if the outer fibers of the board or log dry out faster than the inside. When this happens the wood inside shrinks more than that outside, which can lead to checking, or splits, within the lumber.

End splits

End splits are caused by the ends of the boards drying too rapidly. This can often be prevented by sealing the ends during the air-drying process.

Distortion

Bowing, warping, twisting, winding, or springing can be caused by poor stacking of the

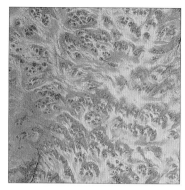

Lumber with burls.

Lumber with shakes.

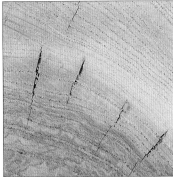

Honeycombing.

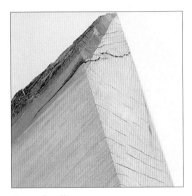

An end split.

Warping and end splits.

A knot.

Lumber suffering from fungal attack.

boards, or from stresses that have built up during poor seasoning. These stresses make the wood difficult to cut.

Ingrown bark

Ingrown bark is unattractive and weakens the structure of the lumber.

Knots

Knots form where the stumps of dead branches have been overgrown with new growth rings. This makes the grain pattern around the knot very irregular and difficult to plane.

Insect or fungal attack

Defects in wood caused by insect or fungal attack are most often found in furniture in old buildings, where systems of ventilation and heating are often antiquated and inadequate. Damp environmental conditions allow pests and fungi to attack. Any sapwood left on the lumber will suffer the worst. New lumber is less likely to suffer, because much greater care is now taken in harvesting, milling, and seasoning, although it may occur when proper care is not taken at source. Remember, however, that if damp conditions are present there is always a risk of infection.

Buying and storing lumber

When buying wood, it is best to visit a lumberyard personally in order to examine the boards for defects and to select the best pieces to suit your needs.

BUYING HARDWOODS

Hardwoods are cut from the tree into planks and the stated thickness of the board is the sawn size. However, the maximum dimensions you have to work with must allow for planing the plank all around so it is flat and square. For example, a sawn plank purchased at 1 in. (25 mm) will finish between 1¾6 and ⅞ in. (21 and 23 mm) depending on how much has to be removed in order to make it flat, straight, and square. In order to arrive at a specific dimension of 1 in. (25 mm), a thicker board would have to be purchased, thus giving more waste. You also need to consider how much width you will get out of a plank.

When buying hardwoods in planks, there may be some resistance to turning over too many boards in a stack to find the best grain characteristics or color, especially if you require only a small amount. However, if you are reasonable about it, generally lumber dealers will be happy to oblige.

When buying lumber, examine any defects that are marked on the wood.

BUYING SOFTWOODS

You will encounter a very similar situation regarding measurements of sawn softwoods, but the dealer will normally allow you to pick out the pieces yourself. Sometimes softwoods can be purchased "planed all around" (PAR) or "dressed all around" (DAR)—that is, planed or dressed on all four sides. But the size given would be expressed in the original sawn size—for example, a board labeled 2 x 1 in. (50 x 25 mm) will actually be about $1\frac{3}{16}$ x $\frac{7}{8}$ in. (46 x 23 mm), but it will not be to an exact measurement. It will be to the nearest size that the lumberyard can plane in order to achieve a reasonable finish on all faces. As a result, a purchase made on one occasion may differ on another.

GENERAL POINTERS

Finished sizes also vary according to the country of origin and the milling standards in that country. Some countries have standard thicknesses and widths, allowing for a consistency of product from one yard to another. This tends to be the case particularly with common building and carpentry grade lumber and milled sections such as moldings and baseboards. The more exotic lumber for fine cabinet work is generally supplied rough sawn. If it needs to be planed, then the maximum thickness and width will be provided.

When purchasing lumber in large quantities the cost is often calculated by its cubic content, although in smaller volumes it may be sold by the length or piece. Be aware of how the dealer makes the calculations. Some dealers may want to charge you by the cubic foot, which can become quite confusing, particularly if you are used to dealing in cubic meters. Remember there are 424 cubic feet in a cubic meter. So ask the dealer for the cubic meter rate in addition to the cubic foot rate and then make sure they both add up correctly.

If you live a long way from a dealer there are mail-order companies that will supply a large range of lumber of varying sizes. The product is obviously more expensive but often there is no alternative, especially if you need a specific species. Generally, however, suppliers have a reputation to maintain and give a good service.

STORAGE IN THE WORKSHOP

Once you have obtained your lumber, you must ensure that it is stored under suitable conditions. Hardwood planks are best stored in a similar way to that found in a good lumberyard—horizontally with spacers in between each board and away from sunlight and direct heat sources. It is sometimes the case that softwoods are stored vertically at the suppliers, but this is best avoided unless it is absolutely necessary as a result of space constraints. In general, make sure that your workshop is dry and well ventilated.

You will find that as you undertake more projects there will be material left over. Not all of this will be waste and you should store any scraps that may be useful to use in later projects. Ensure, however, that this is undertaken methodically so that you know where to find different types.

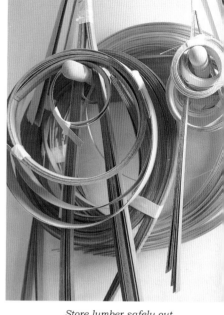

Store lumber safely out of the way on a wall, away from direct heat and light.

Lumber is best stored horizontally and away from heat sources.

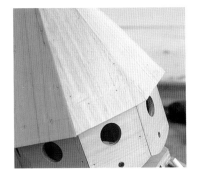

Manufactured boards

Even though the natural characteristics of wood are a major part of its attraction, they also tend to cause problems including shrinkage during mass manufacturing. Therefore, the industry has developed a number of ways of using lumber to make board materials that are much more dimensionally stable than natural lumber and these manufactured boards are readily available to the home woodworker. There are a number of different boards, each with its own uses.

Modular storage cubes made of preveneered MDF (see pages 316–23).

BOARD SIZES

Manufactured boards are usually produced to standard thicknesses, which are precise and expressed either in imperial or metric sizes. The sheet size is generally made to a standard 8 x 4 ft. (2400 x 1200 mm). Larger sheets can be made available to special order— that is, approximately 10 x 5 ft. (3000 x 1500 mm). Some of the thinner thicknesses may be sold at a different size—for example, ¹⁄₁₆ in. (2 mm) aeroply may be found 5 ft. (1500 mm) square. Many outlets, however, will cut standard sheets into smaller sizes, normally increments of the standard sheets—for example, 4 x 4 ft. (1200 x 1200 mm) or 4 x 2 ft. (1200 x 600 mm). When tackling the projects in this book, you may decide to amend the sizes that are given in the accompanying drawings (see pages 66–7). If you do so, it is always important to consider how easily the required size can be cut from the standard sheet with the minimum of waste.

TYPES OF MANUFACTURED BOARD

There are various types of manufactured board available on the market today. These include plywood, particleboard or chipboard, fiberboard, and blockboard. Manufactured board can be used on its own, but also often forms a base for wood veneer (see pages 38–42).

Plywood

Plywood is made from constructional veneers, which are laminated and glued together, with the grain alternating along and across the board. Usually there is an uneven number of layers in a board so that the outside grain directions on the faces of the finished boards are the same. Plywood is available in a range of different thicknesses—from a flexible ⅛ in. (3 mm) sheet to a hefty 1³⁄₁₆ in. (30 mm) board.

Plywood can have various numbers of layers—the thinnest, three-ply, has three layers. As its name suggests, three-ply is made from just three laminates—two face veneers and a core that is sometimes the same thickness.

Thicker boards, or multi-plies, are made of more sheets of laminates—always an odd number and finished to the standard board thicknesses. The performance of plywood is determined by the quality of the laminates and the type of adhesive used in the manufacturing process. Interior grade plywood is normally bonded with a urea-formaldehyde adhesive. These are suitable for most interior work, but other types should be chosen if they are to be used for kitchens or bathrooms. Exterior grade plywood—termed weather and boil proof or WBP—is bonded with phenolic adhesives, which are highly resistant to weather, wet and dry heat, insects and fungi. Marine plywood has laminates that are selected so that they are fault-free. For very special applications resorcinol adhesive can be used in the manufacturing.

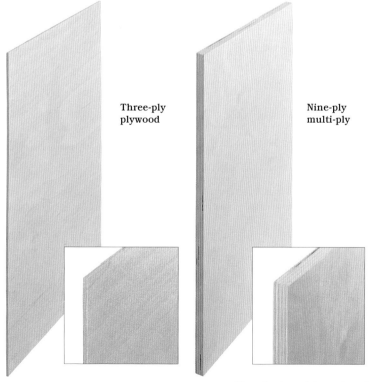

Three-ply plywood

Nine-ply multi-ply

Particleboard or chipboard

Particleboard, also known as chipboard, is made from small wood chips, which are glued together under pressure. It is stable but can be affected by moisture if a waterproof adhesive has not been used. Some boards are made from similar-sized particles, but often you will find boards with outside layers of high-density particles sandwiching a coarser core, such as in graded-density chipboard.

Decorative chipboard is also available with faces of wood veneer or plastic laminates.

Other boards with greater tensile strength are available, but more for building work than furniture making. Oriented-strand board is made from long strands of wood. Flakeboard or waferboard is made from big chips of wood, bonded in layers with random grain direction.

Blockboard

Blockboard is constructed of solid wood strips between laminates. They are suited for worktops and shelves. Boards are normally sold in full 4½ x 4 ft. (1400 x 1200 mm) boards, with thicknesses ranging from ½–1 in. (12–25 mm).

Laminboard is a top quality block construction board. The core strips of solid wood are narrow—about $\frac{3}{16}$ in. (5 mm) wide. It is usually edge-glued with two laminates on either side of the core, with the grain of the outside in line with the direction of the core strips. This is probably the most stable manufactured board available.

Standard blockboard has core strips that are wider than

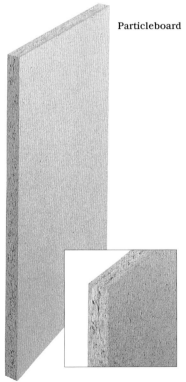

Particleboard

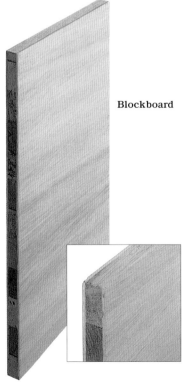

Blockboard

laminboard—about ¾ in. (20 mm). The core strips are not necessarily glued, and are sandwiched between outside laminate faces in one or two layers on each side. A problem with this board is that the strips can show through the outside veneers, particularly if there is only one on each face.

Battenboard is a cheaper blockboard where the interior strips are much wider—from 1¼–1½ in. (30–40 mm). Obviously show-through is much more likely.

In addition to these boards, solid boards made from wood strips, joined end to end and glued together to make a wide board, have been used in the furniture industry and are available in many do-it-yourself outlets. If you can visually accept the pattern of the board's strips, they are stable and are a useful alternative to other boards and solid wood.

Fiberboard
Fiberboard is made out of tiny particles of wood (finer than sawdust) that are fixed together with a tough resin. For many years, the best-known material was standard hardboard, which normally has one smooth and one textured face. Standard hardboard is available in a large variety of thicknesses—from ¹⁄₁₆ to ½ in. (1.5 to 12 mm). Fiberboard is often used for making cabinet backs and childrens' toys.

One problem with hardboard, as well as chipboard and other particleboard, is that lippings, either solid or veneer, have to be applied to the edges. To overcome this problem, medium density fiberboard

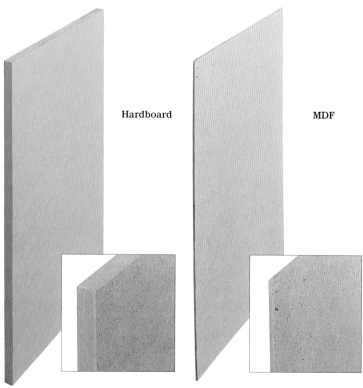

Hardboard

MDF

Opposite: Birdhouse made of exterior grade plywood (see pages 338–42).

(MDF) was developed. MDF has a dense, smooth surface texture that is ideal for routing or painting. The edges can be polished so that there is no need to use lippings. It has now become a standard material for much furniture making and also has certain applications for some interior trim. MDF comes in thicknesses ranging from ¼ to 1¼ in. (6 to 32 mm).

Buying and storing manufactured board

When you wish to depart from the sizes of the projects as given or want to develop your own designs, always remember at the planning stage to reduce waste as much as possible by checking that the components needed can be economically cut from the standard-size sheets.

Unless you are purchasing from a company that carries a large range, the selection available from local outlets may be limited. When buying plywood, birch ply is best for making furniture because of its quality and birch veneer faces. Often the plywood available locally uses low-quality veneers. With blockboard and particleboard, the local quality can also be variable. There are several grades of specialized boards that use different adhesives or resins as bonding agents. The best can be entirely waterproof if required; if you need a high-performance variety, you will need to order from a company that specializes in high-grade board.

Manufactured boards can be stored vertically as long as they are well supported to ensure that they do not bend or warp. Support the boards in a strong shelf rack along one side of the workshop. They must also be stored under dry conditions because they can soak up moisture.

Dining chair back made of plywood (see pages 375–83).

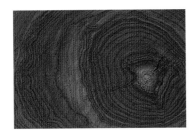

Veneers

A veneer is a thin sheet of wood that is used for structural or decorative purposes. With many types of wood now hard to find in solid form, the use of veneer for decorative purposes is becoming more common.

Veneers range in thickness from ⅟₃₂ to ⅛ in. (1 to 3 mm).

Many types of wood have such interesting and unique characteristics that, in order to conserve and extend their use, they are made into veneer.

There is a vast range of veneer available to the wood-worker today. This is the case with woods that exhibit highly decorative grain patterns, such as curly mahogany.

For structural use they tend to be known as constructional veneers and they are usually cut to thicknesses of between ⅟₃₂ and ⅛ in. (1 and 3 mm).

HOW VENEERS ARE PRODUCED

In early times, veneers were produced by sawing, which resulted in thick veneer—as much as ⅛ in. (3 mm)—and high wastage from the sawdust. Veneer-slicing machines were developed in the 18th century to produce thin veneers.

Sliced veneers
Flat slicing is where the log is supported on a carrier and a series of slices is produced. This can be standard flat slicing, quarter-cut slicing, or flat-sliced quartered. Quarter-cut slicing is used to produce veneer with a more varied grain pattern than flat slicing. Flat-sliced quartered veneer is produced when quartered logs are cut

across the log. Sometimes when slicing, fine cracks, known as knife checks, can occur on the back face of the veneer. This is called the open or loose face. If possible lay this face down, although when using book-matched veneers this will not be possible.

Rotary-cut veneers

The rotary cut is used for constructional veneers and some decorative veneers. The trunk of the tree, after the bark has been removed and softened by steaming, is set on a machine similar to a huge lathe. As the machine revolves, a continuous sheet is cut from the log. The cutting knife reduces in radius to give a sheet of even thickness.

For decorative veneers, the log can be positioned in different

SLICED VENEERS

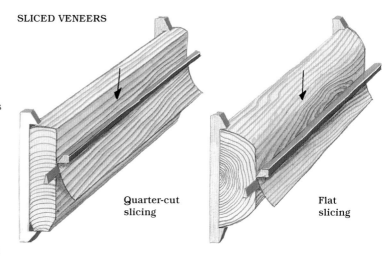

Quarter-cut slicing

Flat slicing

ways so that various grains and figures are emphasized. Rotary cutting can be off-center, half-round, or back cutting. Both off-centre cutting and half-round cutting produce a figure similar to flat-slicing. The back-cutting method is often used to make the most of curly and burl veneers.

ROTARY-CUT VENEERS

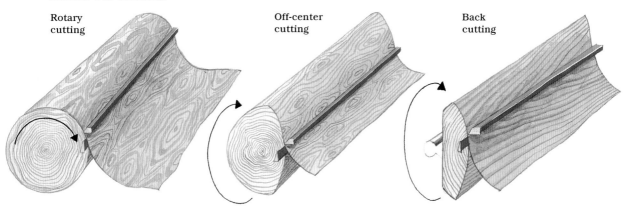

Rotary cutting

Off-center cutting

Back cutting

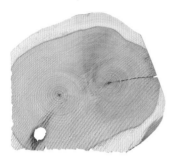

Kingwood oyster veneer

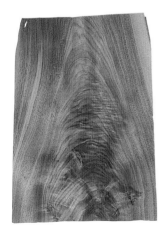

Yew oyster veneer

Veneer types

Many types of veneer are available today and they have been made from a wide range of hardwoods, with varying colors, grains, figures, and textures. The specific type of veneer is obtained by slicing the log in various ways, as was described on pages 38–9. The part of the tree that the veneer comes from—for example, the main trunk, the burls or the fork—will also determine the type of veneer that is produced from it.

Some of the most common types of veneer you will come across in your woodworking are described below.

Crown-cut veneers are the most common veneers used to decorate tables and other traditional furniture. They are produced using the flat-sliced quartered method of veneer slicing.

Curly veneers are produced from the fork of a tree where the trunk divides. They are produced using the back-cutting rotary method. The figure that is found on curly veneers is called a feather figure. Striped veneers are produced using the quarter-cut flat slicing method. This results in a radial cut being made across the width of the tree's growth rings.

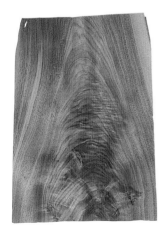

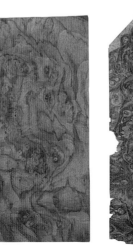

African walnut curly   **American walnut burl**   **American walnut burl**   **Mahogany African striped**

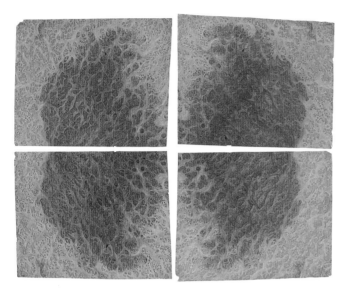

**Book-matched
Veuona burr**

*The surface of this tray
is made with oak veneer
on manufactured board
—the handle and lipped
edge are solid oak.*

Burl, or burr, veneers are often used for smaller pieces such as jewelry boxes or as a decorative focal point on larger pieces.

Some types of burl veneers are highly figured. They are produced using the back-cutting rotary method.

Some interesting veneers are created from hardwood lumber with irregular grain. These are called freak-figured veneers and are rotary cut.

Artificial dyes can also be used to make veneers in a variety of different colors, either to match another piece of timber or as contrast to it.

A veneer hammer and animal glue are used in traditional veneering. Modern adhesives can also be used.

Store veneers in a cool, dry place, away from direct light.

A utility knife and straightedge can be used to cut veneers to size.

Buying and storing veneer

Veneers are available from specialized suppliers who normally carry large stocks of many species. The most common types are normally to be found in fairly long lengths—12 ft. (3.5 m) or more—and between 10 and 14 in. (250 and 350 mm) wide. Thicknesses vary, depending on the intended use. Where exotic veneers are needed, the size will be much smaller and will depend on the log or the side of the log from which they are cut. Calculate how much veneer you require and allow around 15 percent for waste. Every veneer is different, so finding a matching veneer may be tricky.

Veneers are fairly brittle so take care when opening your rolled up sheet or it may crack. If the veneer has end splits, then repair it immediately with paper veneer tape, which is available from veneer suppliers.

Veneers should be stored flat, in a cool and dry environment. They should be stored away from bright light as the colors can deteriorate. If using matched veneers, the leaves should be numbered to make assembling them easier.

Other materials

Even though most of the materials used by furniture makers are wood-based, there are other furniture materials that you will sometimes wish to use. Most of these are listed below and are included in some of the projects in this book.

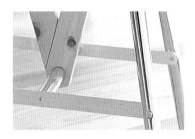

Glass

If you want to use transparent panels in your furniture, then you have the choice between glass and plastic (see page 44). Glass has been used by man for many centuries, is readily available in sheet form and adds an interesting quality to many furniture pieces. Glass is available not only in flat and clear types but in frosted and patterned varieties that can add interesting effects.

Even though it is possible to learn how to cut glass in your own workshop, unless you plan to use it frequently it is easier to have it cut by a professional glazier. Glass is generally available in most areas from suppliers of windows and other glazing materials. When ordering glass, especially if it has to fit into a frame, cut a sheet of board material to the exact size needed, try it in place and then give that pattern to the glazier, asking

for the piece of glass to be cut to that precise size. Whenever glass is to be used without a frame, as in the feature table project (see below and pages 281–6), it is essential to have the edges either finished or polished, and to have the sheet hardened so that it will not harm anyone if an unfortunate

Where glass is used without a frame the sharp edges must be polished.

Below: Aluminum offers a lightweight and sturdy option for chair legs (see pages 300–4).

Bottom: Acrylic sheet makes stylish shelves for this CD rack (pages 287–94).

mishap does occur. These processes can normally be carried out by your glass supplier.

Store glass upright on edge, ensuring that the sheets cannot fall or be knocked over.

Metal

You will often use different types of metal in furniture making, particularly when using screws or other hardware. The projects in this book make frequent use of bolts, machine screws, and threaded studs. Metals include iron and steel, brass, aluminum and other alloys, and precious metals. While there is a large range of different metals, the most usual type in the workshop will be brass, aluminum, or steel.

Brass and aluminum are fairly easy to work and a small metal vice with some basic metalworking tools will suffice for most purposes—the most common are hacksaws, drills, and files (see pages 221–3). Steel requires more effort, but since the work is largely simple fabrication it is easily achievable. Even though adhesives can be used to join metals, it is easier to undertake

the fabrication yourself and to take these components to a local metalworker to have them soldered, brazed or welded.

Metals are available in home-improvement stores or from hardware stores, engineering firms and metal fabricators. Metals can be purchased in many sections or in lengths of rod, bar, or tube.

It is best to store metals in a rack or placed vertically in cardboard tubes.

Plastics

Plastics, which are materials manufactured from chemicals, are generally used and fabricated in factory conditions. A vast range of plastics is available in many forms: sheet, powder/granules, liquids, and both flexible and rigid foams. There is a huge variety of plastics and many are chemically formulated for specific uses. They are very useful in the workshop since many of the modern plastic-based adhesives and finishes can be applied to them.

As a material, however, plastic is most likely to be used in two applications. First, as a cushion for a chair—

polyurethane flexible foam—and second, for drilling and shaping a transparent panel. For example, when making the CD rack project (see pages 287–94), plastic sheets need to be cut to size and drilled. For the sheets, use either acrylic or polycarbonate, which can be worked easily using a combination of woodworking and metalworking tools.

Plastic sheets are sometimes also available from home-improvement stores or plastics suppliers. It is best to store plastic upright on edge, taking care that the sheets cannot fall or be knocked over.

Fabric

Fabric can be derived from chemicals, plants such as cotton, or animals. In woodworking, fabric is normally used as upholstery or as a decorative feature on a piece of wooden furniture.

Ceramics

Ceramics can provide additional interest to furniture. A large range of tiles are readily available from local suppliers and can add interest, color, and a very durable surface to horizontal work areas, such as kitchen cabinets and sinks.

Leather

Leather works well in furniture making. It is not only used as an upholstery material but also as straps for chair arms, such as on the easy chair project (see pages 343–52), and it can be inlaid into the tops of desks. Leather is readily available from saddlers and leather merchants. To store leather, roll the hides into cylinders and place on shelves.

Leather makes comfortable armrests on chairs as it is flexible.

Design and construction

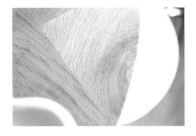

Function

Over the centuries, furniture design has evolved as knowledge, skills, technology, and materials have developed. Good furniture, however, has always represented something more than pure utilitarianism—form is just as important.

Good furniture finds a balance between form and function.

As well as developments in the science of furniture making, there are also the wishes of the client and market trends to consider, and other influences that are found in any historical period. These may be economic, social, or even political, and can be affected by perceptions of other cultures or by fashions of the time. In many periods there is also a desire to look back—to borrow from past styles. The style of projects in this book aims to follow a contemporary route but the design of some pieces—because of material, construction, or memory—may be influenced by the past.

Early in the 20th century the expression "form follows function" was coined by architects and designers. They believed that the function of a piece should dominate how it looks. Some furniture designers are happy to work within this constraint, but many others strive for a different approach. At one extreme, a designer will follow an approach in which function entirely directs the logical form of a piece. At the other, a designer will want to make an individual statement or even make a piece in which

the aesthetics distort or hide the functional requirement.

As well as fulfilling its function, most of us also want our furniture to be pleasing to the eye. The visual attractiveness of a piece can be affected by its intended use, how it is constructed, the material it is made from, and the space in which it will be used. Ultimately, it should look right for the job that it is intended for.

Essential to the skilled woodworker is an appreciation of the function of a piece of furniture. Every piece must suit its purpose and three types of principle must be considered.

• Structural principles: Is the piece strong, stable, and safe?
• Ergonomic principles: Has the piece been designed with the human body in mind? How easy is it to use? Is it comfortable? Does it need to be adaptable to increase its usefulness?
• Construction principles: Does the piece conform to tried and tested principles of construction? Does it take into account the properties of wood and any other material that might be used?

STRUCTURAL PRINCIPLES

In all furniture construction it is essential that structural principles are understood and followed.

Forces and loads

To ensure that every construction is strong, stable, and safe, an understanding of the forces and loads that will act on it is necessary. Structure is concerned with compression, tension, shear, torsion, and bending.

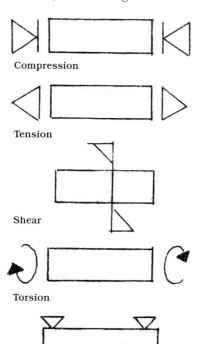

Compression

Tension

Shear

Torsion

Bending

Bracing is used to ensure the stability of this small table (see pages 259–64).

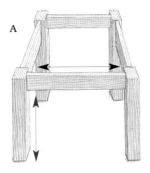

A

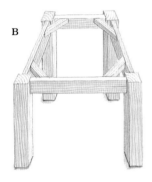

B

Designing with forces in mind

The joints between the rails and legs on a table or chair need to be strong enough to resist shear forces and sideways pressure.

Diagram A shows the forces acting on a bare frame: shear forces mean the legs oppose the load on the rail (red arrow) and sideways pressure increases these forces (black arrow). In diagram B, the frame is held rigid with strong joints and corner blocks to combat opposing pressures.

Strengthening structures

The size of the components and the overall piece, and the type of joints used, are also important. One of the basic principles is that a three-sided structure will always be the most stable and so any component that comprises more than three sides should ideally incorporate an element of triangulation to give it maximum strength.

This, however, is not always possible in furniture making, and other means must be found to provide structural strength. For example, in a frame we can use the relative sizes of the stiles and rails to give structural strength. In the frame door

panel, the bottom rail is often wider than the other three, and this wider rail adds extra rigidity to the structure. Large cabinets follow the principle of the five-sided box, in which one of the six sides can be left open provided the other sides are designed to add structural integrity. A cabinet can be strengthened in a variety of ways, for example, by adding a back panel in a groove or rebate, or corner plates.

A cabinet is strengthened with a wide bottom rail and back panel.

The triangle is the strongest structure.

Corner plates reinforce the cabinet structure.

A strip under a shelf provides extra support.

If a shelf becomes overloaded, it is likely to sag and the compression and tension may even cause it to break. By fitting a strip underneath the shelf, however, strength is added and it can support more weight.

Safety under strain

When designing and making a piece of furniture with structural principles in mind—strength, stability, and safety—also ask yourself if the piece will meet these benchmarks under rather more unusual circumstances. For example, if all the drawers are open in a chest of drawers, is it still stable and safe? Or does a tall, shallow free-standing bookcase require provision for anchoring to a wall to prevent it falling forward? Likewise, will a chair topple if the person sitting on it leans back? Leaning back moves

the chair's center of gravity, and if it becomes unstable it will topple (A). By sloping the back legs outward, the chair's base is widened, thereby increasing its stability (B and C). These points become obvious when the piece is made, but should be resolved at the design stage to avoid compromises.

ERGONOMIC PRINCIPLES

Anthropometrics is the science of the measurement of humankind, which results in data that shows people's sizes and the percentage of the population between the smallest and the largest. Ergonomics is the use of this information to determine the size of spaces, products, and their arrangement to make them as effective and efficient as possible.

Furniture makers need to consider how real people will use a piece of furniture. Ergonomic principles are fundamental and prompt considerations such as whether the relative heights of a dining table and chair work well together or whether high or deep shelves and cupboards can be used easily. For example, in making a cabinet, can items be inserted and retrieved in a convenient and

A

B

C

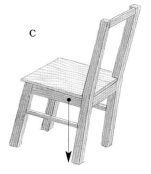

safe manner? Does the storage space work in the most efficient way? Each piece needs to be as safe and comfortable to use as possible.

The projects in this book that are directly related to the human body—such as the chairs, tables, and the bed—have all used standard sizes and should be suitable for most people. However, the dimensions are not set in stone, and in particular, you may wish to alter the proportions of the storage projects in the book. So remember that an advantage to making your own furniture is that you can customize dimensions to suit nonstandard requirements. If you want to change the designs, work out your required dimensions, understand how the pieces fit together, and plan the changes as necessary. You must always ensure that the piece remains structurally, ergonomically, and constructionally sound, as well as aesthetically pleasing, with proportions still harmonious.

CONSTRUCTION PRINCIPLES

The principles of furniture construction have been developed over the centuries as successive generations of makers and designers understand more about the materials with which they are working.

The qualities of the wood itself have a major impact on furniture construction, especially in the way allowances have to be made for wood movement. In this book we look specifically at our main material, wood, and see the ways in which we can use this natural resource—as solid lumber, as manufactured boards, and as veneers. The materials available to furniture makers are varied, and metals, plastics, glass, leather, stone, ceramics, and fabrics can also be used. (See pages 43–5 for a description of the nonwood materials used in furniture making, as well as pages 221–3 for more on using metals and plastics.)

Lumber can be used in furniture making in several different forms. Lengths or strips are available in various sections, including square, rectangular, and round, plus other special shapes. These lengths are often used to make frames and different jointing methods are used according to the material.

This shelf demonstrates the principle that a three-sided structure is always the most stable.

Sometimes panels are added to frames in order to increase their rigidity. Panels can be either flat or curved. They can be used as supplied or shaped in various ways for particular requirements.

Allowing for wood movement

Solid wood moves as it absorbs and exudes moisture according to the humidity level of its immediate surroundings. This characteristic must always be borne in mind, both in the design and in the making of the piece. Wood moves least along its grain, with the movement being almost negligible. Movement across the grain, although varying from species to species, will always take place, the problem becoming worse the wider the panel.

If a component needs to be fitted across the wood grain, it should never simply be glued or jointed in an attempt to fix it rigidly in place. This will put the wood under additional stress as it moves and cause problems. Instead the component should only be fixed in a small area and the rest of it allowed to move.

A good example of this is a solid planked tabletop with restraining battens underneath; the convention is to put the

center screw in a hole, with the other screws in slots. You will see many examples in this book where allowance for some movement has been made.

When using solid lumber for cabinets, or carcasses, the problem of wood movement must always be considered. When the grain runs round the carcass sides, top and bottom, any movement will not affect the structure. However, if any members are to be fitted with the long grain across the main grain direction of the carcass, allowance must be made for the lateral movement of the carcass when fitting these members.

The problem of wood movement can also be avoided by using manufactured board, which do not move and shrink. However, the use of board raises a different construction issue. The nature of the edges of manufactured boards require a lip to be added. If you decide to veneer the board first and then add the lip to cover the edges, the lip will show and will have to match the veneer. Or, you could lip the edges and then lay on the veneer, but if the lip is too wide, a line may start to show after a period of time, particularly across the grain.

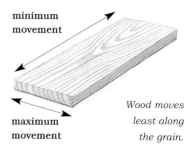

minimum movement

maximum movement

Wood moves least along the grain.

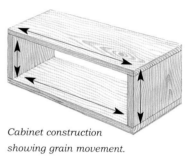

Cabinet construction showing grain movement.

Standard constructions

Standard constructions for different types of furniture have evolved over time. Tried and tested, the following methods can be relied upon to ensure that the pieces of furniture you make are functional.

This section looks briefly at the standard constructions for chairs, tables, cabinets, and drawers, as well as the wood-working joints that also form part of these furniture constructions.

CHAIRS

There are many examples of chair construction, but probably the most common and the most versatile is frame construction. The vertical elements are called legs, or stiles, and the horizontal elements are called rails. The back legs extend upward, and form the main support for the backrest. Chairs also have top, crest or backrest rails, and sometimes lower stretcher rails when the structure calls for it. The frame is usually joined with mortise-and-tenon joints, although sometimes chair frames have dowel joints, which are almost as strong as mortise-and-tenon joints. There are many different options available for forming the seat of the chair, including solid wood or slats, lamination, cane, and upholstery.

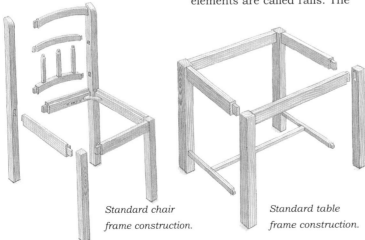

Standard chair frame construction.

Standard table frame construction.

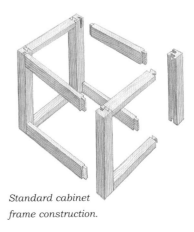

Standard cabinet frame construction.

TABLES

The most common construction for tables is also the frame construction, with either mortise-and-tenon or dowel joints. Lower stretcher rails are sometimes added to the frame for extra strength. The table frame construction is versatile, and a range of options is available for the tabletop, both in shape and materials.

CABINETS

On a solid wood carcass, the rails are usually joined to the uprights with lap dovetail joints, while the side rails are joined to the uprights with mortise- and-tenon joints. The back of the carcass is important for rigidity and stability. Backs have traditionally been located in grooves or rebates. Even though solid wood may be used, these days backs tend to be made from plywood. A carcass's rigidity can be increased by adding fixed shelves and partitions.

DRAWERS

In the traditional method of drawer construction, the sides are joined to the front with lap dovetail joints, and the back is joined to the sides with through dovetail joints. The front and sides can be grooved to accept the bottom of the cabinet, while the back is made narrower in order to allow the plywood to pass underneath it.

In circumstances where design dictates that drawer sides are too thin to accept grooves, drawer slips are fitted. On wide drawers a center rail, called a muntin, may be added. The drawer will usually run along the cabinet sides and between the top and bottom rails. Where these cross-rails are not wanted, one alternative is to run the drawer on a rail that fits into grooves on the drawer sides. Handmade drawers are a feature of quality cabinet work. If, however, you are making fitted furniture and need a lot of drawers, they can be built by using lap joints on the corners, setting the bottom in a rebate, and gluing and nailing. If you need a large number of drawers, use this method and fit false fronts to the drawer boxes.

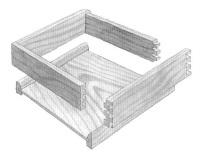

Standard drawer construction.

A drawer with a false front.

Drawer with groove for runner.

WOODWORKING JOINTS

Woodworking joints have been developed and refined over the centuries, and even though mechanical and production methods have led to changes in the furniture industry, the joints are still important, both in general carpentry work and particularly in fine furniture making. They have all been developed for specific purposes.

The history of furniture construction shows us how jointing systems have developed and how many different approaches are now available. The common mortise-and-tenon joint provides many examples of development, much of it concerned with structure, but some with appearance—for example, the stopped mortise-and-tenon, the through mortise-and-tenon, the haunched mortise-and-tenon, and those that are wedged. Joints, as well as being efficient, can also be a very decorative feature of your piece of furniture.

Mortise-and-tenon joints are used most often in frame construction for tables, framed doors and cabinet fronts, and chairs. Chair making, however, developed in its own particular way because of the use of curved shapes, and specific methods of construction were developed where dowels were widely used.

A wide variety of dovetails are used in cabinet and drawer construction. Dovetail joints are generally considered to be the most attractive joints and much is made of their fine proportions. There are also single-lap, double-lap, and secret miters, though the last is now being overtaken with the use of routers and biscuit jointers.

There are other types of joints and this book describes how to make all of the most commonly used joints, including half-lap joints (pages 149–52), mortise-and-tenon joints (pages 153–62), dado joints (pages 163–6), and dovetail joints (pages 167–71).

Dovetail joints are used when strong joints and an attractive appearance are required.

Designing for visual attractiveness

The most important elements of designing are that it should add to the pleasure of your creative experience and satisfy the spirit of your brief. Following the guidelines given here will help ensure the overall attractiveness of your project.

Design is always a challenge, but once you have developed an understanding of the principles of standard construction and function, you will be well on the road to success with your designs.

The way in which a piece is constructed and how it will be used will certainly have an impact on how it will look, but the materials chosen, the details of the design, and the space the piece will occupy are all of equally vital importance. So you should also develop an appreciation of the main principles of design at play. A knowledge of furniture history in its social context will help give you ideas but is not essential.

If you are designing your own furniture it is important to clarify what you want to achieve with your design.

For example:
- Are you constrained by a very specific plan?
- Is there a special type of wood that you would like to feature in the piece?
- Is visual impact paramount?
- Does your design need to cater to particular storage requirements?
- Is comfort your primary concern?
- Do you need to resolve how to fit eight people comfortably around a dining table?

Add to this your own skills, the facilities and materials you have at your disposal, together with a dash of inspiration, and you have the basis for initial design decisions.

Each project is going to be different and require care and clarity in its planning, focusing on general considerations as well as details and maintaining

Opposite: This classic upright chair would look equally at home in dining room or hallway.

the integrity of the whole piece. Once the basic function, scale, and proportions of your design are understood, begin the visual process with drawings to develop the structure and refine proportion and visual weight.

DESIGN INFLUENCES

Your design will inevitably be influenced to some degree by the construction techniques you use and the species of wood you choose to work with—its dimensions, strength, color, and grain, and the way in which it has been cut from the log and seasoned. Using more than one species of wood with either a similar or contrasting color or texture can lend additional scope and interest to a design. However, you will usually find that it is best to avoid using more than two woods, or the piece may become confusing. Simple design statements are often the most successful.

The grain, texture, and color of a particular species of wood can all inspire design choice and influence the size of components and the way in which they are detailed. For example, a dovetail drawer construction that employs a dark wood for the front and

a pale, smooth wood for the sides emphasizes the joint construction.

For both practical and aesthetic reasons, coarse-grained woods are often used with softened edges and corners, whereas the appearance of smooth-textured wood is enhanced by crisper, sharper detailing.

Inspiration for a design sometimes comes from a natural curve in a log or board, a feature in the grain or a change in color. Incorporating them in a structure or as decoration will create a unique piece.

Furniture is not seen in isolation. Whether in a domestic interior or a garden setting, it will be influenced by the scale, light, and color of its surroundings. In turn, a piece of furniture will influence and change the feeling of a space. An interior or a setting requires a focal point—a fireplace, a painting, a rug, an ornament, or an item of furniture. Whether designing to a specific plan or speculatively, it is essential to understand the role of the piece in its environment.

If you are creating a design that will be used more than once,

you will need to take into consideration the constraints such a repetition may impose. A series of wall-mounted cabinets, or dining chairs around a table, will probably need to be simpler than a stand-alone piece.

Spaces created within the frames of chairs, stools, and tables are generally dictated by structural and ergonomic considerations, but offer scope for original interpretation, particularly when introducing angled and curved members. The rear view of a dining chair is seen more than the front, and so should be considered in relation to the tabletop and to other chairs close by, and the backrests of chairs seen across the table. This is a case for simplicity; the shape and any features will be seen in repeat and will also be associated with other furniture.

Above: With this easy chair, a perpendicular frame offers stability, while the curved backrest encourages relaxation.

Opposite: Veneer inlays make a subtle and attractive surface for this coffee table.

Woven strips of timber add visual interest to this bedhead (see pages 331–7).

THE RIGHTNESS OF A DESIGN

Reactions to the rightness of a particular design are mainly a subconscious visual response to its proportion, style, or shape. Such responses are usually based on our experience of the formation of structures in nature. These natural structures have been understood since Classical times, when structural theories were developed into sophisticated formulas and applied in practice to the design of buildings and their details.

Many artists, musicians, architects, and mathematicians, as well as furniture designers, are still developing and using these formulas with pleasing results. The simplest of these are geometric developments of squares and rectangles, used to create linear constructions and calculate numerical sequences, as well as formulas covering the development of circles. In furniture design these are often employed to calculate the basic proportions and subdivisions of a design, and the positioning of the details and hardware.

Alternatively, it is often the apparent "rightness" of a design that dictates much. For example: the subdivision of the face of a cabinet and the position of handles; the position of stretcher rails in a chair frame that creates a satisfying relationship to the seat rail or the floor; or how a piece of furniture relates to the proportions of a wall or the architectural features of a room in which it is to be placed.

SCOPE FOR SELF-EXPRESSION

Developments in the techniques of furniture making, finishes and their application, glues and resins, hardware and fixtures, and the continuous introduction of improved hand and machine tools have all combined to offer great scope for experiment and self-expression in design.

Choosing a finish
The choice of a surface finish should be made with great care. Polish finishes are applied to surfaces to enhance and seal the grain and ease maintenance. Lacquers and varnishes are a film surface finish. Oils are absorbed into the wood to provide an open finish, which, with additional coating, can build from a matte to a gloss finish. A major feature of oil finishes is that

they retain the tactile quality of the wood and can be easily rejuvenated if mars or stains have to be removed. White polish, or sanding sealer, will seal wood surfaces with very little color change. Wax polishes can be applied to unfinished and treated wood. They can be clear, slightly tinted, or colored with proprietary pigments to use as a grain filler in order to accentuate an attractive open grain pattern.

Further options for finishes can change the natural color of solid wood by bleaching, dyeing or fuming. Bleaching and dyeing are achieved with proprietary products, while fuming is done with ammonia in a sealed container, and should be handled with great care. Oak is especially responsive to fuming, as it will increase in darkness the longer it is exposed to the fumes.

Open-grained wood such as oak and ash can be given a limed effect by being coated with either a proprietary liming paste, or with white or colored paints. The coating is wiped from the surface across the grain before it has dried,

leaving the open grain filled. Colored paints can be used on most wood to accentuate the grain of coarse-textured wood, or to fill the grain to provide an even finish.

Veneering

Veneers add a surface to board materials or solid wood where a particular color, grain pattern, or exotic appearance is required. They are cut to different thicknesses to meet specific requirements of decoration or durability. Most are knife cut with the grain and laid in sequence, slipped, or

Veneers can be used to form patterns that can be as simple as this checker design or quite elaborate.

book-matched to create repeating patterns. Plain veneers, often of sycamore, are also available dyed in a variety of colors. Decorative or plain-colored stringing, inlaid in either solid wood or veneered surfaces, can be used to create linear designs and borders. End-grain veneer is cut square or obliquely across the grain to feature growth rings. Often cut from a branch of laburnum or yew and laid in sequence in a grid formation, these are referred to as oysters.

Marquetry is a technique of laying veneers of contrasting colors onto a surface, which offers still more opportunities for decoration. Marquetry introduces color and shading effects, which can create three-dimensional illusions.

Bending and laminating

Techniques of bending and laminating wood have been used to great effect and economy in furniture design and manufacture. Both techniques are used equally in industry and in small workshops, differing from one another only in their scale of operation. Bending wood is a very ancient craft that has been used in furniture making for

hundreds of years. In industry, very complex shapes can now be achieved, while it is possible for the home woodworker to make simple bends. Wood used for steam-bending need only be partially seasoned and prepared for bending with minimal waste and energy.

The technique of laminating was developed in the 20th century to produce shaped components. A series of veneers, or laminates, are glued together—with the grain of each running in the same direction—in a mold that will give the required shape. Preparing laminates of thin slices of solid wood has a high waste factor to set against the final effect. More economic methods use, for example, plywood with a face veneer.

Both bending and laminating offer enormous scope for structural and decorative forms in furniture, whether linear or in broad planes.

Decorative joints

There are various decorative joints, including through mortise-and-tenon, and dovetail joints. End grain and long grain woods are often combined to emphasize the joint, or wedges

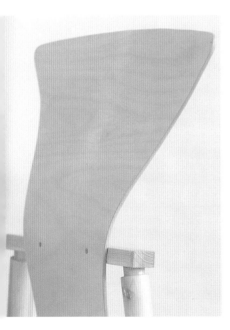

Plywood was shaped in a mold to form a comfortable back on this chair (see pages 375–83).

of two contrasting woods can be used to enhance the decorative effect.

Shaping and carving

Router cutter profiles offer further scope for imaginative decoration. Straight or curved lines with an even depth, or tapering, from a simple jig, are starting points to explore techniques, shadow effects and different grain patterns. Traditional hand-carved motifs, cut with chisels and gouges, are also worth considering.

With preforming, a series of veneers or laminates with the grain at right angles can be formed into shaped sheets. Generally it is only possible to form single curvatures, although double curvatures can be achieved with special presses. Wood is one of the materials that cannot be cast as such, but shapes can be made industrially by using chips and fibers that are pressed in metal-matched molds. Another shaping technique is that of papier-mâché, which predates the more modern fiberglass.

Using contrasting materials

Introducing different materials into a piece of wood furniture can have a big influence on the overall character and tactile qualities of a piece of furniture.

For hard surfaces there are the different colors of slate and the wide, often dramatic, choice of marble colors and patterns. The many forms of glass bring a delicate quality—clear, tinted, or silvered, with polished bevels, square or profiled edges.

Fabrics, available in an infinite variety of colors, patterns, and weaves, offer a sometimes bewildering choice of materials and should therefore always be considered with care. Felt, cane, or rush are other options. Leathers can be both supple or stiff, and also come in a wide range of colors.

Developing an individual style

Look at furniture, in your own home or in illustrations, to discover what approaches to design you find sympathetic to your taste. Note how furniture relates to interiors and vice versa. A scrapbook of sketches will become a valued reference of forms and details, color, decoration, and structure, and will help to develop a way of regarding furniture from the many aspects that combine to create good design.

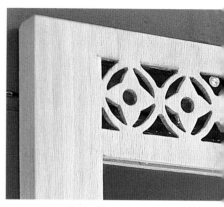

Carved patterns can add visual interest to a simple wooden construction.

Designing for yourself

Once you understand the basics of construction and have explored the possibilities of design, you may feel ready to try designing your own furniture and will need to know how to turn your ideas into practical drawings.

The finished folding chair, for which the drawings are shown opposite.

TOOLS FOR DRAWING

If you have developed your skills to the point of wanting to design your own furniture, you will need to invest in some drawing equipment—including a flat, square-cut drawing board, a large set square for drawing vertical lines, a T-square for drawing horizontal lines, a compass, a protractor for drawing angles, French curves for drawing curved lines, and a scale rule.

WORKING DRAWINGS

Working drawings show how a piece is made and are critical in furniture making. The drawings in this book are more decorative than standard working drawings, with color, grain, as well as shadow added. The imperial and metric measurements given in the book are not direct conversions and so it is important to follow either one system or the other, but not a mixture of the two, or the project may not work.

Views

Working drawings follow a convention that is understood worldwide. A working drawing presents a piece in a series of different views. The plan presents the view from the top, the front elevation presents the view from the front, and the side elevation presents the view from the side. Sections show the internal structure, such as the details of joints, by showing the piece as though it has been cut through on a particular axis. It is sometimes easier to combine an elevation with a section.

Perspective drawings and details

The drawings for each project also include a perspective drawing, which attempts to show how the piece will appear visually. Perspectives are useful in showing how things fit together, particularly if they are either exploded to show the parts separately or sectioned, when some parts are removed to make a construction clearer. Details of important joints or particular features of a piece are also given where relevant.

Scale

For a working drawing to be really useful, it needs to be drawn to scale. It may be drawn full size (or 1:1). Usually, however, the piece itself is of such a size that the drawing must be smaller, in which case you must scale it down. For example, when using imperial measurements the most common scale is one-fourth full size (1:4), where ½ in. represents 2 in. For metric measurements one-fifth full size (1:5), where 10 mm represents 50 mm, is the most common scale, although 1:10 and 1:20 are also used. When using a scaled drawing, a special ruler called a scale ruler is used so that the dimensions of the actual piece can be read from the drawing.

A scale is not given on the drawings that are featured in this book, but annotated dimensions are given throughout. These accurate, full-size dimensions will remove the possibility of doubt and mistakes if you attempt to make the piece yourself.

FRONT ELEVATION

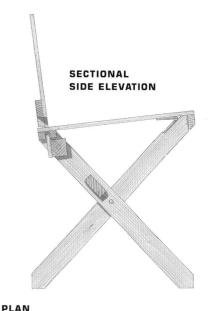

SECTIONAL SIDE ELEVATION

PLAN

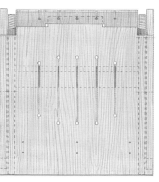

SINGLE-POINT PERSPECTIVE

MODELS AND MOCK-UPS

Once you have designed your piece it is worth trying out the design before you start to build it. This can be done by making either a scale model—for example, using balsawood—or a full-sized mock-up using fiberboard so you can check all the dimensions and proportions of the piece.

Tools and techniques

The workshop

If you are new to woodworking and furniture making, it is important to spend time planning the design of your work space. Initially, you may use any extra space—in your garage, for instance—so that you can try constructing some basic projects before you commit to a long-term workshop and equipment. It is worth temporarily adapting a sturdy table as a workbench and obtaining some basic tools.

When you are sure that you want to develop your skills you will need to set up a dedicated workshop, which will include a good quality workbench, a range of vices and various hand, power, and machine tools.

PLANNING A WORKSHOP

A clean, well-planned, dedicated workshop will provide a safe, effective, and pleasurable environment in which to develop and refine your woodworking skills. To have a fully dedicated space for woodworking may not be feasible, unless at some time you graduate from hobby to professional work. However, it is possible to adapt and dedicate spaces such as basements and garages. Circumstances will dictate the size that will be available to you, but with due consideration, and accepting that you will need to move machinery, most spaces can be made to accommodate a workshop area.

Whether you decide to adapt or dedicate space for your workshop, all of the principles of workshop design described here need to be considered.

The floor surface

The floor needs to have a finish that will enable you to keep it clean and even—a concrete floor painted with floor paint will serve well. The place where you stand at your workbench benefits from having a slightly less hard surface. Industrial-type rubber flooring works well for this.

A well-designed and fully equipped workshop is essential for a woodwork enthusiast.

Power sources

Almost all mechanical equipment is powered by electricity, and so it is essential that the power supply in your workshop meets all of the necessary regulations and that its distribution is suitable and safe for you to use when running your power and machine tools. Also avoid the temptation of buying secondhand industrial machines. While they may be cheap, you may run into problems with them if they require more power than your home is wired for.

Ensure that you have the necessary power supplies and a heat source, such as this wood burner.

It is best to store tools safely near your workbench.

Lighting

It is best to have as much natural lighting as you can. North-facing is preferable, but if this is not possible and you have direct light, you may need blinds to stop the sun's glare. This will no doubt have to be supplemented by artificial light. Fluorescent lights can give an even illumination, but spotlights can be very useful over the workbench and your machinery.

Heating and humidity

Heating and air conditioning may be necessary, depending upon the climate. Furniture makers are always concerned about the fact that wood moves. Ideally the workshop should be at the same temperature, and definitely the same humidity, as the environment where the completed work will stand.

Access

As long as the pieces made are small scale, access might not be a problem. However, larger pieces will need to be moved out of the space when completed and inaccessible places can give rise to severe problems. Try to select a place where materials and equipment can be moved in and completed furniture moved out. Attic or basement areas therefore may not be suitable.

Power tools will soon become covered in dust if left on a bench. Store them in boxes under or near the bench.

Security

As your facilities grow, be sure that your valuable tools are secure because they will be very expensive to replace.

Storage requirements

It is convenient to have many tools, particularly hand tools, hung on the walls near the bench. However, hand power tools should always be stored in cupboards for safety reasons, and drawers are needed for many of the smaller tools to keep them tidy.

You will collect many types of materials. Hardwood planks are

Use a bench shelf for the most useful and commonly used items.

Wherever possible, store tools safely out of the way on a wall.

Label and store containers safely.

best stored in a similar way to that found in a good lumberyard—horizontally with spacers in between each board and away from sunlight or direct heat sources. Softwoods can often be found at the suppliers stored vertically, but this is best avoided unless it is absolutely necessary. In general, ensure that the workshop is dry and well ventilated so the wood does not soak up moisture. Manufactured boards should be stored in a vertical stack against a wall or partition.

As you work, you will find some material will be waste but other, particularly exotic, lumber may be worth retaining for future jobs. It is useful to have some boxes or bins where you can keep small pieces of wood for this purpose. Make sure, however, that this is undertaken methodically so that you know where to find different wood types quickly and easily.

Sundries such as hardware, adhesives, and polishes can be stored on open shelving or in cupboards. Remember, however, that if you are going to have large quantities of finish, it should really be stored outside the workshop in order to reduce the risk of fire.

HEALTH AND SAFETY

Always be aware of the possible problems, but work with caution and confidence. Make sure that you have a first-aid box in your workshop.

Fire

Your workshop should have fire-safety measures built into it. A fire extinguisher or fire blanket should be on hand; install a smoke detector. Prevention is better than cure, and so ensure that dust and shavings are removed daily and that you do not smoke. Also make sure that there are no sparks from electrical or other equipment.

Some materials may be flammable, so store large amounts of such material outside in a metal fireproof box, and bring only enough material into the workshop to complete the current job. When using finishing oils applied by cloth, always unfold the cloth and leave it outside to prevent spontaneous combustion.

Fine dust and chemical fumes

When work is generating fine dust or chemical fumes, ensure that you wear a face mask or respirator, and use safety goggles whenever your eyes may be vulnerable. Some form of exhaust system or extractor is needed when you progress to machine tools and this is also useful for many of the hand power tools. With machines such as table saws and combination planes, exhaust is very important.

Most of your finishing may well utilize oils and waxes, but if you are working with solvent-based finishes that generate noxious fumes it is better to have a part of the workshop specifically dedicated as a small finishing or spray booth. Then you can fit a ventilation system to remove fumes. In this situation you should always wear a suitable mask.

Noise

When using machines or processes that generate high noise levels always wear ear protectors or plugs.

For your health and safety, always use a dust extractor of some kind when working with power tools.

Hand tool safety

Accidents can happen, and so be aware when procedures could be dangerous and take special care.

Machinery safety

With any woodworking machinery safety is paramount. Follow these guidelines:

• Never make adjustments without turning off the power.

• Always follow the manufacturer's instructions for the specific machine.

• Inspect the machine before you switch it on and always check the machine after making adjustments.

• Always use the guards supplied.

• Never attempt to machine small items without adequate jigs.

• If anything happens to your piece of work, switch off the machine before attempting to rectify the situation.

• Most important, when using any cutting machine, be it a table saw, portable power saw or router, wear safety glasses. Safety glasses are also recommended for drilling operations and nailing, particularly when using large nails.

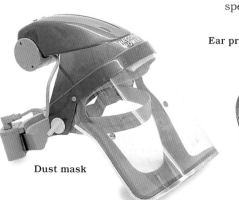

Dust mask

Ear protectors

The workbench

A good, sturdy workbench is an essential element of a woodworker's workshop. A thick, hardwood top is best to use as a work surface, and the underframe should also be of a sturdy hardwood.

Try to make a workbench one of your first major projects (see pages 270–6).

Make sure the worktop is level. The usual height for a workbench is between 32 in. (800 mm) and 34 in. (850 mm), although different heights can be made to order.

WORKBENCH FITTINGS

The workbench should be fitted with well-machined vices. Many workbenches have both side and end vices already installed. However, if you need to purchase and fit vices separately, the most important vice is the main woodworker's vice. Buy as large a capacity as you can afford, and fit the vice as close as possible to one of the legs of the underframe; this will prevent any flexing of the worktop when the working lumber is clamped in the jaws of the vice. It should also be properly set into the bench so that when the wooden vice cheeks are applied, no metal shows and the top of the vice is perfectly flush with the top. You will need to drill large holes or cut mortises in the worktop so that a bench stop can be fitted. These are normally used with an end vice, which can be useful for clamping small jobs as well as holding the work.

A large woodworking vice is useful for holding your work securely while you work on it.

Most workbenches are made with a tool well, which enables a large work piece to be moved across the worktop without sweeping hand tools onto the floor. Many workbenches also come with a drawer or cupboards for the storage of tools or materials underneath.

The workbench project featured later in this book (see pages 270–6) would be a good investment of your time and effort. It has a strong underframe with some substantial lumber for the main working area, a ply well for tools, and a deep backboard to make the structure rigid.

OTHER TYPES OF BENCHES

Proprietary folding benches can also be bought. Although not substantial enough to be your main bench, they can be useful in the workshop if you need to undertake work such as fitting away from your base.

Sawhorses, or trestles, can also be useful when you are initially cutting sheets of manufactured board.

MAINTAINING YOUR BENCH

A workbench needs to be well-maintained to provide good, long-lasting service. Here are a few tips for good maintenance:

• Support the work piece away from the work surface, using padded strips of lumber. This will protect the work surface as well as the piece that you are working on. Specialized rubber mats are available that allow nails, screws, and working debris to fall through the mats to the work surface. As an alternative to these mats, a layer of hardboard can be placed on the worktop surface and changed whenever it becomes damaged.

Folding bench

Sawhorse

- Clean the work surface down regularly with a brush to remove debris.
- Avoid using carpet as a surface protector; it can trap and hide nasty abrasive materials, such as glass fragments, small nails, and screws, in its surface.
- Avoid nailing anything into the surface of the workbench if possible. Try to use a clamp or screws instead.
- When drilling, always make sure that you use a piece of scrap material between the work piece and the worktop.
- Check that the surface of the worktop is straight and without twist. This can be achieved with winding sticks, which are parallel pieces of lumber. Set the wood edge-up at either end of the workbench and sight across the top edges to test. Or you could use a level and a straightedge to test for level. Adjust the workbench with chocks to set the worktop true and flat.

A TEMPORARY WORKBENCH

If you have just started woodworking, you may want to make a temporary workbench initially rather than investing in a permanent one right away.

In this case, you will need to find an existing table that has a strong structure, and make a temporary top.

Take a sheet of manufactured board that is 1 in. (25 mm) thick, and cut it to a size that is 6 in. (150 mm) larger than the existing table all the way around. Fit some baize—a soft, usually green, woolen fabric that resembles felt—to the underside and make four corner blocks so that the surface will not move out of position. On the edge where you wish to work, fit another strip of board 12–16 in. (300–400 mm)—the same length as the base board— and glue this strip of board into position.

You should have enough room to fit a small vice and it would be advisable to use a couple of C-clamps to hold it in place and ensure that it is stable. This should give you a surface that enables you to start work.

Ideally, the workbench should be level with your waist, and so you may have to make some chocks for the legs.

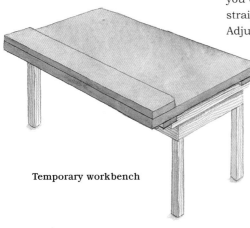

Temporary workbench

The essential tool kit

If you are a woodworker with experience you will already have a set of tools, but if you are starting this pleasurable journey you will need to begin by purchasing some basic tools. The list below is a reasonable starting point.

It is good practice to extend your tool kit by purchasing reasonably priced tools as they are needed for a particular job, and also to have a long-term plan for expensive tools, power tools, and machine tools. Within your budget always purchase the highest quality that you can afford since they will last longer and will be easier to use. A good list of hand power tools would include a power drill, jigsaw, orbital sander, and router. Machine tools would include a pillar drill (drill press), a table saw, a bandsaw, and a combination plane.

Below is a summary of the tools that you will need as you begin your woodworking journey.

MEASURING AND MARKING TOOLS

The importance of accurate measuring and marking is stressed often throughout this book, and it is advisable to obtain the best-quality tools available on the list. The most important are:

• For workshop-based furniture making, a folding ruler is useful, but if you need to do a lot of site work a steel tape can be more useful.

• A good-quality, accurate steel ruler—12 in. (300 mm) long—is essential for measuring and marking work.

• Pencils need to be hard enough to give a precise fine line, but soft enough to be seen. A 2H grade will be adequate.

• Some people use a marking knife that is ground on one face only, but a more traditionally sharpened blade is usually preferable.

• A good-quality try square or combination square is essential. A combination square is a more expensive option, but is preferable since a good-quality tool will give much better results and will last

A selection of chisels is an essential part of your tool kit.

longer if cared for. If money is tight, however, a good-quality try square will suffice.

• A traditional sliding bevel will suit well.

• You will need other gauges later, but a good marking gauge will suffice at first. If you buy a mortise gauge as well, be sure that it is the type with a screw adjustment for setting the space between the points rather than a simple slide, which can slip.

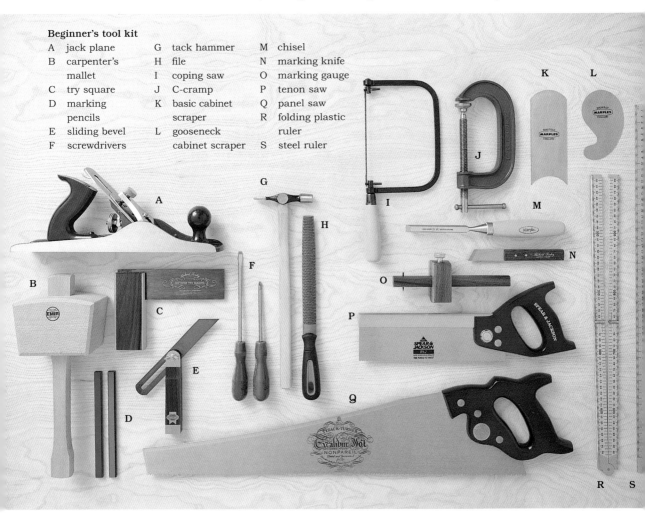

Beginner's tool kit

A	jack plane	G	tack hammer
B	carpenter's mallet	H	file
		I	coping saw
C	try square	J	C-cramp
D	marking pencils	K	basic cabinet scraper
E	sliding bevel	L	gooseneck cabinet scraper
F	screwdrivers		

M	chisel
N	marking knife
O	marking gauge
P	tenon saw
Q	panel saw
R	folding plastic ruler
S	steel ruler

SAWING TOOLS

• A good-quality panel saw cuts both solid lumber and manufactured boards.

• A backsaw, a small tenon saw, or large dovetail saw will be needed for fine work—8 in. (200 mm) will be suitable.

• For curved cuts, a coping saw is essential.

• Even though most power tools will be added to your kit at a later date, if you wish to undertake large-scale or a large amount of work, then a jigsaw will be a welcome addition. It removes much hard work, and can cut both solid lumber—up to 2 in. (50 mm) plus—and manufactured board, and also helps with some fine work. Metal blades are also available.

SURFACING TOOLS

• A jack plane is the most useful to start with.

• A cabinet scraper, for fine finishing on difficult wood, is a must.

CUTTING TOOLS

A range of bevel-edged chisels —¼ in. (6 mm), ½ in. (12 mm), and 1 in. (25 mm)—will suffice at first.

GENERAL TOOLS

• Small cordless electric drills are now so reasonably priced

that they are the best tool for early drilling jobs. You will need a range of drill bits: twist drills from ¹⁄₃₂–½ in. (1–12 mm) or dowel bits from ⅛–½ in. (3–12 mm). You may need to drill holes larger than ½ in. (12 mm) and a set of spade bits from ½–1½ in. (12–40 mm) will tide you over until you can afford more expensive bits.

• Buy a small power router with basic bits.

• For initial shaping work, rasps will suffice until spokeshaves are needed.

• A tack hammer is good for fine work. Heavier hammers will be needed later.

• A carpenter's mallet is essential for both joints and assembly.

• Both Phillips and slot screws are now used, so buy a screwdriver that accepts different-size heads—or use screw bits in your power drill.

• A hacksaw and a range of small files will cover jobs where some modification to metal parts is necessary.

• Holding and assembly tools, including sash clamps and C-clamps, are essential. Purchase a small set of four light sash clamps—30 in. (800 mm)—as a start, and two 10-in. (250 mm) and four 6-in. (150 mm) C-clamps.

More advanced tools

Once you have the basic tool kit, the following are worth considering:

• An orbital sander will help you with finishing large surfaces.

• A floor or bench-mounted drill press (or a large electric drill and a drill stand) is a very useful addition to the workshop.

• A table saw is useful for many precise operations.

• A belt sander is also useful, but it is essential that you get this bench mounted.

• A bandsaw will enable you to cut curved components and thick pieces of lumber.

• A combination planer means that you can purchase sawn wood, and ensure that work is straight, flat, and to the correct thickness.

Measuring and marking

Accurate measuring and marking are vital in achieving quality work. Even the slightest inaccuracies in the early stages will inevitably lead to complications later. There is an old craftworkers' saying: "measure twice, cut once."

TOOLS

As with any aspect of woodworking, the range of equipment available for measuring and marking is vast. However, some tools are more useful and adaptable than others, and so it is worth finding the best ones that can be trusted for the job. A rough measurement is adequate for converting planks into slightly oversized pieces, but precise measuring and marking are essential for tasks such as preparing to cut specific lengths of wood or waste from a joint.

Rulers and measures

A **folding wooden** or **plastic ruler** or a **retractable steel tape measure** are equally suitable for the initial measuring of length, but are not accurate enough for precise marking. A **steel ruler** is best for this. A 12-in. (300 mm) ruler is essential and a longer one in excess of 24 in. (600 mm) is also useful. Buy a quality ruler that has accurately marked measurements. A **steel straightedge**, at least 24 in. (600 mm) but preferably 32 in. (800 mm) long, is useful for marking straight lines or checking the flatness of a surface. A **vernier gauge** is useful for measuring small dimensions. A small plastic one that will measure to $\frac{3}{200}$ in. (0.1 mm) is adequate.

Squares

Precision try squares are essential for establishing a right angle to mark across the grain. The type with a metal blade, rosewood stock (handle), and a brass face, particularly in large sizes, is generally adequate for right angles. A **miter square** can be used for 45-degree angles. A small **engineer's metal square** is often useful when working on very

Precision
try square

Engineer's metal square

Sliding bevel

locking
level

blade

adjustable pins

adjustable pin

Vernier
gauge

stock

Combination
square

thumbscrew

Cutting gauge

Retractable steel tape
measure

beam

thumbscrew

Folding
plastic ruler

Marking
gauge

Mortise gauge

Steel rulers: 12 in. (300 mm) and 24 in. (600 mm)

Measuring equal divisions

You can divide a piece of lumber or board into equal divisions, where the actual width of the divisions is not vital, without using mathematics. Lay a ruler at an angle across the surface so that clear increments mark exactly the required number of divisions.

Marking knives

Marking pencils

small items (a larger version is also available). A **combination square** does the job of a try square, miter square, and level in one.

Sliding bevels

A **sliding bevel** is necessary for marking dovetail joints and for other angled work. They are available with a wooden handle or all in steel, the engineer's version. The screw allows the sliding bevel to be set at the required angle with the aid of an accurate protractor.

Pencils

Pencils can be used for precision marking if they are fairly hard and can be sharpened to a good point or chisel edge that will last. It is best to use a pencil mark for rough guidance and for setting out; use a marking knife to make a cut line when greater accuracy is required, such as when marking joints, or for sawing or chiseling.

Marking knives

Marking knives are much more accurate than pencils and provide a slight indentation for saw teeth. Always use a knife for marking across the grain, running the blade along the waste side of the desired line.

Gauges

A gauge is the best tool for marking along the grain and there are several types available. Each has an adjustable marking device that can be set at the required measurement and used to score a line. A **marking gauge** has one steel pin, whereas a **mortise gauge** has two independently adjustable pins for marking the position of mortise-and-tenon joints. A **cutting gauge** has a small blade that is most suitable for cutting lines across the grain.

PREPARING THE TOOLS

All measuring and marking tools should be used with care or their accuracy can be affected.

Checking a try square

1 To check if a try square is accurate, lay it on a piece of board that has a straight edge. Position the metal-edged stock along the straight edge.

2 Mark a line on the board face against the try square blade, at right angles to the edge. Turn the square over and mark another line a short distance from the first. If the lines are parallel, the square is accurate. If not, repair can be difficult so it is best to replace the tool.

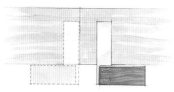

Check with a try square.

Adjusting a sliding bevel

1 Make a mark on the edge of a board and use a protractor to make a second mark at the desired angle. Join the marks to give a line on the face of the board that is at the correct angle to the edge.

2 Loosen the screw on the sliding bevel and align the outer edge of the bevel along the angled line. Retighten the screw to set the bevel.

Adjusting a sliding bevel.

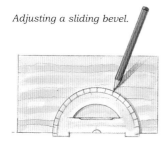

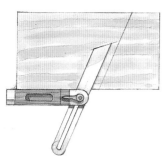

PREPARING THE LUMBER

Before measuring and marking the lumber for a project, it is important that it is perfectly flat, square and straight.

Checking lumber

1 Check to see if the surface is free of pits or bumps by running a straightedge across it. If the surface is not flat, it should be planed true—perfectly flat—before the wood is measured and marked (see Planing, pages 100–14).

Use a straightedge to check for flatness.

2 You can check if the board is straight by positioning two steel rulers across each end. Now sight along the board and, if the two rulers appear parallel, the wood is straight.

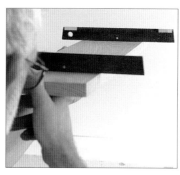

Check that the board is straight.

Using a bevel to determine a ratio

Bevels can also be used to determine a ratio—for example, on dovetail joints. For a ratio of 1:4, square a line across from the edge, measure up four units—say, 2 in. (40 mm); on the edge of the board measure one unit—say, ½ in. (10 mm). Then join the two points with the blade while the stock is against the edge.

Marking the faces of timber

1 Make the face-side mark (usually a scroll shape) on the timber surface, toward the edge to be planed next.

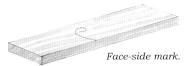

Face-side mark.

2 Plane the edge straight and at right angles to the face side. Check with a straightedge and try square.

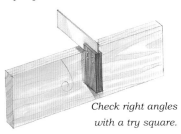

Check right angles with a try square.

3 Apply the edge mark, conventionally a "V" shape, on the face edge.

Apply edge marks.

TAKING MEASUREMENTS

Measure lumber and the accessible parts of projects with a steel ruler. Place the end of the ruler on one edge of the surface and read the required dimension at the other.

Measuring awkward spaces

Some measurements can be difficult to make because a ruler cannot be held in the best position for accuracy, for example, measuring across the internal diagonal of a frame, in order to check for squareness.

1 Cut two strips of wood that, when overlapped, will span the distance to be measured. Cut a bevel at one end of each strip.

2 Hold the strips together, positioning the beveled ends in each corner. Mark a line on each strip to show where they meet.

Use beveled strips across diagonal.

3 Place the strips on a flat surface, match up the lines and measure from point to point. Alternately, measure from the line to the point on one strip and add it to the total length of the other strip.

Marking rough measurements

For approximate measurements parallel to the edge of the lumber, you can make the marks with a pencil and improvise a gauge by using a finger or rule.

Gauging with a finger

1 Hold the pencil between your thumb and index finger. Rest another finger on the edge of the board so that the pencil is at the required distance from the edge.

2 Keeping the hand and pencil steady, run the pencil along the board to make a line parallel to the edge.

Gauge a line with your finger.

Gauging with a ruler

1 You can also use a ruler as a gauge. Place the ruler on the wood's surface so the end is the required distance from the edge.

2 Hold a pencil against the end of the ruler and use your other hand to keep the ruler at the correct distance from the edge. Run the ruler and pencil along the board's length to make a line parallel to the edge.

Marking precise measurements

Precision is best achieved with a marking knife or a gauge, which will give a clean indentation for positioning a chisel or saw.

Using a marking knife

1 Hold a ruler or try square firmly in place and position yourself so that you can see where the edge meets the board.

2 Position the knife blade flat against the edge of the ruler or square and mark the board by pulling the knife along the edge with care.

Using a marking gauge

1 Use a ruler to set the position of the stock at the correct distance from the pin or blade and lightly tighten the thumbscrew. Check this against the board and make any required adjustments by tapping the gauge on the workbench. To increase the gap, tap the base of the beam;

to decrease it, tap the beam at the head. When the pin is in position, tighten the thumbscrew.

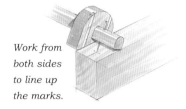

increase

decrease

Use a marking gauge.

2 Position the stock against the face edge, with the pin just touching the surface of the face side. Slightly rotate the marking gauge and run the stock along the edge.

Gauge a line with a marking gauge.

Finding the center point

Marking gauges can also be used to find the center point on a piece of lumber. Set the pin to approximately half the surface width. From each side, make a small mark with the point. Keep adjusting the stock by tapping the beam, as described

at left, and repeat the operation until the marks line up from each side, at which point the mark is perfectly centered.

Work from both sides to line up the marks.

Using a cutting gauge

You can use a cutting gauge in place of a marking gauge in order to achieve a cut line. This tool is used in the same way, but the blade must be very sharp and firmly inserted in the beam.

Using a mortise gauge

Set the pins the required distance apart—that of your mortise chisel. Then adjust the stock along the stem and tighten with the thumbscrew. The gauge is then ready to mark two parallel lines.

Set the pins at the correct position.

Basic sawing

Some saws can be used to cut timber into manageable sizes, and others to cut intricate joints and shapes. It is useful to separate the skills into basic sawing, which is discussed here, and fine sawing, which is discussed on pages 115–21.

HAND SAWS

There are three main types of hand saw—the **ripsaw**, the **crosscut saw**, and the **panel saw**—and all taper in length to assist the blade's movement. The main difference between each of the saws lies in tooth size. Large teeth remove a lot of material, whereas smaller teeth make smaller, finer cuts. Tooth size is generally measured by the number of teeth per 1 in. (25 mm), and is expressed as teeth per inch (tpi). This applies where teeth are measured from the base of one tooth to another, but if you are calculating from point to point instead, the measurement is described as points per inch (ppi).

Saw teeth

The teeth on saws differ to suit the type of sawing that is to be undertaken. However, all but the smallest saws are sharpened and set in a specific way. Each tooth has a leading edge, which makes the cut, and a less upright side known as the trailing edge. The shape produced is known as the pitch. The teeth are also set—that is, bent first to one side, then to the other—so that the cutting is more effective and the blade does not bind in the cut. The cut that the saw makes is called a kerf. Saw teeth are measured as tpi (teeth per inch) or ppi (points per inch).

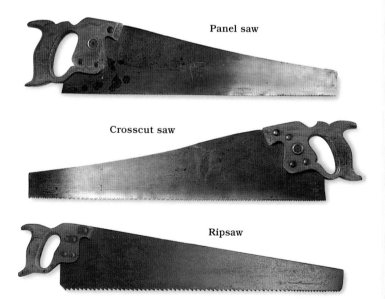

Panel saw

Crosscut saw

Ripsaw

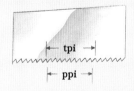

basic sawing

Sharpening a saw

Saws should be sharpened regularly to ensure that they cut smoothly and accurately. While traditional craftworkers used to sharpen their own saws, many modern woodworkers take their tools to "saw doctors." These people specialize in saw sharpening, and work with machines or, for very fine saws, by hand. Some modern saws, especially cheap ones, may have hardened teeth that can be sharpened only by machine, while others must simply be replaced when the teeth become too blunt. It is, therefore, more economical in the long run to buy quality tools that can be serviced regularly, rather than constantly replacing them.

Panel saw

Panel saws have much finer teeth than ripsaws and crosscut saws, with a tpi of 10 to 12. They can be used on solid timber, and are also more suitable than the other saws for cutting manufactured board because of the finer teeth.

Crosscut saw

The crosscut saw is designed for cutting solid lumber across the grain. The leading edge has a greater pitch than a ripsaw's and the teeth are sharpened at an angle so that each tooth has a knife-like cutting edge. These saws have more tpi (8 to 9) than ripsaws, and while many experienced craftworkers will use both types, most enthusiasts find that possessing one crosscut saw is adequate.

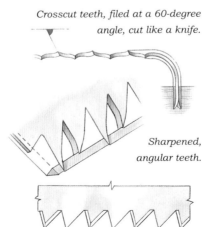

Crosscut teeth, filed at a 60-degree angle, cut like a knife.

Sharpened, angular teeth.

Ripsaw

The ripsaw is normally the largest of the hand saws. It is sharpened for cutting wood along the grain and thus has few tpi (4 to 5). Each tooth has an upright leading edge, which is filed to a chiseled point at 90 degrees to its face.

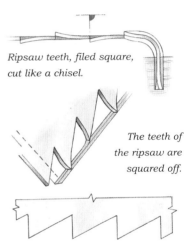

Ripsaw teeth, filed square, cut like a chisel.

The teeth of the ripsaw are squared off.

Using a hand saw

All of the saws described at left are used for cutting material to an approximate size. For this reason, an allowance of about ⅛ in. (3 mm) for planing is needed. Remember this when marking cut lines, both along and across the grain. Always hold the saw firmly, with the index finger pointing in the direction of the cut. This helps keep the handle from twisting as the blade moves.

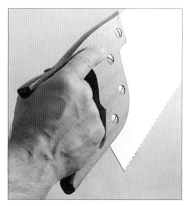

The correct grip for a hand saw.

1 Mark the lines to be cut, both along and across the grain. Cuts along the grain or in manufactured board are generally easier if the material is supported horizontally on sawhorses or trestles.

For cutting along the grain, support the board horizontally on trestles.

For cutting short pieces of lumber along the grain, it may be possible to put the wood in a vice, so that it can be cut vertically.

Cut short pieces of wood along the grain in a vice.

For cutting across the grain, it may be more convenient if the board is cramped to a workbench.

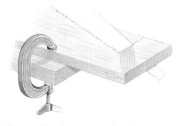

Cramp the timber to a bench to make cuts across the grain.

2 Use your thumb to locate and steady the saw on the waste side of the cut line and make some short strokes to begin the cut. Keep your thumb away from the teeth of the saw.

Use your thumb to steady the saw as you start the cut.

Sawing manufactured board

Use a panel saw to cut manufactured board. Hold the saw at a low angle to prevent breakout on the bottom face, especially on veneer-faced boards. Steady the work with a cramp or your knee.

basic sawing

Safety first

- Always tie long hair back and don't wear loose clothing.

- When using power tools, follow the instructions provided by the manufacturer.

- Cut carefully and do not force the blade—let the saw do the cutting.

- Never lift tools by the cord or disconnect by pulling the cord.

- Before changing blades or making any other adjustments, check that the tool is disconnected from the power supply.

- Don't use faulty tools.

- Always wear the correct protective gear—for example, safety glasses, dust mask, and ear muffs.

- Ensure that the work is held firm and the saw blade will not cut any unintended objects such as the sawhorses.

- Place the power cord over your shoulder so that it is behind both you and the saw.

- Allow the tool to reach full speed before you begin work with it.

- Keep tool cutters and blades sharp.

3 Remove your thumb once the saw has started a small kerf in the wood. Continue to apply pressure to the handle so that you guide the saw along the cut.

4 Gradually increase the length of the strokes that you take and build up a steady rhythm, ensuring that each forward cut stays on the waste side of the line.

5 On some wood, the cut can begin to close as you work farther down the length of the board. This may cause the blade to bind and interrupt the flow of movement. Insert a small wedge in the kerf, so that the cut edges remain separated. You could also add a little wax or even soap to the side of the saw to act as a lubricant and help it slip through the cut.

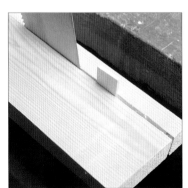

Cut along the grain with a wedge in the kerf to separate the wood.

Cutting cleanly

Generally, sawing along the grain of the wood should not present too many problems with splintering or splitting. However, sawing across the grain can cause the grain to fracture and break out on the underside. This should not be a cause for concern when you are sawing prior to planing, because the damage will be removed later as the wood is refined. However, precautions need to be taken when you are cutting after the wood has been planed true and to size.

If breakout is a particular problem, you could use a finer toothed saw and/or lower the angle of the saw as you work—especially for veneered boards such as plywood.

POWER SAWS

There are two main types of power saw – the hand-held saw and the machine saw. Although these tools are unlikely to remove the need for hand tools and careful, skilled craftwork, they are versatile and can be useful for some woodworking tasks. For example, power saws are ideal for cutting heavy or large pieces of wood, which would need a lot of effort if sawed by hand. The jigsaw is also good for intricate work, helping to ensure accurate and precise cuts.

Hand-held power saws

The **jigsaw** is particularly useful for initial rough cutting wood both along and across the grain, as well as manufactured board. It can also be used for fine work, giving accurate and precise cuts. The tool can be used with a variety of blades, all of which are designed for cutting different materials and producing different results. Most blades cut with a vertical—or reciprocating—motion, although some advanced saws can have an orbital action. The blade always cuts on the upstroke and can saw solid wood up to 2 in. (50 mm) thick. Some varieties have different speeds so they can be used on plastics and soft metals.

Many woodworkers also use a **circular saw** for cutting solid wood and manufactured boards. Light and portable, the saw is suitable for site work, but a hand saw or jigsaw is usually an adequate alternative in the workshop and is much safer to use. However, the circular saw can be useful if it is mounted in a stand as a first table saw. The saw consists of a sole plate that will rest on the work, a saw guard to prevent accidents,

a fence for parallel cuts and a tilt mechanism for angled cuts. Unlike jigsaws, circular saws are always used for straight cuts, though the blade can be set to cut through the material, or work to a set depth.

Using a jigsaw

Jigsaws can be used to cut freehand straight or curved lines, or in conjunction with fences and guides that direct the cut. However, always ensure that there is nothing in its path that is likely to foul the blade.

1 Hold the jigsaw firmly by the handle with one hand. Use the other hand to support the weight of the lumber or board, or cramp the work down.

2 Start the saw and bring the blade up to the edge of the work, resting the sole plate on the work; ease it through the board. Always saw on the waste side of the cut lines—the blade cuts on the upstroke, which can cause grain breakout that will need to be cleaned up later.

Starting the cut from the edge.

Safety first

• Always ensure that you have set the machine correctly.

• Keep all body parts away from the blade, especially hands, which should never be in line with the cut.

• Whenever possible, use fences, jigs, and other guides, keeping your hands away from the cutters at all times.

Power jigsaw

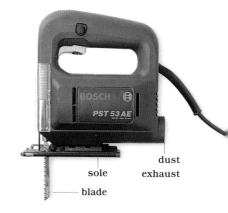

dust exhaust

sole

blade

blades

Table saw

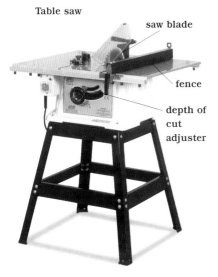

saw blade

fence

depth of
cut
adjuster

Radial-arm saw

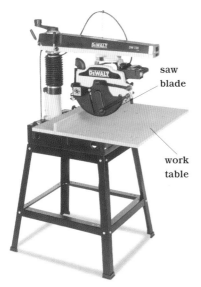

saw
blade

work
table

3 Work slowly, firmly, and smoothly, avoiding any sudden changes in direction that may cause the saw not to cut true or the blade to break.

Making internal cuts
1 Measure and mark the shape on the wood.

2 Drill (see Drilling, pages 140–8) a starting hole in the waste area that is large enough to accommodate the blade of the jigsaw.

3 Insert the jigsaw blade through the hole and use the tool to cut the shape in the normal way.

Use a jigsaw to make a neat internal cut.

Machine power saws
Like hand-held power saws, machine power saws can make light work of large pieces of lumber and board. They can also be set to levels of accuracy for repetitive work that can be hard to achieve with hand-held tools. The **table saw** is the most popular kind of machine tool. This is basically a machine with a rigid, flat table through which a circular saw blade projects. Behind the blade is a riving knife. The blade can be set to produce different depths of cuts and in most models can also be angled. The machine has a secure fence against which parallel cuts can be made, and adjustable fence slides, set in grooves, for crosscutting. There are many types of saw blades, which means that the machine can be used to make both quick cuts as well as precise saw cuts. Always operate the saw with extreme care, checking that it is set correctly, with all the necessary guards in place, before beginning any work.

Radial-arm saws can be used to perform many tasks in woodwork, including crosscutting and jointmaking. They are also used for ripping lumber, although this can be hazardous so always take care. Some machines may also be set up with a sanding disk. Machines dedicated to a specific task often perform better than ones that do multi-tasks.

A **bandsaw** (see pages 120–1) is another useful machine for cutting, especially shaped work.

A **miter saw** is used for precision cutting of angles and square ends. It is used for cutting miter joints for baseboards, moldings, and picture frames. The saw assembly and motor are hinged on an arm, which is lowered to cut the wood. The arm is spring-loaded to return the saw to the "up" position. The saw has a fixed top guard that covers the blade and a lower guard that retracts as the arm is lowered onto the work. The miter saw can be turned to make angle cuts. Most saws turn at 45 degrees to each side, and some turn up to 60 degrees.

Other types of miter saws include **compound** and **compound slide saws**. These allow the motor assembly to turn both vertically and horizontally.

Using a table saw
1 Check that the table saw is set to the correct adjustments before turning it on. To cut wood into parallel pieces, set the fence to the required distance from the blade; be sure the blade is at the correct height.

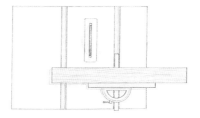

Set the fence securely so that it is at the right distance from the blade.

Saw the wood into parallel pieces.

2 To crosscut, set the adjustable fence to the required angle. Miters and specific angles can also be cut by setting this fence, or by canting the blade. Hold the timber against the crosscut fence. Slide the work towards the blade and cut steadily. Once cut, slide the work away from the blade before bringing the crosscut fence in front of it.

Make angles and miters with the fence.

3 Use push sticks, spare battens, to feed timber through the blade, so that you can keep hands clear of the blade. This should have a notch cut in the leading end to hold the timber down while pushing it forward.

Warning
Many power tools require grounded (3-prong) outlets or ground-fault interrupter (circuit breaker) outlets. Do not attempt to bypass these safeguards.

Miter saw safety
• Check that the guard is working correctly.

• Use the vice at the base of the saw to hold your work.

• Ensure the tilt adjustments are tight.

• Never "cross hands" when operating the saw.

• Always use the correct saw blade.

Use push sticks as a safety measure when using a table saw.

S h a r p e n i n g

Effective woodworking relies on tools that have sharp cutting edges. This is particularly important for hand tools, such as planes, chisels, and gouges, as well as the blades and cutters in machine tools.

Flattening the back of a new blade

New blades will need to have their backs flattened on an oilstone. To do this, lubricate a coarse or medium stone with oil and rub the back of the blade along it. Ensure that the surface is flat by regularly checking it against a straightedge.

The following description of sharpening uses a wide chisel to demonstrate the process, but exactly the same methods are used for plane blades and narrow chisels, although the grinding angle for narrow chisels is smaller: for wide chisels and plane blades, the angle is 25 to 30 degrees, and for narrow chisels the angle is 20 to 25 degrees.

Sharpening is carried out in two stages: the blade is first ground to an angle and then it is honed in order to achieve the sharpest edge.

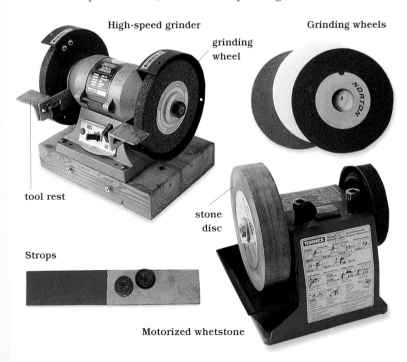

High-speed grinder

grinding wheel

Grinding wheels

tool rest

stone disc

Strops

Motorized whetstone

GRINDING

Chisel and plane blades can be ground to an angle using a high-speed bench grinder or a slow-speed motorized whetstone.

High-speed grinder

High-speed grinders are a quick means of grinding an angle. The blade is held against the rotating wheel. The wheels are usually made from aluminum-oxide and rotate very fast, at around 3000 rpm or more. Make sure that heat does not build up; otherwise the temper of the blade will be removed, rendering the tool useless. If this happens, the metal will change color. Cool the blade frequently in water.

1 Always wear safety goggles when using a grinder even though the tool has protective spark deflectors. Before grinding a bevel, check that the cutting edge on the blade is square by holding it against an accurate try square. If it is not square, sharpen the edge on the grinder, before moving onto the bevel.

Ensure that the cutting edge is square before you start on the bevel.

2 Hold the tool at the correct angle to ensure that you will achieve the correct bevel. For a wide chisel, this is about 25 degrees. Then, adjust the tool rest to match.

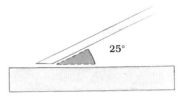

Ensure that the grinding angle is correct before you start.

3 Switch on the grinder, and hold the blade between your index finger and thumb. Position the blade on the rest, ensuring your fingers are well clear of the wheel. Move the bevel forward until it just starts to grind. Move the tool from side to side over the face of the wheel to sharpen the full width.

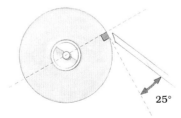

Start grinding, keeping the angle steady at 25 degrees.

4 Inspect the sharpened edge often to check that it remains square and at the required angle.

Sharpening a plane blade

When sharpening plane blades, hold the blade at a slight angle to the stone. This will help to ensure that the whole of the cutting edge makes contact with the stone.

Honing a narrow chisel blade

Use a zigzag or figure-eight action. Move the chisel along the stone to ensure that its surface does not become unevenly worn. If you find this process difficult, honing aids that hold the blade in a given position are available, but it is worth persevering to develop this skill yourself.

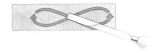

Truing stones

After a great deal of use, an oilstone will become hollow. This makes it difficult to keep a square edge on chisels or blades; therefore, it needs to be flattened. Grind the surface with carborundum powder and oil or water, on a sheet of glass. Continue to rub the face of the stone until it is flat.

Motorized whetstone

Use a motorized whetstone for the same job. This has a horizontally or vertically mounted whetstone, turning at under 500 rpm, which is lubricated by a stream of water or oil. The slower speed and built-in lubrication help to ensure good control, while removing the risk of drawing the temper.

1 Check that the cutting edge of the blade is square. Bring the tool down firmly onto the stone at a 25-degree angle.

2 Inspect the bevel often to ensure that it remains square and at the required angle. The grinding process generates a burr, which will be removed by honing.

Grind the chisel on the whetstone at an approximate angle of 25 degrees.

HONING

Honing produces the final cutting edge on the tool blade. It is achieved by rubbing the ground tool edge up and down a stone that is lubricated with oil. This produces a second bevel, which will give the sharp, cutting edge.

Oilstones

Most people starting out in woodwork use an oilstone made from synthetic materials such as aluminum oxide or silicon carbide. These are available in coarse, medium, and fine grades and are the cheapest varieties on the market. However, as you develop your woodworking skills there are some suitable alternatives. For example, natural stones such as

Japanese waterstone

Oilstone housing tray

Arkansas have a range of hardnesses, while some woodworkers prefer to use Japanese waterstones. There are also manufactured sharpening stones that have hardened particles bonded into them.

Honing sequence

The grinding of the chisel blade will have produced a bevel of 25 degrees. To ensure the tool is ready for use, this bevel now needs to be sharpened or honed to an angle of 30 degrees.

The honing angle must be 30 degrees.

1 Place the edge of the blade flat on the stone, bevel side down. Hold the blade firmly in one hand and place your other hand on the top of the blade. Lift the tool slightly to give the correct honing angle— 5 degrees more than the grinding angle.

2 Work the bevel by rubbing the blade firmly up and down the stone, ensuring that the whole cutting edge is in contact with the stone.

Make the bevel by honing the chisel at an angle of 30 degrees.

3 When you have produced a bevel of about ⅓₂ in. (1 mm), continue the same process on a finer stone. The rubbing action will cause a burr to form on the back of the blade. To remove it, turn the tool over and make a few light strokes, holding the blade perfectly flat. This removes the burr and leaves a sharp edge.

Create a sharp edge by removing the burr.

Using a leather strop

A leather strop helps to remove any trace of a burr and leaves an extremely sharp blade. Hold the blade, and swipe the honed bevel away from the sharp edge. Then turn the tool over and do the same to the back. You should now have a razor-sharp edge. If a fine, shiny line along the cutting edge appears on the blade, continue sharpening.

Planing

Planing is one of the most satisfying woodworking skills to master. It is also one of the key processes; precision and accuracy are vital for achieving a perfectly flat and straight surface with an exact square edge.

HAND PLANES

There is a range of planes available—each developed to carry out a specific function or job. The most familiar is the bench plane, and we will use this to examine the basic structure of all planes, together with the planing process.

Bench planes

The **try** or **jointer plane** is the longest bench plane. It is used to ensure that the board surface is as level as possible, and removes warps or irregularities that may have occurred during seasoning, or may not have been rectified during the sawing and milling processes. The length of the plane, 2 ft. (600 mm), helps to ensure that this first surface is as level as possible.

The **jack plane** is a bench plane of medium length and can be used after the try plane, or to accomplish the same result on a shorter piece of material.

The **smoothing plane** is the shortest of the bench planes and, as its name infers, it is used for final finishing. It is also an ideal tool for dealing with wood that has a rather difficult grain.

Once bench planing is complete, most boards will still require some further finishing with sandpaper in order to achieve a completely smooth surface.

Rabbet planes

A rabbet is a recess cut into the edge of a piece of wood— and it is mostly used for fitting panel boards.

A **bench rabbet plane** is used for cutting large rabbets and is basically a version of the jack or smoothing plane—the blade extends across the whole width of the sole. In order to cut the rabbet accurately, a fence, along which the plane can run, should be cramped in position.

Wooden planes

Planes are made from several different materials. Traditionally they were made from timber by the actual craftworker, the blade component being the only part that needed to be sourced outside the workshop. Although these planes are nowadays mostly confined to the tool collector, they are still used, particularly in Scandinavia and Germany. Japanese wooden planes have also aroused considerable interest in recent years.

Try or jointer plane

Smoothing plane

Jack plane

Shoulder plane

Side rabbet plane

Bull-nose plane

Bench rabbet plane

Wooden rabbet plane

planing

Traditional planes

The planes described here are the traditional ones found in the cabinetmaker's tool chest. However, it must be remembered that, with recent technical developments, much rabbeting, routing, and molding can be carried out by a small, electrically powered hand router (see pages 129–30).

A **rabbet** and **fillister plane** has both a guide fence and a depth gauge, and is suitable for cutting small rabbets. With careful use, it will also cut a rabbet that is square and true. In some models, the cutter can be mounted in two positions; the front position is used when planing a stopped rabbet. Some types of this plane can be fitted with a spur that cuts the wood fibers, so that a rabbet can be made across the grain.

The **shoulder plane** was developed as a means of trimming the shoulders of large joints; although smaller, it can also be used in a similar way to the bench rabbet plane.

A **side rabbet plane** is used for easing the width of a groove because it cuts the vertical edge of grooves, or rabbets.

A **bull-nose plane** is similar to a shoulder plane but the blade

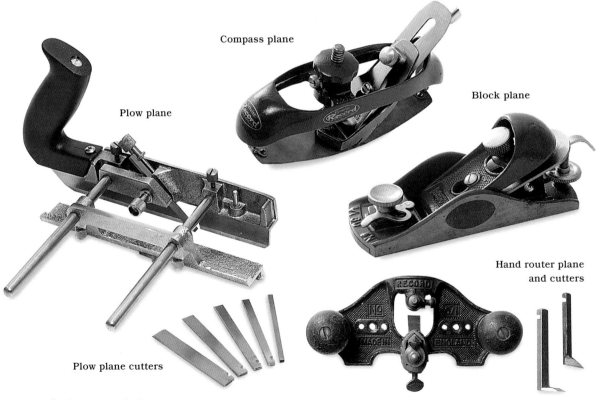

Compass plane

Plow plane

Block plane

Plow plane cutters

Hand router plane and cutters

is very near the front, facilitating the trimming of stopped rabbets.

Plow and combination planes

A simple **plow plane** is designed to cut grooves. It has a range of cutters, usually from 1/8–1/2 in. (3–12 mm) in size, and has both a guide fence and depth gauge.

A **combination plane**, or molding plane, is similar but it has a wider range of cutters and is able to make tongues, beads, and other shapes.

Specialized planes

There are a number of specialized planes available.

Compass planes, as the name implies, are special planes that can be adjusted to cope with both concave and convex curves. Set the flexible sole to the curve that you want to plane and generally try to work with the grain.

Block planes are general-purpose, lightweight planes that can be used with one hand.

A **hand router plane** is very useful for fine work and for special applications such as making small recesses.

PREPARING A PLANE FOR USE

Most new planes, apart from the most expensive, hand-finished varieties, need a few adjustments before they are ready to use. Like many tools, the plane needs to be fettled, or "tuned," to make it fit for precision work. Old planes should be checked and refettled occasionally, as required.

The main part of the plane is the sole (A). This needs to be machined perfectly so that the underneath is totally flat. Unfortunately, mass-produced castings are often not left long enough to "settle" or normalize, before the process of machining takes place, and this can result in a less than flat surface.

Fettling the sole

If a sole is badly deformed it may be easier to find a machine shop that can surface, machine, or grind the sole face flat. If there is not much to be done, though, you can do it yourself.

1 Spread some carborundum powder over a perfectly flat sheet of glass. Alternatively, tape some wet-and-dry emery paper to the glass surface. Use different grades of powder or

planing

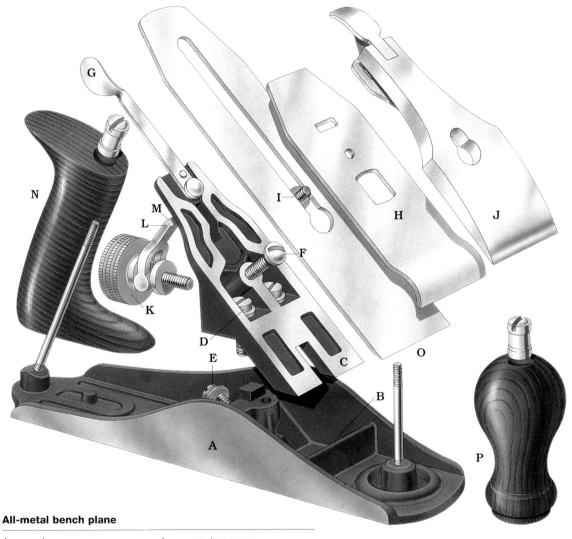

All-metal bench plane

A	sole	I	cap iron screw
B	mouth	J	lever cap
C	frog casting	K	depth-adjustment wheel
D	frog-locking screws	L	depth-control lever
E	frog-adjusting screw	M	Y-lever
F	lever-cap screw	N	handle
G	lateral-adjustment lever	O	blade
H	cap iron	P	knob

paper, working from coarse through to very fine.

2 Hold the plane at the front and rear, and push the tool over the surface. Rub the sole firmly over the surface, using an oil lubricant to enable the powder or paper to cut efficiently. This tends to be an extremely messy job!

3 As the rubbing continues, any high points become increasingly polished. Check the sole frequently to ensure that the whole face slowly develops an even polish and, therefore, an overall flatness.

4 Use increasingly fine powder or paper to polish the sole to the finest finish.

5 Check that the mouth (B) is perfectly square with the edge by using a try square. If it is not true, carefully make the mouth square by using a fine file to remove the unwanted metal.

Reassembling the plane

Having ensured that the sole is correct, examine the frog assembly (C–G), which consists of a casting (C) with various components for adjustment. The frog can slide from front to back, which enables the size of

the mouth to be adjusted—wider for coarse planing and narrower for very fine cuts.

1 Check that the frog is sitting properly—you may need to check the mating surfaces and adjust them with a fine file.

2 Fit the frog with frog-locking screws (D) and an adjusting screw (E). The lever-cap screw (F) will hold the blade assembly in place, and the lateral-adjustment lever (G) allows for lateral adjustment of the blade.

3 Put the blade in position—taking care as it will be sharp—and fit the cap iron (H) over the top. Initially, fit the iron across the blade, before turning it lengthwise and moving it toward the cutting edge. For coarse shavings, fit at $\frac{1}{16}$ in. (1 mm) or more from the edge. For fine shavings, the cap iron must be closer. It has to fit to the blade or shavings will collect under the edge.

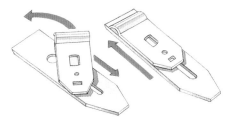

Fit the cap iron to the blade sole.

Expert tip

To ensure that the cap iron fits neatly with the blade, use an oilstone to flatten and straighten its edge.

4 Hold the plane with your fingers covering the mouth underneath the sole. Carefully place the assembled cap iron and blade, ground side down (cap iron up), over the lever-cap screw (F) and rest it on the frog. Move this slightly from side to side to check that the lateral-adjustment lever (G) is fully engaged in the slot on the blade. Ensure that the lug on the Y lever (M) is engaged in the slot in the cap iron, and that the Y is correctly fitting on the adjustment screw.

5 Place the lever cap (J) over the top of the cap-iron assembly with the lever up; slide it down until it fits securely against the lever-cap screw (F). Adjust the depth of the cut so that the blade can be felt just protruding slightly from the mouth. Lower the lever to secure the assembly; if necessary, adjust the level of

The fully assembled blade.

tension by raising or lowering the lever-cap screw, applying firm pressure. Now, close the lever securely, and the plane is ready for fine adjustments.

Adjusting the plane

1 Hold the plane by the knob upside down with the toe facing you. Sight along the sole to assess the position of the blade. Adjust the blade depth, using the depth-adjustment wheel (K) and depth-control lever (L), until a fine margin appears.

Sight along the surface of the sole.

2 Move the lateral-adjustment lever (G) to produce an even margin across the plane.

3 Recheck the depth of the cut and the lateral adjustment.

USING THE PLANE

To check that the plane is ready for use, it is a good idea to try the tool on a sample piece of wood.

Planing stance

Whenever you plane, you need to take a well-balanced stance behind the work with your feet apart. Make sure that the bench is set to a comfortable height, so that when you are holding the plane there is a right angle between your upper and lower arm. The lower arm should be horizontal, which will enable you to make your cuts with the maximum control.

Be sure to adopt the correct stance when planing.

Planing technique

1 Make sure that your stance is correct. Set the board to be planed on the bench. Although it can be held in a vice, you will have more of a feel for the process if the work sits on the benchtop and you plane against a stop. Set the stop lower than the thickness of the wood.

2 Hold the rear handle with your stronger hand, extending the forefinger against the edge of the frog. Wrap the other hand around the front knob. As you plane, the initial pressure will be on the front knob, but as the cut is made, pressure transfers to the rear handle. Practise controlling the plane and adjusting the blade to make fine and coarse cuts. Use a plane adjusted for coarse cuts when starting to level. Adjust for finer cuts as you plane the smoothest surface possible.

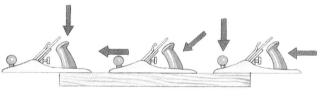

Make sure that you apply pressure at the right time.

Planing the face side

The face side is the first surface prepared to ensure that it is perfectly straight along its length and is totally flat, without any wind or twist.

1 Plane the surface by making a cut along the grain with the plane straight—plane high areas first. It can be an advantage to use the plane at a slight angle so the blade makes a slicing action. On wide or uneven

Planing manufactured boards

Plane the edges of manufactured boards in the same way as you would for lumber, but plane from both ends to prevent breakout.

wood you may need to plane at an angle across the board, as well as planing straight.

2 Regularly test along the length for straightness by tilting the plane onto its edge, which should be perfectly straight. Or you can position a straightedge along the work. Sight between the work and straightedge for any high spots. Plane the highs until no gap can be seen.

3 Position winding strips at either end of the surface. Or use two rulers. Sight across the top edges and check that the two strips are parallel. Any deviation in flatness will be exaggerated by the winding stick. Plane the high corners until the strips are parallel; check again for straightness.

Test the piece for straightness.

Planing the face edge

The face edge also needs to be planed perfectly straight, and should be at a precise angle to the face side—normally 90 degrees. Select the edge and apply a face-side mark to indicate the edge to be worked.

Also plane the face edge of your board until it is straight.

1 Place the work on the bench. If it is too narrow to stand alone, secure it firmly in a vice.

2 Carefully plane along the edge, making sure it is straight. If the face edge is very narrow, curl the fingers of your front

Plane along the edge.

hand under the plane, keeping them away from the blade, to guide and act as a fence.

3 Keep checking the edge for squareness by holding the stock of a try square against the face side. Ensure that you are planing square all along the length.

Mark the required width.

2 Measure and mark the required thickness and plane to this line. Check the surface with a straightedge as before. The board should now be the required shape with straight and square surfaces.

Use a try square to check for squareness.

4 If the edge is not square, mark inaccurate areas with a pencil and replane these until the edge is straight and flat.

Mark the required thickness.

5 Once complete, mark the face edge with a pencil. Most markings or setting out for the job will be made from the face side and edge.

Planing to width and thickness
Once the surfaces are perfectly flat, the wood will need to be planed to size.

1 Mark the exact required width with a marking gauge. Then carefully plane away the waste to meet the gauged line.

Planing at angles
There will be times when you will need to plane angles.

1 Mark the chamfer, or bevel, with a pencil along each edge.

2 Set the work in a vice and plane down to the lines. On a wide bevel use the normal planing action; on narrow pieces curl your fingers under the plane to guide the tool, as described above.

Expert tip

Remember that when marking angles you should use a pencil rather than a gauge because gauge marks will show when the chamfer, or bevel, is planed.

3 Hold the plane at the angle you require. Adjust the angle of the plane as you work down to the line, ensuring that the planed edge remains even and parallel.

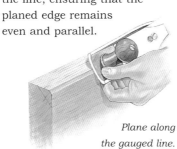

Plane along the gauged line.

Planing difficult and interlocked grain

The description just given will normally suffice when the wood you are working has a straight grain, but wood that has interlocking or other difficult grain features requires special attention.

1 Ensure that the plane blade is extremely sharp and put it on a very fine setting.

2 Plane across the face at an angle and, if necessary, square to the edge. It may also pay to plane in various directions. The surface will need to be finished

Plane in various directions.

Interlocked grain after planing.

off with a scraper and/or abrasive paper.

Planing end grain

With end grain you must ensure that the planing action does not break out the end of the cut. If there is sufficient width on the surface, plane a chamfer on the edge toward which you are planing. Otherwise, clamp a block to the material to provide sufficient planing length. Then plane across both pieces to create a smooth, even surface. Alternatively, plane into the center from both directions.

Plane the end grain into the center from both directions.

HAND POWER PLANES

There is a range of hand power planes on the market, although they are less suitable for precise work than the hand plane. These tools remove material relatively quickly and need to be carefully adjusted. It is also very important to realize that these planes cut by means of a rotating block of knives, so always keep both hands on the handles and never try to hold the tool in the same way as a hand plane, with your fingers around the toe. Never try to plane small material with one.

MACHINE PLANERS

One of the first machines many furniture makers invest in is a machine planer. Industrial workshops tend to have two separate machines—a surface planer or jointer, which is used for accurate, flat planing of the face side and edge, and a thicknesser for planing the width and thickness. However, most home woodworkers use a machine that performs both of these functions—it is called a combination plane, or a planer/thicknesser. The wood is fed in one direction over the top table for surfacing, and the opposite way underneath for thicknessing.

Combination planer or planer/thicknesser

These machines come in a variety of sizes, so aim for one that is adequately large—a width over 8 in. (200 mm) is best. Long infeed and outfeed tables are also preferable.

The surfacing part of the machine has two tables—the infeed table and the outfeed table. A rotating cutter block with sharp cutters is located beneath the gap between these two tables. The infeed table is adjusted to produce different depths of cut, and the outfeed table is appropriately adjusted, so that it is level with the top of the cutters.

A guard covers the cutter block and is adjusted to accommodate the thickness of the timber, so that the board safely passes beneath. The fence enables edges to be planed and can be tilted at an angle for beveling. The thicknessing part of the machine is similar to an old-fashioned mangle. The cutter block and

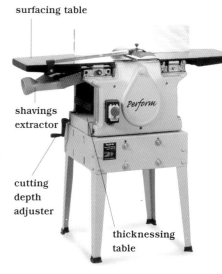

surfacing table

shavings extractor

cutting depth adjuster

thicknessing table

Combination planer

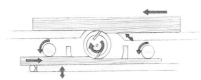

Section of planer showing surfacer and thicknesser.

Safety first

• Never make adjustments without turning off the power.

• When planing always be aware of the possible problems. Work with caution and confidence.

• Always follow the manufacturer's instructions for the specific machine.

• Inspect the machine before you switch it on—always check and recheck adjustments.

• Always use the guard supplied.

• Never attempt to plane short or thin pieces without using adequate jigs.

• The material you are planing must be at least as long as the distance between the two feed rollers.

• Feed only one piece of board through the machine at a time.

• Never try to remove too much material in one pass—it is better to use several fine cuts.

• If anything happens to your piece of work, switch off the machine before attempting to rectify the situation.

the feed rollers are at the top and the feed table is adjustable in height so that the wood can be planed to an exact thickness.

Cutter block and cutters

To achieve the best quality finish, ensure that the cutters are very sharp and that they are correctly installed in the cutter block. High-speed steel cutters can be used, but if there is a lot of planing to be done, tungsten carbide-tipped knives are preferable. Most cutter blocks provide for two cutters whereas larger, industrial machines tend to take three or four. Always follow the manufacturer's instructions for fitting the cutters into the block.

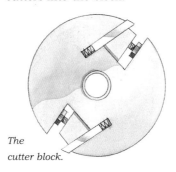

The cutter block.

Always double-check to ensure that the cutters are tightened in position and that the power is off. When fitting the cutters into the block you must adjust them so that all cutters and all parts of the cutting edge are working

together. So, when inserting the knives ensure that they project from the block evenly. Positioning a perfectly straight piece of wood on the outfeed table should make this easier.

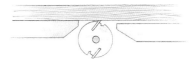

Fit the cutters and tighten in place.

Surfacing with a combination planer

It is essential to adopt the correct stance when surfacing—planing the face side—with a planer. This is both for safety reasons and to ensure that you apply even pressure when passing wood across the plane.

1 Stand to the right of the table and position your right hand flat on the work.

2 Feed the work under the guard, maintaining pressure with your right hand. As it emerges, shift your body weight slightly and use your left hand to apply pressure to the work on the outfeed table.

3 Continue to feed the work through, with pressure on both ends, before shifting your right hand to the work on the outfeed table.

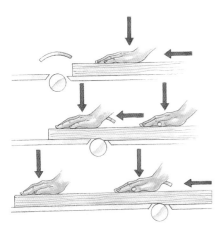

*Apply varying pressures to
your work while surfacing.*

Planing the face side

1 Adjust the infeed table to
determine the thickness of the
shaving that will be planed.
Slide the bridge guard into
place over the cutter block.

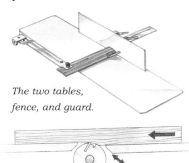

*The two tables,
fence, and guard.*

*Change the thickness of the cut
by adjusting the infeed table.*

2 Position the board on the
infeed table and raise the guard
so that the wood can pass
beneath. Stand to the side of
the infeed table and, with the

machine switched on and at
operating speed, apply pressure
on the board so that it does not
rock. Slowly feed the wood
through the planer. As the
piece passes under the guard,
transfer pressure to the outfeed
table so that the cut will give
the flattest possible surface.

3 Continue to apply pressure
until the whole of the wood has
passed through the planer.
Continue passing it through
until the surface is flat. If it is
cupped or bowed, make several
passes so it is stable on the
planer tables, before achieving
a finished surface.

Planing the face edge

1 With the machine switched
off, check that the fence is at
a right angle—90 degrees—to
the tables. Or, for a beveled
edge, set the fence to the
required angle. Lower the guard
and slide it across, so that the
wood can pass between it and
the fence.

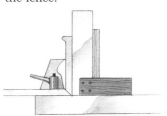

*Set the fence at a 90-degree angle
for the face edge.*

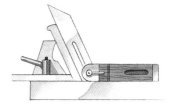

*Set the fence at the appropriate
angle for a bevel.*

planing

Turn to pages 226–9 and use the small shelf exercise in order to practice and develop your planing skills.

2 Switch the machine on and position the timber on the infeed table. Hold the face side firmly against the fence and feed it over the cutter block, passing it from one hand to the other.

Pass the wood from hand to hand as you feed it over the cutter.

Thicknessing with a combination planer

With a perfectly flat face side and face edge, it is now possible to plane the board to the required width and thickness.

1 Remove most of the excess material with a table saw in order to help make the board manageable.

2 Ensure that the surfacing tables are correctly adjusted and that the cutter-block guard and shavings deflector are in position.

3 Stand slightly to one side of the machine. Position the board on the infeed table and use push sticks to feed it through the thicknesser—keep your hands away from the rollers.

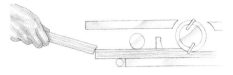

Use push sticks when the wood nears the base and the feed rollers.

4 As the board moves across the rollers, move to the other end of the machine to receive it. Do not force the board by pulling or put your hands anywhere near the rollers— make sure that you wait for the board to feed through naturally, keeping your hands well away.

Planing thin pieces

To plane the edge of thin wood, use a special jig to hold the board safely. Set the machine fence at the correct angle and take extra care. Very thin pieces of wood can be difficult to plane to width because they may not stay upright. Either make a special jig to ensure their stability or carry out this operation using the method described in "Surfacing with a combination planer," having first sawed almost to width.

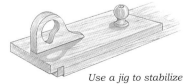

Use a jig to stabilize very thin material during planing.

Dust/chip extraction

Even small machine planers produce a lot of waste chips. Most machines have attachments by which an extraction unit can be fitted to remove waste, thus keeping both the job and surrounding air clean. Although the unit is normally a separate investment, most woodworkers find that it is well worth the additional expense.

Fine sawing

In addition to rough sawing lumber to size, you will also need to be able to perform much finer saw work. This section looks at the tools and skills needed for fine work, such as cutting precise joints and difficult shapes.

HAND TOOLS

There are many saws available to the woodworker for fine cutting.

Backsaws

Backsaws are used for precise work. They have a strip of brass or steel attached to the top of the blade—this both keeps the blade straight and adds weight to the tool, to help make cutting easier.

A **tenon saw** is the largest of the backsaws. Its blade ranges between 10 and 14 in. (250 and 350 mm) in length, with a 12 to 14 tpi. As its name suggests, this saw is used mainly for cutting fairly large joints, particularly tenons.

A **dovetail saw** is similar to a tenon saw, though it is slightly smaller. The blade is 8 in. (200 mm) long, with 15 to 21 tpi. The teeth on this saw are generally set very fine. Again, its use is quite specific—for cutting dovetails and other fine sawing work.

A **bead saw**, or gents saw as it is also known, is designed for very delicate work. It normally has a straight handle and is a much finer backsaw than the dovetail. The blade is about 6–8 in. (150–200 mm) long, with 15 to 25 tpi.

Curve-cutting saws

There are several saws used for cutting curves.

The **bow saw**, although not used very much these days, is a traditional curve-cutting saw that has a lightweight wood frame. The removable blades are between 8 and 12 in. (200 and 300 mm) long with 8 to 16 tpi. The blade is tensioned with a tourniquet and can be turned through 360 degrees.

A **coping saw** has a sprung metal frame, which holds the blade in position by tension.

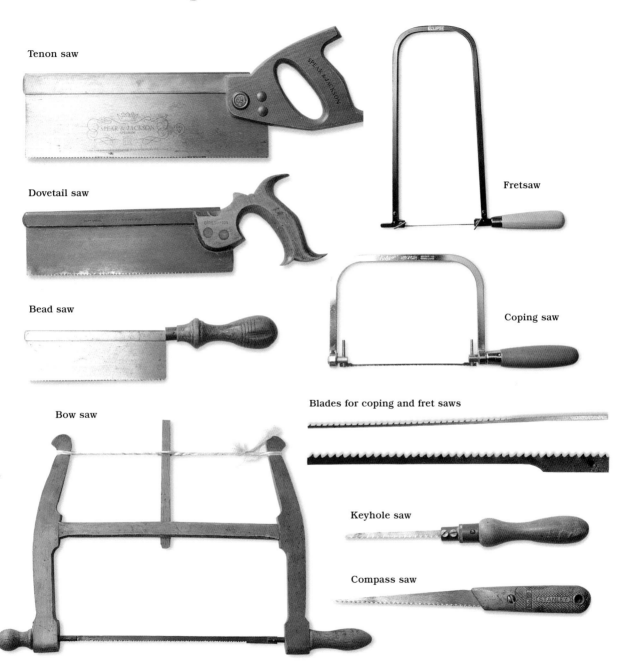

Tenon saw

Dovetail saw

Bead saw

Bow saw

Fretsaw

Coping saw

Blades for coping and fret saws

Keyhole saw

Compass saw

The handle turns to add or release tension. The blade is 6 in. (150 mm) long, with approximately 15 tpi. The blade is very narrow, and can be disposed of when blunt since it is inexpensive to replace. The blade can be revolved in the frame by turning the end fittings. Unusually, this saw cuts on the pulling stroke.

A **fretsaw** is similar to the coping saw but it has a deep throat in the steel frame and is designed for cutting very tight curves. The blade is 6 in. (150 mm) long, with about 15 tpi. The fretsaw uses very thin blades—as thin as ⅛ in. (3 mm)—that are held in with thumbscrews at both ends and are very fragile.

A **keyhole saw**, or **pad saw**, is used for internal cuts when a bow saw is unable to reach the area to be cut. It has a straight handle, which can be more comfortable for some tasks. You may come across a compass saw with a shaped or straight handle, which performs the same operation as the pad saw.

Using a backsaw

Backsaws are generally used for fine, accurate saw work.

1 Measure and mark the lines with a marking knife.

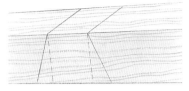

Use a marking knife to mark the saw lines on your board.

2 Secure the work in a vice. Use the tip of your index finger to position the saw blade on the waste side of the cut line. Begin with a few backward strokes, guiding the saw with your finger.

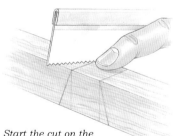

Start the cut on the waste side and guide the saw with your finger.

3 Extend the strokes along the cut line, keeping to the knife mark. The saw cuts on the forward stroke, and so release pressure on the return stroke. Guide the saw on the forward stroke; the weight of the back strip will aid the actual cut.

Hand power tools

The best hand power tool for fine sawing is the jigsaw (see page 93). This is able to saw relatively tight curves, both on the inside and the outside of the curve, and with care can handle very intricate work. The main problem is that the saw cuts on the upstroke, and when cutting across the grain, this can cause grain breakout or pickup. The tool must be held flat against the surface of the work. Always cut on the waste side of the line.

Japanese saws

Japanese tools have become increasingly popular with Western woodworkers in recent years. Japanese saws have superb cutting performance and cut on the pull stroke rather than needing pressure to cut the way European saws do. The range of Japanese saws shown here includes the most commonly known example to Westerners, the *ryoba noko* (double-edged saw), shown in the center. It is used for work where both crosscutting and ripping are necessary. A small *ryoba noko* is often employed in the making of cabinets or when framing doors. The unusual-looking saw on the left is known as *azebiki nokogiri*; it has a short blade with curved edges. The curves allow the woodworker to begin in the center of a piece of wood, which can be useful. It is also used to cut sliding dovetails.

Using a bow saw

1 Begin by fitting the blade into the bow saw. Do this by loosening the tourniquet and positioning the blade in the slots in the handle rods. Carefully insert the pins through the holes in the blade and rods and take up the slack on the tourniquet.

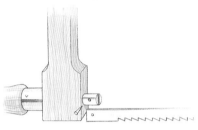

Fit a blade in a bow saw.

2 Turn the handles to adjust the blade to the required position in relation to the frame for the intended cuts. The blade may be revolved as for a coping saw.

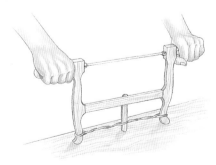

Turn the handles to adjust the blade position.

3 Tension the blade by twisting the tourniquet with the center piece of wood, or the toggle. Ensure that the toggle is sitting against the center rail.

4 Hold one end of the saw with both hands. It is vital to have a proper grip on the tool, with the index finger of the first hand extending in line with the blade. Even though the saw has a handle at both ends, it is normally used holding one end only with both hands; make careful strokes making sure that you keep to the line.

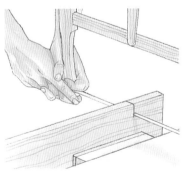

Hold the bow saw correctly.

Using a coping saw

1 To replace a blade, unscrew the handle to bring the pins closer together and release tension. Insert the blade in one end and slightly flex the frame against the bench; insert the blade in the other end and tighten by turning the handle.

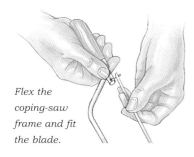

Flex the coping-saw frame and fit the blade.

2 Secure the piece of wood in a vice, grip the handle of the saw firmly, and position the blade on the waste side of the cut line. Pull the saw toward your body in order to make the cut.

Pull the coping saw toward you as you make the cut.

3 To change the direction of the blade or to prevent the frame from falling foul of the edge, loosen the handle slightly, rotate the blade in the frame, and retighten before continuing with the sawing. This allows the frame to be turned over the nearest edge without changing the cutting direction.

Using a fretsaw

1 To fit a blade, loosen the thumbscrews at each end and insert the blade. As you retighten the thumbscrews, spring the frame closed; this will give the blade tension.

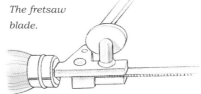

The fretsaw blade.

2 Clamp the wood to the bench with the work area overhanging, and sit so that you are near the cutting area.

3 Position the blade on the waste side of the line, so that it cuts on the downstroke and you can cut to the marks on the top surface. These saws cut with a pulling action, not pushing as other saws do.

Use a pulling action with a fretsaw.

fine sawing

Safety first

• Wear the appropriate safety equipment.

• Always ensure that the blade is properly tensioned, and that the blade guides and rear thrust wheel are properly positioned.

• Never force the work. The blade should be sharp enough to do the cutting; you are only directing its path.

Turn to pages 230–3 and use the mail rack exercise to practice fine sawing.

Using a compass saw or keyhole saw

1 To make an internal cut, drill a hole in the marked area of the piece, on the waste side.

2 Insert the saw blade and use the forward, thin edge of the blade to start the cut. Gradually increase the length of the strokes.

Use a compass saw to cut a hole, inserting it in a drilled hole.

BANDSAW

The best machine tool that you can use for intricate, fine sawing is a bandsaw. Unlike most other types of machine saws, this has a continuous band of metal with teeth on the leading edge. The band runs around two or three wheels and the blade itself passes through a slot in a machine table.

The blade is tensioned by the top wheel, and it is powered by a motor working on the bottom wheel. Various thicknesses of blade and different sets of teeth mean that very small curves can be sawed, and the large blade makes it an extremely good general-purpose machine. The machine is supplied with various fences, but once mastered, it is often easier to use by sight than with guides or fences.

Using a bandsaw

1 Before starting the machine, select the correct blade that you need for the job. It is important to check this for faults before you start work. The blade needs to be tensioned and the top wheel needs to be tracked in order to keep the blade running in the center of the wheel. A hand wheel or knob tilts the top wheel to align the blade. Set the guide blocks so that they just miss the sides of the blade; usually there is a set above and below the table.

2 Next, the friction wheel needs to be set approximately $\frac{1}{16}$–$\frac{1}{8}$ in. (2–3 mm) from the back of the blade—too far back and the blade may come off, while if it is put too far forward, it could break the blade.

3 Once the saw is set-up test run it for 5 to 10 seconds on full speed; stop the saw and check that the blade is still set in the correct position; adjust as required.

4 Before sawing, adjust the blade guides so that there is only about ⅛ in. (3 mm) between them and the work.

5 Switch on the machine and align the saw blade with your marked line, ensuring that it is on the waste side.

6 Carefully feed the work into the blade, constantly checking that it is following the line.

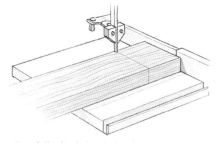

Carefully feed the timber into the blade of the bandsaw.

7 At the end of the cut, use a push stick to feed the remaining edge of the work through the blade. Always be sure that your fingers are out of the way when the saw breaks through.

Bandsaw

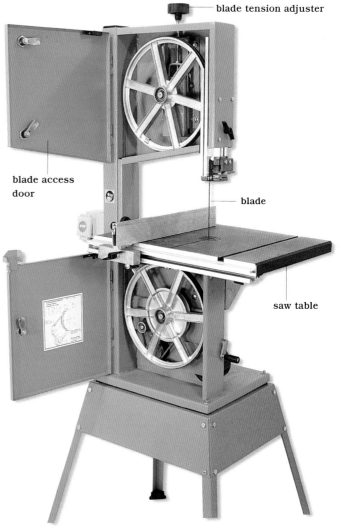

blade tension adjuster

blade access door

blade

saw table

Chiseling

Together with saws and planes, the chisel is one of the most important tools in a woodworker's workshop. It is used for creating neat, accurate joints and also for removing waste material.

CHISELS

Chisels come in a wide range of sizes, and it is important to have a good selection in your tool kit to cover the full range of tasks. Like all edge tools, chisels function best when they are very sharp. This ensures less effort is needed to cut, and the tool is easier to guide, which means you get greater accuracy. Paring—the removal of very fine shavings with the chisel—can be carried out either horizontally or vertically.

A **firmer chisel** is the strongest chisel and has a rectangular shaped blade. It comes in sizes ranging from ⅛–2 in. (3–50 mm) and is used for general-purpose chiseling tasks.

Bevel-edged chisels also come in various sizes and have two shallow bevels ground along the edges of the upper face. This makes the chisel more suitable for joint making.

A **paring chisel** is the same as a bevel-edged chisel, although it has a much longer blade, which is particularly useful when paring housings. One type of paring chisel is cranked (has the blade at an angle) so that the blade can be kept flat, even when you are paring very wide boards.

Gouges

A gouge is, essentially, a type of chisel, which has a curved cross-section to the blade. There are two types of gouges available for different purposes: an out-cannel gouge and an in-cannel gouge.

The **out-cannel gouge** has a cutting edge ground on the outside and is used for paring convex shapes.

The **in-cannel gouge** has a cutting edge ground on the inside and is used for paring concave shapes.

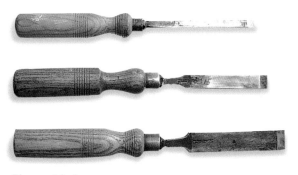

Firmer chisels

Bevel-edged
chisels

Paring chisels

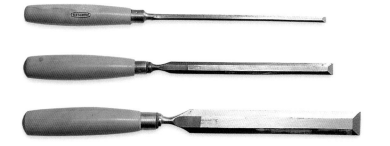

**Robert Thompson's
mouse**

Robert Thompson,
also known as the
"Mouseman of Kilburn,"
(1876–1955) is one of
the best known British
craftsmen of the 20th
century. He became
entranced by medieval
carved woodwork while
he was an apprentice
and spent his spare time
experimenting with
traditional tools and
techniques. His work is
characterized by the use
of naturally seasoned
oak, solid shapes, and
hand-finished adzed
surfaces. He also gave
each piece his very own
distinctive touch—a
hand-carved mouse. He
began using this
"signature" about 1920
when a comment was
made about him and
another carver being as
poor as mice. On the
spur of the moment he
carved a mouse on the
piece he was working
on. From then on
everything he worked on
was given a mouse.

Gouges

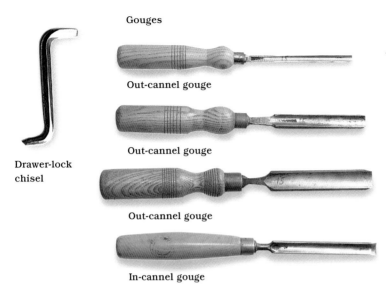

Out-cannel gouge

Out-cannel gouge

Out-cannel gouge

In-cannel gouge

Drawer-lock
chisel

Sash-mortise chisels

Registered mortise chisels

Mortise chisels

Mortise chisels are stronger than the chisels described on page 122, and are designed for tougher work, such as cutting deep mortises. Whereas most chisels are normally used only with body pressure, mortise chisels may require a mallet to drive the tool firmly into the work, so these chisels normally have some form of cap, such as a metal ferrule, to protect the top of the handle from splitting. However, keep the mortise chisel sharp, so that only a slight tap with the mallet works.

The **sash-mortise chisel** has a thick, substantial blade for very heavy-duty work. It has wide sides that help to keep the blade straight. This enables it to lever out waste from deep mortises.

The **registered mortise chisel** is a heavier pattern, having a thicker blade, and is used for cutting larger joints.

A **drawer-lock chisel** may be used to cut mortises or housings in tight spaces.

JAPANESE CHISELS

As an alternative, you may want to invest in some Japanese chisels for your tool kit. They are made up of a lamination of

A selection of Japanese chisels.

Safety first

• Never place any part of your body in front of the cutting edge.

• Secure all your work before working on it.

• Never hit a chisel with your hand as this may inflict an injury.

a thin bottom layer of very hard steel and a thicker layer of softer steel. The *oire nomi* (butt chisel) shown above on the left is a general, all-purpose chisel. It has a thin blade and the top face has a wide chamfer on both edges to make it lighter and easier to reach corners with. The *kama nomi* (sickle chisel) on the right gets its name because of the way it looks. It has beveled sides and is used to clean up the insides of dovetails and the side grooves of plane blocks.

USING CHISELS
Paring horizontally

1 Lay the work flat on the bench and secure it with C-clamps or, if it is a suitable size, in the vice.

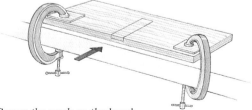

Secure the work on the bench,
ready to be pared horizontally.

chiseling

2 Stand with your chest and shoulders at right angles to the board, with your legs apart and the elbow of your dominant hand tucked into your body.

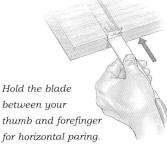

Hold the blade between your thumb and forefinger for horizontal paring.

The correct stance to adopt when paring horizontally.

3 Hold the chisel handle in your dominant hand. Hold the blade between the thumb and forefinger of your other hand, behind the cutting edge. Apply pressure with the forearm of your dominant hand in order to make the chisel cut. Use the other hand to steer and guide the direction of the chisel.

Guide the chisel carefully and pare away the waste.

Paring vertically

1 Place the work on the benchtop and secure in position with a C-clamp. It is preferable to fix a piece of spare wood underneath the work.

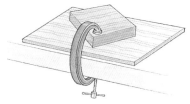

Secure the work on the bench, ready to be pared vertically.

2 Bend over your work so that your shoulder is directly over the chisel, and apply a controlled, downward pressure on your hand. This action will help you to keep the chisel straight while cutting.

Control the blade with your thumb and forefinger.

The correct stance to adopt when paring vertically, with your shoulder directly over the chisel.

3 Grip the handle of the chisel firmly in your dominant hand by placing your thumb over the end of the handle. Use the thumb and forefinger of the other hand to control the blade carefully, as before when paring horizontally. Apply a firm downward pressure in order to chisel out the waste.

Apply a downward pressure as you chisel away the waste.

Cutting mortises with a chisel

1 To remove the bulk of the waste, hold the chisel in one hand with the blade positioned between the gauge lines— approximately ⅛ in. (3 mm) in from the end of the mortise—

chiseling

Turn to pages 234–6
to practice chiseling
to make animal shapes.

and apply pressure. Repeat several times along the mortise to chop out the initial layer.

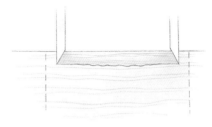

Remove the first layer of waste from the mortise.

2 To remove deeper levels, strike the handle of the chisel squarely with a mallet. Do this first at each end of the mortise, with the bevel facing the center of the recess. The chisel will cut straight down. Then hold the chisel at a slight angle a little farther in from the end and strike the chisel with the mallet. This will raise the waste from the bottom of the mortise.

Use a mallet to raise the waste from the bottom of the mortise.

Pry out the waste and continue these steps until the required depth has been reached. If cutting a through mortise, work from both sides.

3 Finally, finish the mortise by cutting it back to the required shoulder lines. Do this by paring away the waste to the end of the mortise, using the technique shown in "Paring vertically," on page 126. It is important that you keep the chisel square during this process.

Using gouges

Use gouges in the same way as chisels, ensuring that the cutting edge is sharp. Use the in-cannel gouge when you are trimming curved shoulders, and the out-cannel gouge for hollowing out shapes.

Use an out-cannel gouge for hollowing out shapes.

Making grooves

Grooves are long narrow channels cut either along or across the grain. They can be used for joints that fit pieces of wood together or for decorative effect. Grooves are often used to hold drawer bottoms and cabinet backs.

HAND TOOLS

Before power tools were introduced into the workshop, grooves were cut with a hand plow plane, or one of the more complex tools that derived from it, such as the combination plane (see page 103).

The plow plane has bits ranging from ⅛ to ½ in. (3 to 12 mm), held with a screw at the correct cutting angle. The tool is fitted with a depth gauge and a fence, which means that it will only cut straight grooves parallel to a given edge. The combination plane has features that make it suitable for tongue-and-groove work, while the multi-plane has extra bits for moldings.

POWER TOOLS

Good quality hand power routers can be used for carrying out grooving and operations such as rabbeting and molding. For people starting out in woodwork, a small power router is ideal because it is more versatile than a plow plane.

Power routers

Power routers consist of a motor held in a mounting, beneath which is fixed a socket to hold varying sizes of bits. The baseplate guides the tool over the work surface and is fitted with clamps for securing rods and accessories. The depth stop is used to adjust the projection of the bit from the baseplate, while the handles are used to steer the tool.

Most large routers work by a plunging action. The motor body rises and falls on a pair of columns. The bit is plunged into the wood and retracted at the end of the job. The motor size varies but all routers give a speed without load of between 22,000 and 27,000 rpm. Because the speed drops as soon as the bit touches the work, high-powered ones are best for high-quality finishes.

Safety reminder

- Always follow the manufacturer's instructions.

- Hold the router firmly when starting up and operating.

- Use both handles.

- Use safety glasses, ear protectors and a dust mask.

- Never start the router when the bit is in contact with the work.

- Always disconnect the power supply when you are making any adjustments, especially when changing bits.

- Use sharp bits.

- When cutting, the router should move from left to right.

- Secure the work well.

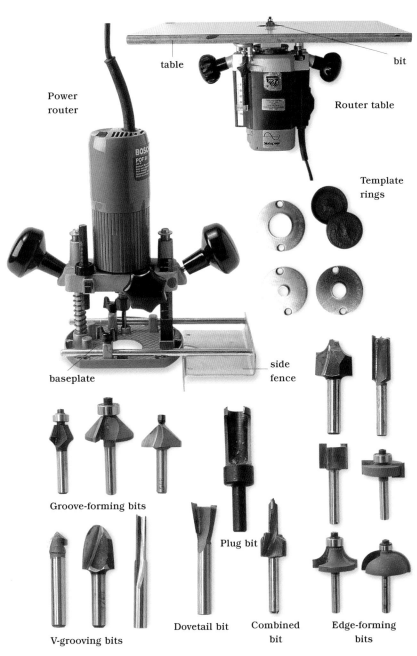

table

bit

Power
router

Router table

Template
rings

baseplate

side
fence

Groove-forming bits

Plug bit

V-grooving bits

Dovetail bit

Combined
bit

Edge-forming
bits

The socket accepts the shank of the router bit and is found in several sizes. The lightest routers have sockets of either ¼ or ⅜ in. (6 or 8 mm) in diameter, while larger ones have ½ in. (12 mm) ones. The larger the socket capacity, the larger the bits that fit.

Router bits

While high-speed steel bits are adequate for most jobs, tungsten-tip bits maintain their sharpness for longer. However, when these bits do need sharpening, they must be sent to a specialist. There is a wide range of bits available, and these can be categorized as either groove-forming (straight) or edge-forming (molding).

Groove-forming bits come in a range of styles. Straight bits cut square grooves, while V-grooving bits create a V-shaped indent, largely for decorative work. Veining and core-box bits produce round-bottomed grooves, while a dovetail bit is used for dovetail housings and joints.

Edge-forming bits can have pin- or ball-bearing race guides. The latter is preferable as it reduces the risk of damage along the edge of the wood. The most common types are rabbet, chamfer, rounding and trimming varieties. For shaping edges, cove, ogee, and beading bits create decorative edges along the wood.

Router table

One main advantage of the router is that it can be mounted upside down in a frame so that the bit projects from the surface, with safety fences in place. This is a very useful and safe way of working. Instead of taking the router to the work, the wood is fed over the router, in the direction of the bit.

Proprietary **router tables** can be bought, but you can also make one using material such as plywood. Cut and construct a box with one open side so that the router is readily accessible. Cut a hole in the top of the box for the bit to protrude through and fix the router baseplate in the box, directly below the hole in the top.

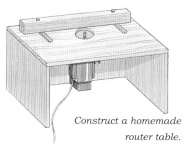

Construct a homemade router table.

Biscuit jointers

Even though the furniture maker can use the jointing methods described previously, if you need to make a lot of cabinets or boxes, the biscuit jointer is a very useful tool.

The **biscuit jointer** is a small circular saw that cuts slots into both faces of a joint. A wood oval—the biscuit—available ready-made of compressed beech, is inserted into the slots. The biscuit joint is often used in place of tongues and grooves or dowel joints and can even replace some traditional cabinet- and drawer-making joints.

The biscuit jointer can make butt joints, both from edge to face and from edge to edge, as well as miter joints. It can also be used to cut small grooves and to trim panel edges.

Dust extraction

Routers produce a lot of very fine dust, so try to have some form of exhaust system as you work. Many machines have a facility for attaching extraction tubes, so take advantage of this whenever possible. You should always wear safety glasses, and a dust mask is also advisable.

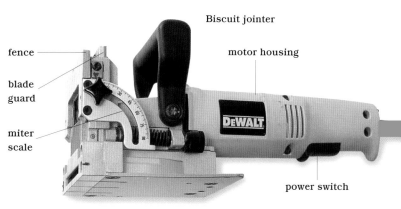

Biscuit jointer

fence

blade guard

miter scale

motor housing

power switch

Using a power router

Compared with some tools, power routers are relatively safe to use, provided you maintain them properly and follow the manufacturer's instructions.

Fitting a bit

When fitting a bit into a socket, first unplug the router from the electrical supply.

1 Lock the spindle, using either the button provided, or the metal rod that passes through a hole in the spindle. Some routers have two wrenches—one for the spindle and one for the socket nut.

2 Use a wrench to loosen the nut and unscrew the socket.

3 Insert the bit into the socket, carefully pushing it into position. Be careful not to cut your fingers.

Insert the bit with the retaining nut into the socket.

4 Then, tighten the socket nut using the wrench and unlock the spindle.

5 Use your fingers to check that the bit is tight. Test-run the router, so that it gains full speed for 5 to 10 seconds. Turn off the router and recheck the bit.

Cutting grooves with a side fence

To produce a straight, grooved line, parallel with the edge of the wood, use a side fence. This should be positioned to the right side of a clockwise-rotating bit, so that the force of the blade does not pull the fence too much toward the work. It is a good idea to test-run a scrap piece of wood first before routing your work.

Position the fence to the right of the clockwise-rotating bit.

1 Choose the required bit for the job and insert it into the tool as explained above.

2 Adjust and lock the fence in the correct position.

3 Set the depth of cut so that the bit will plunge only as far as you require. In many instances, it is better to make deep cuts in small stages. This will help to prolong the life of the bit and prevent the machine from overheating.

4 Hold the router firmly, using both handles. Switch on the machine, with the router motor in position above the base. Twist the locking handle to unlock the router body and plunge the bit into the work to the preset depth. Lock the router into position.

Cut a groove, using a router and side fence.

5 Continue the cut to the end of the piece of wood. To make a stopped groove, plunge the router at the start mark, guide the tool until the bit reaches the end mark, and release the plunge mechanism.

Cutting a groove using guide battens

Guide battens can be used for making grooves that are some distance from the edge of the wood. You can use any straight pieces of wood that are long enough to project beyond the start and finish marks of the groove.

1 Using C-clamps, fix the guide battens to the work. The bit has to line up with the center of the router base, so that the groove will end up being midway between the battens.

2 Select the required bit and then fit it carefully into the power router.

3 Plunge the router and cut as before. Remove the battens when finished.

Cut a groove, using a router and side battens.

Cutting housings

Provided the router is fitted with sharp bits, the action of routing across the grain—cutting a housing—is very similar to that of routing with the grain. However, you may encounter problems with certain types of grains since an open texture or dry wood may split or chip easily. In this case it may be necessary to work to a marking knife line, although this should not normally be necessary.

Safety first

• The router is generally a very safe machine, but remember always to keep your hands away from moving bits.

• Always switch the machine off and wait for it to stop completely before laying it down on a bench.

• If you need to make adjustments, disconnect the machine from the power supply.

• Wear safety glasses and a dust mask, and secure your work.

Expert tip

When molding the edges of solid wood panels, particularly across the grain, there may well be some breakout at the end of the pass. For this reason, use the tool on the two sides of the end grain first. Then, as you mold the long sides, this breakout should be removed.

Cutting edge moldings

Edges are molded for decorative effect or to soften sharp corners.

1 Select the required bit and insert it in the socket. Use molding bits with a bearing at the tip, rather than a simple steel tip, because this reduces the risk of burning the wood.

2 Fit the fence securely, bearing in mind that the bit will tend to draw the fence to the edge.

3 Clamp the work to the bench as shown below, ensuring that nothing is obstructing the fence.

The edge to be molded needs to overhang the bench sufficiently.

4 Plunge the router to the correct depth, lock, and start the motor. Bring the bit up to the edge of the wood, and holding the fence or bearing against the work, cut the molding, moving from left to right.

Routing with a template

In addition to using fences and battens, shaped edges and internal shaping can be carried out using a template. Most routers have a collar or ring that can be fixed to the tool's faceplate, which will act as a guide when using a template.

The diagram below shows a section of the collar of the router and the bit, and how the aperture along the edge and inside the template has to account for the differences in diameter. For example, a ⅜-in. (10 mm) bit with a ⅝-in. (16 mm) outside diameter collar will need the template cut ⅛ in. (3 mm) bigger than the size of the finished cutout.

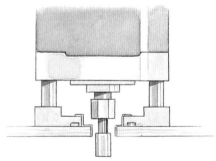

The collar and template.

1 Mark a template on a piece of ¼-in. (6 mm) medium density fiberboard. Draw out the whole pattern that you want to reproduce, with the outer line representing the edges of the final job. Remember you can cut shaped outside or inside edges. Now measure the bit and the collar to determine the required differences in diameter, as described above.

2 Make the template, cutting as closely as you can to your second line with a bandsaw or jigsaw. Finish off with a rasp, file, or sandpaper.

3 Fix the template in position. If the surface has not been finished, you can use nails to secure it. If any finish or veneer has been applied, use double-sided tape. In some instances, depending upon the desired shaping, it may be possible to use C-clamps.

4 Switch the router on and plunge the bit into the piece to the required depth. Then guide the collar against the template as you rout around the edges.

Cutting joints

The router is a versatile tool that can be used to cut many types of joints—even some of the complex ones such as mortise-and-tenons and

dovetails. Unless you need to cut a number of joints, these can be done by hand. However, any joints based on rabbets and grooves, such as tongue-and-groove, lap, and housing joints (both barefaced and dovetail) are suitable for the router.

Using a biscuit jointer

The instructions below show you how you can make a simple butt joint.

1 Set the cutting depth to suit the biscuits you are using, and adjust the fence so that the blade aligns with the center line on the first component. Press the fence against the work.

2 Start the machine and plunge the blade to make a cut. Use the same procedure to cut the rest of the slots. Then cut those on the edge of the second component.

3 To assemble the joint, spread adhesive into the slots and insert the biscuits. The adhesive will make the biscuits swell, producing a very strong joint. You will need to work rapidly to apply the adhesive, insert the biscuit, and clamp the joint.

Turn to pages 237–9 where the hot plate stand will give you practice in grooving.

Machine tools

A machine tool equivalent of the power router is a large industrial machine with a fixed head containing the motor with larger capacities and speeds. Nowadays the hand power tools are so efficient that you may never need to investigate the machine alternative. Another industrial machine is the spindle molder, and again the power router is so efficient for most purposes that this industrial equivalent will not be necessary.

Shaping

The ability to shape curved surfaces and edges moves furniture away from the solely functional. When you want to introduce a freer approach to your work, you will need to use the tools and techniques described in this section.

SHAPING TOOLS

Even though some work on convex and other curved surfaces can be carried out with planes and chisels, narrow edges require a smaller tool to prevent slipping. Spokeshaves are ideal for such work. Rasps and files are also used for shaping work, particularly when curves are tight.

Spokeshaves

Although spokeshaves are ideal for shaping, they can be quite difficult to control and will require some practice. There are two main types—one for convex shapes and the other for concave. Spokeshaves are usually made of metal but, traditionally, furniture makers would have made their own tools from wood—normally beech—into which a metal blade was then fitted.

Round-face spokeshaves have convex blades that are ideal for use on wood with a concave

face. The blade is held in position by a cap iron, and the depth of the blade can be adjusted by loosening this cap and jiggling the blade into the required position. Alternatively, some spokeshaves have screws at the top two corners of the blade, which can be loosened and tightened for making precise adjustments.

Flat-face spokeshaves are the same as round-face versions, except that they have flat, narrow faces. This feature of the tool makes it suitable for skimming a convex curve.

A **half-round spokeshave** has a deep, concave blade and face, and is suitable for rounded tabletops and chair legs.

A **chamfer spokeshave** can be used to cut bevels up to 1½ in. (38 mm) wide.

A **combination spokeshave** is dual-purpose, and has both a

Using a second-cut file

The distribution and size of teeth on rasps and files determine the degree of coarseness—or cut—of the tool. A bastard cut is the coarsest, a smooth cut is the finest, and a second cut is in between the two.

Metal spokeshaves

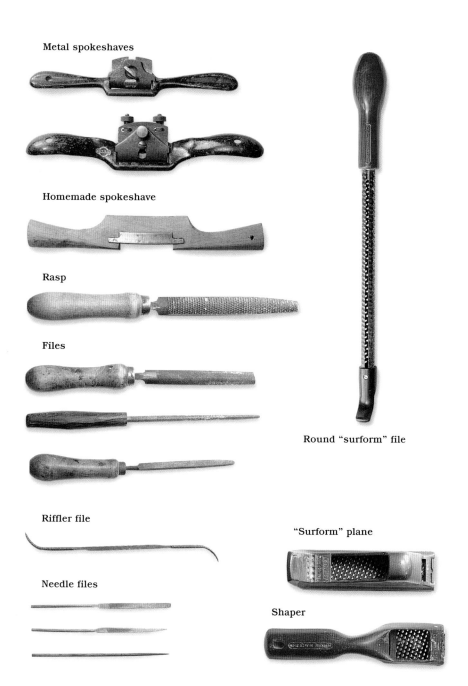

Homemade spokeshave

Rasp

Files

Riffler file

Needle files

Round "surform" file

"Surform" plane

Shaper

Drawknives

A traditional tool used by chairmakers, wheelwrights, or coopers, drawknives have similarities to axes, and remove wood very quickly. They do not produce a very refined finish, and are most suitable for initial shaping before using a plane or spokeshave. The tools are now not really in general use, and tend to be found only in specialized trades. The one pictured here is a curved drawknife.

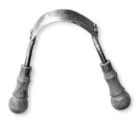

straight and half-rounded blade. Because it is useful on work with a range of surfaces, it saves changing blades as you move from one area to another.

Rasps and files

Most commonly used by carvers for initial shaping, rasps and files also remove a lot of material. Rasps produce a fairly rough surface, which then needs to be smoothed with a file. The teeth on rasps range from coarse to quite smooth, and the tool is available in flat, round (rat-tail) and, most usefully, half-round shapes.

Files are much finer than rasps and help to remove roughened wood left by the other tool. For a finer finish, they can be used with abrasive paper wrapped around them. **Riffler files** are designed for use in tight curves, while **needle files** are used for metalwork and are useful when adapting hardware such as hinges.

"Surform" files are available in a range of plain or file types. The main difference lies in their carefully punched teeth, which enable wood shavings to pass through the metal. This means that the tool can move over the wood's surface more quickly,

because it is less likely to get clogged. The most commonly used surform tools are the flat surform file and the round surform file.

ADJUSTING THE BLADE ON A SPOKESHAVE

1 Remove the blade by undoing the locking screw on the cap iron. Sharpen the blade by grinding and honing, as required (see pages 96–9).

2 Carefully reposition the blade ground-side down and tighten the lead screw. If this screw is the sole means of adjustment, tighten the blade gradually and position the blade with your fingers until it protrudes at the correct depth. If the tool has adjustment screws, use these to achieve a more precise setting.

Adjust the blade in the spokeshave to the desired projection.

USING A SPOKESHAVE

Effective shaping with a spokeshave can take time to master. It pays to practice on scrap wood, before attempting a job on a piece of furniture. Keep the cutting edge of the blade sharp to ensure the best results, and remember to adjust the position of the blade to vary the depth of cut as required.

1 Secure the work in a vice. Hold the tool with both hands, so that your fingers curl over the front of the handles, and your thumbs rest at the back.

Secure the work in a vice and hold the spokeshave with both hands.

2 Rest the tool on the work and move it forward and backward, so that the blade cuts a shaving. Work in the direction of the grain, changing the position of the wood in the vice as you go, if necessary.

USING RASPS AND FILES

There are frequently occasions when curves are so tight that edge tools are not suitable for the job. In these instances, it is best to use a file or rasp.

1 Fit a handle to the rasp or file. If possible, secure the work in a vice. Use your spare hand to hold the wood securely, preferably with your fingertips near the area to be filed, to maximize the pressure.

2 Hold the rasp firmly with your dominant hand and apply forward pressure in order to cut away the wood.

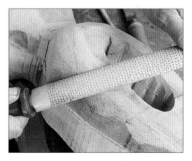

Cut away the timber with a rasp.

3 After making a series of rough cuts with the rasp, use a wood file in order to remove the rough surface.

4 Finish with sandpaper wrapped around a file or a piece of hardwood.

Cleaning rasps and files

When rasps and files become clogged, use the wire bristles on a file cleaner—or file card—to loosen the shavings. Then remove the shavings with the coarse fiber brush on the other side of the file cleaner.

Drilling

In woodwork and furniture making, you often need to make holes, either to use with special saws or to insert a range of screws, dowels, and other hardware. It is important to be able to drill accurately to a specific depth and angle.

HAND TOOLS

With the advent of the power drill, hand drills and braces are less commonly used today. However, they still have an important role to play in the woodworker's workshop.

A **bradawl** is a simple tool for marking pilot holes for small screws, or for creating the center-mark for drilling.

A **gimlet** is similar to the bradawl, but it creates deeper holes by actually cutting into the wood.

Hand drills

A **hand drill** is the simplest type of drilling tool. By operating the handle, a series of gear wheels rotates the chuck shaft. The drill bits, which are held in the chuck, are subsequently rotated. There are several types of drill bits that can be used in this tool and powered varieties to perform different functions.

Drill bits

The following bits can be used in hand or powered drills.

Twist drills come in a range of sizes. It can be difficult to drill precisely with these bits—they can easily move off course with the vibration of the tool. You could mark the drilling location with a bradawl, making a slight recess in the surface for the bit.

Dowel bits, or centerpoint drills, also come in a range of sizes and have a point at the center of the tip and two spurs. The center tip can be placed exactly on the drill mark, and the two spurs help to prevent the bit from moving off course.

A **countersink bit** cuts a tapered recess around the main hole. This provides a useful home for the head of a screw, so that the top of the screw sits flush with the surface of the wood. This makes for a very clean and smooth finished look.

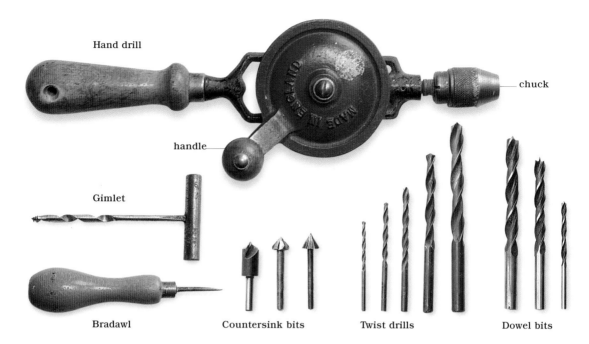

Hand drill

chuck

handle

Gimlet

Bradawl

Countersink bits

Twist drills

Dowel bits

Braces

A **brace** is also used to drill holes, but the whole frame of the tool is rotated in a clockwise direction while pressure is at the same time applied to the rear, domed handle. Most types of braces have a ratchet mechanism, so that the tool can be used in restricted spaces. The chuck of a brace has jaws that are designed to house bits with square shanks. However, some braces can accept the same round-shanked drill bits that are used in power and hand drills.

Brace bits

Center bits come in a range of sizes from ¼–2 in. (6–50 mm).

A single spur on one side of the bit scores the edge of the hole. Then the cutting edge on the other side of the bit cuts into the wood. A lead screw protruding from the center pulls the spur and then the cutting edge into the wood. This ensures that a neat, crisp hole is made.

Auger bits are similar to center bits but cut deeper holes. The long, spiral body behind the cutting edge keeps the drill in line and removes waste wood.

Expansion bits are similar to center bits, but have a cutter that can be set to different

drilling

BRACE BITS

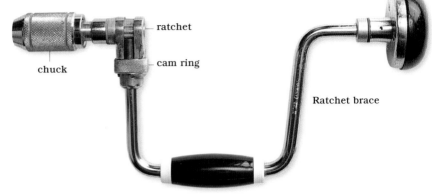

ratchet

cam ring

chuck

Ratchet brace

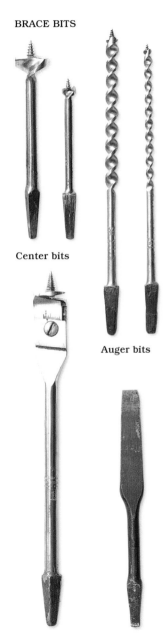

Center bits

Auger bits

Expansion bit   Screwdriver bit

diameters. Available in two sizes, the total cutting capacity ranges from ½ in. to 3 in. (12 to 75 mm).

Countersink bits work in the same way as those for drills, but they have square shanks to fit in the brace chuck.

Screwdriver bits enable braces to be used as a heavy-duty screwdriver for long screws. However, many people use electric screwdrivers or light power drills with screwdriver bits instead.

POWER DRILLS

One of the first electric tools, the power drill is now available in a large range of sizes and features. Heavy-duty versions are suitable for such work as masonry and concrete, while

lightweight, rechargeable types are ideal for fine drilling, such as for small screws.

Like hand drills, power drills have a chuck that holds the required bit. It is worth remembering that the shank of the bit corresponds with the diameter of the hole that the bit cuts. So large drills, which tend to have a large chuck capacity —up to ½ in. (12 mm)—can take larger bits, which means that they are capable of drilling larger holes. Smaller, lighter drills have less chuck capacity and are used for making smaller holes.

Most drills come with a speed selector. Some larger drills have a hammer action, which is useful when attaching battens to masonry walls.

Power drill bits

There is a wide range of drill bits available.

Twist and **centerpoint drill bits** are the same as those used for the hand drill, although if they are to be used on metal at any stage, it is worth investing in high-speed steel types. Large twist drills are made with reduced shanks, so they can fit in standard power drill chucks.

Spade bits have long points for positioning on the exact center of the hole mark. This is especially helpful when you are drilling at an angle to the face surface, since the point prevents the drill from wandering.

Forstner bits are high-quality drill bits that have a special serrated ring around the main point. These teeth help the bit to stay on course, boring through difficult areas and preventing knots from deflecting the drill.

Countersink bits with reduced shanks (again designed to fit ordinary power drills) are also available, as are drill-and-countersink bits, which produce both a hole and countersink in one action.

Drill-and-counterbore bits perform similar actions to the drill-and-countersink bit, except that they also produce a neat counterbored hole, which can be plugged with a piece of wood, to conceal the screw beneath. To cut the plug, use a plug cutter, which will cut a cylindrical piece of wood exactly the right size for the hole made by the drill-and-counterbore bit.

Drill bits

Forstner bits

keyless chuck

forward/reverse switch

torque selector

trigger

battery pack

Cordless power drill

drilling

A vertical drill stand

This is another useful attachment, as it transforms a hand-held power drill into a temporary drill press. The feed lever is used to lower the drill, with its rotating bit, into the work. When this lever is released, a return spring brings the drill back to the starting position. A depth gauge on the stand can be used to limit the movement of the tool, so that stopped holes can be drilled. To drill through holes, position a piece of plywood under the work. This helps to prevent the underside surface from splintering as the drill passes through.

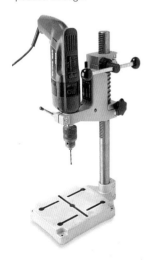

PILLAR DRILL

Usually known as a drill press, the **pillar drill** is a heavy-duty machine tool and is very useful in the workshop. In fact, unless you are planning to carry out a lot of site work, a pillar drill is probably the next step after a small power drill, rather than investing in a large tool and separate stand. Pillar drills can be either bench or floor mounted, and are ideal for precise, repetitive drilling.

Pillar drill

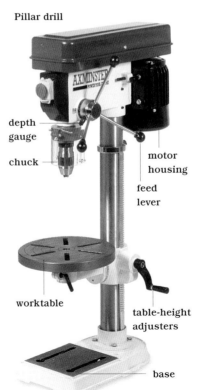

depth gauge

chuck

motor housing

feed lever

worktable

table-height adjusters

base

The tool has an adjustable table to accommodate a range of sizes of wood, and a feed lever that works in much the same way as the lever on a vertical drill stand (see far left). A depth gauge can be set to determine the depth of the hole, while a guard helps to prevent any obstructions or clothing from getting in the way of the rotating chuck. Remember never to wear loose clothing while you are using a piece of machinery.

USING A HAND DRILL

It is possible to use a hand drill from most positions. However, it is most common, and generally easier, to drill from a vertical position, so that you can apply a steady pressure to the rear handle.

1 Select the drill or bit you require. Open the jaws of the hand drill by holding the chuck with one hand and rotating the drive wheel counterclockwise with the other. Alternatively, some hand drill chucks are opened with a chuck key, just like power drills.

2 Insert the bit into the chuck and tighten the jaws, either by turning the drive handle clockwise or, if appropriate, tightening with the chuck key. Check that the bit is centered in the chuck jaws.

3 Mark the center of the hole on the wood's surface, preferably with crossed hairlines. Twist a bradawl on the exact center of the mark, which will produce a starter hole.

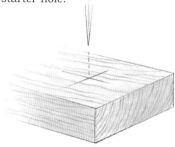

Mark the center of the desired hole before you indent it with the bradawl.

4 Put the tip of the drill on the starter hole. Bring the body of the drill to the correct angle—

Rotate the hand drill's drive wheel.

normally square with the face. Stand two try squares near the mark so that you can sight the drill bit to ensure accuracy.

5 Hold the drill steady by applying a moderate amount of pressure to the rear handle. Begin to rotate the drive handle, so that the drill cuts into the surface. Continue rotating the handle while holding the drill steady and at the correct angle. You should not require a great deal of pressure or speed—experience will teach you how all the different woods respond and how much pressure is required for each.

USING A BRACE

1 Select the required bit for the job. Center the cam ring so that the brace ratchet is locked in position. Then hold the chuck and rotate the frame clockwise, to open the jaws.

2 Insert the bit and tighten the jaws of the chuck by rotating the frame counterclockwise. Ensure that the tapered shank of the bit is firmly in the chuck.

3 When you are drilling horizontally, place the work in a vice so that you are drilling at lower chest level.

4 To drill vertically, secure the work on the bench or in a vice. Hold the brace upright with one hand while you turn the brace with the other hand.

Hold the brace with one hand and turn the frame of the brace steadily.

5 Hold the brace steady. Most drills have a screw that pulls the bit into the work, so only the minimum amount of pressure is required. Turn the frame with your other hand, taking care to keep the tool level. Remember that the bits used in a brace are designed for slow and methodical cutting.

6 At the required depth, reverse the handle a couple of times to release the screw. Then gently pull the tool away from the hole, rotating the brace at the same time in order to clear the waste from the hole. If you are boring through

holes, stop drilling as soon as the lead screw shows on the opposite side. Remove the brace and drill bit, as described, and then reverse the work to repeat the drilling from the other side.

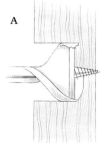

A

When the drill bit pierces the work (A), reverse and drill from the other side (B).

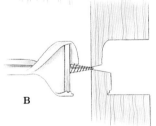

B

7 If there is not enough room to make a full sweep with the

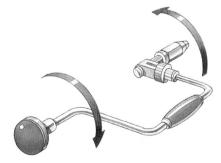

Turn the ratchet brace with a quarter sweep to cut and then return.

frame, set the cam ring on the ratchet. When the ratchet is set, it will turn the bit about one-quarter of a turn. Then reverse the handle direction and make another cut. This technique is useful when you are forced to work in confined spaces.

MAKING A DEPTH STOP FOR A TWIST DRILL

Even though it is possible to buy metal depth stops for twist drills, it is very easy to make your own version. Take some square scraps of hardwood and drill a hole of the required size down the center. Slip the wood over the drill bit, and mark the length of the hole required. Cut the wood on the mark. Slip the depth stop back on the drill and drill the hole until the stop touches the surface. You can keep several lengths of wood

Homemade depth stops.

drilled to fit the drill sizes that you most commonly use so that you can cut suitable lengths when needed.

USING A POWER DRILL

Power drills are relatively easy to use—on wood there is less vibration than on materials such as concrete or masonry.

1 Select the required bit and fit it into the chuck. This is usually done with a chuck key, in the same way as a hand drill, but some power drills have keyless chucks. Pull back the casing of the chuck, insert a bit with an appropriately grooved shank, to fit the type of drill, and release the chuck casing. The chuck will automatically grip the bit.

2 Select the required speed on the drill. With some tools, the speed of the rotating chuck will depend on the amount of pressure applied to the trigger. Although knowledge of the desired speed comes with experience, it is generally best to have a fast setting for drilling holes in wood, and a slower speed for masonry.

3 Hold the rear handle with your dominant hand and the secondary handle, if there is

Safety first

- Wear safety glasses.
- Secure the work.
- Do not wear any loose clothing.
- Keep hands well away from drill bits.
- Tie back long hair securely.
- Always select the correct speed.
- Never use a tool to do a job for which it was not designed.
- Make sure that you use sharp drill bits.
- Never force the tool— let the bit do the work.

drilling

Position the drill bit and start to apply pressure to the trigger.

one, with the weaker hand. Stand comfortably with your body squarely facing to the work. Position the tip of the bit on the drill mark and steadily pull the trigger.

4 As the drill bit moves into the wood, keep the tool steady and at the required angle to the work.

5 When you have achieved the depth of hole required, gently pull the tool away, with the bit still rotating, and release the trigger when the bit is clear of the work.

The power drill is used in a similar way when fitted with a screwdriver bit, although a slower speed is usually required to ensure accurate results. All power drills also have a reverse-action switch, so that the tool can be used both to tighten and loosen screws.

USING THE PILLAR DRILL

When using a pillar drill (see page 144), take extra care to hold the work securely. If possible, use C-clamps to hold it in position, and use a fence and end stop to drill identical holes in separate pieces of work.

1 Select an appropriate bit and unlock the chuck of the drill with the chuck key. Insert the bit, tighten the chuck, and be sure to remove the chuck key. It is extremely dangerous to leave the key in position when the machine is switched on.

2 Lower the safety guard and switch the machine on. Holding the work securely, use the feed lever to lower the bit onto, and through, the wood. Keep your hands well away.

3 After you have achieved the required depth, use the lever to raise the bit. Once the bit is completely clear of the workpiece, you can turn off the machine.

Now turn to pages 240–3—the wine rack will be a good exercice to practice precise drilling.

Making half-lap joints

Learning to make joints is a fundamental skill in woodwork, and marks the first step of proper construction. Half-lap joints are among the simplest to make, although they still require accurate skills in measuring, marking, sawing, and planing. They are used when two pieces of wood cross each other; the joint is made by removing half the thickness of the wood from each piece.

TYPES OF HALF-LAP JOINTS

There are several types of half-lap joints. The most common that you might come across in your woodworking are described below.

Cross half-lap joints are used when two rails meet square to each other. It is usual for the vertical piece to look as though it continues through,

but both halves are actually the same.

Corner half-lap joints are similar to cross half-lap joints, but the pieces meet at the corner, rather than in the main body of the rail, and may need additional reinforcement.

Oblique half-lap joints are made in a way similar to cross half-lap joints, but the cutouts are set at an angle.

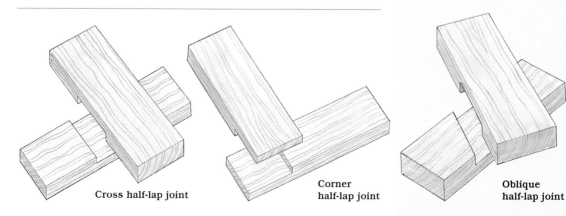

Cross half-lap joint

Corner half-lap joint

Oblique half-lap joint

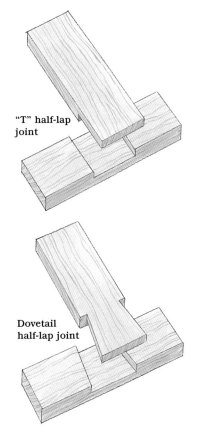

"T" half-lap joint

Dovetail half-lap joint

"T" half-lap joints are used when the end of a rail meets flush with the outside edge of another.

Dovetail half-lap joints are virtually the same as "T" half-lap joints, but the pieces are cut to a specific dovetail shape—giving the joint additional strength.

Note that half-lap joints are not integral structural units and so they will need to be secured with either adhesive or screws.

The illustrations show examples of half-lap joints where each joint is cut on the wood's thickness. However, you will find the joint is often cut the other way around for certain types of underframes—for example, on the small table project (see pages 259–64).

Making a cross half-lap joint

1 Take two pieces of wood of the same width and thickness and lay one across the other in the position of the finished joint.

2 Use a try square and marking knife to mark the width of one piece on the face side of the other where the material will be removed, and square those lines halfway down the edges. Repeat on the other piece. Note that

the top half is removed from the first piece, while the bottom half is removed from the second.

Mark the face sides.

3 Use a marking gauge, set to half the thickness of the wood, in order to scribe a line in between the knife marks. Work from the face side of both pieces of wood.

Gauge the edges.

4 Use a tenon saw to saw across the two shoulder lines down to the gauge line, working on the waste side of the lines.

5 Make some extra saw cuts across the joint to make it easier to chisel out the waste.

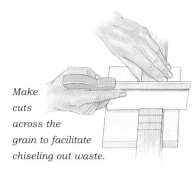

Make cuts across the grain to facilitate chiseling out waste.

6 Secure the piece in a vice or clamp. Pare away the waste across the grain until you have a flat surface. Chisel from both side edges to stop breakout and pare the shoulders of the joint to ensure a good fit.

Pare away the waste.

7 Repeat on the other piece. To ensure that the joint is square

Dry test the half-lap joint.

and flush, dry-test it before gluing the pieces and clamping them together.

Making corner or oblique half-lap joints

A corner half-lap joint is made in the same way as a cross half-lap joint. However, all cuts can be made with a saw, so little chiseling should be required.

Oblique corner half-lap joints.

The photograph above shows oblique corner half-lap joints. Exactly the same principles apply but the cross is angled rather than square.

Making a "T" half-lap joint

This joint is made in a way similar to the cross half-lap and corner half-lap joints.

1 Put one wood piece in place on the other and mark its width. Mark the area to be cut out, including the depth.

2 Measure and mark the end of the other butting piece, and use a marking gauge to mark the depth of cut on all three sides.

Gauge and mark the depth of cut.

3 Saw away any excess from the lower cross piece, then use a chisel to cut the wood to depth.

4 Secure the butting piece in a vice and saw down the gauged line, then across the shoulder.

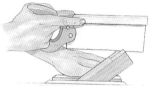

Saw down the gauged line.

Making a dovetail half-lap joint

Although the principle behind this half-lap joint is similar to that of a "T" half-lap joint, this joint requires very precise measuring and setting out. If possible, use a template for accurate results.

1 Measure and mark the butting piece, preferably using a template for the dovetail shape.

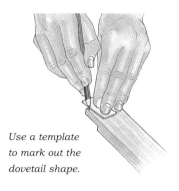

Use a template to mark out the dovetail shape.

2 Cut out the dovetail with a saw.

3 Trace the cut dovetail on the face side of the cross piece and square the lines down the edges. Gauge the depth of the joint. Use the dovetail as a template for drawing the area to be removed on the cross member.

Draw around the dovetail shape.

4 Cut the half-lap across the angled lines with a tenon saw down to the gauge lines.

5 Chisel away the material until the two pieces fit snugly.

Making mortise-and-tenon joints

The mortise-and-tenon is generally a joint between a vertical piece, a stile or a leg, and a horizontal piece, a rail. When glued, it makes a very strong structural unit. The two components are usually the same thickness and both mortise-and-tenon are one-third of that thickness. The tenon can travel right through the vertical piece, a through joint, or be stopped within its width, a stopped joint.

THROUGH MORTISE-AND-TENON JOINTS

Through joints are mainly used for decorative effect. The tenon on the end of the rail projects right through the stile or leg and shows on the outside. It can be wedged from the outside for extra strength.

Wedged through mortise-and-tenon joints
Through joints can be strengthened by inserting wedges in the end of the tenon. This forces the tenon to splay and lock tight in the mortise.

Loose-wedged through mortise-and-tenon joints
This is an old joint that is used on benches and tables.

It can be assembled dry and therefore can be pulled apart and put back together—a knock-down capability.

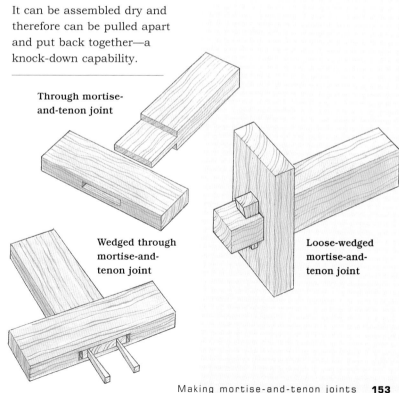

Through mortise-and-tenon joint

Wedged through mortise-and-tenon joint

Loose-wedged mortise-and-tenon joint

STOPPED MORTISE-AND-TENON JOINTS

If a through mortise-and-tenon joint is not required, and this will be true in many frames, a stopped mortise-and-tenon joint can be used instead. In this type of joint, the tenon and the mortise stop short of the outside face. This is the most common type of mortise-and-tenon joint. It is usually strong, but for extra strength it can be fox wedged. Wedges can be inserted into the mortise-and-tenon joint before it is closed.

width of the rail. With a simple tenon, the rail could break away from the stile at the top. Therefore, to give the mortise-and-tenon as much contact as is possible, an angled haunch is made on top of the tenon to help keep the rail in line but this joint does not show on the top surface.

Square-haunch mortise-and-tenon joints

This kind of joint is used where the components are either grooved or rabbeted. When making a frame with a groove on the inside edges, the groove is normally worked the whole way a long each edge. Therefore, the haunch of the tenon must be square, thus filling the outside end of the joint and the groove.

Long-and-short shoulder mortise-and-tenon joints

This joint is also used for grooved or rabbeted components. In traditional cabinet making the rabbet is made before the tenon is cut. When making a frame with a rabbet, one shoulder of the tenon needs to be long in order for it to reach across the rabbet into the mortise and the other needs to be short so that it will

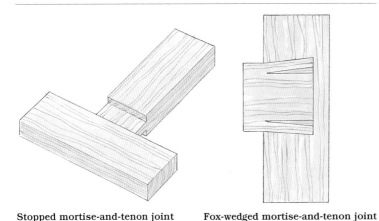

Stopped mortise-and-tenon joint   Fox-wedged mortise-and-tenon joint

Sloped-haunch mortise-and-tenon joints

When the top of a stile has to be level with the outside face of a rail, the tenon will only usually be two-thirds the

sit against the top of the rabbet. In this situation it is possible to make a square top on the haunch.

Corner mortise-and-tenon joints

When two rails join together at the top of a leg the mortises will intersect at the center point. Therefore the ends of the two tenons are cut at an angle so that they do not foul each other when the piece is assembled, and the tenons are then inserted into the relevant mortises.

Wide mortise-and-tenon joints

Sometimes in a frame a rail has to be quite wide and it will weaken the joint too much to have one wide tenon going into a wide mortise. Therefore, two tenons and two mortises are made so as to retain the strength in the stile or leg. This joint can be through as well as stopped.

Twin mortise-and-tenon joints

On wide, thick components, the two mortises and tenons sit side by side rather than in vertical alignment as they are in the previous joint. This joint can be a through joint as well as a stopped one.

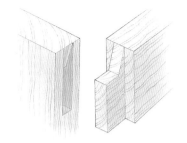

Sloped-haunch mortise-and-tenon joint

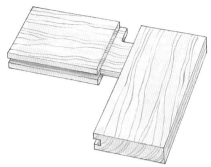

Square-haunch mortise-and-tenon joint, with grooved frame

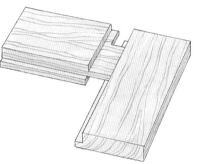

Long-and-short shoulder joint with rabbeted frame

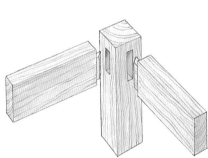

Corner mortise-and-tenon joint

Wide mortise-and-tenon joint

Twin mortise-and-tenon joints

Expert tip

With your first mortise-and-tenon joints you may have to pare the faces of the tenon slightly so that it fits in the mortise, but with practice the joint should fit together directly from the saw.

MAKING A THROUGH MORTISE-AND-TENON JOINT

When making a mortise-and-tenon joint, it is best to start by making the tenon and then the mortise. Mark all the lines to be cut with a knife and gauge. Other marks can be made with a pencil.

Marking the tenon

1 With the rail length slightly oversized, mark the shoulders all round with a knife. Then mark the length of the tenon plus ⅛ in. (3 mm) waste.

Mark the shoulders and length of the tenon.

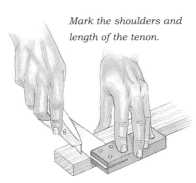

2 Set a mortise gauge to the exact width of a mortise chisel, which is close to one-third the thickness of the wood.

3 Gauging from the face sides, mark the thickness of the tenon from the shoulder lines toward the end of the rail,

using a mortise gauge. Ensure that the mortise marks are in the center of the rail.

Mark the thickness of the tenon with a mortise gauge.

4 Cut the tenon to length and mark across the end with the mortise gauge.

Cut the tenon to length and mark out the end.

5 If the tenon is to have a haunch or side shoulders, mark these on the face of the rail.

Mark the waste area of the tenon with a pencil.

Cutting the tenon

Place the work in the vice and cut as follows with the tenon saw, ensuring your saw is just on the waste side of the line.

1 With the tenon upright make some careful cuts across the end grain to a depth of about ⅛ in. (3 mm).

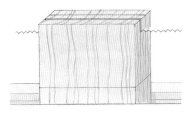

Make a series of careful cuts across the end grain.

2 Now reposition the rail and saw at a 45-degree angle from the first cut down the tenon, stopping short of the shoulder line.

Make the first cut and stop just short of the shoulder line.

3 Turn the tenon around and saw down the other side. This will give you sawn lines across the top and down both sides.

Secure the rail vertically in the vice and saw directly down to the shoulder line.

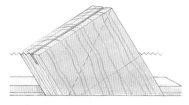

Turn the tenon around and cut from the other side.

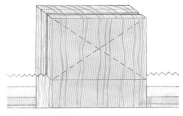

Make the final cut and remove the waste from each side.

4 When both sides of the tenon have been cut, lay it flat against a bench hook. Saw across the shoulder line with a tenon saw in order to remove the waste from each side of the tenon.

The finished tenon.

Marking the mortise

1 Mark the position and width of the mortise all round. Use a pencil initially to mark all around the stile.

2 If the stile is the same thickness as the rail, use the mortise gauge as already set to scribe the mortise on the face side.

3 If the stile is thicker than the rail, reset the mortise gauge so that it marks the mortise in the center and mark on the joint face.

4 In this situation most tenons will have shoulders all the way around. The shape of the mortise will therefore need to account for this. With this in mind, mark the actual width of the mortise with a cut line on both the mating and outside surfaces of the piece of wood.

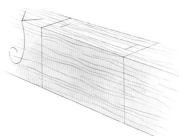

Mark out the mortise, ready to be cut.

Cutting the mortise

1 To cut the mortise, start approximately ⅛ in. (3 mm) from the cut lines at each end, which indicate the mortise's true width, and make a series of cuts in the wood using a mortise chisel to about ⅛ in. (3 mm) deep.

Make a series of cuts in the mortise using a chisel.

2 Remove the waste from your first series of cuts.

3 Make several more cuts and remove the waste until you get about half to two-thirds of the way through the piece.

4 Turn the piece of wood over and then start to cut from the other side.

5 Make another series of cuts until the two parts meet in the middle.

6 Pare the faces within the mortise, if required.

7 Pare the ends of the mortises back to the cut line, working from both sides.

If you are making a stopped mortise rather than a through mortise, you will need to stop chiseling when you reach the required depth (see page 160).

Alternatives for cutting the mortise

There are alternative ways of cutting a mortise.

Bench constructed with mortise-and-tenon joints (see pages 353–65).

Using only a mortise chisel, start from the center of the mortise and take a series of cuts so that you make a "V" in the center of the mortise; then turn the chisel around and cut out the edges. Always leave the final cut to the end of the mortise until the rest has been cleared of waste.

Or, remove the bulk of the waste from the mortise by drilling a series of holes along the mortise (a pillar drill or drill in a stand is best and set a guide on the drill table). Use a mortise chisel at the ends, and a wider paring chisel to true up the inside faces of the mortise.

Choosing the best method

There is little to distinguish between different methods of cutting a mortise—it is a matter of preference. However, the methods using the mortise chisel are suitable if you have only a few mortises to cut. The drilling method has great advantages where you have a pillar drill or drill in a drill stand and have a lot of mortises to cut. Square mortise drill attachments are also available for pillar drills.

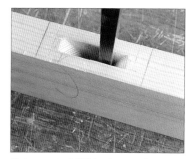

Cut a central "V" in the mortise with a chisel.

Chisel away the waste from the mortise after drilling a series of holes.

Making a wedged through mortise-and-tenon joint

A wedged through mortise-and-tenon joint is made in a way similar to a through mortise-and-tenon joint. Note that the tenons are marked and cut over length so that the projection can be planed flush with the outside face after assembly. Adapt the basic method as follows.

1 Make saw cuts in the end of the tenon that are two-thirds the length of the tenon.

2 Slightly enlarge the mortise aperture from the outside face, by ⅛–3⁄16 in. (3–5 mm) at each end, to two-thirds the width.

3 Make the wedges. Fit the joint and glue and clamp it before driving the wedges into position. The clamps can be removed after the joint has been wedged if you prefer.

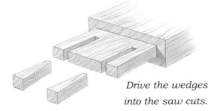

Drive the wedges into the saw cuts.

Making a loose-wedged through mortise-and-tenon joint

A loose-wedged mortise-and-tenon joint is made in the same way as a through mortise-and-tenon joint, but the proportion of the tenon has to allow for the removable wedge. Therefore, it needs to project out of the mortise some distance.

1 Make a hole in the tenon, ensuring that its position will enable the wedge to tighten the joint. The outside edge of this hole or mortise must be at the same bevel as the wedge.

2 Make the wedge, and when the joint is clamped, tap it into the joint. As the wedge is driven in, the tenon is pulled forward and secured in place.

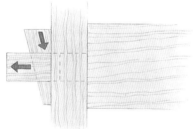

Tap the loose wedge into the mortise-and-tenon joint.

MAKING A STOPPED MORTISE-AND-TENON JOINT

All the steps for making this joint are similar to the description for a through joint as detailed above except:

1 The tenon will be shorter than the width of the piece into which the mortise is cut.

2 The mortise will be cut only to a specific depth—that is, approximately two-thirds of the rail's width.

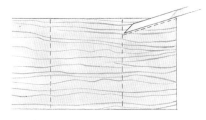

Use a chisel to pare away the waste wood.

Making a sloped-haunch mortise-and-tenon joint

A sloped-haunch mortise-and-tenon joint is commonly used in constructions such as frames, where the outside rail is level with the top of the stile and you do not want the haunch to show.

1 Cut the mortise to match the full length part of the tenon, two-thirds the width of the rail. Make the space for the haunch by making two saw cuts at an angle from the top edge of the stile into the mortise.

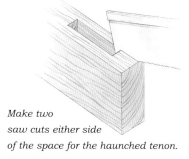

Make two saw cuts either side of the space for the haunched tenon.

2 Pare away the waste wood from the mortise with a chisel.

3 Cut a full tenon. Then saw the sloping haunch across from the outside edge to two-thirds the width. Finally cut along the tenon to remove the waste.

Making a square-haunch mortise-and-tenon joint

When making a frame that has a groove on the internal face it is easiest to cut that groove right through from end to end; the square haunch is made so that it exactly fits the groove.

1 Carefully mark out the square-haunch joint to allow for the groove. Remember that the mortise will be shorter than the width of the rail.

Mark out the square-haunch mortise-and-tenon joint.

The small table on pages 259–64 was designed especially as an exercise in mortise-and-tenon joints. It is good practice and a lovely piece of furniture in its own right.

2 Cut the mortise as before.

3 Mark and cut the square haunch on the tenon.

Making a long-and-short shoulder mortise-and-tenon joint

Making a frame with a rabbet on one face will require a tenon that has one shoulder shorter to fit on the top of the rabbet. The longer shoulder fits into the mortise. The face of the tenon should line up with the face of the rabbet because this makes for easier construction.

1 Carefully mark out both the mortise-and-tenon of the long and short shoulder joint.

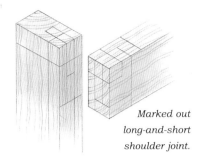

Marked out long-and-short shoulder joint.

2 Cut the mortise as before.

3 Cut the tenon with one long and one short shoulder to match the depth of the rabbet.

Making a corner mortise-and-tenon joint

A corner mortise-and-tenon joint is used when two rails meet a leg at the same level.

1 When the mortises are cut, ensure that they meet in the center of the leg.

2 When the tenons have been cut, make a 45-degree bevel on the end of each tenon, ensuring that they are cut the right way so that the mortise will be filled.

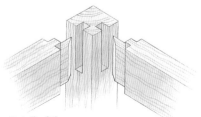

Detail of the corner mortise-and-tenon joint.

Chair with stopped and through mortise-and-tenon joints (pages 343–52).

Making dado joints

Dado joints are grooves that are cut across the grain of the wood and are generally used when installing intermediate shelves or dividers in cabinets. There are a number of varieties for different purposes. The through dado joint is the most common and easiest to make. The dovetail dado joint is more complex and requires more practice, but it is much stronger and more stable than the through joint.

THROUGH DADO JOINTS

A **through dado joint** is a very simple joint. It consists of a groove—or dado—that accepts the full thickness of the shelf or divider. Through dado joints will show on both the front and the back edges of the side panel.

STOPPED DADO JOINTS

The **stopped dado joint** is the same as the through dado joint, except that one end of it stops short and so the dado cannot be seen on the front edge of the side panel. It, therefore, gives a neater finish than a through joint.

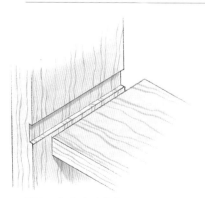

Through dado joint

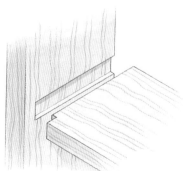

Stopped dado joint

DOVETAIL DADO JOINTS

In a dovetail dado joint, the end of the shelf is cut to a dovetail to run in the dado in the side panel.

Dovetail joints can show on the front but they are usually created as stopped dovetail joints—that is, cut short of the front edge so that the joint cannot be seen.

The dovetail can be on one side only—a barefaced dovetail dado—or on both sides.

When long dadoes are needed for a piece, a tapered dovetail dado joint is frequently used so that the dovetail "bites" in the last few fractions of an inch (or the last few millimeters).

CUTTING A STOPPED DADO JOINT

1 Start by marking your guides on the inside face of the side to be cut. Use a marking knife to cut lines in order to indicate the desired position of the shelf —that is, the shoulders. Square these lines down the edge.

2 Then, use a marking gauge to mark the depth of the dado—one-third the thickness is normal—and also the stopped part of the dado.

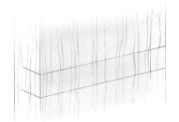

Mark the position of the shoulders.

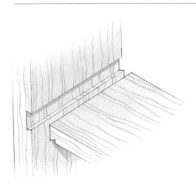

Through dovetail dado joint

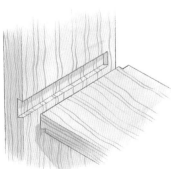

Stopped dovetail dado joint

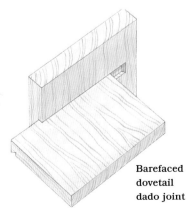

Barefaced dovetail dado joint

3 To cut the dado joint, chisel a cutout at the end of the stopped groove, working to the required depth of the dado. This will enable you to saw the groove from the rear.

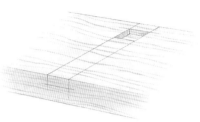

Chisel out the end to the required depth.

Saw the sides of the dado.

4 Chisel out the waste a little at a time across the grain down to the gauge line. Check the bottom for flatness.

5 Now mark the end of the shelf using a marking gauge along the two faces and the front. Then you can gauge the waste at the stopped end.

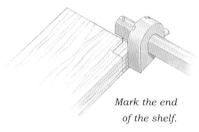

Mark the end of the shelf.

6 Cut away the waste with a tenon saw and fit the joint. Adjust as required.

CUTTING A STOPPED, TAPERED DOVETAIL DADO JOINT

1 Mark the dado as for the previous joint.

Mark the shelf position in pencil.

2 Mark the dovetail on the edge with a sliding bevel. Mark the stopped end of the dado with a marking gauge. Mark the tapered and straight shoulders of the dovetail groove with a knife—a taper of about ⅛ in. (3 mm) on the bottom; the top is usually square to the edge.

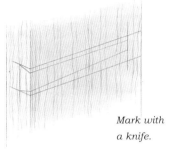

Mark with a knife.

3 In order to be able to saw the joint, cut out a pocket at the end of the stopped groove to the required depth.

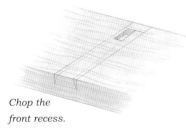

Chop the front recess.

4 Saw the dovetail angle from the rear on the waste side of the shoulder lines. Place an extra saw cut in the center to help remove the waste.

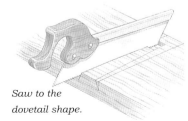

Saw to the dovetail shape.

5 Now chisel out the waste by paring across the grain, taking care because the waste will be hard to remove since it is wider than the top of the dado.

6 Now mark shoulders for the dovetail on the shelf using a cutting gauge along the two faces. Use a pencil and square for the back edge.

7 Gauge the stopped end. Then, mark the taper of the dado, and using the sliding bevel as set for the dado, mark the dovetail angles on the back edge of the shelf.

8 Cut away the stopped part with a tenon saw. Then saw the shoulders and pare the dovetail angles across the grain.

9 The shelf should now slide in smoothly from the back, making for a very sturdy and securely fitted joint.

Slide the shelf into the dado.

The small mirror and shelf on pages 254–8 is an ideal project to practice both dado joints and fretwork.

Making dovetail joints

The dovetail is considered to be the most beautiful of decorative joints. Fine craftworkers proudly use dovetail joints when making a piece of furniture to demonstrate the highest levels of their craftwork. So, in this case the joints should definitely be seen and the most common type is a through dovetail.

THROUGH DOVETAIL JOINTS

The **through dovetail joint** is the simplest of the dovetail joints, but still requires careful marking and cutting. It is a traditional joint used for joining the ends of solid-wood pieces, and is often seen on cabinets and other box constructions. The pins and the tails show on the outside faces of the piece, giving a decorative effect.

SINGLE-LAP DOVETAIL JOINTS

The **single-lap dovetail joint** is a common joint in cabinet making. It is mostly used for connecting drawer sides to a thicker drawer front—cases in which the dovetail joint is required for strength but must not interfere with the finish of the piece. With the single-lap, the dovetails are visible on the sides, but the front piece is unbroken and clean-looking.

Pins or tails first?

Some craftworkers prefer to cut tails first, but it is easier when making a double-lap dovetail or a secret-miter dovetail to cut the pins and mark from them to the tail side. This description is for the latter method, but the step-by-step instructions for the small casket project (see pages 265–9) describe making the tail first and then marking the pin.

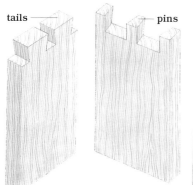

tails — pins

Through dovetail joint

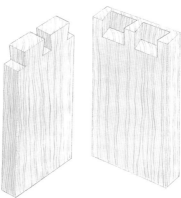

Single-lap dovetail joint

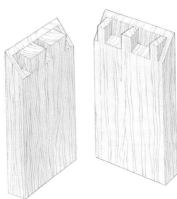

Double-lap dovetail joint   **Secret-miter dovetail joint**

DOUBLE-LAP AND SECRET-MITER DOVETAIL JOINTS

Although great satisfaction can be derived from making double-lap and secret-miter dovetails, the craftwork will never be seen unless it is a demonstration joint that will be taken apart.

The growing use of routers—for making tongue-and-groove joints—and biscuit jointers makes these joints an interesting, but not very practical option.

The **double-lap dovetail joint** is used on cabinets or boxes where you do not want the joint to be seen. You will only see a thin strip of end grain on one lap—either the tail or pin member.

The **secret-miter dovetail joint** is a strong joint often used in very fine woodworking and requires extremely careful marking and cutting. In this instance, the dovetail joint is completely enclosed and will never be visible from the outside.

DOVETAIL ANGLES

The angle of the dovetail should not have too much slope; otherwise it will be weakened by short grain. Not enough slope will reduce the potential strength of the joint.

Experience has shown that in hardwood the angle should be 1:8 and in softwood the angle should be 1:6.

Too much slope.   *Too little slope.*

Hardwood angle.   *Softwood angle.*

MAKING A THROUGH DOVETAIL JOINT

There are different approaches to dovetailing. The main options are to mark and cut to the exact length of the dovetail as described here or to mark the length, but add an extra ¹⁄₁₆ in. (2 mm) waste to be cleaned off.

1 Mark the lengths of the wood pieces, including the dovetail. Cut to length and carefully plane the ends straight and square on both halves of the joint.

2 Set the gauge to the thickness of the wood and mark the shoulder lines on both of the pieces.

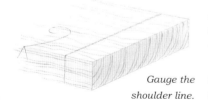

Gauge the shoulder line.

3 With a pencil, set out the pins on one piece to the required spacing and number. To do this, mark the full width of the first pin (a) parallel to the edge (b). Divide the remaining width of wood into equal parts (c).

4 Transfer these marks to the top edge and set out the wider ends of the pins (d). Set a sliding bevel to the required pitch (1:6 or 1:8) or use a dovetail template and mark the beveled sides of the pins, back to the narrower ends, where the tails will fit (e). Make sure you mark the bevel on the end pin marked in step 3 and that all the bevels slope the correct way.

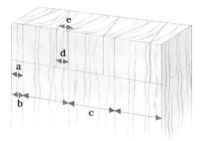

Set out the pins and check all bevels slope the correct way.

5 When you are satisfied, mark the pins on the end of the wood with a knife.

6 Using a knife and square, mark the pin sides down to the shoulder line. With a pencil, mark the areas to be removed.

Mark the waste areas carefully, ready to saw.

***Nejiri arigata –
Japanese
dovetail joint***

This traditional Japanese joint is fascinating because it looks so mysterious and intricate. It is extremely strong and, unlike a conventional dovetail, cannot be taken apart in a straight pull in either direction once it is assembled. Although it may look incredibly difficult to make, it is not that hard to cut because all the angles are based on 75 degrees. It is just important to make sure that each piece is accurately marked before cutting. This joint was introduced into British furniture making by Alan Peters in his own Devonshire workshop. He was taught the secret of how to do it by Japanese furniture maker Kintaro Yazawa.

7 With a fine dovetail saw, saw down the waste side of the cut lines. Be sure to stop before you reach the shoulder line.

Saw carefully down the marked pin lines.

8 Using a coping saw, remove most of the waste from between the pins.

9 Pare right down to the shoulder line using a sharp chisel. After some practice, you will be able to pare from one side only. But when you are starting out, you may find it easier to pare from the shoulder lines on both faces.

10 Mark the tails from the pins. Lay the wood that will have the tails on the bench. Hold the pins upright in the correct position between the shoulder line and edge of the wood. Mark the tails using a knife or a scriber.

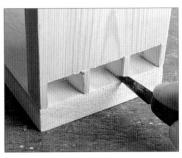

Mark the positions of the tails by drawing around the pins with a knife or scriber.

11 Square the lines across the ends of each joint and use a pencil to mark off the waste (the pin areas).

Square the lines across the ends of the joints.

12 Cut the tails carefully on the waste side of the cut mark.

13 Remove the waste and pare between the tails as before.

MAKING A SINGLE-LAP DOVETAIL JOINT

Since the dovetail in this joint is stopped short of the front face of the wood, you must chisel as well as saw to remove the waste.

1 First, gauge the thickness of the side—the tail piece—on the inside face and edge. Then, you can mark the dovetail pins using a sliding bevel or a dovetail template and a steel square.

Mark the pins with care and accuracy.

2 Next, place the wood in the vice and secure in place. Saw down the dovetail angle and the square line. Remember to make sure that you are sawing on the waste side of the cut line.

3 Make some saw cuts in the waste area to relieve the wood and to make the process of chiseling easier.

Saw out some narrow cuts, ready for paring.

4 Pare the waste at an angle from shoulder to shoulder, and then pare away the remaining waste in order to produce the dovetail socket.

5 Mark the position of the tails from the pins, holding the pins upright between the shoulder line and edge of the wood. Then, cut the tails carefully on the waste side of your mark.

The small box on pages 265–9 is a good way for you to practice your dovetail joints.

The simple through dovetail joint can be an attractive feature on wooden boxes, and when cut to a beveled edge as on this box (see pages 265–9), it is also an impressive illustration of quality work.

Using abrasives

You may produce a satisfactory surface with a plane or scraper, but in most cases, before you apply a finish, you will need to smooth with abrasive paper, also called sandpaper—sheets of paper with a variety of abrasive materials glued to the face.

ABRASIVE PAPERS

There are different "sandpapers" available, usually named for the type of abrasive grit that is used.

Glasspaper is used on softwoods but not usually in fine cabinet making.

Garnet paper is generally a reddish-brown color with hard particles that form sharp cutting edges. It is a good general-quality abrasive.

Aluminum-oxide paper is harder than garnet paper, and is widely used as the abrasive sheet for power sanders.

Silicon-carbide paper is generally used for finishing metals or for smoothing paint surfaces between coats. It is usually lubricated with water and therefore called wet-and-dry paper. For woodwork, a silicon-carbide paper dusted with zinc-oxide powder is used, with the powder acting as a lubricant. This gives a very good finish between coats when using lacquers and polishes.

Grades of abrasive papers

You should always work from the coarse to the fine grades, the idea being that the next finer grade will remove the scratches caused by its rougher predecessor. Generally, with good planing and scraping, you should not need to use the very coarse grades. As well as being graded from very coarse to very fine, sandpaper is also graded by number—the higher the number, the finer the grit.

Medium grades, and some fine grades, are used for general cabinet making, while some fine and very fine grades are used when finishing. Abrasive papers can also be termed closed-coat, where the particles are closely grouped for fast sanding, whereas open-coat papers have larger gaps between the particles and thus clog less readily.

Abrasive paper grades

Very coarse	50–60
Coarse	80–100
Medium	120–180
Fine	220–280
Very fine	320–600

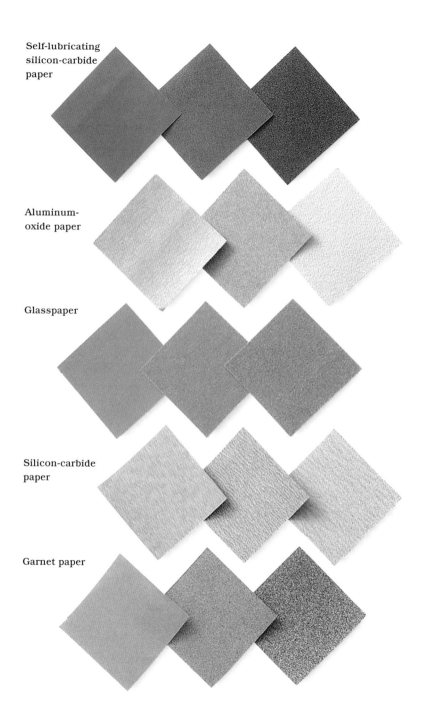

Self-lubricating silicon-carbide paper

Aluminum-oxide paper

Glasspaper

Silicon-carbide paper

Garnet paper

De-nibbing

The coarser abrasive papers are used for smoothing the surface. The finer grades are used after a finish has been applied to remove any slight runs or blemishes in the finished surface. This is known in the trade as de-nibbing.

Using steel wool

A small pad of very fine steel wool can be used after applying a finish, to obtain a final smooth surface or to apply a coat of wax polish for a surface that is attractive to touch. Dip the steel wool in the wax and apply with the grain. Finish with a soft cloth.

Belt sander

An orbital sander

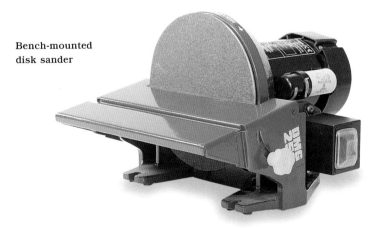

Bench-mounted disk sander

POWER TOOLS

Generally it is best to sand by hand since you can see and feel how the surface is changing. However, when confronted with large areas, a power tool will save much effort. Some hand-sanding is generally still required to remove any minute scratches left by a power sander.

Orbital sanders

The orbital sander is a useful tool and has the advantage of being unlikely to remove too much material by accident and spoil the surface. Care must be taken, however, when using it on veneered surfaces. Most machines are similar in that the rubber-covered baseplate has the sandpaper stretched over it, and the motor causes this plate to move in an orbital, elliptical or a reciprocating pattern. Although special abrasive sheets are available, standard sheets can generally be cut to fit.

Belt sanders

The belt sander needs very careful handling because it is very easy to remove more material than you intend, unless you have extremely careful control over the tool when working on flat surfaces.

However, it is a useful tool when bench mounted and used to undertake specific small sanding jobs, either along the grain or when shaping parts.

Bench-mounted disk sanders

As with the belt sander, disk sanders can be very fierce on flat surfaces. A disk sander is best used as a bench-mounted tool for sanding and shaping small pieces. Orbital disk sanders are also available and are ideal for finishing because they produce virtually no surface scratches.

SANDING BY HAND

It is advisable to use a sanding block for most work. Very occasionally you may want to use the abrasive paper without a sanding block, either for curved work or very light sanding. If you need to sand moldings, make a block to the appropriate shape to match the face of the mold.

1 Choose your starting grade of sandpaper depending on the work that you are planning to sand.

2 Fold the paper backward and carefully tear it to fit the block. When using standard sized sheets, you can generally tear each into four pieces.

3 Before you begin, wrap the abrasive paper tightly around the sanding block.

Wrap abrasive paper securely around a sanding block.

4 Always sand with the grain of the wood and work down through the various different grades of abrasive paper until you achieve the desired finish.

5 Turn the sanding block at 90 degrees to the surface grain in order to avoid catching the grain with the edge of the sandpaper.

Sand with the grain.

Sanders for working in tight spaces

The principle of orbital sanders has been applied to special models that have small bases—often triangular in shape—so that they can be used in corners. They should be needed only occasionally.

Safety first

• Grip the machine with both hands.

• Adopt a well-balanced stance. Do not overreach.

• Work should be held firm, especially when using a belt sander.

• Do not apply additional pressure to the sander.

• Disconnect the power before changing the sandpaper.

• Wear a dust mask, or connect a dust-extraction system to the baseplate.

• Wear safety glasses.

• If using a sander for long periods, use ear protectors.

• Check, clean, and if required, change the sandpaper as the work surface may burn if the abrasive is clogged or worn out.

USING POWER TOOLS
Using an orbital sander

Cut or tear the paper in half lengthwise and fit on the sander. When using an orbital sander, grip the tool with both hands and maintain an even balance.

1 Switch the sander on before placing it on the work surface. Carefully lower the sander flat onto the surface and guide it over the work before applying a light pressure only. Too much pressure will tear or wear out the abrasive paper prematurely.

2 Use long and slow backward and forward strokes, keeping the sander moving evenly over the whole surface of the piece. Do not dwell on one spot or lift the sander up on one edge; you will create an indentation in the surface.

3 Lift the sander clear of work before turning it off. You may want to finish sanding by hand.

Using a belt sander

1 Before you begin, hold the sander upside down on a firm surface and inspect the belt carefully. If it is damaged or worn, be sure to replace it before starting work.

2 Start the sander and note any sideways movement. Operate in short bursts, and correct any sideways movement by turning the tracking adjustment knob until the belt runs evenly, flush with the outer edge of the baseplate.

3 Secure the work. Hold the sander above the surface with both hands, maintaining a well-balanced stance. Lower the sander onto the surface. Move the sander backward and forward along the work, maintaining an even contact with the baseplate.

4 There are times when you will find it easier to secure the belt sander to your workbench and lower the work onto the belt. This is particularly useful for sanding long edges or end grain, or for shaping wood pieces.

Using a disk sander

1 Make sure the supporting table is square with the face or set it at the required angle. Start the sander, allowing it to reach full speed.

2 Press the wood carefully against the sanding disk. Make sure that you apply only short bursts of moderate pressure, otherwise the wood may burn.

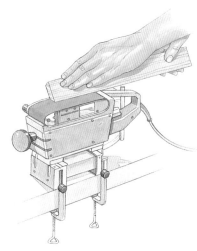

Sand long edges by mounting the belt sander on a worktop and securing with C-clamps.

Scraping

On some wood the grain will make it difficult to achieve a good finish with a plane and the final surface finishing will have to be carried out with a scraper. A scraper will take very fine shavings from difficult surfaces.

SCRAPING TOOLS

The basic **cabinet scraper** is a thin rectangular sheet of tempered steel. It is very useful for finishing surfaces of irregular or interlocked grain where the cut of a plane is not fine enough.

Continued use of the scraper may cause your thumbs to become sore. If you have a lot of scraping to do, use a **scraper plane**. This is a cast-metal tool with a double handle that holds a scraper blade in the right position and at the correct angle. While a cabinet scraper is sharpened on four edges, the blade for the scraper plane is generally sharpened on only one edge of the two long faces.

A **hook scraper** is a versatile tool that can be used instead of a scraper plane and will also remove paint or varnish.

Another useful tool is the **burnisher**. This is made from hardened steel with a round, oval, or triangular section. It is used to form a burr on a scraper.

Gooseneck cabinet scraper

Basic cabinet scrapers

Scraper plane

Hook scraper

Burnishers

SHARPENING A SCRAPER

The long edges of the scraper have to be sharpened to produce a burr that will remove small amounts of wood when pushed across the surface.

1 Ensure that the edges of the scraper are square by drawing a file along the edge.

Square the edge of the scraper using a file.

2 Use an oilstone box to smooth the edge and remove the file mark. Simply place the edge of the scraper between the top and bottom parts of the oilstone box and move the scraper backward and forward a number of times.

3 True the sides of the scraper on the stone to produce a perfectly square edge.

True the sides of the scraper on the side of the oilstone box.

4 You now need to create a burr on the edge of the scraper. To do this, run a burnisher or a small gougel along the flat edge at an angle in order to create the burr.

Smooth the edge of the scraper in an oilstone box.

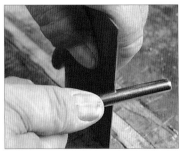

Create a burr on the edge of the scraper with a burnisher.

5 You will probably have to practice this technique a number of times in order to produce a satisfactory edge on the scraper.

6 When using the tool, you will frequently have to re-raise this cutting burr, so use the burnisher in order to flatten the edge of the scraper. Re-turn the edge over the face before starting the sharpening process over again.

Burnish the edge of the scraper.

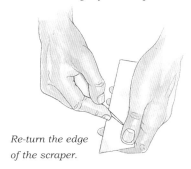

Re-turn the edge of the scraper.

USING A SCRAPER

1 Hold the scraper in two hands with the fingers positioned as shown. Bend the scraper slightly, and keeping it at an angle, carefully take thin shavings from the wood's surface. The angle will depend on the burr and wood's surface.

2 Cabinet scrapers usually have four edges on which burrs have been created, but if you are scraping a very hard wood with difficult grain you will have to resharpen your cabinet scraper quite often.

USING A SCRAPER PLANE

1 First, take the blade out of the scraper plane so that you can sharpen it. Now, carefully work a burr on the edges of the blade, as described above.

2 When you are happy with the burr that you have produced, set the blade back into the scraper plane. Make sure that you allow the scraper to protrude just a little above the surface.

3 Holding the two handles of the scraper plane, carefully scrape the tool over the wood's surface until you achieve the desired finish.

4 You will probably find that you have to sharpen the blade of your scraper plane frequently.

Hold the scraper with both hands.

Work a burr onto the blade of the scraper plane.

Carefully scrape the plane across the surface.

Using adhesives

Adhesives were traditionally derived from natural substances and could suffer degradation if exposed to moisture or heat. During the last century, however, adhesives were developed for industrial applications and these became available to the woodworker.

TYPES OF ADHESIVES

The first popular synthetic adhesive developed was based on urea-formaldehyde (UF). Another very popular adhesive is polyvinyl-acetate (PVA). UF and PVA have become the mainstay for cabinet makers, although special adhesives are available for specific purposes.

Urea-formaldehyde

Urea-formaldehyde (UF) usually comes as a powder that has to be mixed with water before use. It is essential to ensure that the correct balance of water and powder is used and that it is well mixed in order to remove all lumps. The curing takes place by moisture evaporation and chemical reaction. This adhesive can be supplied as two liquids—one being a separate catalyst or hardener. The two liquids are applied to the two different mating faces of a joint, with curing taking place by chemical reaction.

Polyvinyl-acetate

Polyvinyl-acetate (PVA) is available as a white liquid and, when applied to a joint, sets by water evaporation. Initially, it had poor water and mechanical resistance, being limited to interior applications. It was not deemed suitable for laminating purposes. Now, however, there have been many developments and PVA can achieve high standards of moisture and mechanical resistance.

Epoxy-resin adhesives

Epoxy-resin adhesives are useful for joining different materials together, but are less satisfactory for general woodwork. They are ideal for exterior work, although they are very expensive.

Contact adhesives

Contact adhesives are generally solvent based and are applied to both surfaces, left until tacky and then brought together under pressure. They

Safety first

- Always store adhesives in tightly closed containers.
- Some adhesives can harm the skin, so you should use a combination of barrier creams and gloves.
- Always wash your hands after using adhesives.
- Some adhesives give off toxic fumes, so always use these in a well-ventilated area.
- Some adhesives are flammable; keep fire or any source of ignition away.

Double-container glue pot

Pearl glue

Urea-formaldehyde

Polyvinyl-acetate

Epoxy-resin adhesive

Contact adhesive

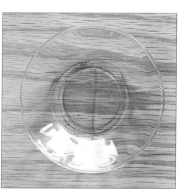

Cynoacrylate

Early adhesives

Early adhesives or glues were often made from animal skins and bone. A **double container glue pot** was used. The inside container held the glue and the outside held the water, which, when boiled, softened the adhesive. It would usually come in slab or cake form, which first needed to be softened in water, and then brought to the right temperature and viscosity in the double container. Later, adhesive was available in the form of fine granules or **pearls**. These glues are seldom used today and generally only in the restoration trade or when laying veneers by hand. They have little resistance to heat and solvents.

are often used for applying decorative plastic laminates to manufactured board or when gluing fabric. It is not advisable, however, to use such adhesives for laying veneer because the latex rubber base allows too much movement to occur.

Cynoacrylates

Cynoacrylates are instant glues and are available in different consistencies. The thinnest variety is like water and is used for parts that fit together snugly. It cures in 5 to 10 seconds. Then there is a somewhat thicker liquid—the consistency of syrup—that can fill small gaps between ill-fitting parts. Its setting time is slightly longer, at 10 to 25 seconds. The thickest of the glues is molasses-like and has the best gap-filling ability. Its slow cure rate (30 to 50 seconds) means that you can realign components after you have assembled them. But you can use an accelerator spray with the glue so that it cures instantly.

Hot glue

Hot glue is available in cylindrical sticks, which can then be applied using a convenient hot glue gun. The gun is electrically heated, and the adhesive sets within seconds, making it ideal for constructing mock-ups.

Glue brushes

Plastic glue syringe

Adhesive spreader

Electric glue gun and glue sticks

Glue roller

APPLYING ADHESIVES

Adhesives can be applied with a **brush, flat stick**, or **roller**. A plastic glue syringe is useful when trying to reach inaccessible joints. When applying UF or PVA, a **hand-held adhesive spreader** can save time and help to ensure a thin, even spread of adhesive. An **electric glue gun** is an extremely useful applicator to use for large jobs. Used with solid glue sticks, it melts the adhesive and forces it out through the nozzle in a liquid form.

USING ADHESIVES

Choose the adhesive that will best suit the assembly process, considering factors such as drying time, moisture resistance, and strength.

Apply adhesive to flat surfaces using a brush, spreader, or roller. Apply the adhesive to joints using a brush or a stick.

Almost all assemblies will need clamping to fix the pieces together securely. Pressure will need to be maintained until the adhesive has cured completely. The curing time of the different adhesives varies from product to product so be sure to check the packaging. It is worth remembering that heat will accelerate the curing of most adhesives.

Removing excess

When assembling work adhesive will invariably squeeze out of the joint when finally clamped. If adhesive is left in place until it has cured, the surface of the work is bound to be damaged by its removal. You could remove the excess when the adhesive is still wet, using a cloth and water to remove all traces. Or, wait until the adhesive has cured to a "rubbery" state, when it can be removed easily by scraping across the surface with a chisel. It will still need to be wiped down with a damp cloth to remove all traces of the adhesive. Do not drown the work with too much adhesive or water as this can stain wood, especially hardwoods.

Remove adhesive with a chisel.

Assembling projects

Whatever the piece of furniture being made, a crucial stage is that of assembly. It can be a complex operation. You need to plan the process carefully, often putting a piece together in separate stages to make handling easier. Most joints and assemblies use an adhesive that will need to cure under pressure.

Jig work

In industry clamping jigs are often used to apply all the necessary pressure to the assembly of a specific piece. Although not generally appropriate for small-scale work, some element of jig work can be useful if you have many similar components to assemble.

When assembling furniture, it is recommended that you always try out the process first with dry joints—that is, without any adhesive. This is a good method of finding and solving any fitting problems that may arise before you are committed to final assembly with adhesive.

CLAMPS

There is a wide range of clamps, and even though they will mainly be used for dry or final assembly, they are often useful to hold components on a bench during the making process.

Sash or bar clamps

For assembly the most common type of clamp is the **sash** or **bar clamp**. Sash clamps have a bar with a screw pressure shoe at one end and a moveable shoe, which will accommodate different lengths, at the other. A rectangular bar is adequate for light use, but a T-bar is better where larger or heavier pressures are needed.

It is possible to make your own sash clamp using clamp heads that can be used on a wooden bar (some woodworkers use a round pipe for the bar). Clamps that have a rapid action enabling them to slide along the bar until pressure is applied are also available, but their very construction means that it is not possible to obtain the same pressure that is achieved with traditional sash clamps.

Sash clamp

Sash clamps can be used for assembling frames or cabinets. Always remember to use wooden clamping blocks between the work and the shoe to prevent bruising the work surface. When used for frames, ensure that the clamps close the joints and remember to check that the assembly is square. To do this, use a try square or, preferably, measure across each diagonal. If both are the same, the frame is square. If a frame is out of square, a slight adjustment of the position of the clamp in order to shorten the longest angle should bring it square.

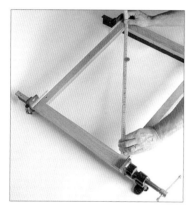

Measure across the diagonal to see if the clamped frame is square.

It is worth investing in a number of clamps rather than just one. When assembling cabinets more than one clamp may be needed at a time, and arranging their position to achieve pressure in all the necessary directions will make it essential to try a dry run first. It may also be necessary to make special clamping blocks.

It is useful to have a number of clamps on hand for assembling large projects.

C-clamps

Smaller clamps will often be needed for both assembly and holding operations and the most useful is the **C-clamp**. The basic C-clamp is a casting, which has a screw at one end that applies pressure.

This type of clamp comes in a range of sizes for different scales of woodwork, and can have a deep throat for use when pressure away from an edge is needed.

Large C-clamp

Small C-clamp

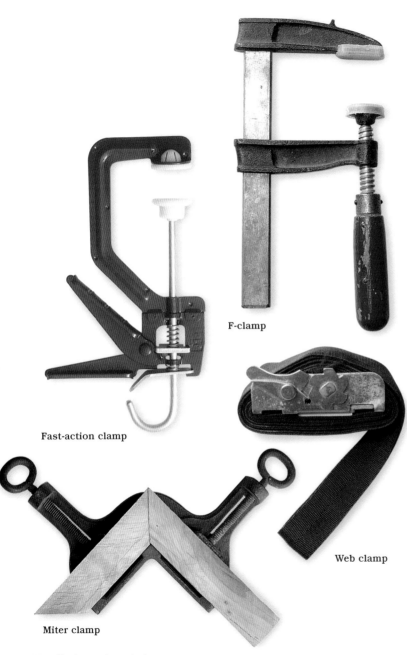

F-clamp

Fast-action clamp

Web clamp

Miter clamp

Other small clamps

An older tool is the wooden handscrew, and although less adaptable, it can still be used for holding and clamping operations.

An **F-clamp** has an F-shaped adjustable jaw, which slides on a steel bar. It is quicker to use than a C-clamp but it does not exert quite as much pressure.

There are also small **fast-action clamps** available, with sliding shoes, cam, or ratchet action. These clamps also have large clips, but since the amount of pressure they give is limited they are better used simply as holding devices. They should, however, not be used to hold any work that is to be subjected to vibration since they tend to slip.

For curved work another option is the **web** or **strap clamp**, which works by using a ratchet to tighten a woven nylon strap around the work. This is then tightened to apply pressure.

When clamping a mitered corner, such as a light frame, use a miter clamp or a web clamp with right-angle corner blocks.

HAMMERS AND NAILS

Most cabinet making uses well-cut glued joints. However, a selection of hammers is useful for some joints and for building mock-ups.

The **cross-peen hammer** is a useful general hammer. It is good for tapping assemblies together or apart, will insert nails and larger brads and the peen end will start off small nails and brads. Hold the hammer at the end of the handle and be sure that its face hits the top of the nail vertically.

The **tack hammer** can be used for light work—to drive small finish nails or brads.

The **claw hammer** is normally used by carpenters and woodworkers because it performs two functions. The round, flat head is used to drive

in nails while the claw at the back is used to remove nails when necessary. Always use a piece of scrap lumber under the head when removing nails to protect the surface of the work.

Use a tack hammer to drive in a small nail, held in place with some paper.

Pincers are also used to remove nails and brads before they have been driven home; again protect the surface of the work when using pincers.

Cross-peen hammer

Pincers

Tack hammer

Claw hammer

Rubber mallet

Carpenter's mallet

Hand sledge

A **nail set** is used to drive finish nails and brads under the surface of the work, enabling the small hole to be filled.

Hammer a small brad using a nail set so that the wood is not damaged.

NAILS

Common nails are seldom used in fine cabinet making except perhaps when making molds and jigs. However, small finish nails or brads are often used. Their heads are punched below the wood's surface and the hole is filled.

MALLETS

A **carpenter's mallet**—or wood mallet—is used with firmer and mortise chisels to protect their wooden handles and during some assembly operations.

The **rubber mallet** is used for light work and the **hand sledge** for heavier assembly work.

SCREWS

Screws are essential to woodworking and you will find a good range available. Screws come in different metals, with steel and brass being the most commonly used for fine woodwork. The conventional screw has a head, a shank, and a thread.

A flat head screw sits flush or slightly under the wood's surface.

The growth in the use of manufactured boards has seen the introduction of the twin-thread screw where a double thread grips the material and there is no shank between the thread and head.

Three types of screw head are normally available, the most useful for cabinet making being the **flat head**, which fits flush or slightly under the wood's surface, allowing the hole to be filled and completely disguised. The **round head** sits proud of the surface and the **oval head** is a combination of the two.

The slots in the top of the screw heads also vary. Simple **slot screws** have one groove for the screwdriver. **Phillips head screws** have a cross pattern, sometimes with an extra set of shallower indents between the four points of the cross. These provide greater grip and less chance of damaging the screw head when using a screwdriver.

 Slotted Phillips head

Using brass screws

When you are using brass screws you should always first insert a steel screw of the same size and gauge in order to cut the thread. Remove this and insert the brass screw. It is often useful to apply a lubricant, such as wax or petroleum jelly, to the brass screw to ease it in.

Drilling pilot holes

When making fine furniture, always drill pilot holes prior to inserting screws. First, drill the clearance hole that will accept the shank. This must be right through the material that is to be held down. Next, drill a pilot hole to guide the thread shank as the thread cuts into the bottom piece. When using flat head screws countersink the top surface.

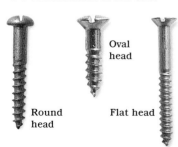

Round head   Oval head   Flat head

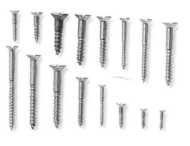

A range of brass screws

A range of metal screws

The traditional slot head uses an ordinary screwdriver blade, while the Phillips head screw requires a Phillips screwdriver. To avoid damaging the screw head—and your work—always match the screwdriver to the type of screw.

Never overtighten screws, particularly twin-thread screws, because their heads tend to break off more easily with this type of screw than they do with the regular slotted screw.

Modern Phillips head screws are often referred to as chipboard screws. They have a sharp point and a thin thread that makes them easier to drive into manufactured boards.

Screws are bought according to their length and gauge (shank diameter). The gauge is expressed as a number from 0 to 20—0 is the smallest and 20 the largest.

Screwdrivers

The tip of a screwdriver should fit the screw slot exactly. This avoids damage to either the work or the screw head. You will find a range of screwdrivers useful.

The **cabinet screwdriver** is used with traditional slotted screws, and a range is needed for different sizes of screw.

The **ratchet** and **spiral ratchet screwdrivers** are useful tools when a number of screws have to be inserted.

Phillips screwdrivers are specifically for use with Phillips head screws.

The **stub screwdriver** or **stubby screwdriver** is useful when space is limited, and the

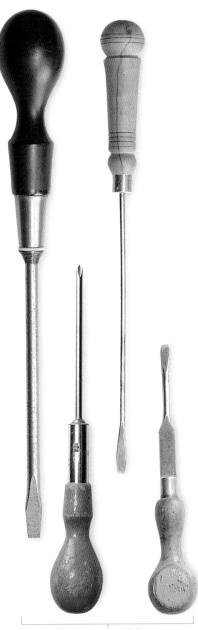

Cabinet screwdrivers

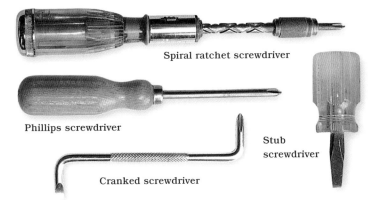

Spiral ratchet screwdriver

Phillips screwdriver

Cranked screwdriver

Stub screwdriver

cranked screwdriver when there is very little space at all.

The cabinet and ratchet screwdrivers have largely been replaced by the cordless drill/ driver (see page 143). For screwdriving, choose a drill with a two-speed gearbox so the speed can be controlled. You can buy sets of differently sized screwdriver heads and a quick-change holder that is fitted in the chuck.

HARDWARE
Poorly made or unattractive hardware can ruin the appearance of your craftwork. Always plan ahead and choose hardware that will enhance the appearance of your work.

Hinges
Many hinges are available, and only the most common are described here.

The **butt hinge** is the traditional cabinet maker's hinge. Those with wide leaves are suitable for larger pieces of furniture, such as cupboards, while those with smaller hinges are more suited to small cabinets and boxes.

A **piano hinge** is a long hinge, which is made in continuous lengths and then cut to size. It is used where an especially strong hinge is needed.

The **cylinder hinge** is used for doors, such as folding doors, which need to open to a full 180 degrees.

The **soss hinge** is similar to the cylinder hinge, but is used for very heavy doors. It is invisible when the door is closed.

The **cranked hinge** is normally used for finer work with lay-on doors. The door can swing through 180 degrees, allowing clear access to the cupboard.

Steel flap hinge

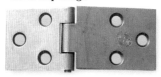

Brass butt hinge

Butt hinge

Flush hinge

Soss hinge

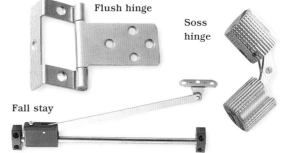

Fall stay

Piano hinge

Hinges can be used to make falls (see pages 366-74).

The **flap hinge** is an adjustable hinge where the flap lies flush when open.

The **backflap hinge** has wide leaves recessed into the wood, and is used for attaching writing desk door flaps. The hinged door "falls" down to provide a desk work surface.

Fitting a butt hinge

When fitting hinges, precise marking, cutting, and screw positioning are essential.

1 Set two marking gauges from the center of the hinge pin—the first to the outer edge of the leaf to gauge its width and the second to the face of the hinge to gauge its thickness.

2 Mark the length of the hinge with a square and knife in position on the door or flap, and then gauge the width and thickness of the recess.

3 Chisel out the recess, keeping inside the set-out lines, by first tapping the chisel ⅛ in. (3 mm) within the squared lines. Hold the chisel at a 45-degree angle and lightly tap it to raise the grain. Pare across the recess from the depth-gauge line, guiding the chisel by hand and leveling the

bottom of the recess. Test the hinge to make sure that it fits and adjust as required.

Chisel out the recess for a butt hinge.

4 Using the hinge as a guide, mark the center of the screw holes with an awl. Remove the hinge and drill pilot holes for the screws. If using brass screws, insert steel screws first as guides to prevent damage to the softer brass. Then remove the guide screws, and place the hinge in position using the brass screws.

5 Fit the other leaf of the hinge using the same technique.

The fitted butt hinge.

Locks and catches

A variety of locks can be fitted to furniture and boxes.

The traditional **cabinet lock** is normally used to secure cupboards and drawers. The **fall**, or **fall-flap lock**, is a cylinder lock that is designed to fit flush with the inside surface of a fold-down desk. The key can be removed only when the flap is shut.

The **sliding-door lock** is another type of cylinder lock that can be used to lock overlapping sliding doors. A variety of catches are also available, including the magnetic catch, the ball catch, and the magnetic latch.

Cabinet lock

Fall lock

Sliding-door locks

Specialist ironmongers may also produce individual fixtures.

Stays

Stays are designed to support a fall-flap in a horizontal position, and take the strain off the hinge. The simplest fall-flap stay is the **joint stay**. The sliding stay is a better-quality version, which slides on a bar fixed to the inside of the cabinet. The friction stay controls the movement of the flap so that it moves smoothly under its own weight.

Joint stay

Escutcheons

Escutcheon is a heraldic term to denote either a whole coat of arms or the field on which the arms are painted. The term is used in cabinet making to describe the carved armorial shields that are sometimes used as a central feature on the pediments of large pieces of case furniture. It also refers to the ornamental metal plate and pivoted metal cover that surrounds a keyhole. When a key is inserted in a lock it very rarely locates on its pin at once without striking the drawer front first—the escutcheon protects the drawer from damage. This type of escutcheon was used on cupboard doors as well as on desk and drawer fronts. They are often found in brass, which was first used from about 1650. By 1770 escutcheons began to vary in size and often formed part of larger designs found on the overall piece. For example, late 18th-century backplates had Neoclassical motifs embossed on them and the escutcheons were often made to match.

Knock-down hardware

It is often convenient to be able to disassemble large pieces of furniture for transportation. The industry has developed a range of hardware so that furniture can be sent flat-pack. You will probably not have access to a wide range of these but the following might be available in your local hardware store.

It is better to use **machine screws** than wood screws since with frequent assembly and disassembly wood screw threads and holes can become slack. The machine screw has a metal thread—like a bolt—and different lengths, gauges, and thread size can be found. However, some type of insert such as a screw socket needs to be placed in the wood component to act as a nut. It has a thread in the center that accepts the machine screw, but

A machine screw and socket.

on the outside has a screw that can be driven. The insert cannot be seen.

The **tee-nut** is used in material where there is not enough depth for a screw socket to be used. It is often used when attaching upholstered seats to chair frames. The nut is a disk with a central threaded socket. The socket accepts a machine screw and four prongs that bite into the surface. This keeps it in position when it is inserted into a clearance hole on the side that will not be seen.

A **barrel nut** is used when connecting a rail to an upright— for example, when fitting rails between a bed's headboard and foot. It is a cylinder that has a thread drilled and tapped perpendicular to the barrel direction. To fit, drill a longitudinal hole for the bolt, and a cross-hole in the rail for the barrel nut. Insert the barrel nut, align the thread and tighten the bolt. You can also use bolts with nuts and washers if you cut a square mortise or recess to accept them. Another extremely useful approach is to use metal studding—lengths of threaded rod—that can be cut to the necessary lengths to suit the size of the job in hand.

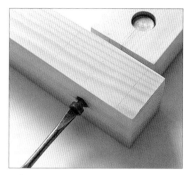

A barrel nut and screw.

Saw sets can be used for connecting cabinets together and are a development of the saw sets that are used to hold saw blades in saw handles.

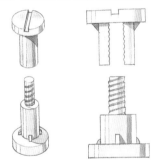

A saw set

Handles

Even though many woodworkers prefer to make their own handles as part of the overall design, there are very many proprietary handles available in all shapes, styles, materials, and colors.

Proprietary handles include **traditional door** or **drawer**

knobs, which are available in wood, metal, or ceramic. These are usually fixed from behind, where a screw passes through the cabinet front into the knob. **D-shaped handles** are modern-style handles, which are fitted in the same way and available in metal, plastic, or wood.

Cabinet handles are available in many forms, including the swan neck. This type of handle is suspended from two pivots—one at each end of the handle.

Drawer-pull handles are very strong handles, and are often used for large or heavy drawers. For smaller drawers, the **drop handle** is common. Both the drop handle and the drawer-pull handle are fitted from the front.

The **flush handle**, as its name suggests, fits flush with the surface. Used for drawers, it is fixed with flat head screws.

Drawer pull

Traditional drop handles

Modern knob with backplate

Swan neck drawer handles

Knob

Modern cabinet handle

Wood finishing

Wood finishing is sometimes viewed as the final but brief operation of a woodwork project. However, it actually needs to be carefully considered at the outset in order to decide on the most appropriate finishing method and when during the assembly it will be best to apply it. Make sure that you leave enough time for finishing, and prepare and plan thoroughly before you start any project.

Safety first

• Make sure that during the finishing process the area is well-ventilated. When using the toxic materials wear protective clothing and gloves, a face mask, and a respirator.

• It is a good idea to use barrier creams.

• Your surroundings must be clean. Remember that most finishing materials are flammable, so keep only enough for the work at hand.

• Store bulk finishes in a separate building away from your home and workshop.

• Make sure that an extinguisher and/or a fire blanket are readily available nearby.

• Do not smoke.

• Keep finishes away from children.

• Always follow the manufacturer's instructions.

Even though finishing is generally the final process that you will undertake in any woodworking project it can often be useful—and sometimes essential—to prefinish your wood components before assembly. This is so that the finish can be applied to all the nooks and crannies that cannot be reached after assembly.

Finishing technology has developed to meet two criteria that must be satisfied when the object is in use—practicality and appearance.

Use may often dictate the finishing strategy—for example, the amount of physical or environmental wear that the piece will have to resist. Will it be used indoors or outdoors, or will it be subjected to some form of continuous wear?

There is a wide range of finishes available today: natural clear, synthetic-colored, as well as some unusual surface finishes. Before you apply finish though, it is important to prepare the wood surface as necessary.

FILLERS

You will often have to fill small cracks and holes in order to prepare the wood for finishing. There is a range of filling materials available.

A **putty**, or **filler, knife** is used to apply a filler. It is a thin, flexible piece of stainless steel fixed to a handle. It is used to work the putty or filler into the defect within the surface of the work before sanding and applying a finish. Putty knives come in a range of widths to suit different situations.

Small cracks and holes can be filled with a **putty** as near as possible to the wood's color. You can also use preparations based on shellac. **Shellac sticks** come in wood colors and are ideal for repairing small cracks or knotholes.

Wax sticks are made from carnauba wax and mixed with resin and coloring pigments. Wax sticks are normally used for repairing small hairline cracks in the wood surface. Remember that you should use wax sticks only when you intend to use a wax finish on the work (see page 200).

Wood filler is made from natural and/or synthetic materials, and is normally used to fill wood defects, such as splits and knotholes. It can be readily sanded down to provide a smooth surface for a polish. It is available in a variety of colors to match

Putty/filler knives   Paintbrush

Solvent-based putty

Wax sticks

Water-based putty

Shellac sticks

Plastic wood filler

Fine surface filler

almost any wood, and can also be mixed with lighter or darker filler or paint pigments for a perfect color match. Most filler for cabinet work is water-based although alcohol-based types, which dry more quickly, are also available and can be useful in fine cabinetmaking.

Grain fillers are much the same as wood fillers, except that they are more watery. Grain fillers are rubbed into the surface with a cloth, left to dry, and then fine sanded. Even though powdered grain fillers are available, it is preferable to use successive coats of lacquer cut down between each application.

When using softwoods take care as the resin can bleed, especially from knotholes. **Shellac**—a resin dissolved in denatured alcohol—will prevent the bleeding.

PREPARING THE SURFACE

Decisions made as to the practicality and appearance of wood finishes are closely linked, and the brief history of finishes (see far right) will help explain the reasons for some of the choices we have made over the centuries.

1 Before applying any finish, be sure that the surface is well prepared by planing, scraping, and using abrasive papers.

2 Ensure that the surface is free of dust or other fine particles by wiping it over with a tack cloth.

3 In some situations you may need to fill the grain, or any defects, with a filler. Place the filler between the putty knife and the defect. Apply pressure with the knife while dragging it across the surface. This forces the filler into the defect. As with any putty or filler, slightly overfill the defect. When dry, sand back to a flush finish.

If you are using a softwood that has knots you may need to use shellac at this stage.

Tack cloth

Shellac

Wood partially filled with filler.

NATURAL CLEAR FINISHES

When quality wood is used nowadays, there is generally no need to change the color, but only to bring out the natural qualities of the wood species. It is worth remembering that on exposure to light the color of most will usually tend to darken anyway. For this reason, the clearest finish possible is often the most desirable.

French polish

French polish is made out of shellac, a natural substance made from beetles dissolved in denatured alcohol. It has been used for many years and used to be the furniture maker's standard finish during the 19th and early 20th centuries. It can be finished to a very high gloss but unfortunately is vulnerable to both water and alcohol. There are various types of French polish available today.

Button polish is the highest grade of French polish and is a golden-brown color.

Garnet polish is a dark red/brown and is used on cheaper wood so that it will look like mahogany.

White polish is made from bleached shellac and is used for pale-colored woods.

Transparent polish is used where minimum color change is required on light woods such as ash and sycamore.

Colored polish contains an alcohol-based stain and is used in order to modify the color of the wood.

Penetrating oils

Oils soak into the wood, giving a beautiful rich finish that enhances the grain rather than simply coating the surface. When applying oil finishes, it is best to thin the first coat to encourage penetration into the wood, and then follow this with several coats to build up a good finish. This is better than simply flooding on a thick coat. Oil is the most easily repaired of all wood finishes. Simply sand down and re-oil. A range of oils is available today.

Linseed oil can be raw or boiled. Raw oil takes a long time to dry, boiled less so. Since drying has to be done naturally, the resulting finish is not as hard as with other oils. Its performance can be improved by adding dryers, such as gold size or terrabin.

A brief history of finishing

During the earliest times there were few finishing options available—those that were around were natural and often based on waxes or oils.

As society developed and furniture became a mark of status, quality furniture finishes became more important. Finishes enhanced the grain and color of wood as well as serving a protective function. This was especially the case with the introduction of woods such as walnut and mahogany, the use of veneers and inlays, and the appearance of special finishes such as gilding. It was during this time that French polish, based on shellac, became the main finish for most types of indoor furniture. Fashion, however, caused other systems to be introduced. The popularity of Japanese and Chinese furniture led to the use of opaque lacquer with painted as well as inlaid decoration. Society furniture was usually given a high-gloss finish and French polishers became expert at achieving this. Vernacular furniture did not always follow fashion and oils and waxes were often used.

Danish and teak oils have dryers already added. Different formulations will give very good results in terms of penetration and hardness.

Tung oil is from the tung tree, and is also known as Chinese oil. It is very durable and is also heat and alcohol resistant.

Waxes

Wax polish is made from beeswax or carnauba wax in turpentine. Each of these waxes can be used alone but it is generally better to seal the grain with a thin lacquer or with white shellac before building up wax coats. Wax is often used as a final finish on top of other materials. A very fine steel wool is used to apply a soft wax, giving a semi-matte surface. The surface is then buffed with a soft cloth. With so many ready-made preparations available, waxes are no longer so popular.

French polish on maple.

Button polish on beech.

Tung oil on teak.

Tung oil on maple.

Limed wax on oak.

Brown Boot Tan wax on teak.

Applying French polish, oils, and waxes

Some of these finishes are combustible and prone to self-ignite, so after you have applied the finish, be sure to unfold the cloth or pad and leave it outside to dry completely.

Application by cloth pad

French polish is applied with a thick, soft pad. Other finishes such as oils can also be applied in the same way.

1 Make the pad from a square of white linen cloth with a ball of batting cotton

Fold the cloth over the batting to make a pad.

placed over the cloth. Fold the cloth over the batting, and then turn in the edges. The pad is then held in the palm of the hand.

2 The batting can be charged with shellac, oils, or some of the other finishes.

3 Dip the pad in the finish, letting it soak up a reasonable amount of the finish; it should not be dripping wet.

Apply polish with a cloth pad.

Application by cloth

A cloth is usually used for applying waxes and oil. Cotton is best for this process.

1 When applying oil, soak the cloth thoroughly in a finish of your choice.

2 Rub the cloth over the wood surface with even strokes. It is very important when you have

Finishing in the twentieth century

In the 20th century synthetic materials were developed that could be applied more rapidly and were more resistant to the elements and general wear and tear. These were originally based on cellulose, a natural substance, but chemical developments enabled the use of synthetic resins based on melamine, polyester, and polyurethane, among others.

Ebonizing

This is the European process of staining and polishing wood to give a surface finish that resembles ebony. It was particularly popular in the 18th and 19th centuries and was influenced by the craze for all things Asian. Edward Godwin, for example, had an intense interest in Japanese art and used ebonized wood to create a lot of his designs. In fact, he pioneered what came to be known as Anglo-Japanese furniture. In the late 19th century Japanese mania was at its height within furniture design. European shapes were retained but Japanese details added, and ebonized wood was used a lot to create the furniture. Ebonized furniture very quickly became an accepted part of the Victorian interior. English furniture makers had also been heavily influenced by France, which had ébénistes—specialized carvers who worked mainly in ebony. The English makers relied heavily on ebonized oak and mahogany in their designs but borrowed techniques and ideas from the French.

finished with the cloth to unfold it and leave it outside to dry to avoid spontaneous combustion.

Apply oil with a cloth.

Application with steel wool
This method is used for applying wax.

Steel wool

1 Wax can initially be applied with a pad of very fine steel

Apply wax with steel wool.

wool, rubbing in the general direction of the grain.

2 Subsequent burnishing is made with a lint-free cotton cloth formed into a pad. This is then used to rub the wax to a dull shine.

SYNTHETIC CLEAR AND COLORED FINISHES

With the rapid developments that have taken place in the manufacturing processes in recent years, there is now a wide range of different types of synthetic finish available: stains, resins, lacquers, and paints. Each is suitable for a particular purpose and so be sure to choose carefully.

Stains
Staining was traditionally done to modify the color of wood when the original did not suit the maker's requirements. More recently, makers have chosen woods for their specific virtues, and a small range of other colors has been developed. They add an overall finish that will color the wood but still show the grain. These stains are available in water-, alcohol-, and oil-based forms. Water-based stains have been formulated to give results

as close as possible to traditional products, without using dangerous substances. The table below shows the variety of effects that you can achieve by applying the same stains to two different base woods.

Lacquers (varnishes)

Lacquers, or varnishes as they are sometimes called, also have a long history, but are not as popular today. They create a fairly hard, resistant surface and can be used in clear form over another surface or as a flat, opaque color that disguises the grain. They are available in gloss, semi-gloss and matte finishes and can be water- or solvent-based. Water-based lacquers have the same benefits as water-based stains.

Paints

Interesting effects can also be produced with paint, either completely disguising the grain allowing some hint of the wood to show through, or with a

Pine alcohol stain on beech.

Canadian Cedar alcohol stain on beech.

Burmese Teak alcohol stain on beech.

Pine alcohol stain on oak.

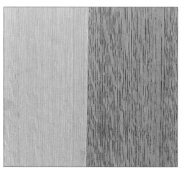
Canadian Cedar alcohol stain on oak.

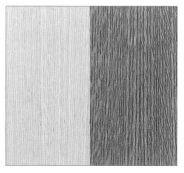
Burmese Teak alcohol stain on oak.

Test a strip of wood with varying degrees of stain.

broken finish. Traditional paints have been oil-based but water-based and more recently plastic-based paints have become very familiar, and all come in a wide range of colors. When completely dry, finish the effect with wax for a soft finish or a clear lacquer for a more durable finish.

Applying lacquers, stains, and paints

These finishes are often applied with a brush, although stroking a stain on with a cloth is also effective. Taking the care to achieve an even finish is always a priority.

Application by brush

1 Take a scrap piece of the same wood as that used in the project you are working on and apply your chosen stain to check if it gives a suitable result. You can create a deeper color by applying more coats.

2 When you are happy with your test piece you can then proceed with your project.

3 Apply the finish with straight strokes of the brush along the grain and let the film settle naturally. When using paint you need to brush initially in different directions, finishing off

with light strokes in one direction. This should be with the grain if the piece is solid wood. If you are painting up to an edge always brush outward.

Apply the finish with a brush.

4 Wipe off any excess with a cotton cloth. Lightly take the brush across the grain again to avoid leaving any cloth marks.

5 When it is dry, rub down with self-lubricating silicon-carbide paper.

6 Remove any sanding dust and apply additional coats of finish as needed.

7 When you have achieved the color that you want, a clear finish can be applied.

Spraying wood finishes

Setting up spray equipment in a proper working environment is expensive. It is essential that the area is clean, that there is adequate extraction/ventilation for the noxious chemicals and that lighting is suitably flameproof. Unless you already have experience in spraying or want to turn your hobby into something more, it is preferable to use the other techniques described here.

UNUSUAL SURFACE FINISHES

If you are seeking an interesting finish for your work, a variety of options are available, including fuming, blasting, scrubbing, and scorching.

Fuming oak

Oak and other woods that contain a proportion of tannin can be fumed effectively when exposed to ammonia, which makes the wood darken. Take an airtight container into which the project can be placed after final finishing. Place some saucers of strong ammonia in the compartment with the project and seal it. After a time the oak will change color to an attractive gray. When the desired color is obtained, remove the ammonia and apply a transparent finish. Take the utmost care when using ammonia because the fumes

are very toxic. Always wear a face mask and goggles.

Sand blasting

Sand blasting is an industrial method of cleaning components prior to other finishing treatments. When wood is sand blasted the softer grain is removed and the hard grain remains. It is then usual to apply a transparent finish. This process should be carried out by a specialist.

Scrubbing

Until recently, wooden work surfaces in kitchens were scrubbed for cleaning purposes. The resulting finish was a light, bleached wood surface. As with sand blasting, this is because the soft grain was worn away. For the right piece of woodwork this can be a very interesting effect.

Scorching

Scorching is not normally a method that is used on fine furniture because this finishing technique uses a blowtorch in order to burn the surface of the wood. The resulting charred material is then carefully wire brushed away. Subsequent finishing with a lacquer or an oil gives an unusual finished effect, particularly when used on softwood species of wood.

Fumed finish

Sand-blasted finish

Scrubbed finish

Scorched finish

Veneering

Although not widely used these days, hand veneering is an important process in furniture restoration. When using modern adhesives a constant pressure needs to be exerted over the area to be veneered. In industry, large presses are used for this task, but it is possible to make your own caul, or press.

VENEERING TOOLS

Veneer work uses many of the basic woodworker's tools, including measuring and marking equipment, planes, a fretsaw, chisels, scrapers, and sanding equipment. If veneering is something you would like to do, then a number of more specialized tools are also needed.

Specialized veneering tools include a selection of **craft knives**. For intricate work, use a fine scalpel blade; for cutting a straight edge along the grain, use a curved blade; for cutting across the grain, use a straight, pointed blade, and for preparing veneers ready for jointing, a bevel blade is best.

The **veneer saw** is a fine-toothed tool, which is used to cut through any thickness of veneer. Use it with a straightedge for accuracy. The saw is about 6 in. (152 mm) long and has a curved blade.

A **veneer hammer** is used for hand-laying veneers and for squeezing excess adhesive, air, and moisture out from under the veneer.

Veneer punches come in a variety of sizes and are used to fix any defects in the veneer.

Veneer nails are used to hold the veneer temporarily in place while the joints are taped with veneer tape.

A **toothing plane** provides a key on the groundwork surface ready for gluing. The blade of the plane is set almost vertical.

A double-container glue pot, adhesive granules and other adhesives (see pages 180–3) are also needed for veneering.

PREPARING THE BOARD

You will need a good-quality board upon which to lay the veneers—a waterproof plywood or blockboard is preferable. Prepare the board by applying lips—edge strips—to all four edges. These are made from solid wood, which is normally of the same species as the veneer. They should be mitered at the corners.

1 Plane all the edgings, but leave the width over size to the thickness of the board.

2 Trim the board to accept the edgings so that the finished size of the project will be correct.

3 Carefully mark and cut the miters on the ends of the edgings so that they fit exactly.

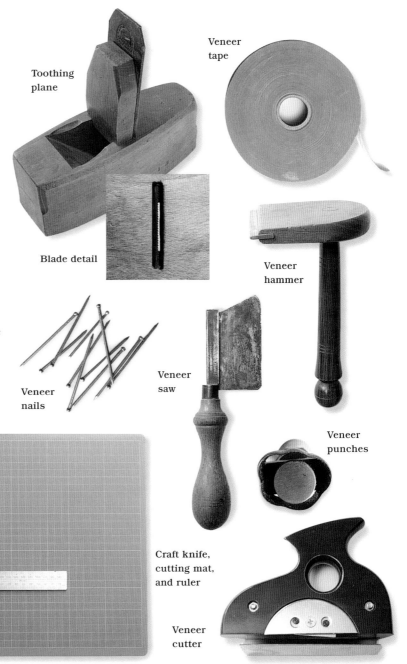

Toothing plane

Veneer tape

Blade detail

Veneer hammer

Veneer nails

Veneer saw

Veneer punches

Craft knife, cutting mat, and ruler

Veneer cutter

4 You can join the edgings to the board with loose tongues or by simply gluing them to the board's edges. If using tongues and grooves, work these with a router prior to cutting the miters.

5 Glue the edgings in place, and make sure that the miters match perfectly.

6 When the adhesive has cured, carefully plane the excess edging flush to the surface of the board on both sides, taking care not to round over the edging.

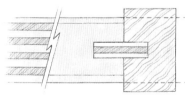

Glue the edgings into place and trim them to shape.

Since veneers can exert a pull on the face of a board, you must put a backing veneer on the secondary face.

PREPARING THE VENEER

Many common veneer woods are available in flat sheets with very little ripple or distortion. These can be used without preparation. When using exotic veneers, and those with difficult grain, the sheets may be distorted with curls and burls. In this case, dampen the veneers and press them between two boards to make them flat.

LAYING THE VENEER BY HAND

1 Begin by soaking the adhesive granules in a little water, using a double-container—either a double-container glue pot or use a can and an old saucepan as an alternative.

2 Heat the water in the outside container so that the soaking granules are heated until they dissolve and the adhesive has reached the correct consistency. You can tell if the consistency is right when there are no lumps present and the adhesive runs evenly off the brush.

Soak and then heat the adhesive granules gently.

3 Texture the faces to be veneered on the baseboard with a toothing plane to provide a key.

4 Brush some slightly thinned adhesive onto the surface of the board—the ground or groundwork—to act as sizing, or a coat to seal the surface. Let this soak in and leave it to dry.

5 Next, apply the adhesive to the top surface of the groundwork and the back of the veneer. While the adhesive is still tacky to the touch set the veneer in place.

6 Use a veneer hammer to press the veneer down; squeeze any air and excess moisture from under it. Use zigzag strokes and always work from the center to the outer edges.

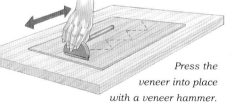

Press the veneer into place with a veneer hammer.

7 If the adhesive begins to cure, place a damp cloth over the veneer and use an old iron set to a low heat to soften the adhesive. Press down with the hammer again.

Soften the adhesive using a cloth and iron.

8 Check for blisters under the veneer by tapping the surface with a fingernail. You will hear if there are any areas that have not adhered correctly.

9 If you are applying extra veneer pieces, such as a border, prepare the new veneers for application.

10 Working from the center to the edges, lay the new pieces of veneer overlapping the original.

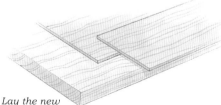

Lay the new pieces over the original layer.

11 Using a sharp craft knife and a metal straightedge, cut along the required line.

Cut the veneer with a veneer knife.

Stringing

When veneers were first used they were usually banded to make a decorative border and the veneer just ran to the edge of a piece of furniture. But by about 1780 it had become fashionable to inlay furniture with boxwood and ebony stringing, which strengthened the edges of a piece with very tough, durable wood. Stringing, therefore, is basically made up of thin square strips of colored, patterned woods, which range from tiny lines only as thick as paper up to about ⅛ in. (3 mm). Stringing had been used earlier, on its own, in Tudor and Elizabethan furniture purely as decoration, but is most often used in combination with veneer banding. The wire-like, linear stringing becomes the framework to the borders or marquetry panels on veneered furniture. The most common designs found on stringing are rectilinear or radiating and they are usually made from satinwood, boxwood, purplewood, or ebony.

12 Soften the adhesive with the cloth and iron, remove the waste pieces and press down with the veneer hammer using zigzag strokes.

13 Continue to lay the veneer to complete the desired pattern.

CAUL, OR PRESS, VENEERING

A caul is a press that applies pressure to the groundwork and veneer. It is made from two sheets of manufactured board at least 1 in. (25 mm) thick, which should be slightly larger than the piece of work to be veneered. For small areas it is possible to use C-clamps on the caul as long as their throats are deep enough to give some pressure near the center. For larger areas, however, you need to make clamping strips or bearers that have a slight curve in the center to span the caul. As clamping force is

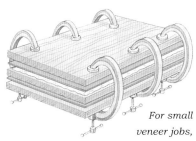

For small veneer jobs, clamps should be sufficient.

applied, maximum pressure is initially concentrated on the center, while subsequent pressure spreads to the outside.

Making the caul

The caul is quite easy to make.

1 Having decided upon the size of the component you want to veneer, cut the two thick sheets of manufactured board, which need to be approximately 2 in. (50 mm) larger than the work.

2 Make some bearers that will apply pressure to the two boards. In order to ensure that the initial pressure is at the center of the boards and progresses toward the edges as the clamps are tightened, make a slight curve on one face.

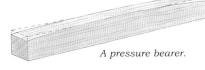

A pressure bearer.

3 Prepare two sheets of polyethylene to place between the work and the boards to keep the veneer from sticking to the caul face.

Pressing veneer in a caul

1 Prepare the package that is to be pressed. There will be the element to be veneered, normally called the groundwork, a face veneer on the show side and a backing veneer on the other face, all sandwiched between two sheets of polyethylene. A paper pad or rubber sheet can act as a softening pad, and sometimes an aluminum sheet that is able to be heated can be inserted to help the adhesive cure.

Prepare the veneer package.

The layers of veneer in a caul press.

2 The two boards of the caul are then placed on the top and bottom of this package.

3 To ensure pressure is applied in the center, place the bearers in position with the curved faces against the caul. Using C-clamps, apply initial pressure.

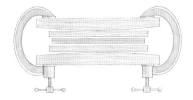

Apply the initial pressure.

4 When the clamps are tightened, the pressure applied by the shaped bearers will start from the center and will spread to the outside on further tightening.

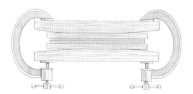

Tighten the clamps to apply the final pressure.

5 If the caul is to be used frequently to press similar size veneered work, then it is advisable to use threaded rods, nuts, and washers in place of clamps.

The arrangement of threaded rods, nuts, and washers on the caul.

6 When the adhesive has completely cured, the veneer package can be carefully removed from the caul.

A chessboard, veneered using the caul method (see pages 244–7).

Carving

Carving is a specialized craft, often used to produce items that are carved in the round. These may represent animals, people, or a variety of other objects. In relief carving, a pattern is applied to a panel or an edge—a simple form for the beginner.

CARVING TOOLS

A wide range of carving tools is available to the specialist who will have many unusual ones for particular jobs. The furniture maker can generally manage with a small number of carving tools. The carver will also have a variety of different types of holding tools, especially where the work being undertaken is of a sculptural nature.

Here we look at simple forms of carving, rather than more sculptural work. The focus is on how decoration can be applied using chip carving, where a pattern is cut into the work. Carving chisels, carving gouges, and special knives are generally used for this.

Carving chisels and gouges are usually beveled on both sides so that the wood can be cut at a variety of angles. The cutting profile of each tool is different—ranging from a straight chisel for cutting straight lines through

to special fluting, parting, and veining tools. There are also a number of blade shapes to make special operations easier, including **straight, curved, spoon-bent, back-bent, skew, and fish-tailed blades.**

A **carver's mallet** is needed for driving chisels and gouges when cutting across the grain or when working difficult pieces.

Carver's punches are made of steel and used to produce a wide variety of patterns and textures. Look for them in secondhand tool stores.

TOOL SHARPENING

It is particularly vital that carving tools be very sharp. Sharpening is covered in an earlier section (pages 96–9), but for carving tools a set of **shaped slipstones** is essential.

Sharpening a (carving) chisel

The honing angle should be the same as the ground bevel.

Cutting curves

When making curved cuts, work the gouge by hand. Straight cuts can be helped by using a carver's mallet.

1 Place the bevel on an oilstone, lowering the handle as you pull backward and lifting it as you push forward. This will result in a rounded bevel.

2 Repeat until the bevel is smooth and rounded, and a fine burr is made on the cutting edge.

Make a fine burr on the cutting edge.

3 Remove the burr from the cutting edge and polish with a leather strop.

Sharpening a (carving) gouge
1 Hone the outside of the gouge on a flat slipstone and work the inside with a slipstone that fits the curved shape.

Work the inside of the gouge using a slipstone.

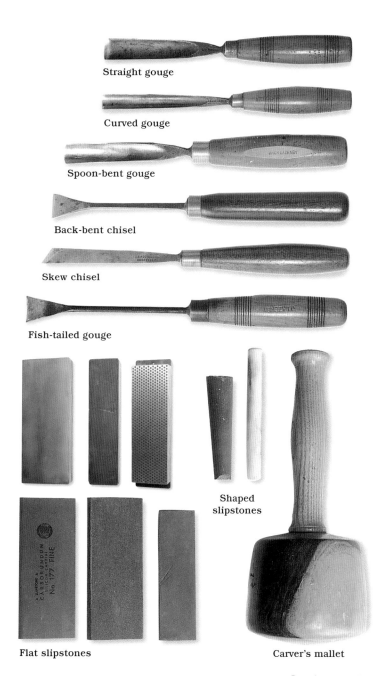

Straight gouge

Curved gouge

Spoon-bent gouge

Back-bent chisel

Skew chisel

Fish-tailed gouge

Shaped slipstones

Flat slipstones

Carver's mallet

2 Finish sharpening by polishing the carving gouge using a leather strop.

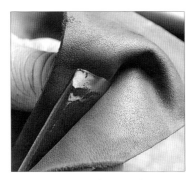

Polish the gouge with a leather strop.

CHIP CARVING

Decide the pattern that you want to carve to add interest to your work.

1 Begin by marking off the design of your choice onto the surface of the wood using a pencil. If you draw it first on a piece of paper it can then be transferred using carbon paper. Alternatively, you may find it easier to use a stencil to mark out your pattern directly onto the wood.

2 Next, cut the pattern with a cutting knife and ruler, or combination square. Select the best shaped chisel for the cut you want to make. Start to remove the waste; you may want to start the cutting by

using a mallet to drive the chisel, but final cuts should be made with hand pressure only.

Cut the pattern with a knife.

3 Continue and complete the pattern as required. It is best to work with the grain.

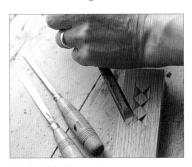

Work with the grain as you carve.

TEXTURING

Use carver's punches to create interesting patterns or textured effects. Decide the effect you want to achieve. Position the punch and tap with a hammer. This is a tricky skill that may take some time to perfect.

Turning

The object of turning is to make round objects, either in the form of spindles, by turning between centers, or in the form of disks, by turning on a faceplate. Turning is unique because the wood revolves and the cutter is held steady.

LATHES

The lathe is a simple machine. It consists of a motor that drives a headstock through a series of belt-type gears. A drive mechanism is attached to the headstock, which holds and turns the wood.

The wood can be fixed to the spindle in different ways. On most lathes, you will be able to turn both between centers (for shaping long, thin pieces of wood) and on a faceplate (for turning boxes and bowls, for example).

An adjustable tool rest supports your turning tool in front of the spinning wood.

Lathes can be free-standing or small enough to be bench mounted. The capacity of a machine is judged by the size of material that can be accommodated between centers and the "swing," which represents the diameter of

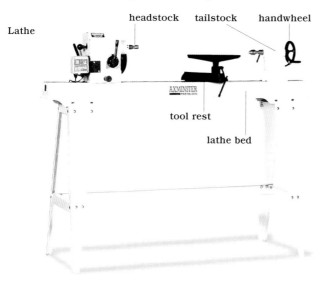

Lathe

headstock   tailstock   handwheel

AXMINSTER

tool rest

lathe bed

Safety first

• Do not use any defective wood or faulty tools.

• Do not wear loose clothing when you are operating machinery.

• Never thrust a chisel into the work.

• Always wear a full face shield.

• Be sure that the work and the tool rests are completely secure.

• Maintain a firm grip on the tool with a well-balanced stance.

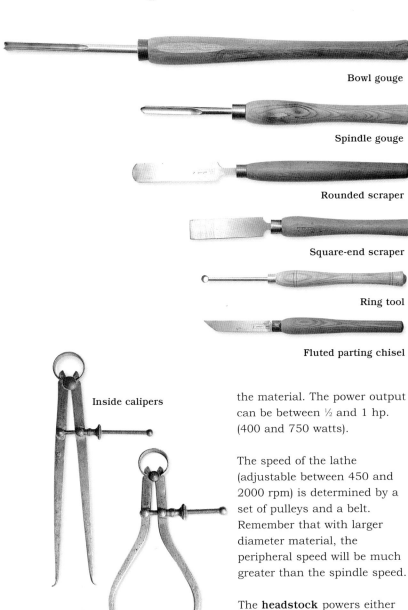

Bowl gouge

Spindle gouge

Rounded scraper

Square-end scraper

Ring tool

Fluted parting chisel

Inside calipers

Outside calipers

The **tailstock** supports the end of the woodwork for between-center turning. It moves along the lathe bed, so that it can accept different lengths of wood.

The **lathe bed** allows adjustment of the tailstock and supports the tool rests.

The **tool rests** are adjustable and support the turning tools.

TURNING TOOLS

Special ranges of turning tools are available that are strong enough to withstand the particular stresses involved. Turning gouges are used for the initial roughing out when turning square stock into round. **Spindle and bowl gouges** are for those respective operations. Chisels, such as the skew (see page 212), are used for smoothing spindles, while **full-round and square-end scrapers** are used to work the inside and outside of bowls when turning. For measuring, inside and outside **calipers** are needed. **Parting tools** are used for cutting through a piece of wood and removing it from the lathe.

the material. The power output can be between ½ and 1 hp. (400 and 750 watts).

The speed of the lathe (adjustable between 450 and 2000 rpm) is determined by a set of pulleys and a belt. Remember that with larger diameter material, the peripheral speed will be much greater than the spindle speed.

The **headstock** powers either a drive center for turning between centers or it can accept a faceplate.

Turning tools are generally sharpened on the whetstone or grinder; with the latter, do not overheat the tool tip.

SPECIAL CHUCKS

Sometimes neither between centers nor the faceplate will be appropriate for particular jobs. A wide range of chucks has been developed for holding the work, particularly when doing small turnings. They include the **screw chuck**, **cup chuck**, and **internal pin chuck**, which can be used inside or outside.

Guide the cutter with your hand.

Screw chuck

Cup chuck

Internal pin chuck

USING A LATHE

When using a lathe you need to make sure that you are working accurately and safely at all times.

Gripping the tools

The tool is controlled by holding the long handle with the working hand, while guiding the cutting edge with the other.

For rough cutting, grip all your fingers firmly over the top of the blade while you work.

Use an overhand grip for rough cutting on a lathe.

For finer woodwork, however, you will need to place your thumb on top of the blade and wrap your fingers around underneath. This underhand grip will give you more control over the blade as you work.

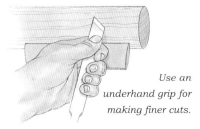

Use an underhand grip for making finer cuts.

Turning stance

When it is operating, the lathe should be set at such a height that the center of the turned object is approximately at the height of your elbow. Stand face on to the lathe with your feet apart, and tuck the tool into your body. If you stand too far away from the lathe, you will be forced to lean forward and will lose some control.

Using the tools

When you are cutting, set the tool rest just below the center of the work. Check that the work will clear the rest completely as it turns. Then, place the blade on the rest, hold the tool at an angle and start the cut. The tool should then be positioned in the direction of the movement, which will induce a slicing action. At the same time, roll the blade in the direction of the movement as you work.

Place the blade on the rest.

Hold the tool at an angle and start the cut.

Use an extractor when sanding while the lathe is in operation.

Sanding

The safest way to sand while the lathe is in operation is to hold a piece of sandpaper with one hand underneath the work. However, make sure that your hand does not actually make contact with the piece of work. You can apply pressure to the free end of the sheet by using your other hand.

Turning between centers

1 Prepare the material by marking the center of both ends with diagonals and center punch the crossed lines. It can be an advantage to plane square wood to an octagon

Position the blade in the direction of the movement.

before you begin turning—this will reduce the amount of work you will need to do on the lathe.

2 Tap the drive center firmly into one end of the work.

Tap the drive center into the work.

3 Place it in position in the headstock and bring the tailstock to the other end. Make sure that you locate the revolving center on the center mark.

4 It is important that you lock the machine into position.

5 Cut to the required diameter with a roughing gouge, then

Use a roughing gouge to cut to shape.

smooth with a chisel. Finish by using sandpaper to smooth and then apply a suitable finish.

6 Mark the object's length. Then, use a parting tool to cut a deep slot in the work. Leave a small spindle at the center of the workpiece at each end.

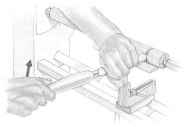

Use a parting tool to cut a slot.

7 Remove the object from the lathe and cut with a saw. In addition to producing straight-forward cylinders, many different patterns can be cut.

Turning on a faceplate

On larger lathes the faceplate may be fitted to the opposite side of the headstock, or in some cases, the headstock itself may revolve to give greater access for bowl turning.

1 If you have a bandsaw, cut the disk of wood to the size you require, plus ¼ in. (5 mm).

2 Mount the faceplate onto the center of the work. Screw it directly or glue a thick piece of scrap wood to the work with a sheet of paper between the two to facilitate easier removal when turning is finished, and screw the scrap piece through the back to the faceplate.

3 If you are turning a bowl, mount the faceplate on the inside; turn the outside shape and the scrap to the same diameter as the faceplate.

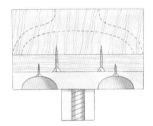

Turn the outside of the bowl.

4 Turn this outside face first. Remove the bowl from the scrap and faceplate.

5 Turn a small recess on the scrap face, the same size as the base that you have already cut, and remove it from the faceplate.

6 Fit the turned side to the scrap wood recess with screws; replace it on the faceplate and turn the inside.

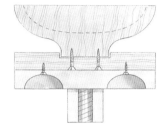

Turn the inside of the bowl.

7 If you are using a balk where the grain crosses the disk, work from the outside inward—otherwise the work can split.

8 If you have wood that presents end grain, work from the inside out.

Faceplate turning requires practice. Turn between centers until you gain experience.

Turning on a faceplate.

A turned plant stand (pages 295–9).

Using metals and plastics

Nonwood materials are now common in the furniture industry. You will also find materials like sheet plastic and metal sections such as studding and steel bars and tubes useful in your own projects.

TOOLS FOR METALS

The most likely process that you will undertake with metal is cutting. For cutting thick metal, both tubes and rods, you will need a **hacksaw**. You will also require a scriber—a sharp steel point in a holder—to mark the line to be cut on the metal.

Metal shears or **snips** can be used for cutting thin pieces of metal. There are left- and right-handed, straight and offset, and large and tight curved shears available for almost any shaped cut required.

Metalworking files are used for metal finishing and there is a range of grades from coarse to fine. There is also a wide range of shapes, including flat, half-round, and round in different sizes.

For very fine metalwork a set of **needle files** is useful.

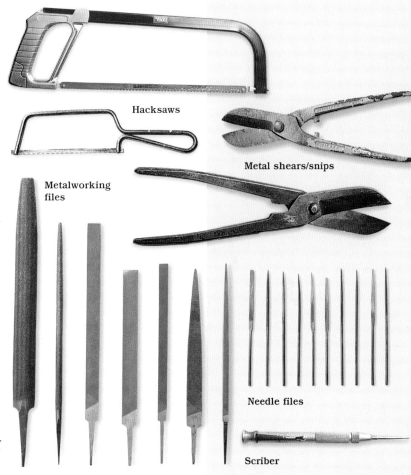

Hacksaws

Metal shears/snips

Metalworking files

Needle files

Scriber

Metalworking vice

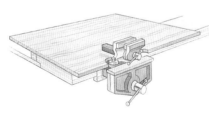

Workbench cover for metalwork

Tools for plastics

The main types of plastics that you will come across are acrylics and polycarbonates. They can be worked with most woodworking tools.

PREPARING TO WORK WITH METALS

It is not recommended that you work metals in your woodworking vice or on your bench. You need a separate metalworking vice, which is mounted on a block of wood that is held in your woodworking vice. Cut and fit a sheet of ply over the work area; swarf and filings laying on or embedded in the work area can ruin later woodwork. Some metals are much easier to work than others—aluminum is soft and bends and works easily, brass is harder but can still be worked and bent, while steel can be much more difficult.

SAWING A METAL BAR, ROD, OR TUBE

Use a hacksaw for cutting a metal bar, rod, or tube with any substantial thickness.

1 Mark the line to be cut with a scriber. Take care not to mark or damage any finish on the metal.

2 Cut with firm strokes; hacksawing will take much longer than sawing wood.

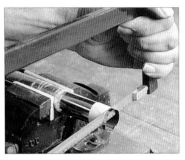

Cut the metal tube with a hacksaw.

3 When the cut is almost finished, support the waste.

CUTTING SHEET METAL

If you are using sheet metal that is not too thick, it can be cut with metal shears or snips, used in the same way as scissors.

1 Mark the shape to be cut.

2 Cut to the line. The sheet will bend as it is cut and you will probably have to beat the sheet flat with a hammer on a rigid surface if it curls up too much. However, if you use the correct shears this should not be too much of a problem.

FINISHING AND FILING

The cut edge will nearly always need some finishing with metalworking and/or needle files.

1 Set the work in the vice.

2 Holding the file firmly at both ends, use it to remove material in a forward motion. With a little practice you will be able to file accurately to a line. Always be sure the handle is on the file.

File across the metal tube.

JOINING METALS

It is quite difficult to join metals with most adhesives, and the two main methods are heat and hardware. Very high levels of heat are needed to melt and fuse most metals together. Unless you happen to have an engineering background or facilities, you will most likely need to have this type of work undertaken by a metal workshop.

Hardware is more easily used, and can range from screws to bolts and nuts for structures to rivets for sheet materials. Screws can be self-tapping and/or self-drilling.

USING PLASTICS

Plastics, other than adhesives and finishes, are less likely to be used even though it may often be better to use transparent clear plastics than glass. Plastics are generally easy to work. Some plastics can be joined with solvent adhesives, and modest heat can be used to soften local areas so that sheet can be bent. After sawing plastics, smooth the sawn edges first with a fine metalworking file and then with wet-and-dry paper.

Filing a plastic edge.

Sanding a plastic edge.

Expert tip

Take care when working plastics as they tend to become brittle and can crack or chip. When sawing, keep the saw at a low angle to avoid breakout. Use safety glasses, especially when machining. If drilling, use metal twist bits, not augers or spade bits.

The projects

Small shelf

This small shelf has no apparent supports, which helps to give it a compact, attractive appearance. Provided it is hung on a substantial wall, the shelf is perfectly safe and should be able to take the weight of normal household items. However, do not place very heavy articles on it, or extend the shelf width, as this will reduce its strength.

Tools

Jack plane

Drill and ½ in. (12 mm) and countersink bits

Tenon saw

Smoothing plane

Screwdrivers

Measuring tools

For all projects, a ruler or tape measure is needed for setting out. A try square is needed to square any set-outs across an edge or face.

MATERIALS

Part	Materials and dimensions	No.
	Hardwood	
Shelf	28 x 5 x 1½ in. (750 x 128 x 38 mm)	1

Other materials: one 12 x ½ in. (300 x 12 mm) diameter dowel; four 2-in. (50 mm) 10 gauge flat head screws; adhesive (PVA recommended); wax; finish.

1 Plane all of the surfaces of the wood to the correct overall length, width, and thickness with a jack plane. Ignore the bevels for the moment—you will not complete these until steps 8, 9, and 10. Using a try square and ruler, measure and mark a line ⅝ in. (16 mm) in from one of the long edges of the piece. This is the line where the wood will later be cut into two pieces to make the shelf and its support (rear strip). Following the measurements given on the drawing below, mark on the back edge of the wood the position of the three support dowels and the four screw holes in the center.

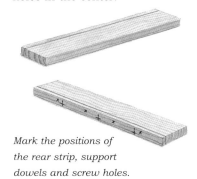

Mark the positions of the rear strip, support dowels and screw holes.

2 Use a ½-in. (12 mm) drill bit to drill four holes through the wood for the support dowels. Drill at an angle of 15 degrees so that

Finished size

28 x 5 x 1½ in.
(710 x 128 x 38 mm)

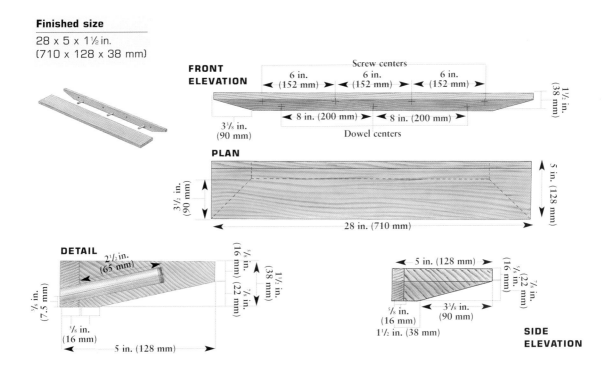

FRONT ELEVATION

Screw centers

6 in. (152 mm) 6 in. (152 mm) 6 in. (152 mm)

1½ in. (38 mm)

8 in. (200 mm) 8 in. (200 mm)

3⅛ in. (90 mm)

Dowel centers

PLAN

3½ in. (90 mm)

5 in. (128 mm)

28 in. (710 mm)

DETAIL

2½ in. (65 mm)

⅝ in. (16 mm)

1½ in. (38 mm)

⅞ in. (22 mm)

5/16 in. (7.5 mm)

⅝ in. (16 mm)

5 in. (128 mm)

5 in. (128 mm)

⅝ in. (16 mm)

⅞ in. (22 mm)

⅝ in. (16 mm)

3⅛ in. (90 mm)

1½ in. (38 mm)

SIDE ELEVATION

once the dowels are in place, they do not protrude through

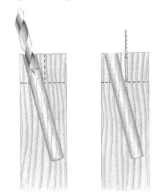

Drill the dowel holes at a 15-degree angle and then the screw holes.

the beveled face of the shelf. These holes should be 3¼ in. (80 mm) deep so that when the board is sawed into two pieces they will be deep enough to accommodate the dowels. Next, drill the screw holes in the rear of the board to a depth of ⅝ in. (16 mm). Make sure the holes are square with the face side.

3 Next, clamp the wood to a bench and use a large tenon saw to cut down the marked line to separate the rear strip from the front

section. Work carefully so you remove the minimum amount of material. Then plane the two new faces so that they fit precisely together.

4 Finish the screw holes by countersinking them on the joining face.

Cut to separate the two sections and countersink the screw holes.

5 Cut three dowels. Chamfer one end of each dowel. On the opposite end, cut ⅜ in. (10 mm) along its length with the tenon saw. Insert the dowel into the front half of the shelf, applying some wax to the holes and the dowel so that they can be separated again easily.

Wax the dowel and insert it into the shelf.

6 From waste material cut wedges that are approximately ¾ in. (20 mm) long and ¼ in. (6 mm) thick to match the diameter of the dowel.

Cut wedges to match the size of the dowels.

7 Next, bring the two sections together to wedge the dowels into position. Apply adhesive to the dowel holes in the rear strip. Push the rear strip panel onto the dowels and secure them with adhesive. Drive the wedges in from the back to spread the dowel ends. Once the adhesive is

dry, clean off the face of the dowel flush with the wood.

Push the rear part onto the dowels, ready to be wedged in firmly.

8 Mark the bevel with a pencil on the bottom of the shelf, 3⅝ in. (90 mm) in from the ends and front edge. Again, on the ends and front edge make a pencil line ⅝ in. (16 mm) down from the top of the shelf.

9 Hold the wood vertical in a vice with the bevel face toward you. Using a sharp, finely set jack plane—with the shelf and support strip together —shape both ends. Hold the plane so that it cuts at a slight angle to prevent any breakout.

Plane a bevel on both ends of the shelf and support strip.

10 Turn the wood horizontal on the bench and use a bench stop to hold the work; plane the bevel along the length of the shelf.

Plane a bevel onto the bottom and sides of the shelf.

11 Sand and finish the shelf. Separate the parts and attach the rear to the wall using flat head screws. Finish by placing the shelf back on the dowels.

Fix the rear strip to the wall and position the shelf on the dowels.

basic

Mail rack

This simple project should enhance your sawing ability, particularly your fine-sawing skills. The slats are held in place on the battens with dovetail joints, so you will need a dovetail saw as well as a curve-cutting coping saw.

Tools

Smoothing plane

Sliding bevel

Drill and ⁹⁄₁₆-in. (4.5 mm), ⅛-in. (3 mm) and countersink bits

Marking knife

Dovetail saw

Coping saw

1in. (25 mm) paring chisel

Straightedge

Screwdriver

MATERIALS

Part	Materials and dimensions	No.
	Hardwood	
Slats	30 x 8½ x ½ in. (750 x 210 x 12 mm) to make seven	1
Battens	14 x 3 x 1 in. (350 x 50 x 20 mm) to make two	

Other materials: fourteen 1½-in. (40 mm) 6 gauge flat head screws; finish.

1 First, measure, mark, and cut the seven vertical slats 4 in. (100 mm) high x 8 in. (200 mm) wide. Make sure that the grain direction is vertical. Plane the face side, face edge, width, and thickness.

Prepare the wood slats, ensuring that the grain direction is vertical.

2 Carefully plane the bottom edges to ensure they are square, checking with a try square. You will not cut the top edges to shape until step 10.

3 Plane the two supporting battens, face side, face edge, width, and thickness. Mark the dovetail angles by gauging a pencil line along the bottom face ⅛ in. (4 mm) in from each edge and then across the face edge to the top corner. Hold the batten in a vice and plane the bevels on each edge.

Make the dovetail angles on the two supporting battens.

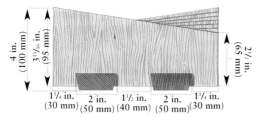

FRONT ELEVATION

4 in. (100 mm)
3¹³/₁₆ in. (95 mm)
2½ in. (65 mm)
1¼ in. (30 mm) | 2 in. (50 mm) | 1½ in. (40 mm) | 2 in. (50 mm) | 1¼ in. (30 mm)

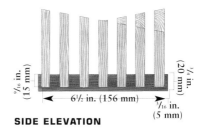

SIDE ELEVATION

⁹/₁₆ in. (15 mm)
³/₄ in. (20 mm)
6½ in. (156 mm)
¹/₁₆ in. (5 mm)

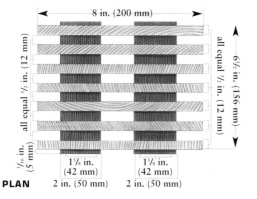

PLAN

8 in. (200 mm)
all equal ½ in. (12 mm)
6½ in. (156 mm)
all equal ½ in. (12 mm)
³/₁₆ in. (5 mm)
1⅝ in. (42 mm) | 1⅝ in. (42 mm)
2 in. (50 mm) | 2 in. (50 mm)

Finished size

4 in. (100 mm) high, 8 in. (200 mm) wide, and 6⅞ in. (166 mm) deep

4 Set up a sliding bevel to measure the angle of the dovetail on the batten. You will then be able to repeat this angle in step 6 to make sure that the slats are cut to exactly the right shape.

Use a sliding bevel to work out the angle of the dovetail battens.

5 On the battens mark where the slats will be positioned at ½-in. (12 mm) intervals (see the drawing above) and, for each slat, drill a ³/₁₆-in. (4.5 mm)

clearance hole for the screws. Countersink the screw holes on the bottom of the rack. All the slats will be held in the center of the dovetails.

6 Take the slats and use a marking knife to mark precisely the positions of the dovetails that will accept the supporting battens. From the bottom of each slat, measure up ⅝ in. (15 mm) and square a pencil line right around the wood. Use the measurements on the drawing above to mark off the position and width of the dovetails on the slats. Set a

sliding bevel to the angle of the dovetail on the battens that you measured in step 4. Use this and a marking knife to mark the dovetail angles. Gauge a line between these to represent the top cut-line of the dovetails.

Mark the dovetails on the slats.

7 Cut down the shoulder lines with a dovetail saw; remove the waste from the center with a coping saw. Pare to the top cut-line with a 1-in. (25 mm) paring chisel, ensuring a square cut. Cut one dovetail at a time; check each fits.

Use a paring chisel to pare out the waste from the dovetail joints.

8 Try all the slats dry on the battens to check that they are square with the battens.

9 Next, drill a ⅛-in. (3 mm) pilot hole from the existing clearance hole into the slats; insert and fix the screws in place.

Join the slats and battens together with screws.

10 Now that the slats are held firmly, mark the angles on the top surfaces. Measure up 3¹³⁄₁₆ in. (95 mm) on the two diagonally opposite corners of the end slats. Then mark 2½ in. (65 mm) up on the other two diagonally opposite corners. To find the heights of all the middle slats, lay a straightedge along the outside of the rack and join the 2½-in. (65 mm) mark at one end with the 3¹³⁄₁₆-in. (95 mm) mark at the opposite end. Mark with a marking knife. Number the bottom of each slat in sequence.

Use a straightedge to mark the heights of the middle slats.

11 Remove the screws and, having marked the positions of all the slats, slide them off the battens.

12 Cut the angles on the top surfaces of the slats. Saw carefully as the surface does not have a right-angled edge but twists from side to side. Hold in a clamp, saw end angles a short way, and then follow the line along the face to the center on both sides. These will act as guides for planing.

13 Plane and sand these top edges. Then sand all the faces and apply a finish to all the components before assembly.

14 Now slide the slats, one by one, onto the battens and align with your marks. Reinsert the screws.

15 Apply another coat of finish to the areas that you can still reach if desired.

The top edges of the slats are angled for best effect.

basic

Animal shapes

A basis of all work is cutting precisely to a line, and then chiseling—or paring—vertically or horizontally. This project gives the opportunity to practice chiseling skills and, since the design is so simple, achieve a very crisp result.

Tools

Smoothing plane

Marking knife

Marking gauge

Tenon saw

Bevel-edge paring chisel

Drill and drill bit

Dovetail saw

MATERIALS

Part	Materials and dimensions	No.
All pieces	Hardwood length and width to suit the scale of the animals chosen (8¾ x 8 in./220 x 200 mm used here) x 1 in. (25 mm) thick.	

Other materials: abrasive paper; finish.

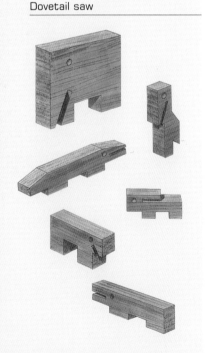

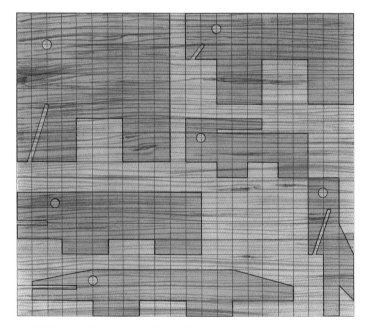

Maximum size

6¾ in. (170 mm) long and 4 in. (100 mm) high

Each square represents ⅜ in. (10 mm).

1 Use the drawing on page 234 in order to choose the scale at which to make the animals. The size of the grid can be changed to suit your own individual requirements—if you want to make the animals twice as big, then simply double the size of the grid that you use.

2 When you have chosen your scale, true the timber with a smoothing plane by working systematically all around. Then you are ready to mark the grid on the timber with a pencil.

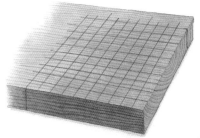

Mark out the grid on the timber.

3 Draw the animal shapes onto the grid with a pencil. Then mark the outside edges and details of the animal shapes across the grain with a knife and along the grain with a gauge. Also mark centers for the eye positions and cut lines for the slot detail.

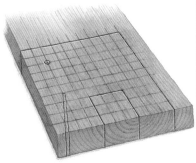

Mark out the animal shapes in the grid, including centers for the eyes.

4 Cut out the rectangle that contains each animal using a tenon saw. Where there are square or rectangular portions to be removed from the main block, cut them out, sawing to the waste side of the line.

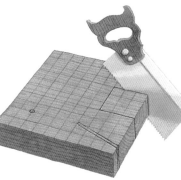

Saw away the bulk of the waste.

5 Carefully pare to the cut lines, vertically paring the end grain and either horizontally or vertically paring the long grain.

Use vertical strokes to pare back to the marked line carefully.

6 Now drill out the holes for the animals' eyes and cut the thin slots with a fine dovetail saw.

7 If your planing, sawing, and paring have been done well, then you may not wish to use abrasive paper on the faces and edges of each piece, but the sharp arrises on all corners will need removing at this stage.

8 If the animals are to be handled by children, then do not apply a finish. As an alternative, you could use a vegetable-based oil.

The finished animals.

Hot-dish stand

This project provides an easy way to develop your skill at creating grooves. This is quite a simple technique, but a very useful one. You can use either a hand plow plane or an electric router.

MATERIALS

Part	Materials and dimensions	No.
Whole piece	39 x 1¾ x ⅜ in. (1000 x 45 x 10 mm)	2

Other materials: adhesive; sandpaper; finish (oil).

Tools

Tenon saw

Two sash clamps

Hand plane

Either a plow plane or an electric router with ⅜ in. (10 mm) blade or cutter

Two C-clamps

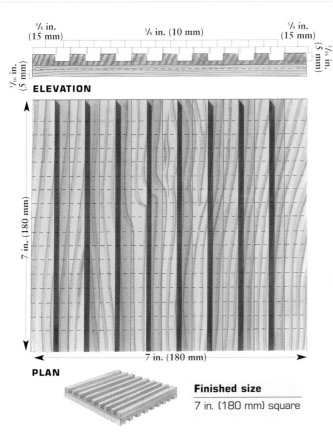

⅝ in. (15 mm)   ⅜ in. (10 mm)   ⅝ in. (15 mm)

³⁄₁₆ in. (5 mm)

³⁄₁₆ in. (5 mm)

ELEVATION

7 in. (180 mm)

7 in. (180 mm)

PLAN

Finished size

7 in. (180 mm) square

The stand is made out of two pieces of wood ⁵⁄₁₆ in. (7.5 mm) thick, cut into strips and joined with adhesive. It is better to use two pieces of wood rather than one, even if it is available in the correct width, and to cut them into strips. This is because heat causes wood movement, which is minimized by alternating the direction of the grain. Also, grooving is carried out along the grain, and turning the two squares through 90 degrees will provide you with a more stable board.

1 Cut the wood with a tenon saw into 18 strips, each ¾ in. (20 mm) wide x ⅜ in. (10 mm) thick and approximately 8 in. (210 mm) long.

2 Join nine strips together to make a square. Arrange the grain so that it is as near as possible to a quarter-sawn board—with growth rings at not less than 45-degree angles to the base. Glue these strips together: apply adhesive to one side of a strip; lay the next one on top and move it from side to side until you feel the suction of the adhesive holding the pieces together. Bring the faces and end flush. Repeat for all the other pieces of the stand. Place in sash

clamps, but take care not to overtighten the clamps, as this will cause the work to bow. Repeat with the other nine strips and allow to dry.

Clamp together the nine strips of wood.

3 With the hand plane, plane each square to give a perfectly flat face side. Test by placing one on top of the other, with the grain at right angles to each other.

4 Once you have fitted the two squares face to face, glue them together with the grain at right angles.

Glue the top and bottom together.

5 With a hand plane, plane the outside edges of the piece so that each face is true and perfectly square. Test with a try square.

6 Insert a ⅜-in. (10 mm) bit or blade into your plow plane or router; set the depth to ¼ in. (5 mm), and the fence to guide the groove ⅝ in. (15 mm) in from the edge. Run the groove along the grain; rotate the work and repeat. Turn the work over and run the groove along the grain on the opposite side; rotate the work and repeat.

Use a router to run the grooves on each side of the piece.

7 Move the fence over an additional ¾ in. (20 mm)— 1⅜ in. (35 mm) in total—and run the next groove. Repeat as explained above in step 6. Then, move the fence another ¾ in. (20 mm)—2⅛ in. (55 mm) in total—and run those grooves. Move the fence by another ¾ in. (20 mm) and complete the central grooves.

The finished corner.

8 When you have completed cutting the grooves on both sides of the stand, finish the piece by smoothing off the rough ends of wood carefully with sandpaper, removing the arris.

9 Any synthetic finish that you apply to the hot plate stand will probably suffer from the heat of pots and pans, so it is best simply to oil the stand lightly to minimize any future spotting.

basic

Wine rack

This stylish wine rack requires accurate drilling work. You can achieve good results slowly with hand tools, but if you are making a large rack, it will be easier to use a drill press or power drill. The steps below describe a method where each hole is individually marked. For a larger rack, it would be easier to use a jig to drill the holes in the correct position without needing to mark each piece.

Tools

Tenon saw

Marking gauge

Drill and ⅜-in. (10 mm) dowel bit

Smoothing plane

MATERIALS

Part	Materials and dimensions	No.
	Hardwood	
Slats	1³/₁₆ in. (30 mm) square—the total length depends on how many bottles you wish to store; for a four-bottle rack you need nine slats, 7½ in. (190 mm) long	1

Other materials: ⅜-in. (10 mm) diameter dowel—for a four-bottle rack you will need 24 lengths each 3¾ in. (94 mm) long; sandpaper; adhesive; finish.

1 First, decide how many bottles you want to store in your wine rack. Then use a tenon saw to cut the required number of wood pieces, each measuring 1³/₁₆ in. (30 mm) square and 7½ in. (190 mm) long. To make the four-bottle rack shown here, you will need nine slats.

2 Next, mark the positions of the holes at each end of the slats. Select a face side and face edge on each piece, marking one set of holes on the face side and its opposite face 1 in. (25 mm) from each end. Then mark holes on the face edge and its opposite face 1⅜ in. (35 mm) from the ends. Square a pencil line across each edge and face at these locations.

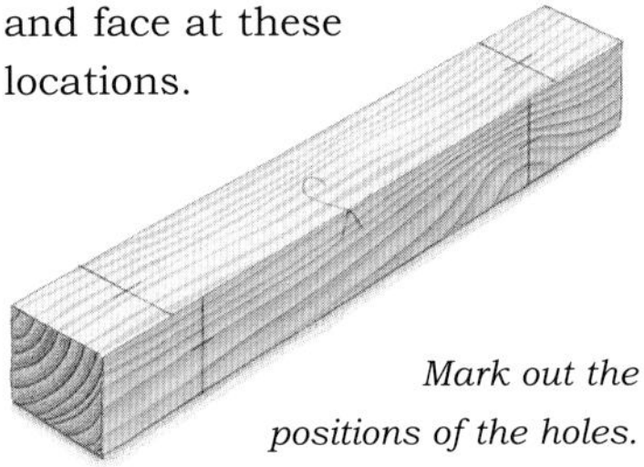

Mark out the positions of the holes.

3 Set a marking gauge to ⅝ in. (15 mm), half the width of the wood. Mark the hole center on each pencil line.

FRONT ELEVATION

9¼ in. (230 mm)

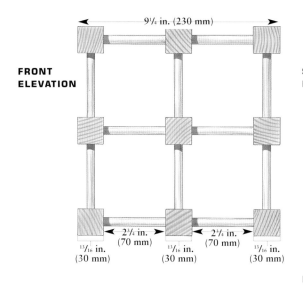

2¾ in. (70 mm) 2¾ in. (70 mm)

¹³⁄₁₆ in. (30 mm) ¹³⁄₁₆ in. (30 mm) ¹³⁄₁₆ in. (30 mm)

SIDE ELEVATION

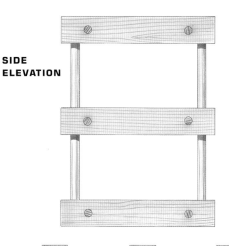

PLAN

Finished size

Approximately 9¼ in. (230 mm) high and wide, and 7½ in. (190 mm) deep

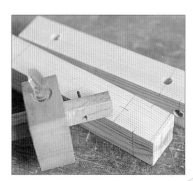

Use a marking gauge to mark the hole centers.

4 It will be easier to locate the drill if you mark the hole centers first with a center punch or an awl.

Mark the hole centers with an awl first so that it will be easier to locate the drill.

5 Drill all the holes with a ⅜-in. (10 mm) dowel bit. You will need to use a proprietary tool or make your own depth stop to be sure all the holes are at the correct depth. The simplest way to make your own drill stop is to drill a hole through a piece of wood and then cut it to size so that the drill bit protrudes ½ in. (12 mm) out the end.

Drill through a piece of wood to make a drill stop.

This will enable you to drill the correct depth in each piece of wood. Drill all the holes as marked—two in each face.

Drill holes in each piece of timber.

6 Next, prepare the dowels to hold the slats together. Each should be 3¾ in. (94 mm) in length with a shoulder ½ in. (12 mm) in from each end. If your holes have been drilled correctly, you will not need to mark the shoulders.

7 Before assembly, sand the surfaces of all components and remove the arris on the square components. Plane and sand the end grain. Create a

small chamfer on each end of the dowel. This will help to locate the dowel in the hole when assembling the rack.

8 Lay out the pieces and start assembling in units of two slats and two dowels. Insert adhesive into the holes and tap the dowels in place. To ensure that the dowels sit in the holes, use a clamp to squeeze the joints tight.

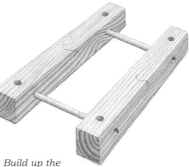

Build up the rack two pieces at a time.

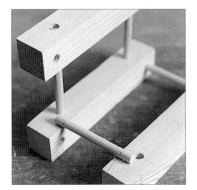

Place adhesive into the holes and press the dowels into place.

9 Assemble to the size of rack you require and remove any adhesive that has exuded from the holes. Check the frame for wind and square. Apply a finish if you wish.

10 To stabilize a large rack and to tip bottles forward to keep the corks moist, insert a thin batten, about ¼ in. (6 mm) under the front edge, and tack into place so that the rack leans backward against a wall. Or, you could use furniture glides.

Stabilize the rack by inserting a batten under the front edge.

The planed and sanded end grain adds visual interest to the rack.

basic

Veneered chessboard

The checkered pattern of dark and light face veneers is made with a caul (or press) and adhesives to attach the veneer to the base.

Tools

Smoothing plane

Miter square

Straightedge

Router

Sash clamps

Toothing plane

Veneer knife

Caul, tools, and materials

MATERIALS

Part	Materials and dimensions	No.
Base	**Manufactured board** 16 x 16 x ¾ in. (420 x 420 x 20 mm)	1
Lips	**Hardwood** 17¼ x ⅞ x ½ in. (450 x 22 x 12 mm)	4
Checkered pattern	**Veneer** Dark and light face veneers both approximately 12 in. (300 mm) square	
Border	17¼ x 2½ in. (450 x 65 mm)	4
Underside	Backing veneers	

Other materials: sandpaper; veneer tape; polyethylene; finish.

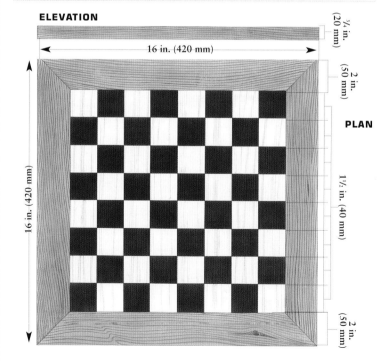

ELEVATION

¾ in. (20 mm)

16 in. (420 mm)

2 in. (50 mm)

PLAN

16 in. (420 mm)

1½ in. (40 mm)

2 in. (50 mm)

Finished size

16 in. (420 mm) square

1 The first stage of the process is to apply lips to all four edges of the board. The final size will need to be 16 in. (420 mm) square—see measurements on the drawing on page 244 as a guide. Use a smoothing plane to plane all the lips, but make sure that you leave the width over size to the board's thickness. Trim the board to 15¼ in. (400 mm) in order to accept them. Using a miter square, carefully mark miters on the ends of the lips so that they will fit exactly in the corners.

2 You can either join these lips to the board with loose tongues or simply glue them to the edges. If using tongues and grooves, work ¼ x ¼-in. (6 x 6 mm) grooves with a router prior to cutting the miters.

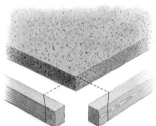

Apply lips to the board, mitering the edges to allow for the corners.

3 If using adhesives, glue the lips in place. Hold with sash clamps as required.

4 When the adhesive has completely cured, use a smoothing plane to very carefully plane the excess lip flush to the surface of the board on both sides.

Plane the lips so that they are flush with the board.

5 Key the top and bottom of the board with a toothing plane. Veneers can exert a pull on the face of a board, so put a backing veneer on the underside.

6 Select the veneers for the underside of the board. Carefully cut the light and dark veneers for the top face into precise 1½-in. (40 mm) wide strips. Join nine of these strips in alternating colors with veneer tape.

7 Now carefully cut another nine 1½-in. (40 mm) wide strips at right angles to the first set so that you are left with strips of alternating light and dark squares.

Cut nine more strips at right angles to the first set.

8 Next, shift every other strip up by one square so that you end up with a checkered effect. Fix in position with veneer tape.

Move every other strip up by one square to create a chessboard effect.

9 Lay this matrix in the center of the board and trim the excess squares off the end so that you end up with a chessboard of eight squares by eight squares. Lay the four border strips in position with veneer tape, overlapping and trimming the mitered corners as necessary with a veneer knife.

10 Ensure that, as well as face and backing veneers, you have two polyethylene sheets about the same size. Spread adhesive onto the undersurface of the board and place the backing veneer in position.

11 Apply more adhesive to the top surface of the backing board and place the top veneer assembly in position on it.

The top veneer assembly kit consists of polyethylene sheet, caul, backing veneer, core board, and top veneer.

12 Lay a sheet of polyethylene on the bottom of the caul and lay the package of backing veneer, core board, and top veneer on it. Lay another

polyethylene sheet on top of this and place the top caul in place.

Clamp the assembly together.

13 Apply even pressure to the clamping bearers all the way around.

14 When the adhesive has cured, remove the veneered board from the caul and trim all the edges.

15 Carefully remove the veneer tape, sand all surfaces, and finish the board.

The contrasting border veneer accentuates the checkered design.

Parquetry

Parquetry consists of mosaics of different colored wood veneers, which are glued onto a groundwork to form geometric patterns. Checkered or diamond shapes are the most common parquetry designs. By skilful manipulation of the color and grain of the wood, an optical illusion of a 3-D image can be created with this technique. Parquetry was most fashionable in walnut furniture from 1670 to about 1715.

basic

Triangular trivet

A trivet is a small frame that can be put beneath a hot platter or dish to protect the table or kitchen surface. This is a relatively straightforward project, which is put together with oblique halving joints and adhesive.

Tools

Smoothing plane

Sliding bevel

30/60-degree set square or protractor

Marking gauge

Marking knife

Tenon or dovetail saw

1-in. (25 mm) bevel-edged chisel

C-clamps

MATERIALS

Part	Materials and dimensions	No.
	Hardwood	
Side	24 x 1¼ x ¾ in. (610 x 32 x 20 mm)	3

Other materials: adhesive; sandpaper; finish.

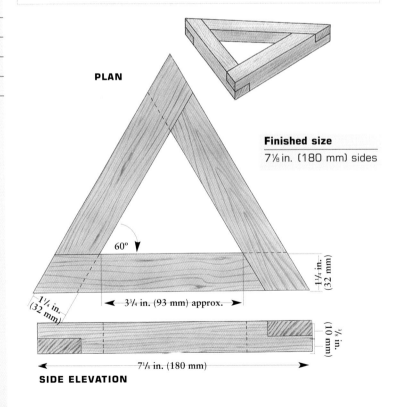

PLAN

60°

1¼ in. (32 mm)

1¼ in. (32 mm)

3¾ in. (93 mm) approx.

Finished size

7⅛ in. (180 mm) sides

¾ in. (10 mm)

7⅛ in. (180 mm)

SIDE ELEVATION

1 Plane the wood until it is rectangular in shape. Measure and cut the three side pieces of the trivet to length, using the drawing on page 248 as a guide. Apply face-side and edge marks.

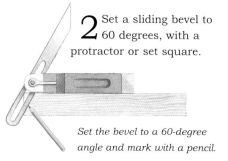

2 Set a sliding bevel to 60 degrees, with a protractor or set square.

Set the bevel to a 60-degree angle and mark with a pencil.

3 First, mark the piece of wood that will be sawed off the end of each piece of wood (A)—measure from one corner up to the opposite edge at a 60-degree angle. Carefully saw off these sections.

4 Next, mark the shoulder—the piece of wood that will be sawed partway through each end to make the half-lap joint (B). Mark a line 1¼ in. (32 mm) in from one end at a 60-degree angle across the face side, parallel with the end that you cut in step 3. Turn the piece over and mark the shoulder at the opposite end in the same way. Check that the distance between the shoulders is 3¾ in.

(93 mm). Use a try square to square these lines across the edges. Gauge a center line from the shoulder lines out and around the end of each piece and back to the first shoulder line. Repeat until all the pieces of wood are marked up.

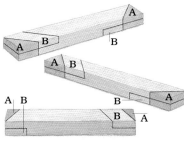

Marking shoulder lines.

5 Go over the shoulder marks with a marking knife, then carefully saw partway down the shoulder lines until you reach the center line. Be sure to saw across the grain.

Saw the shoulder lines across the grain.

6 Hold one of the pieces of wood in a vice so that the shoulder line is vertical. Saw down the gauged center line on the waste side of the shoulder. It should be possible to saw accurately to the line but, if

you are new to woodworking, you may have to trim the faces of the joints with a chisel. Repeat to achieve shaped ends on all the pieces of wood.

Saw down the center lines on the shoulders.

7 Lay the three components of the trivet together and check that the joints are tight. Adjust as required.

Check the fit and adjust if necessary.

8 Apply adhesive to the joint faces and clamp together with C-clamps.

9 When the adhesive has cured, smooth the outside edges with a plane.

10 Use abrasive paper to sand the trivet and apply the finish of your choice.

Carved mirror frame

The construction of this piece is very simple and the carving on the face is particularly effective. Here the frame has been used to hold a mirror but you could adapt it if necessary to fit a particular picture or photograph.

MATERIALS

Part	Materials and dimensions	No.
	Hardwood	
Uprights	23 x 2 x 1 in. (575 x 50 x 25 mm)	2
Horizontals	12¾ x 2 x 1 in. (325 x 50 x 25 mm)	2

Other materials: one 18½ x 12⅝-in. (470 x 320 mm) mirror; one 18½ x 12⅝-in. (470 x 320 mm) sheet of ¼-in. (6 mm) plywood and hardwood strips removed when making internal rabbets for use as retaining strips (if you rout rabbets you will need more material for strips); adhesive; sandpaper; finish; ¾-in. (20 mm) 6 gauge flat head screws.

Tools

Smoothing plane

Router with ½-in. (12 mm) straight bit

Mortise gauge

Tenon saw

Mortise chisel

Carving tools

Carver's mallet

Clamps

Drill and ⅛-in. (4 mm) and ¹⁄₁₆-in. (2 mm) bits

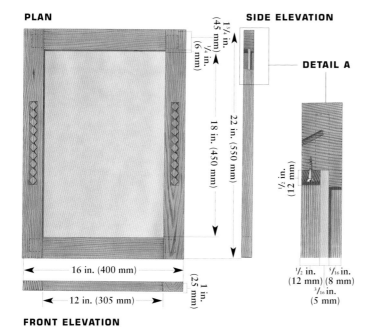

PLAN

SIDE ELEVATION

1¼ in. (45 mm)

¼ in. (6 mm)

22 in. (550 mm)

18 in. (450 mm)

DETAIL A

½ in. (12 mm)

16 in. (400 mm)

12 in. (305 mm)

1 in. (25 mm)

½ in. (12 mm) ⁵⁄₁₆ in. (8 mm)

³⁄₁₆ in. (5 mm)

FRONT ELEVATION

DETAIL OF CARVING

Finished size

22 in. (550 mm) high and 16 in. (400 mm) wide

1 First, prepare the wood for the basic frame. Plane the two uprights and two horizontals face side and face edge. Apply marks and plane the width and thickness to 2 x 1 in. (50 x 25 mm). The finished horizontals will be 14¾ in. (374 mm) long (the internal size of the frame plus the two tenons) and the finished uprights will be 22 in. (550 mm) long. Cut these pieces to length.

2 Use a router to cut the rabbets on the back edge of the internal faces ½ in. (12 mm) wide and ⅝ in. (17 mm) deep.

3 Mark the long-and-short-shouldered mortise and tenons to suit the rabbet size in their respective positions. Mark the tenon with the mortise gauge ⁵⁄₁₆ in. (8 mm) wide. Grip the horizontals vertically in a vice and cut down to the set-out shoulder lines with a tenon saw. Lay them on a bench against a bench hook and cut

the shoulder. Place each horizontal vertically in the vice again and cut ⅜ in. (10 mm) off the outside edge of each tenon. Remove waste by cutting across the long shoulder line.

4 The mortise lines up with the rabbet on one face. Hold each upright on the edge and chisel out the mortise for each—1 in. (25 mm) deep to suit the stopped tenons. First, pare away the waste within the mortise to the required depth, and then pare back to each shoulder. Check each joint for fit and adjust as required.

5 Mark the shapes of your pattern. Using the relevant carving tool, make cuts to the required pattern. You can practice on some scrap lumber.

6 When the carving is complete, assemble the frame with adhesive and clamp the joints. Ensure that the frame is square and free of wind. Adjust as necessary.

7 When the adhesive has cured, prepare the frame for finishing and apply the required finish.

8 Make the four retaining strips to fit in the rabbet. Place the mirror or picture in the frame. Lay a couple of sheets of paper over the back to protect it, then a sheet of plywood. Drill holes for the screws through into the rabbet and screw the four strips in place. An angled hole can be drilled at the top of the frame for wall mounting.

Cut the long and short shoulders of the mirror frame.

Use a chisel and mallet to practice carving on a piece of scrap lumber.

The finished carving should look crisp and neat.

basic

Small mirror and shelf

This simple mirror and shelf, ideal for a bathroom wall, will enable you to put several key skills into practice. You will need to make a dovetail dado joint to attach the shelf to the frame, use an electric router to remove the wood to fit the mirror in place and use a fretsaw to produce the fine fretwork detailing.

Tools

Marking gauge

Smoothing plane

Marking knife

Tenon saw

Sliding bevel

Paring chisel

Straightedge

Cutting gauge

Electric router or Forstner drill bit and hand router

Fretsaw

Drill

FRETWORK TEMPLATE

MATERIALS

Part	Materials and dimensions	No.
Frame and shelf	Hardwood to make both the backboard and the shelf: 22 x 8 x ¾ in. (550 x 210 x 20 mm)	1

Other materials: one 8⅛ x 5½-in. (205 x 140 mm) mirror; adhesive (PVA); silicon; double-sided tape or mastic to fit glass; sandpaper; finish.

1 Prepare the wood face side and face edge. Use a marking gauge and then a smoothing plane to plane to a width of 8 in. (200 mm) and a thickness of ¾ in. (20 mm).

2 First, mark the finished lengths of the two pieces— 16 in. (400 mm) for the backboard and 4½ in. (112 mm) for the shelf. Square all round with a marking knife. Set out the position for the dovetail dado 2 in. (50 mm) from the bottom of the backboard. Use a pencil to square the top and bottom of the shelf across the backboard.

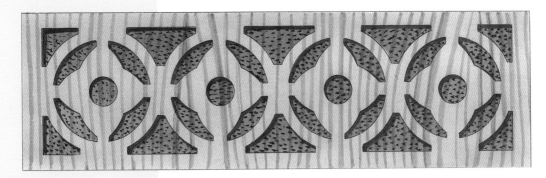

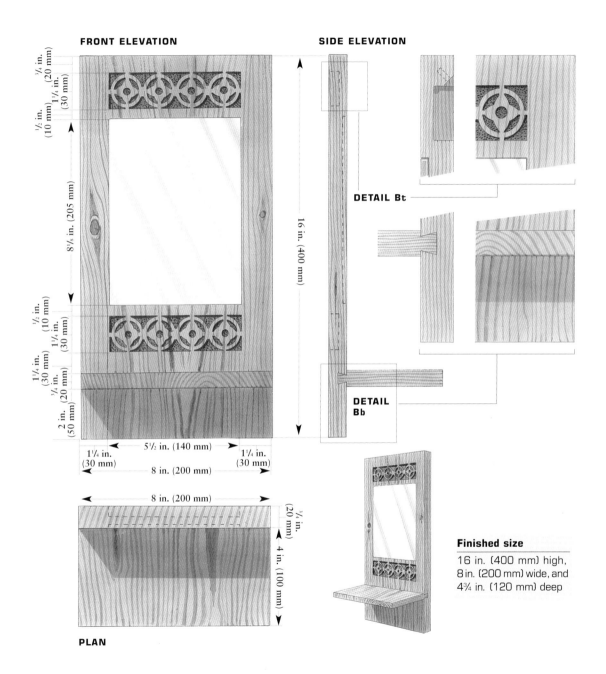

FRONT ELEVATION

3/4 in. (20 mm)
1/4 in. (20 mm)
1 1/4 in. (30 mm)
1/2 in. (10 mm)
8 1/8 in. (205 mm)
1/2 in. (10 mm)
1 1/4 in. (30 mm)
1 1/4 in. (30 mm)
3/4 in. (20 mm)
2 in. (50 mm)

16 in. (400 mm)

1 1/4 in. (30 mm)
5 1/2 in. (140 mm)
1 1/4 in. (30 mm)
8 in. (200 mm)

SIDE ELEVATION

DETAIL Bt

DETAIL Bb

8 in. (200 mm)
3/4 in. (20 mm)
4 in. (100 mm)

PLAN

Finished size

16 in. (400 mm) high,
8 in. (200 mm) wide, and
4 3/4 in. (120 mm) deep

basic

Square the other lines on the board with a pencil. Gauge a line 1¼ in. (30 mm) in from each edge to represent the ends of the fretwork and the recess for the mirror, as shown in the drawing on page 255.

3 Cut the backboard and shelf with a tenon saw and carefully plane the end grain true to the finished length.

4 Square the two set-out lines for the shelf across each edge of the backboard. Use a marking gauge to gauge a depth of ⅜ in. (10 mm) between these squared lines. Set a sliding bevel to a pitch of 1:4 and mark the dovetail on the edge from the gauge line (see detail Bb on the drawing on page 255).

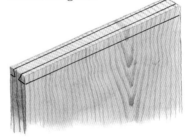

Set a sliding bevel to pitch of 1:4 and mark the dovetail dado on the edge of the backboard.

5 Use a marking knife to square the shoulder lines where the bevel line meets the face. Clamp the piece flat on the bench and cut on the waste side of the line with a tenon saw to the gauge line. Place another saw cut in the center, stopping short of the gauge line.

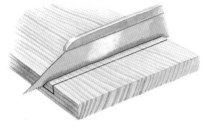

Use a tenon saw to cut away the dovetail dado.

6 Use a paring chisel in order to remove the waste from both sides; work carefully to the gauge lines. Place a straightedge along the bottom to be sure it is perfectly flat.

7 Next, set out the dovetail on the shelf across each face with a cutting gauge set to ⅜ in. (10 mm), the depth of the dado. Using a pencil, square these lines down each edge of the shelf. Then reset the sliding bevel to the correct pitch and mark the angle of the dovetail from the corner back to the squared line.

8 Square the lines all around the shelf edge. Hold the shelf flat on the bench and cut each shoulder on the waste side of the cut line to the required depth. Pare away the waste with a sharp paring chisel, working from each side across the grain.

Square the dovetail lines all round the shelf edge and cut to size.

9 On the backboard make gauge marks along the grain and knife cuts across the grain to the precise dimensions of the mirror. It is always better to choose the mirror first and make the recess fit it, because you cannot always rely on obtaining glass that is cut precisely to size.

Measure the dovetail on the edge of the shelf.

10 Now cut away the recess, which will house the mirror. The best tool to use for this is an electric router. Set the router to the correct depth and the fence to enable the tool to cut to the gauge lines. Take a cut from each edge, stopping short of the total length. Leaving the depth setting the same, adjust the fence so that a series of cuts from each side will remove the bulk of the material. When this has been completed, pare to the top and bottom cut lines. If you do not have an electric router, you can remove the bulk of material with a flat-bottomed bit such as a Forstner, setting the depth in a drill press and making a series of holes in the waste area. Use a hand router to remove the remaining waste and carefully pare squarely to the four edges.

Use a Forstner drill bit to cut the recess for the mirror.

Fretwork

Fretwork is made from thin wood that has been cut with a very fine saw, called a fretsaw, to form patterns—usually interlocking geometric designs. These are used decoratively on furniture: They are sometimes left open, or applied to a background or can be backed with a different material, such as silk, which shows through the holes. Fretwork was used widely on bookcases, cabinets, commodes, tabletops and chair backs and the term often refers specifically to the mid-18th century Chinese-style of furniture. At this time there was a craze for Oriental designs and chinoiserie (a general term for Chinese decorative work such as motifs or carvings) was applied to a range of furniture. Fretted galleries were added to tables, pagoda-like fretted tops put on cabinets, and fretwork chair backs were designed.

11 The thickness of the board is designed to give a stable piece and still allow for jointing. Some material will be removed from the back where the fretwork details will be cut, thus giving a thickness of about ⁵⁄₁₆ in. (8 mm). Remove this as described in step 10.

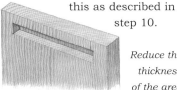

Reduce the thickness of the area where you will do the fretwork.

12 Use the template (see drawing on page 254) to mark out the fretwork detail carefully on the prepared area of the mirror frame. Make knife lines and drill holes to accept the fretsaw blade in each of the areas to be removed. This can be easily achieved by tracing the pattern with carbon paper. Alternatively, photocopy the design and glue it down in the required location. The latter is by far the best method to use because the glued-down paper will hold the surface firmly and help prevent chipping.

13 If you have not used a fretsaw before, practice on scrap lumbers. Cut the patterns. Take your time and follow the lines exactly.

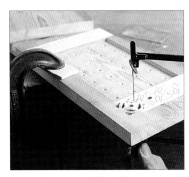

Cut the pattern with a fretsaw.

14 To hang the mirror, make a chamfer and drill a hole at an angle in the center of the top fretwork recess on the back. This can then be located on a screw or nail in the wall.

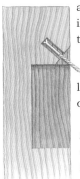

Fix a screw at an angle on the wall. Position the mirror over the screw.

15 Sand all the wood components, taking care to remove all set-out marks. Glue the shelf in place on the backboard with PVA adhesive. Apply the required finish of your choice.

16 Glue the mirror in position by placing three or four lumps of mastic on it, or use silicon or double-sided tape.

Small table

This small table was designed by Rupert Williamson, one of the top late 20th century designers/makers in the UK, as an initial exercise for students of fine woodworking. It is a simple and classic piece but requires precise work to complete well, particularly when making the legs and the mitered top frame.

MATERIALS

Part	Materials and dimensions	No.
	Hardwood	
Legs	20 x 1¼ x 1¼ in. (510 x 30 x 30 mm)	4
Top rails	10⅝ x 1¾ x ⅝ in. (270 x 45 x 16 mm)	4
Cross-rails	13½ x 1¼ x ⅝ in. (340 x 30 x 16 mm)	2
Top frame	15 x 3 x ¾ in. (375 x 75 x 20 mm)	4

Other materials: the top can be plate glass, stone, tile, slate, metal, or cork—¼ in. (6 mm) thick, 9 x 9 in. (220 x 220 mm); four 1¼-in. (30 mm) 6 gauge flat head screws; adhesive (PVA); sandpaper; finish.

Tools

Smoothing plane
Combination square
¼-in. (6 mm) mortise chisel
Mortise gauge
C-clamp
Box square
Tenon saw, or if you have machinery, radial-arm saw or saw bench
Six small sash clamps
Drill and ³⁄₁₆-in. (4.5 mm), ⁵⁄₁₆-in. (8 mm) and ⅛-in. (3 mm) bits
Miter square
Marking knife
Hand plane or miter shooting board
Screwdriver

1 Begin by planing all the components face side and face edge to the correct width and thickness, as shown in the drawing on page 260.

Making the underframe

2 Keeping each leg square for the moment, mark a pencil line around each to indicate the length of the leg. Also mark the sloped-haunched mortises for the top rails at the top of each leg. Each is 1⁵⁄₁₆ in. (33 mm) long and there are two in each leg, at 90 degrees to each other. Use the mortise gauge to set the width—¼ in. (6 mm)—

between the shoulder lines. On the end of each leg, set out the octagonal shape (see page 339).

3 With a combination square or rule used as a pencil gauge, draw a line along each edge of the leg to indicate the amount to be removed from each corner to create the octagonal shape.

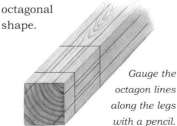

Gauge the octagon lines along the legs with a pencil.

basic

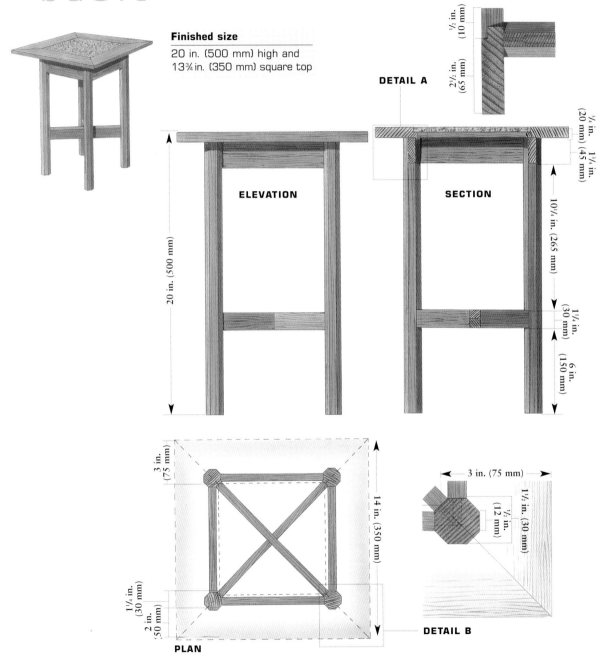

Finished size

20 in. (500 mm) high and
13¾ in. (350 mm) square top

DETAIL A

½ in. (10 mm)

2½ in. (65 mm)

ELEVATION

20 in. (500 mm)

SECTION

¾ in. (20 mm)

1¾ in. (45 mm)

10¼ in. (265 mm)

1¼ in. (30 mm)

6 in. (150 mm)

PLAN

3 in. (75 mm)

14 in. (350 mm)

1¼ in. (30 mm)

2 in. (50 mm)

DETAIL B

3 in. (75 mm)

1½ in. (30 mm)

½ in. (12 mm)

4 Cut the sloped-haunch mortises with a ¼-in. (6 mm) mortise chisel. They will meet in the middle of the wood as this is a corner joint.

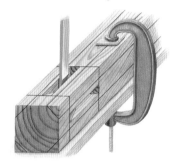

Use a chisel to cut the mortises.

5 Plane each leg precisely to an octagon by holding each one in a vice and planing to a 45-degree angle at each pencil line.

6 Mark the position of the mortises on the diagonal faces for the cross-rails. These are on the face between the two mortises that you cut in step 4. Measure and mark up from the bottom 6 in. (150 mm), and then a further 1¼ in. (30 mm). These mark where the top and bottom of the cross-rails will sit. Square a line ⅛ in. (3 mm) in from each line to represent the shoulder lines of the mortise. Use a box square and pencil to produce these squared shoulder lines (see box on page

262). Set a mortise gauge to leave a gap of ¼ in. (6 mm) between the pins and mark the mortise in the center between the shoulder lines. Leave the gauge set at this position.

7 Secure the legs on the bench with a C-clamp and cut the mortises to a depth of ¾ in. (20 mm). From this stage, it is best to give each joint a number or letter and be sure that this is also marked on the corresponding ends of the six rails. When fitting, always check that the markings match.

Finished leg with mortises at top and bottom.

8 Next, mark and cut the four top rails to length— 7½ in. (190 mm) plus tenons (10¼ in./265 mm)—and mark the tenons with haunches: ¾ in. (20 mm) each.

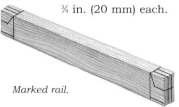

Marked rail.

9 Using a tenon saw, cut the tenons, including the mitered end where they will meet inside the leg.

Legs and rails in the various stages of marking and cutting.

10 This is the best time to drill the countersunk holes that will enable you to screw the underframe to the top frame. There should be one hole per rail. From the underside of the rail drill a hole that will accept the screw head, and then a clearance hole right through.

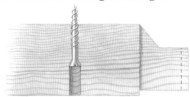

Drill the screw holes into the rails.

11 Fit these four rails into the four legs, ensuring that the joints are a good fit; you may use a little pressure with the sash clamps at this stage. Do not use any adhesive, and make sure that the assembly is perfectly square.

Making and using a box square

A box square is a very useful marking tool for squaring lines around oddly shaped sections, such as pipes or octagonal sections. It can also be used for squaring lines over rabbets or chamfers. It is a very easy tool to make. Simply cut off a section of aluminum or steel angle perfectly square, or use two pieces of wood joined at right angles with the ends perfectly square. Hold the square against both surfaces and align the end with the set-out line on the face. Use a pencil or marking knife to transfer the marks to the edge.

12 Next, mark and cut the two bottom cross-rails to length. Mark the shoulders and check that the pre-assembled frame is square by laying one cross-rail over the top diagonally. Square a line up onto the face of the rail to correspond with the face of the leg. Square these lines around the rail. Use the mortise gauge to set out a ¼-in. (6 mm) tenon in the center with ⅛-in. (3 mm) shoulders top and bottom.

Check that the preassembled frame is completely square.

13 Cut these tenons, checking that the shoulder length is the true diagonal length. Disassemble the top rails and legs, and fit the cross-rail tenons into the

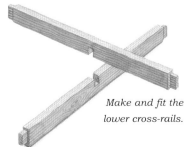

Make and fit the lower cross-rails.

mortises. Repeat with the other joint at the centers of the cross-rails. Cut this joint and fit.

14 Assemble the whole underframe dry.

Assemble the underframe dry.

Making the top frame

15 Prepare the wood for the top frame by planing to size—3 x ¾ in. (75 x 20 mm). Place all four pieces together—on edge, face edge up and flush on one end. Mark the inside edge 3 in. (75 mm) in from the flush end. Measure along 8 in. (200 mm) and square a second line across the edge with a marking knife. Lay each piece flat and mark the miters on the face side with a miter square.

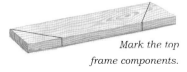

Mark the top frame components.

16 Cut the miters; you may use a tenon saw or, if you have machinery, a radial-arm saw or saw bench. To ensure that the miters fit exactly you will probably have to plane them, using either a hand plane with the wood held in the vice or a miter shooting board.

17 Mark and work a rabbet (½ in./10 mm wide and ¼ in./6 mm deep) on the inside edges of the top frame to suit the material chosen for the top.

18 Try the joints together dry, checking that the miters meet and that the frame is square. Adjust with the plane.

19 A joint will be needed to hold each miter, and this can be a tongue set in a groove or dowels.

For the mitered corners, use either tongue-and-groove or dowels.

20 Try the assembly dry. If the joints are correct, disassemble, apply adhesive to each joint and clamp, ensuring it is square and free of wind.

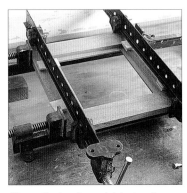

Clamp the top frame joints together.

21 The table looks more delicate if the underside of the mitered top frame has a long bevel planed on it, visually reducing the thickness of the edge. Ensuring that the top surface is flat and smooth, plane the four outside edges and then work the long bevel.

22 Before assembly, ensure that all the components are smooth. You may have achieved this when planing but may want to sand it again.

Assembly and finish

23 Assemble the sash clamps. Apply adhesive to the joints and clamp the underframe. When the adhesive has cured, check the top frame and underframe, and apply finish.

Clamp the underframe together.

24 The underframe can now be fitted to the top using the pocketed screws between the top rails and the top frame. Drill the clearance hole ³⁄₁₆ in. (4.5 mm) through the top rails, 1¼ in. (30 mm) in from each end. Then counter-bore from the underneath about half way through the rail with the ⁵⁄₁₆ in. (8 mm) bit. Hold the top in position with an even overhang on all four sides, and drill through the holes into the bottom face of the top with the ⅛-in. (3 mm) bit for a pilot hole. Fix in place with the screws.

25 One of many options for the panel in the top frame is a glass panel located in the rabbet around the inside top edge. To ensure the glass fits, cut a piece of plywood or thick cardboard that fits the space exactly, and give it to the glazier as a template. You could also use slate, metal, or cork.

Small box

The methods used to construct this box can be used to make containers in many different sizes. Through dovetails are used for their decorative quality—the bevels are planed to improve the shape of the box and demonstrate the precision of the dovetail joints. The whole box is initially made as one piece and split to give a top and bottom after assembly.

MATERIALS

Part	Materials and dimensions	No.
	Hardwood	
Sides and ends	27 x 5½ x 1 in. (700 x 140 x 25 mm)	2
	one side and one end in each piece	
Top and bottom	16 x 10 x ½ in. (400 x 250 x 12 mm)	1
	to be cut into strips and joined together	
Lining	27 x 1¾ x ¼ in. (700 x 45 x 6 mm)	2

Other materials: one pair of 1½-in. (38 mm) brass butt hinges; lock; screws to suit hinges and lock; adhesive (PVA), sandpaper; finish.

Tools

Jack plane
Marking gauge
Marking knife
Cutting gauge
Miter square
Sliding bevel
Dovetail saw
Coping saw
½-in. (12 mm) and ¼-in. (6 mm) paring chisels
Smoothing plane
Plow plane or router
Sash or C-clamps
Tenon saw

1 Prepare all the components for the box. First, select the hardwood strips that will make up the top and bottom of the box and line them up, alternating the grain for

Glue the strips for the top and bottom together.

stability. Glue them together, and when dry, plane the face side and face edge with the jack plane. You should then gauge and plane to thickness.

2 Next, make the sides and edges of the box. The two lengths of hardwood will each make one side and one edge. Plane, test, and mark the face side and edges of each of the lengths. Gauge and plane these pieces to a width of 4 in. (100 mm) and a thickness of ¾ in. (20 mm).

basic

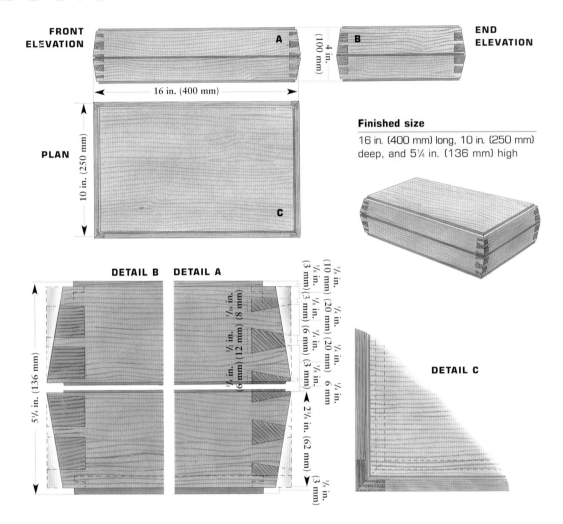

FRONT ELEVATION

A

B

END ELEVATION

4 in. (100 mm)

16 in. (400 mm)

PLAN

10 in. (250 mm)

C

Finished size

16 in. (400 mm) long, 10 in. (250 mm) deep, and 5¼ in. (136 mm) high

DETAIL B **DETAIL A**

5¼ in. (136 mm)

⅜ in. (10 mm) (3 mm)

¾ in. (20 mm) (3 mm)

¾ in. (20 mm)

¼ in. (6 mm)

⅛ in. (3 mm)

⅛ in. (8 mm)

½ in. (12 mm)

¼ in. (6 mm)

¼ in. 6 mm

2⅜ in. (62 mm)

⅛ in. (3 mm)

DETAIL C

3 Place the two pieces together in the vice, with the face sides out and the face edges on top. Mark the length of the sides and ends, leaving some waste at each end and between the pieces. Marking both pieces together ensures that both sides and both ends are exactly the same length.

4 Square all the lines around each piece with a marking knife and try square.

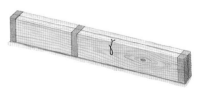

Mark one side and one end in each length.

5 Use a tenon saw in order to cut the sides and ends of the box to length, just outside the marked lines. Plane the pieces to the exact length, at the knife lines.

6 Next, mark out the shoulders for the dovetail joints. Set the cutting gauge to the thickness of the wood—¾ in. (20 mm)—and gauge around all the ends.

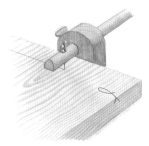

Gauge the shoulders on the ends.

7 Start by marking the tail joints in each end of the side pieces as shown in the drawing opposite (see Detail B), leaving the allowance for separating the lid later. Set out one end and transfer these lines to the opposite end as

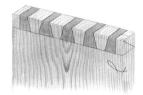

Mark the dovetails and miters.

well. At the top and bottom of each end mark a miter on the edge with a miter square from the outside corner. Set a marking gauge to half the pin width and scribe a line from each inside shoulder line across the ends. Return this line to the outside shoulder of the sides with the dovetails.

8 With a dovetail saw, cut down to the shoulder line; remove most of the waste with a coping saw and finish with a paring chisel exactly to the line. Do not cut the miters yet. Be careful to cut straight and square to the line or ugly gaps will be revealed when the outside of the box is planed down to the finished shape.

9 Place the sides and ends in their correct positions—face sides inside and face edges on top—and number or letter each corner to ensure that the corresponding sides match up.

10 Next, mark the pins by placing one of the end pieces in the vice, face side inside. Place one of the sides on top and mark along the tails with a pencil. Mark each corner independently with its corresponding miter.

Use the cut-out tails to mark the positions of the corresponding pins.

11 Saw pins to the shoulder line, remove most of the waste with the coping saw and pare back to the line. At each edge there is a small pin socket.

The cut-out tails and pins.

12 Hold each piece in a vice and cut the miter at each corner with a dovetail saw. Partially assemble the box, by putting each joint together about halfway.

Partially assemble the box sides.

13 Check that the top and bottom edges of the box are exactly level at each corner; adjust with a smoothing plane if necessary. This is important to ensure that the grooves for the top and bottom coincide perfectly when the box is fully assembled.

14 Mark and plane to size the top and bottom of the box—15 in. (380 mm) long and 9 in. (230 mm) wide. You will need to cut a groove into all the edges of the top and bottom pieces using a plow plane or router. Set the groove ⅛ in. (3 mm) in from each face, ⅛ in. (3 mm) wide and ⅜ in. (8 mm) deep. Hold the work on edge in a vice and run the bit along the top edge from the face side on the end grain, and then along the grain. Cut grooves at the top and bottom of each inside face of the four side pieces.

15 Clean up the inside surfaces of all the pieces and apply the required finish to all six inside surfaces. Since it is necessary for the top and bottom to be able to move slightly in the grooves, rub a little wax onto them.

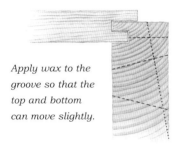

Apply wax to the groove so that the top and bottom can move slightly.

16 Assemble the box by applying adhesive to the dovetail joints. Tap two short sides onto one long side. Slide in the top and bottom and fit the last long side and clamp the joints with sash or C-clamps.

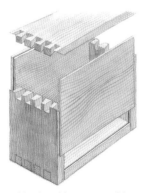

Assemble the sides, top and bottom.

17 Next, separate the top and bottom of the box. When the adhesive has cured, run a groove around the middle of the box. Hold it on edge and use a marking gauge to score a line 2 in. (50 mm) in from each face, leaving a space of ¼ in. (6 mm) between these lines. Use a tenon saw to start a cut at each corner—saw about ¾ in. (20 mm) along both sides between these gauge lines. Do not separate the two parts yet.

Score a line around the box to mark the top and bottom pieces.

18 To give the tapered shape, pencil gauge a line around the top and bottom ⅜ in. (8 mm) from each face side. Hold the box on edge in a vice and use a smoothing plane to produce the taper, planing in from each end so as not to break out any end grain. At this stage the outside of the box can be cleaned up and a first coat of finish applied.

19 Complete the separation of the top and bottom with your tenon saw and then carefully plane the two mating surfaces.

20 Around the inside of the box a thin lining sits ³⁄₃₂ in. (2 mm) proud of, or higher than, the edges. Plane the wood to 1¾ in. (45 mm) wide and mark it to length to match the inside face of the sides. Square the lines across the outside face of each piece of lining with a marking knife. Set out miters on each edge and return them back across the inside face. Make sure the miters face the correct way.

21 Hold the lining pieces on edge against a bench hook and cut the miters with a tenon saw. Check each piece for fit inside the box and adjust by planing. Round over the top edge of each piece with sandpaper. Apply a little adhesive and position each one.

22 Fit hinges and a lock of your choice. Fit the hinges slightly away from the edge of the box so that the box lid will only open to a chosen angle. Apply a finish of your choice.

All-purpose workbench

A sound and sturdy workbench is essential in order to achieve the best possible results in your woodworking. As such it is advisable to make this sturdy workbench one of your first major projects. The joints used in this project are basic mortise-and-tenon joints, held secure with dowels and bolts.

Tools

Jack plane

Straightedge

Marking gauge

Hand saw

Mortise gauge

C-clamps

Power drill and ⅛-in. (3 mm), ³⁄₁₆-in. (4.5 mm), ¼-in. (6 mm), ⅜-in. (10 mm), ¾-in. (20 mm), and countersink bits

⅜-in. (10 mm) and ¾-in. (20 mm) mortise chisel

1¼-in. (32 mm) firmer or paring chisel

Tenon saw

Sash clamps

Sanding block

Screwdriver

Wrench

Electric router with ½-in. (12 mm) straight bit

MATERIALS

Part	Materials and dimensions	No.
	Solid wood: softwood can be used for the underframe, but hardwood is needed for the backboard and the worktop.	
Underframe		
Legs	35⅝ x 3 x 2½ in. (900 x 75 x 65 mm)	4
Cross-rails	24 x 3 x 2½ in. (600 x 75 x 65 mm)	4
Front/back rails	52 x 3 x 1¼ in. (1320 x 75 x 32 mm)	2
Backboard	60 x 8 x 1¼ in. (1500 x 200 x 32 mm)	1
Worktop	60 x 12 in. (1500 x 300 mm)	1
	Plywood	
Tool well	60 x 12⅝ x ½ in. (1500 x 320 x 12 mm)	1

Other materials: eight 15 x ⅜ in. (125 x 10 mm) bolts/nuts/washers; ten 1-in. (25 mm) 8 gauge flat head screws; four 2-in. (50 mm) 8 gauge flat head screws; four 3 x ⅜-in. (75 x 10 mm) coach screws with washers; woodworker's vice; adhesive (PVA); sandpaper (120-grit); finish (oil).

1 Prepare all the wood by cutting and planing the components to size. Apply face and side marks. Wood that has been already planed is available for purchase.

Making the underframe

2 The first parts of the bench to be made are the two end frames, which consist of the front and back legs and two cross-rails each. These are held together with wedged mortise-and-tenon joints.

3 Measure up 4 in. (100 mm) from the bottom of one leg and square a line around the wood to represent the top of the cross-rails. Mark a second line on the face edge 3 in. (75 mm) down from this point and square as before. A mortise will be set out between these lines with a ⅜-in. (10 mm) shoulder.

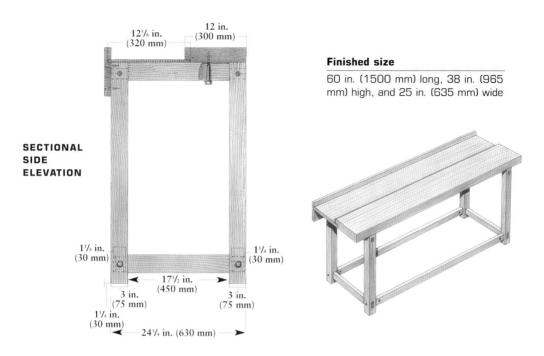

SECTIONAL SIDE ELEVATION

12⅝ in. (320 mm)

12 in. (300 mm)

1¼ in. (30 mm)

1¼ in. (30 mm)

17½ in. (450 mm)

3 in. (75 mm)

3 in. (75 mm)

1¼ in. (30 mm)

24¾ in. (630 mm)

Finished size

60 in. (1500 mm) long, 38 in. (965 mm) high, and 25 in. (635 mm) wide

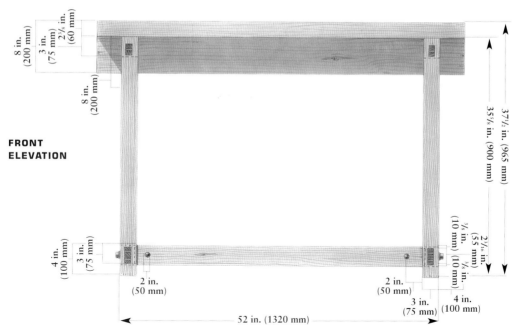

FRONT ELEVATION

8 in. (200 mm)

3 in. (75 mm)

2⅜ in. (60 mm)

8 in. (200 mm)

37½ in. (965 mm)

35⅜ in. (900 mm)

2³⁄₁₆ in. (55 mm)

⅜ in. (10 mm)

⅜ in. (10 mm)

4 in. (100 mm)

3 in. (75 mm)

2 in. (50 mm)

2 in. (50 mm)

3 in. (75 mm)

4 in. (100 mm)

52 in. (1320 mm)

4 For the shoulder, measure in ⅜ in. (10 mm) from the marked out lines and square around all faces of the leg. Set a mortise gauge to scribe a ¾-in. (20 mm) wide mortise between the shoulder lines.

5 Set out a second mortise of the same dimensions for the top cross-rail on the same face. The top edge of the rails will be level with the top of the legs. Mark the other three legs.

6 Hold each leg in turn face up on a firm flat surface with a C-clamp. Use a power drill with a ¾-in. (20 mm) bit, and drill out the bulk of the waste from the mortise. Drill in the center of the mortise and keep the drill straight. Drill halfway from both sides. Clean out the waste with the ¾-in. (20 mm) mortise chisel, by cutting back to the shoulder lines from the center of the mortise. Pare the sides with a 1¼-in. (32 mm) firmer or paring chisel. Work from both sides of the leg, cutting a little at a time back to the set-out lines.

7 To cut the tenons, mark the shoulders by squaring a line around the four cross-rails 3 in. (75 mm) in from both ends. Using the already-set mortise gauge, gauge the tenons toward each end, down and back to the shoulder line.

8 Hold each in turn firmly on edge in a vice or on a saw stool and cut the tenons using a tenon saw. Clean up the face of the tenons with a sharp chisel. Remove ⅜ in. (10 mm) off each edge of the tenons to reduce its width to match the mortises. Check for fit and adjust as required.

9 The mortise-and-tenon joints are secured with wedges. Place a saw cut for the wedge along the tenons ⅜ in. (10 mm) from each edge, and approximately two-thirds the length of the tenons. You can either make the wedges out of the waste from the tenon (as shown here) or cut them from another waste piece of wood.

Mark the wedges that will be cut from each edge and make a saw cut into which they will be secured.

10 Dry fit each end frame. If satisfactory, they may now be glued with PVA. Do not use an adhesive that is brittle

when set because the joint will be subjected to a lot of vibration. Apply the adhesive to the tenons and place in their respective mortises.

Fit each end frame together.

11 Place one of the frames in a pair of sash clamps and apply a light pressure. Check that the rails are parallel and the whole frame is square and not in wind. Adjust the job as needed so that the frame is true. Tighten the clamps and recheck. Lay a straightedge along the rail across each leg to make sure the joint is flat. The sash clamps may need to be adjusted to correct any faults. Repeat with the other frame.

12 Once the adhesive is dry, clean up the faces with the plane, and 120-grit sandpaper and sanding block. Cut any excess length off at the top to finish flush with the rail.

Making the front and back cross-rails

13 Mark and cut the mortises for the front and back cross-rails, which will join the two end frames together. These have a stopped mortise-and-tenon joint that is secured by a nut and bolt. Set these out as before on the face side of the legs using the measurements on the drawing on page 271. The mortise only needs to be chiseled out ⅜ in. (10 mm) wide and ⅜ in. (10 mm) deep. Cut the 3 x 1¼-in. (75 x 32 mm) rails 52 in. (1320 mm) long, and set out the stopped tenons on each end ⅜ in. (10 mm) long. Fit each into the corresponding mortise and adjust as required.

14 Drill a ⅜-in. (10 mm) hole right through the leg from the outside to correspond with the center of the mortise just cut. Hold the rail in its mortise and place the drill back in the hole. Start the drill to make the location on the end of the rail. Remove the rail and drill the hole in the end 2¾ in. (70 mm) deep.

15 Lay the rail flat and set out a mortise 2 in. (50 mm) in from the shoulder, ⅜ in. (10 mm) wide and approximately ¾ in. (20 mm) high to allow for fitting the nut. Chisel this deep enough so that the bolt will align correctly with the thread of the nut.

16 Fix each rail in place by putting the nut and a washer into the mortise. Position the rail and insert the bolt with the washer through the leg into the end of the rail. Tighten with a wrench and check for square.

Making the backboard

17 Make the backboard, which is 8 x 1¼ in. (200 x 32 mm) and set at the same height as the front work surface. Set up a router to cut a ½ in. (12 mm) wide groove ⁵⁄₁₆ in. (8 mm) deep and down 1⅞ in. (48 mm) from the top edge. Secure the board on a flat surface and run the groove.

18 Fit the backboard to the back of the underframe. Cut the backboard to 60 in. (1500 mm) long and set out a dado joint 4 in. (100 mm) in from each end to attach to the back legs. Square these lines from the groove down and across the bottom edge. Gauge the dado ⁵⁄₁₆ in. (8 mm) deep between the lines. Cut the dado with a tenon saw, or with the router, which should already be set at the correct depth.

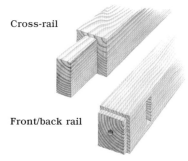

Cross-rail

Front/back rail

Cut the tenons in the cross-rails and the front and back rails.

Fix the lower rails to the end frames with a nut and bolt.

Components of back of bench.

A simple bench stop

On some traditional benches a rectangular strip of wood is located in a mortise in the worktop in a position where it runs against a leg. It is held in place with a wing nut that runs in a groove so that it can be both adjusted and held in place. An alternative and simpler system is to make the stop so that it is a tight fit in a hole—square, rectangular, or round. They are adjusted simply by tapping them to the required height.

19 Place the backboard in position. It will be fixed to the back legs with two 2-in. (50 mm) 8 gauge flat head wood screws at each end. Keep the groove clear of the top frame to enable the plywood well to slip in easily. Drill ³⁄₁₆-in. (4.5 mm) clearance holes through the backboard and use a ¼-in. (6 mm) pilot hole into the leg. Countersink the outside for the screw heads. Secure the backboard in place with screws.

Making the worktop

20 Next, make and fix the worktop and tool well to the bench. First, cut a rabbet in the back bottom edge of the worktop, into which the tool well will slot. Set the router to cut a rabbet ½ in. (12 mm) wide and ½ in. (12 mm) deep. Square a line around each end of the worktop and cut with a hand saw to 60 in. (1500 mm) long.

21 Cut the plywood for the tool well 12⅝ in. (320 mm) wide and 60 in. (1500 mm) long with a hand saw. Straighten the edges with a plane. Test the ply and the worktop for fit. Turn the worktop over and fix the ply into the rabbet with 1-in.

(25 mm) 8 gauge flat head screws 6 in. (150 mm) apart.

22 Drill two ⅜-in. (10 mm) holes through each top cross-rail to enable coach screws to be used to hold the worktop down. Position the worktop on the top of the underframe, with the tool well in the groove in the backboard. Drill a ¼-in. (6 mm) pilot hole through the cross-rail into the bottom of the work surface. Fix in place from underneath with 3 x ⅜-in. (75 x 10 mm) coach screws.

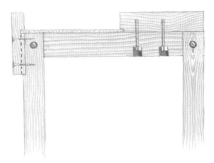

Secure the worktop in place with coach screws.

23 You should now be left with a strong, rigid workbench. Ensure that the working surface is perfectly straight and flat, planing if necessary. Sand the surface in order to remove any sharp corners and apply several coats of oil to finish.

Fitting a vice

24 Next, you should unscrew and remove the main work surface again and fit the vice. Calculate the final position of the vice so that the cheek will be in line with the front of the worktop. Make bearers for the vice casting to sit on. These will go through, into the underside of the worktop so make them thick enough. Drill holes for the coach screws to go through, into the underside of the worktop. When you are ready, replace the worktop and fix the vice cheek on the bench side so that it is in line with the front of the bench. Fix the outer vice cheek to the front of the vice.

Fix the vice in position.

Fix the vice so the inner cheek is in line with the front of the worktop.

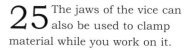

25 The jaws of the vice can also be used to clamp material while you work on it.

Clamp materials while you work.

26 Fit bench stops, against which wood can be planed, to your worktop. Metal ones are available or you can make your own wooden ones (see box on page 274). Another method is a rectangular lumber cam that is fitted to the end of the bench and can be turned against the steel pin.

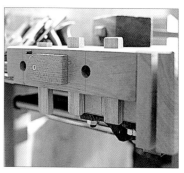

Lumber cam bench stops.

The vice fixed to the bench ready to hold your wood components.

Garden pergola

The design of this pergola is such that it can be added to at any time, by building extra bays or horizontal elements. The wood is supported above ground level, removing the likelihood of wood degradation and thus ensuring a long life.

MATERIALS

Part	Materials and dimensions	No.
	Sawn or planed treated softwood, or exterior hardwood	
	to make one bay of four uprights	
Uprights	83 x 2 x 2 in. (2100 x 50 x 50 mm)	16
Cross-pieces	32 x 6 x 1½ in. (800 x 150 x 40 mm)	4
Horizontal beams	7 x 6 x 1½ in. (180 x 150 x 40 mm)	4

Other materials: sixty-four 3-in. (75 mm) 10 gauge galvanized flat head screws; four 8 x ⅜-in. (200 x 10 mm) steel threaded/studdings; sixteen nuts and washers; four 4 x 4 x ⅛-in. (100 x 100 x 3 mm) steel plates; adhesive (exterior-grade); finish (exterior-grade). Note: use galvanized metal and hardware.

Tools

Marking gauge
C-clamp
Coping saw
Power saw
Hand saw
1³⁄₁₆-in. (30 mm) firmer chisel
Drill and ³⁄₁₆-in. (4.5 mm) and ⅜-in. (10 mm) bits
Hacksaw
Smoothing plane
Screwdriver
Wrench

Making the wood components

1 Mark the length of the four uprights for each leg and square a line around the wood. Mark the positions of the joining cross-pieces ¾ in. (20 mm) up from the bottom and 12 in. (300 mm) down from the top.

2 Each upright requires four cross-pieces, 6 x 1½ in. (150 x 40 mm) per section. Set out four lengths of 7 in. (180 mm) on the 32 in. (800 mm) lengths and then a series of cross half lap joints in the center of each piece—2¾ in.

(70 mm) in from each end and 1½ in. (40 mm) wide. Use a knife and try square in order to transfer the set-out round onto both faces of all four cross-pieces. Use a marking gauge to mark the depth 3 in. (75 mm) from one edge.

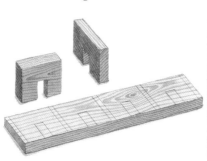

Mark and cut out the cross-pieces.

ELEVATION

1½ in. (40 mm)

2 in. (50 mm) 2 in. (50 mm) 4 in. (100 mm)

2 in. (50 mm)

6 in. (150 mm)

6 in. (150 mm)

6 in. (150 mm)

8 in. (200 mm)

6 ft. 6 in. (2000 mm)

6 in. (150 mm)

¾ in. (20 mm)

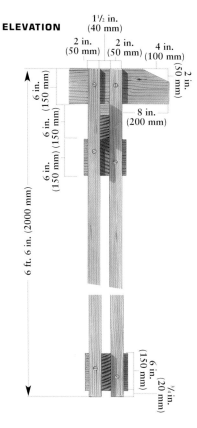

Finished size

6 ft. 6 in. (1980 mm) high and approximately 32 in. (812 mm) square

DETAIL PLAN

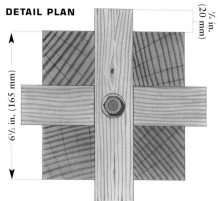

¾ in. (20 mm)

6½ in. (165 mm)

3 Place the wood in a vice with the marked dadoes on top. Saw down the waste side of the cut lines as far as the center gauged line. Remove the waste with a coping saw. Finish the joint by paring down to the gauged line with a 1³⁄₁₆-in. (30 mm) firmer chisel.

4 Cut all cross-pieces to the required length—7 in. (180 mm)—with the power saw. Check that each pair fits snugly to form a finished cross-piece. Adjust as required.

5 Use exterior-grade adhesive to assemble the half lap joints to form the finished cross-pieces. Apply the adhesive in each half lap joint and press the two halves together until the tops are flush. Check that each cross-piece is square and allow to cure.

6 Drill a ⅜ in. (10 mm) hole through the center of the bottom cross-piece.

Making the metal leg bases

7 Cut a ⅛-in. (3 mm) thick galvanized steel plate 4 x 4 in. (100 x 100 mm) with a hacksaw. Your supplier may be able to cut these to size.

8 Drill a hole to accept the threaded studding in the center. Mark the diagonals on the face of the plate and use a center punch to create a small dent in the surface for the drill. When drilling through steel, first drill a pilot hole. This will help the larger drill bit stay in place and will also keep it straight.

9 Secure the work in a vice on a drill press. Use a sharp bit at a low speed and, if available, use cutting fluid to lubricate the drill. Coat all surfaces of the metal with a preservative before assembly to prevent rusting.

10 Fix the steel plate in position with washers and nuts about 2 in. (50 mm) from the bottom of the studding. Place another nut

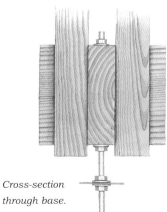

Cross-section through base.

followed by a washer on the long end of the studding, approximately 6⁵⁄₁₆ in. (160 mm) down. Insert the studding through the bottom of the cross-piece. Fix in place with a washer, followed by a nut on the top. Be sure that all nuts are tight so that they will not become loose.

Fix the nut and washer through the base cross-pieces.

Assembling the legs

11 Before assembling the pergola, remove all the sharp edges with a smoothing plane. To make each leg of the pergola, lay one pair of uprights on a sawhorse face down. Place two cross-pieces in the correct position using the marks that you set out in step 1: the studding of the bottom cross-piece should be on the ¾-in. (20 mm) set-out line and the top cross-piece on the 12 in. (300 mm) set-out

line. Place the other pair of uprights on top and push them firmly into the corner of the cross.

12 To join the wood components together, drill two ³⁄₁₆-in. (4.5 mm) holes through each upright and insert the galvanized flat head screws into them. For extra strength you may also choose to add some adhesive to the joint before assembly. Repeat this process at the top cross.

13 Turn the half-constructed leg over and fix the other uprights to the cross-pieces in the same manner. Repeat steps 11, 12, and 13 in order to assemble the other three legs in the same way.

Screw the four uprights into the cross-pieces to make each leg.

14 Next, decide on the length of the horizontal beams. Check with your local building codes as to any regulations specifying span or section sizes. Allow for an 8-in. (200 mm) overhang past each leg and cut them to length. Finish off with bevels cut on the top edges.

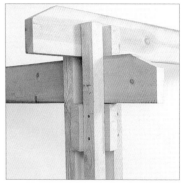

The horizontal beams overhang the uprights and have beveled edges.

15 Lay the beams flat on a sawhorse and sight along the wood to detect any bowing. If bowing is evident, place the bowed edge as the top edge. Mark and cut the bevel on the top edge with a power saw. Apply a finish as required.

16 Finally, install the uprights by drilling additional holes in the baseplate for bolting down or setting them into a concrete footing.

Feature table

This is an interesting and unusual feature table that is constructed from solid wood. It shows the wood to excellent effect and, with its glass top, gives an open visual space, which creates a useful display area. Its simple and effective appearance requires the marking and cutting of extremely fine dovetail dado joints.

MATERIALS

Part	Materials and dimensions	No.
	Any stable hardwood—elm was used here	
Structural shelf	36 x 26 x 1 in. (900 x 400 x 25 mm)	1
Legs	18 x 13 x 1¼ in. (450 x 330 x 30 mm)	4

Other materials: Other materials: one 40 x 20 x ⁵⁄₁₆, or ⅜-in. (1000 x 500 x 8, or 10 mm) toughened glass top with polished edges; eight furniture glides; eight self-adhesive clear plastic buffers; four 2-in. (50 mm) 8 gauge flat head screws; adhesive; sandpaper (150-grit); finish.

Tools

Smoothing plane
Straightedge
Winding sticks
Steel square
Power saw
Marking gauge
C-clamps
Hand saw
½-in. (12 mm) and 1³⁄₁₆-in. (30 mm) chisels
Marking knife
Tenon saw
Router
Miter square
Drill and ⅛-in. (3 mm), ³⁄₁₆-in. (4.5 mm) and countersink bits
Screwdriver

1 Prepare the lumber for the shelf and legs, which must be dry and stable. If you are unable to find boards wide enough, you may need to join strips together, ensuring that the grain direction is as near quarter-sawn as possible (see box on page 283).

2 Plane the wood's face side, face edge, width, and thickness. Test it for square with a straightedge, winding sticks and try square. Plane all pieces so that they are true as required. Apply face-side and face-edge marks to the pieces.

Making the legs

3 To determine the height of the legs, use a pencil and steel square to square two lines across the legs 18 in. (450 mm) apart on the face edge. Hold the material firmly in place on a pair of sawhorses and cut each leg to length using a power saw.

4 Next, mark the slots in the legs into which the shelf will fit. Square a line across the face of one leg 10 in. (225 mm) up from the bottom and then another 1 in. (25 mm) up to take the thickness of the shelf. Repeat on the other legs.

intermediate

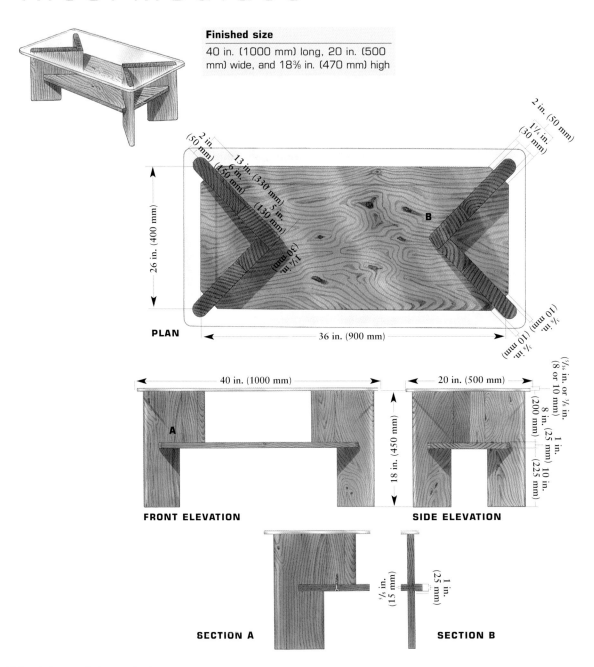

Finished size

40 in. (1000 mm) long, 20 in. (500 mm) wide, and 18⅜ in. (470 mm) high

PLAN

2 in. (50 mm)

13 in. (330 mm)

6 in. (150 mm)

5 in. (130 mm)

1¼ in. (30 mm)

2 in. (50 mm)

1¼ in. (30 mm)

⅜ in. (10 mm)

⅜ in. (10 mm)

26 in. (400 mm)

36 in. (900 mm)

B

FRONT ELEVATION

40 in. (1000 mm)

A

18 in. (450 mm)

SIDE ELEVATION

20 in. (500 mm)

(⁵⁄₁₆ in. or ⅜ in. (8 or 10 mm)

8 in. (200 mm)

1 in. (25 mm)

10 in. (225 mm)

SECTION A

SECTION B

⅝ in. (15 mm)

1 in. (25 mm)

5 The shelf is held in place in dovetail dadoes, with ³⁄₁₆ in. (5 mm) high dovetails. Set out two more lines on the legs ³⁄₁₆ in. (5 mm) in from the two lines already marked out in step 4. Square all lines around the edge back to the other face.

6 Square a line 3¾ in. (95 mm) from the inside edge to mark the wood that is to be removed from the bottom inside corner of the legs. The waste wood is represented by the shaded area in the diagram below.

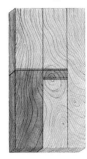

Mark the legs. The shaded area shows the waste wood and the double lines the dovetail joint.

7 Remove the waste wood from each leg—lay them flat on a pair of sawhorses and hold firm with a C-clamp. Use a tenon saw to remove the waste from the corners.

8 Next, cut the waste away from the slots, remembering to leave ³⁄₁₆ in. (5 mm) at the top and bottom to make the dovetail joint marked out in step 5. Use the tenon saw and

then a ½ in. (13 mm) chisel to remove the waste.

9 To cut the dovetails, score a line with a marking knife on the existing set-out lines on each leg. The dovetail pitch must match the router bit you are going to use to cut the dado in the shelf. Hold the leg firm on a flat surface and cut down on the waste side of the line the required depth with a tenon saw. Take care not to damage any wood on the other side of the line as this will be difficult to hide and will look unsightly. Remove the waste from the dovetail with a 1³⁄₁₆ in. (30 mm) chisel. Chisel at an angle in order to make the pitch of the dovetail.

Make the dovetail for each dado joint.

Making the shelf

10 Next mark, cut, and plane the shelf to size. Cut each corner at a 45-degree angle. The length of the cut is equal to the thickness of the leg—1¼ in. (32 mm) plus an extra ⅜ in. (10 mm) each side.

Joining solid wood to make a wide board

It is often necessary to join several strips to make a wide board of solid wood. A suitably wide plank may not be available, or the grain direction in through and through-cut planks may make them unsuitable because of the likely movement of the wood. When joining strips, ensure that they are perfectly square, straight, and flat. It is advisable to have some form of jointing method between the faces to be glued, such as tongues in grooves or dowels. To ensure that the board stays flat, it is essential to place sash clamps on both the top and bottom faces.

11 Now, cut the dovetail dadoes in the shelf. Make a router template (jig) from a piece of manufactured board. The slot up the center will need to match the collar and bit for your router. Set the bit to cut ³⁄₁₆ in. (5 mm) deep into the surface of the shelf. As always when routing, test-run a cut in scrap lumber to ensure the set-up is correct.

Make a router template or jig.

12 Fix a stop under the jig so that the router will cut the dado 11 in. (275 mm) long. When the jig is set correctly, lay it on the surface of the shelf and secure it at a 45-degree angle at the corner with a C-clamp. Before cutting, check it again with a miter square. Rest the router on the template. Start it up and slowly move the bit into the work. Keep the collar against the

left-hand side of the slot, pushing the router forward to the end. Move the router across the end of the slot and pull it back toward you, ensuring the collar stays against the right-hand side of the slot. Repeat on all four corners of the shelf top.

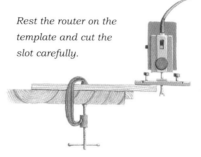

Rest the router on the template and cut the slot carefully.

13 Adjust the stop on the template so that the router will only cut a dado 5¾ in. (145 mm) long. Turn the shelf over and cut the bottom dado in the same way.

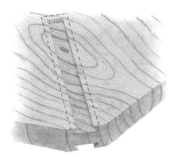

Turn the shelf over and make the dovetail dado in the other side.

14 Before you assemble the table you will need to fix the internal corners where the two pairs of legs meet. Cut 1¼ in. (32 mm) off one of each pair so that when they are slotted into place, the shorter leg can butt up against the longer leg.

15 Check the fit of the joints and adjust as required. Sand and apply a first coat of finish to all components, masking the joint areas.

16 To assemble, slide one long leg into its dado and apply adhesive to the edge that its matching leg will butt against. Slide in the second leg and press together firmly. Apply adhesive to the butted edges only, not the dovetail dado.

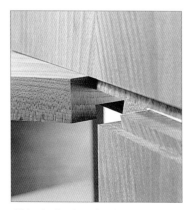

Slide the leg into the dado.

17 Remove any excess adhesive with a damp cloth before it is set. When dry, turn the table over and then screw each leg in place from underneath the shelf. Drill a $\frac{3}{16}$-in. (4.5 mm) hole through the shelf followed by a $\frac{1}{8}$-in. (3 mm) pilot hole into the leg. Countersink the top of the hole and insert the screw in place.

18 Sand the table with 150-grit sandpaper and apply the wood finish of your choice.

19 Fasten two furniture glides to the bottom of each leg. At the top of the legs, position small, clear

self-adhesive plastic buffers to prevent the glass top from sliding. For safety, the glass top must be manufactured from tempered glass, with all the edges ground and polished by a specialized glazier. Do not use standard glass for this purpose.

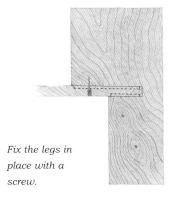

Fix the legs in place with a screw.

Use a power drill to fix the screws in placc.

A glass top allows the structure of the table to be seen.

Free-standing CD rack

As CD collections grow ever larger, safe storage with easy access to CDs becomes an important concern. The design for this CD rack allows for convenient access with CDs stacked alternately to right and left. It is also flexible because you can add extra spacers as necessary by lengthening the rods and make some spacers to a different thickness to accommodate double CDs.

MATERIALS

Part	Materials and dimensions	No.
	Solid lumber – hardwood or softwood of your choice to make a rack for 29 CDs	
Length for triangles	82 x 2 x ½ in. (2100 x 50 x 12 mm)	1
Base	6 x 6½ x 1⅝ in. (150 x 165 x 40 mm)	1
Handle (optional)	4 x 2 x ½ in. (100 x 50 x 12 mm)	1

Other materials: one 150 x 5½ x ⅛ in. (3750 x 140 x 3 mm) acrylic sheet; scraps of lumber for jigs; two 23 x ¼ in. (585 x 6 mm) threaded rods; four with washers (two standard and two dome); six 1-in. (25 mm) 6 gauge flat head screws; sandpaper (120-grit, and 400- and 600-grit wet-and-dry); finish.

Tools

Backsaw
Miter box (optional)
Miter square
Block plane
Table saw or radial-arm saw
Screwdriver
Drill press and ⅛-in. (3 mm), ³⁄₁₆-in. (4.5 mm), and ¼-in. (6 mm) bits
¼-in. (6 mm) dowelling bit, ½-in. (12 mm) Forstner bit, and 1³⁄₁₆-in. (30 mm) hole saw
Smoothing plane
Jigsaw
Second-cut file

You will often be faced in woodworking with the need to produce batches of components of the same size and this project demonstrates some simple jigging methods, which will show how you can achieve this.

This free-standing CD rack can be made with hand tools but in order to use the jigs effectively, some machinery would be useful—for example, a table saw for making the wood triangles and cutting the acrylic precisely to size, and a drill press for drilling the holes in both the wood and acrylic.

Once you have made the necessary jigs it will be easy to add to existing racks or make matching ones at a later stage. The only dimensional change will be the length of the threaded steel rods or spacers of different thicknesses.

Making the wood triangles

First, cut the wood triangles to size. There is a variety of ways to do this.

intermediate

1 If you are going to use a hand saw (or backsaw) mark the triangles with a cut line. On a scrap piece, make a saw cut, measure the width of the kerf and ensure that the two cuts between each triangle are the same dimension as the kerf, so that you will only need to make one cut between each piece.

Mark the triangles and then cut with a hand saw.

2 Alternatively, if you decide to use either a traditional miter box (see box on page 290), or a miter frame with your backsaw, make a stop that is fixed to the fence face that will enable each cut to produce a triangle to the required size. After the first cut, turn the wood over so that the new 45-degree corner fits into the stop. Be sure that the edge is hard against the fence face. Continue cutting to make the required number of pieces. Clean up the cut ends with a sharp block plane and/or 120-grit sandpaper wrapped around a sanding block. If planing, secure the end in a vice and plane with the grain. Check the edge for square

with a try square, and the miter with a miter square. Be careful to keep the pieces the same size.

3 On the other hand, if you are using a table saw, use the adjustable sliding fence and adjust precisely to 45 degrees. Make a wood fence that fits to it at least 1 in. (25 mm) high and fix with screws. Adjust the height of the saw blade to slightly more than the thickness of the wood and make a cut in the wood fence. Now make an extra piece that will fit to the fence to create a stop. Cut one end of this piece at 45 degrees and align it with the saw cut on the right-hand side. Fix in place with two 1-in. (25 mm) 6 gauge screws through the back of the fence.

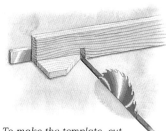

To make the template, cut a stop with a 45-degree corner and fix it to the fence.

4 When cutting the triangles, make a first cut and then turn the wood over and slide it

up to the stop. To make the next cut, hold the triangle carefully in place, passing the fence and wood right over the saw before removing the cut piece. Remove the cut piece from the fence. Slide the wood back from the cut line and return the fence to the starting position. To make the next piece, turn the wood over and cut as before. Continue to cut all the pieces you require for your stand. You will need 58 triangles for 29 CDs.

Drilling the holes

Again, the best way to drill the holes in both the triangles and acrylic sheet is to make a jig.

5 Make a base from scrap manufactured board—8 x 12 in. (200 x 300 mm). The base will be fixed to the table of the drill press or drill stand.

6 Make sure you mark the exact position of the drill center and the edges where the blocks will be fixed. With a pencil and try square, square a line across the width of the board in the center. Mark a parallel line on the face 1 in. (25 mm) in from the back edge of the board. Where these two lines meet, mark two 45-degree

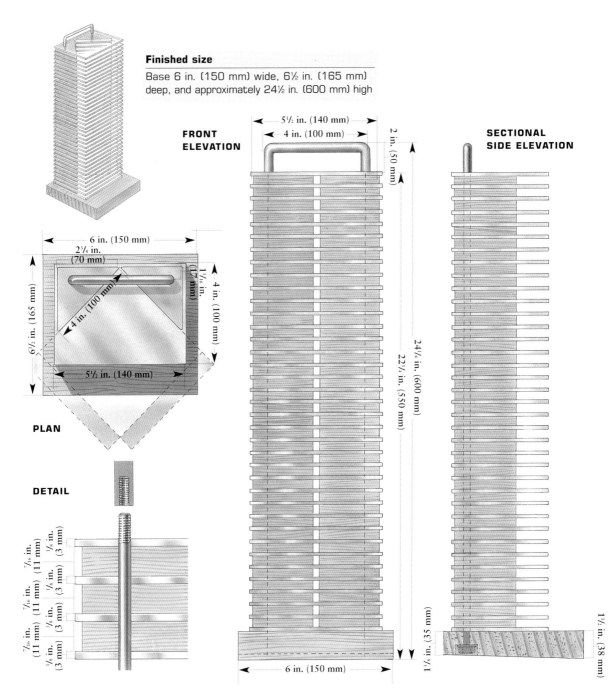

Finished size

Base 6 in. (150 mm) wide, 6½ in. (165 mm) deep, and approximately 24½ in. (600 mm) high

FRONT ELEVATION

5½ in. (140 mm)

4 in. (100 mm)

2 in. (50 mm)

SECTIONAL SIDE ELEVATION

6 in. (150 mm)

2¼ in. (70 mm)

1¹⁄₁₆ in. (17 mm)

4 in. (100 mm)

4 in. (100 mm)

6½ in. (165 mm)

5½ in. (140 mm)

PLAN

24¼ in. (600 mm)

22¼ in. (550 mm)

DETAIL

⅛ in. (3 mm)

⁷⁄₁₆ in. (11 mm)

⅛ in. (3 mm)

⁷⁄₁₆ in. (11 mm)

⅛ in. (3 mm)

⁷⁄₁₆ in. (11 mm)

⅛ in. (3 mm)

⁷⁄₁₆ in. (11 mm)

⅛ in. (3 mm)

6 in. (150 mm)

1⅜ in. (35 mm)

1½ in. (38 mm)

intermediate

Using a miter box

A traditional miter box is a simple wooden jig, which is used with a backsaw to cut square ends and miter joints. It has two raised sides with slots cut in each side. The backsaw is then placed in the slots, which guide the saw.

lines out to the front edge of the jig. These are the lines indicating the block positions.

7 Mark two lines parallel to and ¾ in. (20 mm) inside the first pair. The intersection of these two lines is where the hole will be drilled.

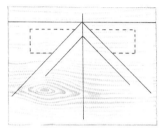

Mark out the jig for drilling holes in the triangles and acrylic.

8 Now make the two blocks from scrap that will form the fence. Make sure that the top edge is perfectly flat. Drill two ³⁄₁₆-in. (4 mm) holes through both blocks. Place one on each side of the first 45-degree lines and drill a ⅛-in. (3 mm) pilot hole into the baseboard through the block. Fix into place with 1-in. (25 mm) 6 gauge screws, ensuring the blocks are fitted precisely on the lines. The jig is made open at the back so that the waste can be removed easily between operations. If you do not make sure the waste is cleared after each drilling, particles will

probably keep the work from sitting precisely against the blocks—causing the hole to be drilled in the wrong place.

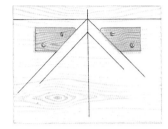

Fix the blocks to the jig.

9 Fix the base in place so that the drill is positioned exactly over its mark and clamp the jig to the drill table.

Fix the jig to the drill stand.

10 Place a ¼-in. (6 mm) dowel bit in the drill press. Adjust the depth stop and/or table height to drill a hole just into the baseboard of the jig. Test that the center of the bit lines up with the center mark on the base. Adjust as required. Hold the wood triangle firmly in position against the fence of the jig and drill the hole right through. Produce a clean cut and avoid breaking out the bottom face. Clean away any waste and repeat for each section of the job.

Drill holes in the wood triangles.

Making the acrylic dividers

11 Prepare the acrylic for the dividers. This usually comes with a protective paper layer on both faces. Do not remove this until you are ready to assemble the finished project. First, prepare the sheet of acrylic with one straight edge and saw strips 4 in. (100 mm) wide. When cutting acrylic sheets, use a wooden push stick on top of the sheet to hold it down firmly; it tends to jump as it passes the back edge of the saw. The waste particles from the cut may be statically charged, so wear a face mask. Hold against the rip fence and cut at a steady speed.

12 Next, set up the cross-cut fence on the saw to cut each strip into the required number of divisions (30), each 5½ in. (140 mm) long. To ensure the divisions are all the same size, set a stop on the right-hand side of the blade. This stop must not be past the leading edge of the blade; if it is, then the cut piece may twist and jam between the blade and the stop. It may also fly up and cause injury. Hold the strip down firmly and slide it across to the stop. Carefully push the strip forward to the blade to make the cut. Remove the cut division, slide the strip away from the blade and return the cross-cut fence to the starting position. Repeat the cutting process for all the acrylic divisions.

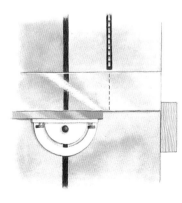

Set the stop on the right-hand side of the blade.

13 Next, drill holes in the acrylic. Since the wood sits slightly in from the acrylic, the drilling position needs to be adjusted (see drawing on page 289). Change the doweling bit in the drill press for a sharp ¼-in. (6 mm) twist bit. The drill speed must be quite fast (1500–2000 rpm). Hold the acrylic down firmly while drilling, or damage may result. Both holes are drilled on the long edge. Feed the acrylic sheets into the jig used for the wood. Drill the first hole and then turn through 90 degrees to drill the second hole.

Drill holes into the acrylic pieces.

14 Clean up the edges of the acrylic divisions by placing them in a vice and then sanding them with a 120-grit sandpaper. Finally, to produce a very fine, clean edge, you should resand with

400-grit wet-and-dry sandpaper and then finish with a 600-grit sandpaper. Remove the sharp edges with the finer paper once you have finished the edge.

Making the base

15 Cut and plane the base to the dimensions shown in the drawing on page 289—1⅝ in. (40 mm) thick 6½ in. (165 mm) long x 6 in. (150 mm) wide. Position the two holes by marking a line ½ in. (12 mm) in and parallel to the back edge. Lay a piece of predrilled acrylic on top so that the back edge lines up with the line. Be sure the acrylic is in the center and mark the hole position through the top onto the base. Drill a ¼-in. (6 mm) hole into the base. Then use a clean-cutting Forstner bit to drill a larger hole—approximately ½ in. (12 mm)—underneath, which will accept a washer and nut.

16 Now plane the taper on the bottom of the base. Pencil gauge a line ⁵⁄₁₆ in. (8 mm) up from the bottom. Join this line to the bottom front corner on each end of the base. Lay the face side down on the bench against a bench stop. Hold a smoothing plane at a slight angle to match the

taper, and plane the base to shape. Turn the base over when finished and lay it on a true flat surface to check for any twist. Adjust as required by planing.

Drill and shape the base and fit two nuts with washers into the bottom.

Making the handle

The handle used here is a proprietary version, the thread of which matches the metal rods into which the wood and acrylic pieces are threaded. Or you could make a wooden handle fitted to the top of the metal rods.

17 Cut and plane the handle to size—5½ in. (140 mm) long x 2 in. (50 mm) high x 1 in. (25 mm) thick. Using the drill press, drill a ¼-in. (6 mm) hole at each end through the width to match the holes in the acrylic divisions. These should be ½ in. (12 mm) in from each face.

18 On the face of the handle, drill a 1³⁄₁₆-in. (30 mm) hole—2 in. (50 mm) in from each end and in the center. The hole should be 1 in. (25 mm) down from the top edge. Again, drill this on the drill press with the hole saw. Hole saws can be used in either a power drill or a drill press. They are used to drill large size holes and are available in sets ranging from 1 to 3½ in. (25 to 90 mm). Interchangeable circular cutters fit into a collar, which in turn fits onto the drill bit. Cut between the 1³⁄₁₆-in. (30 mm) holes with a jigsaw to create a slot in the handle. Hold the handle firmly in a vice while cutting out the center.

19 Clean up the inside edges with a second-cut file if required, and finish it with 120-grit sandpaper. Plane a ³⁄₁₆ in. (5 mm) taper on the face in the same manner as for the rack base.

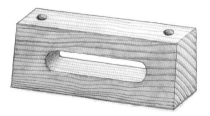

Make a wooden handle for the rack.

Assembly and finish

20 Cut the threaded rods to the correct length— 23 in. (585 mm) each. Place a nut on the rod before cutting to length. Once cut, remove the nut and this will clean the thread on the end of the cut. This can also be smoothed off with a second-cut file. Sand the base and the wood triangles with sandpaper to remove any marks and sharp edges.

21 All the wood pieces can now have a finish coat of lacquer or other finish of your choice. It is not recommended that you use an oil finish as this may find its way onto the CDs.

22 Fit the nuts and washers onto the bottom of the threaded rod and insert this into the base.

23 Now start the assembly of the CD rack by removing the protective cover from the acrylic. Place a piece of acrylic in position on the base and then fit two triangular blocks on the rods, Repeat this process until you have the required number of spaces for the CDs. In order to ensure that everything is straight, it may be necessary

to use some small pieces of double-sided tape when initially placing blocks onto the acrylic rectangles.

Slot the wood triangles and acrylic rectangles onto the threaded rod.

24 Now position the handle, fit the domed nuts and washers, and tighten the stack. If you are using a proprietary handle, the studding—threaded rod—will screw directly into it. Make sure that you purchase studding that will fit the handle chosen, and if necessary, change the diameter of the drilled holes to suit.

25 If you use your own wooden handle, fix the nut and washer onto the bottom of the threaded rod and insert this into the base. Then assemble the acrylic sheet and

wood triangles, finishing with the wooden handle, and top the whole assembly with nuts and washers.

26 If you are using a purchased metal or plastic handle, screw the studding into this first and then assemble the acrylic and spacers before applying the base, and the nuts and the washers.

Hanging the CD rack on the wall

If you want to hang your CD rack on the wall, the rear projection of the base will ensure the stack is held away from the vertical surface so that the CDs slope slightly toward the rear. Make a wooden support to attach to the wall with a groove into which the wooden handle can fit. Drill holes through the support for the screws.

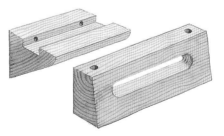

Make a wall support into which the wooden handle can fit.

Circular plant stand

The elegant curves on this plant stand are produced by turning the wood on a lathe. There are two main turning methods—faceplate turning and between-center turning. This project will give you a chance to practice both because the top and bottom of the plant stand are turned on a faceplate while the connecting spindles are turned between centers. The pieces are joined together with adhesive and clamped.

MATERIALS

Part	Materials and dimensions	No.
	Solid wood, preferably hardwood	
Round balks	10½ in. (260 mm) diameter x 2 in. (50 mm) thick	2
Spindles	12 in. (300 mm) long x 5½ in. (140 mm) diameter	2
Connecting piece	6 in. (150 mm) long x 2¾ in. (70 mm) diameter	1
Other materials: adhesive; sandpaper; finish.		

Tools

Bandsaw

Lathe with faceplate and between-center capacity

Full face shield

Set of turning tools

Smoothing plane or hand saw (optional)

Calipers

Three-jaw chuck

Lathe drill

Clamps

If you purchased your wood from a specialty supplier, it may be a slice of a log where the grain travels from face to face. If you purchased it from a lumberyard it is likely to have come from a sawed board and therefore the grain will run lengthwise along the board. In either case make sure the wood is free of splits and defects (see pages 26–8). Also see the section on turning (pages 215–20) before you start.

Wood balks with different grain directions.

Making the top and bottom

1 First, mark out the circumference of the top and bottom of the plant stand on each balk. Use a bandsaw to shape the wood to approximately ¼ in. (6 mm) bigger than this circumference.

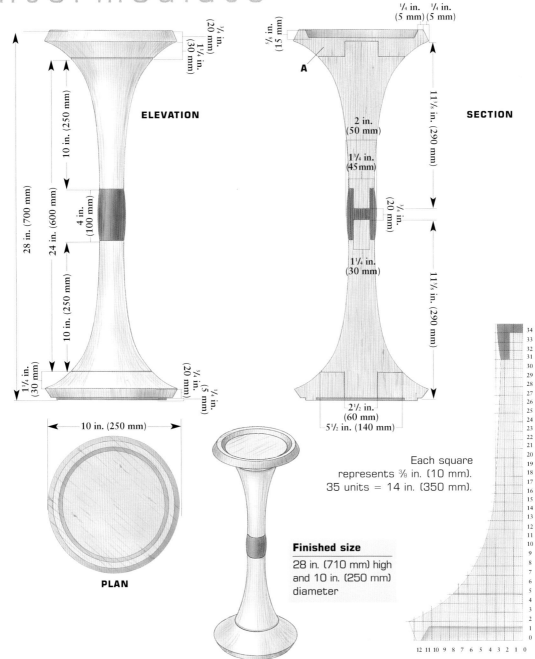

ELEVATION

¾ in. (20 mm)

1¼ in. (30 mm)

10 in. (250 mm)

4 in. (100 mm)

24 in. (600 mm)

28 in. (700 mm)

10 in. (250 mm)

1¼ in. (30 mm)

¾ in. (20 mm)

¼ in. (5 mm)

SECTION

¼ in. (5 mm)   ¼ in. (5 mm)

⅝ in. (15 mm)

A

2 in. (50 mm)

1¾ in. (45 mm)

11⅜ in. (290 mm)

¾ in. (20 mm)

1¼ in. (30 mm)

11⅜ in. (290 mm)

2½ in. (60 mm)

5½ in. (140 mm)

10 in. (250 mm)

PLAN

Each square represents ⅜ in. (10 mm). 35 units = 14 in. (350 mm).

Finished size

28 in. (710 mm) high and 10 in. (250 mm) diameter

2 To make the top, select the best face of one balk and screw it onto the faceplate. Remember you are going to make a rim ⅝ in. (15 mm) deep on top and so ensure the screws do not project into the wood beyond ½ in. (12 mm).

Fix the balk face to the faceplate.

3 Mount the faceplate on the machine and adjust the tool rest just under halfway from the center.

4 Ensure that the plate runs freely and make some marks to give you a guide to the curved base and the center hole that you will be turning. Making sure that you are wearing a full face shield for protection, start the lathe and begin your cut with the roughing gouge.

5 First, follow your markings to shape the end of the balk into what will become the joint with the spindle in step 18 (see drawing opposite). Turn a flat surface in order to produce the shoulder of the joint and then turn the large hole that will accept the spindles in the center.

6 Next, turn curve A (see section on drawing opposite), placing the tool rest at an angle across the corner of the piece as you work. Since the top and bottom are the same up to this stage, turn the bottom in the same way.

Turn the curve on the stand top.

7 Next, you will need to turn the outside face of the top and bottom sections of the stand. Begin by fixing the shoulder face of the top to the faceplate. Make sure that it is centered on the faceplate by checking that the overhang on the work is even all the way around. Screw into position and replace on the lathe.

8 Turn a small bevel on the outside edge of the top. Then carefully turn out the center recess, making sure that it is flat.

Turning

Wood turning began with the invention of the lathe in Egypt some time before the 13th century AD. It was practiced widely by the Egyptians, Assyrians, and Romans and also flourished throughout medieval England. Turned chairs with triangular seats were made of indigenous woods from Norman times through the 17th century with little change and turners were one of the earliest types of craftsmen. Before the end of the 16th century, turners had produced legs, posts, balusters, and spindles; turned decoration on furniture was widely used during the Renaissance period. Turners really came into their own in the 17th century when they began to produce graceful columns. From the 19th century onward, more complex spiral turnings appeared as a result of the development in turning tools. However, classic, simpler styles, such as bobbin and ball turnings, have also retained their popularity.

9 Take the top off the faceplate and fix the bottom of the plant stand in place. Turn a small bevel on the outside edge, a rim on the bottom surface, and a shallow recess, as shown below. It is better not to have a flat base because this may later distort.

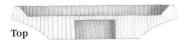

Top

Bottom

The finished shape of the top and bottom of the stand.

Making the spindles

This stand has been designed with two upright pieces with a joint in between, in case the lathe does not have the required length to turn the center spindle in one. If your lathe has the length capacity, you can turn the centre spindle as one. If your lathe will not accept a 5½ in. (140 mm) diameter, adjust the curve.

10 Mark the center at each end of one piece. Fix one end to the driving center in the headstock, with the other end held in the tailstock with a revolving center.

11 It can be helpful, if you have the equipment, to saw or plane the square into an octagon; this means less material to remove. It is possible, however, to turn from a square shape as long as you are very careful.

It is easiest to cut the spindle to an octagon shape before turning.

12 Adjust the tool rest, making sure that the revolving wood will not be in contact with it; very carefully start initial cuts that will remove corners and make the work cylindrical.

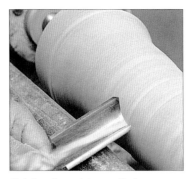

Cut the shape into a cylinder.

13 Make a template from the grid given with the drawing on page 296 so that you can measure off diameters needed at any stage easily.

14 Set the calipers to the thickest end and turn down to the correct diameter. Do the same at the thinner end. Turn along the full length until you achieve the required shape.

15 Both ends need to be turned down to fit into the holes—the thick end into the top or bottom of the stand and the thin end into the connecting piece. Repeat process on second piece.

The bottom half of the spindle.

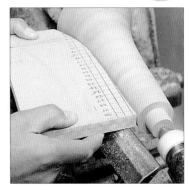

Ensure that you are cutting the right shape by using a template.

16 First, turn the connecting piece to a simple cylinder and then turn the shape of the outside.

Shape the connecting piece.

17 Hold the piece in a three-jaw chuck, and drill or turn the holes that will accept the spindles.

Assembly

18 The parts can now be assembled. Join the two spindles to the connecting piece, applying adhesive and then clamping. The top and bottom of the stand can now be fixed; glue and clamp these in place.

19 When the adhesive has cured, the whole piece can be sanded down and you can apply required finish.

The top lip ensures items are secure.

intermediate

Barstool

This is a good introductory project for combining metal with more traditional wood construction. The metal legs and wooden seat give the stool a pleasing look and are not difficult to achieve with careful measurement and cutting.

Tools

Protractor

Sliding bevel

Jigsaw

Chisel

Drill and ⁵⁄₁₆-in. (4.5 mm), ⅛-in. (3 mm), ¼-in. (6 mm), and countersunk bits

Hacksaw

Smoothing plane

Metal file

Screwdriver

MATERIALS

Part	Materials and dimensions	No.
	Solid wood	
Side and cross-rails	16 x 3 x ¾ in. (400 x 75 x 20 mm)	4
Slats	16 x 2 x ½ in. (400 x 50 x 12 mm)	11
Footrest	12 x 2 x 1½ in. (300 x 50 x 38 mm)	1
V-supports	20 x 2 x ¾ in. (500 x 50 x 20 mm)	2

Other materials: four 24 x 1-in. (600 x 25 mm) diameter steel tube legs; one 12 x 1-in. (300 x 25 mm) diameter cross-bar; two 16 x 1¼ x ⅛ in. (400 x 32 x 3 mm) flat bars; thirty-six 1½-in. (40 mm) 6 gauge brass flat head screws; four 1¼ x ¼ in. (32 x 6 mm) nuts and bolts; eight 2 x ¼ in. (50 x 6 mm) bolts plus barrel nuts; wooden dowels; sandpaper; adhesive; finish.

1 Make the basic seat unit. Mark out the two side rails. The sloping back is at an angle of 65 degrees; set this out with a protractor and sliding bevel. Measure along the bottom edge 13½ in. (335 mm) and mark a second beveled line at an angle of 85 degrees. Set out the curved shape on the top edge and cut with a jigsaw. Clean up edges with sandpaper.

2 Next, mark the front and back cross-rails, first cutting the mortises into which the side rails will fit and then the shaped ends that will receive the metal tube. Cut the shape with a jigsaw as per the drawing on the right and clean up the edges with sandpaper. Chisel from both sides.

Mark out the pattern and cut the two side rails.

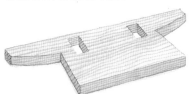

Mark and cut the front and back cross-rails, adding the mortises.

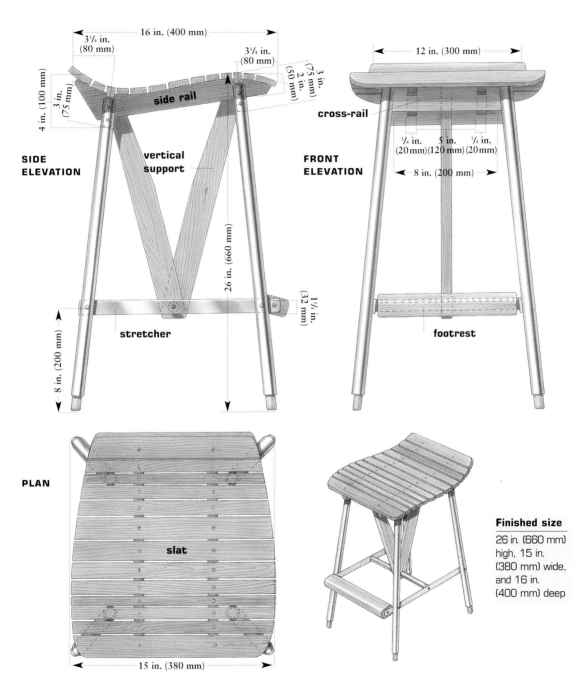

SIDE ELEVATION

16 in. (400 mm)

3¼ in. (80 mm)

3¼ in. (80 mm)

4 in. (100 mm)

3 in. (75 mm)

side rail

3 in. (75 mm)

2 in. (50 mm)

vertical support

26 in. (660 mm)

1¼ in. (32 mm)

stretcher

8 in. (200 mm)

FRONT ELEVATION

12 in. (300 mm)

cross-rail

¾ in. (20mm)

5 in. (120 mm)

¾ in. (20mm)

8 in. (200 mm)

footrest

PLAN

slat

15 in. (380 mm)

Finished size

26 in. (660 mm) high, 15 in. (380 mm) wide, and 16 in. (400 mm) deep

3 Insert the side rails through the mortises in the cross-rails. The mortises are cut so that the front of the side rail will pass through the rear mortises but each will notch into its place. Ensure that the frame is square.

Assemble the base of the seat.

4 Next, make the slats, which will go across the base to make the seat. Cut the 11 slats as shown in the drawing on page 301, rounding the ends of the front slat first and shaping the others to fit. Drill ³⁄₁₆-in. (4.5 mm) screw holes through the slats and then the ⅛-in. (3 mm) pilot hole in the side rail. Assemble the seat dry with flat head brass screws but no adhesive.

Position the slats on the side rails to make the seat.

Part-assembly of the seat.

5 Cut the metal legs to 24 in. (600 mm) with a hacksaw. Insert wooden dowels in the tubes to prevent the bolts crushing them. Drill holes in the top of each leg for the two fixing bolts. Mark from these onto the side of the cross-rails. Drill them for the bolts and barrel nuts.

Assemble the seat unit.

6 Next, turn your attention to the bottom half of the stool. Mark the holes for the stretchers in the lower legs 8 in. (200 mm) up and drill them, ensuring they are in line with the holes that fix the seat.

7 Cut two metal stretchers from the flat bar to 16 in. (400 mm) and round the ends with a file. Mark four holes in each as shown on the drawing on page 301 and drill them. Drill corresponding ¼-in. (6 mm) holes through the legs. Fix the stretchers in position and secure with nuts and bolts.

8 Cut the footrest to length and plane it to shape, ensuring that the angles are correct so that it fits between the two metal side rails.

Assemble the stretchers and footrest.

9 Make the cross-bar that goes across the middle between the two metal stretchers. Mark and cut the tube to fit—the ends will need to be angled to fit against the stretchers. Insert wood dowels in the ends of the tube and screw the cross-bar in place.

10 Next, glue the basic seat frame together, making sure that the components are located correctly. Screw the seat slats in position one by one and then bolt the top ends of the legs to the cross-rails.

Fix the legs to the seat unit.

11 With the stool upside down, bolt the stretchers to the legs and then screw into the footrest and cross-bar.

12 Next, make the feet. You can finish the metal legs with plastic caps on the tubes. Or, you can use leftover

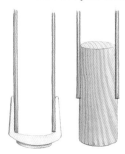

Use plastic leg caps or wood plugs to finish the feet.

wood to make plugs to fit inside the tube.

13 Place the stool upright on a flat surface. Using a pencil on a small block of wood, mark all around the bottom of the legs to show where to angle them at the base so that the stool sits on a flat surface.

Angle the feet so that the stool will sit on a flat surface.

14 Cut to these marks and then work a small bevel around the cut edge. Sand so the edges are not damaged.

15 To ensure that the structure is rigid, make the V-support between the cross-rails and the bottom cross-bar. The two supports are different, and so measure, mark, and label each individually. With the stool assembled, mark the top angle that will connect with the inside face of the cross-rails, and mark the position of the bottom cross-bar.

16 Drill a hole in the V-support to accommodate the cross-bar. Remove the cross-bar from the stool, position both supports and replace it. Check the angled faces against the inside faces of the cross-rails and adapt as necessary.

17 Next, mark the half lap joint between the two supports as they fit over the bar. Dismantle, cut the half laps and glue the supports together.

Assemble the V-support.

18 Clean up the supports and replace them and the cross-bar on the stool. Fix the angled faces to the inside faces of the seat cross-rails with adhesive and screws.

19 Disassemble, sand and finish all wood parts; then reassemble to complete.

Circular dining table

The circular dining table is made from solid wood and has an interesting structural pattern on the top, which is made with interlinking planks of wood. The table will seat four people with ease, but it can seat up to six. If you require additional seating places, then simply scale it up. It has been designed to match the dining chair on pages 375–83.

MATERIALS

Part	Materials and dimensions	No.
	Solid wood, species of your choice	
Legs	27½ x 2½ in. (695 x 60 mm) diameter	4
Top rails	24 x 3 x 1¼ in. (600 x 75 x 32 mm)	4
Lower cross-rails	37 x 3 x 1¼ in. (920 x 75 x 32 mm)	2
Top cross-rails	37 x 2 x 1¼ in. (920 x 75 x 32 mm)	2
Planks for solid top	18 x 3 x 1 in. (460 x 75 x 25 mm)	4
	15 x 3 x 1 in. (380 x 75 x 25 mm)	4
	14½ x 3 x 1 in. (370 x 75 x 25 mm)	4
	11½ x 3 x 1 in. (290 x 75 x 25 mm)	4
	11 x 3 x 1 in. (270 x 75 x 25 mm)	4
	8 x 3 x 1 in. (200 x 75 x 25 mm)	4
	9½ x 4¾ x 1 in. (240 x 120 x 25 mm)	4
	Ply strips	
Table top	36 x 36 x ¼ in. (900 x 900 x 6 mm)	1

Other materials: sixteen 2-in. (50 mm) 8 gauge flat head screws; masking tape; adhesive (PVA); sandpaper (120-grit); finish.

Tools

Smoothing plane

Marking gauge

Radial-arm saw

Mortise gauge

C-clamps

Drill and ⅜-in. (10 mm) bit

½-in. (12 mm) mortise and 1-in. (25 mm) bevel-edged chisel

Box square

Marking knife

Sash clamps

Tenon saw

Router with ³⁄₁₆-in. (5 mm) grooving bit

Straightedge

Jigsaw

Belt sander or spokeshave

Try plane or orbital sander

Making the underframe

1 First, prepare the four legs square. Plane the face side and face edge. Gauge and plane to width and thickness. Cut the four legs to length with the radial-arm saw.

2 Mark on the legs the length and position of the mortises for the top rails, which are fixed to the legs with stopped mortise-and-tenon joints. On one face, measure down 3 in. (75 mm)—the height of the top rail. Set out a mortise from this line. Measure back up 2 in. (50 mm) and square across the face of the leg. Set a mortise gauge to

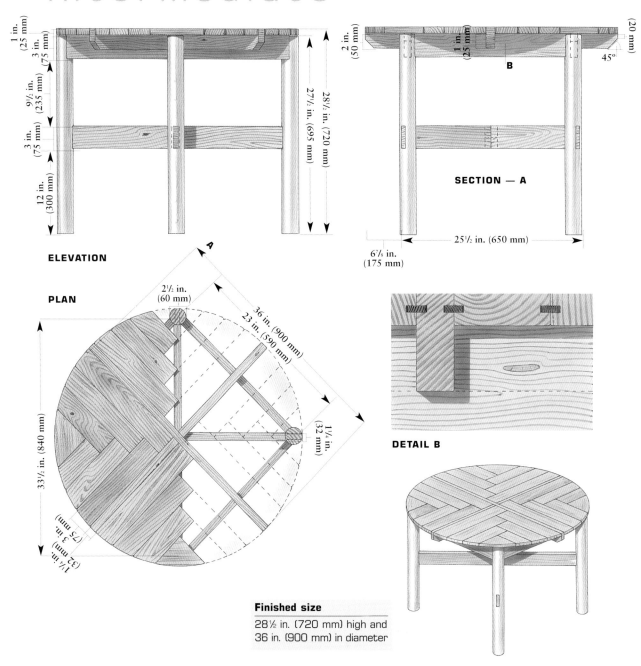

1 in.
(25 mm)

3 in.
(75 mm)

9½ in.
(235 mm)

3 in.
(75 mm)

12 in.
(300 mm)

28½ in. (720 mm)

27½ in. (695 mm)

ELEVATION

2 in.
(50 mm)

1 in.
(25 mm)

B

(20 mm)

45°

SECTION — A

25½ in. (650 mm)

6⅞ in.
(175 mm)

PLAN

A

2½ in.
(60 mm)

36 in. (900 mm)

23 in. (590 mm)

1¼ in.
(32 mm)

33½ in. (840 mm)

3 in. (75 mm)

1¼ in. (32 mm)

DETAIL B

Finished size

28½ in. (720 mm) high and
36 in. (900 mm) in diameter

scribe a mortise ½ in. (12 mm) wide between these lines. Transfer the lines around to the face edge to mark the mortise for the adjacent top rail.

3 Secure the work on a firm surface with a C-clamp. Use masking tape wrapped around the drill bit as a gauge for the depth and drill out the bulk of the waste with a ⅜-in. (10 mm) bit to a depth of 1³⁄₁₆ in. (30 mm). Keep within the set-out lines. Remove the waste with a ½-in. (12 mm) mortise chisel, working back toward the end. True up the sides with a 1-in. (25 mm) bevel-edged chisel. Repeat for the other mortise on the face edge. Mark and cut mortises on the other three legs.

4 It is easier to plane or turn the legs round if you first cut each square leg to an octagon shape. Set out an octagon on the end of one leg (see page 339). Pencil gauge the octagonal sides along the faces. Hold each leg firm in a vice and plane away all four corners to produce the octagonal legs.

5 It is best to cut out the mortise for the lower cross-rails at this stage before

making the legs round. Set out a mortise for the lower cross-rails on the face immediately between the two mortises that you cut in step 3. Measure up 12 in. (300 mm) from the bottom to set out the bottom of the mortise and then measure up 3 in. (75 mm)—the height of the rail—to mark the top of the mortise. Square a line across the leg ¼ in. (6 mm) high. Scribe the width (same as top cross-rails) with the mortise gauge. The lower cross-rails are fixed to the legs using mortise-and-tenon joints. Therefore, use a box square (see page 262) to set out around the leg to the opposite side so that you can drill and cut the mortise from both sides.

6 Now, make the legs round in shape. If turning, you will need a lathe with a long enough bed to accept the length needed; it may make turning easier if the mortises are temporarily filled with softwood plugs inserted dry. If planing, mark the final round on each end and carefully plane the octagon round. The pencil marks on the ends will give you a good guide as to how the rounding is proceeding. Repeat the process to make the other legs round.

7 Next, prepare the four top rails by marking shoulder lengths and the stopped tenons. Square a line around the rail 1³⁄₁₆ in. (30 mm) in from one end, another 21 in. (530 mm) along, and then 1³⁄₁₆ in. (30 mm) for the tenon. Cut to length on the radial-arm saw. Square the shoulder lines all around the first rail with a marking knife. Set up the mortise gauge to the width of the mortise—½ in. (12 mm)—and ⅜ in. (10 mm) in from each face. Scribe the tenon around the rail from shoulder to shoulder line. Hold vertically in a vice and cut down the sides of the tenon on the waste side to the shoulder lines.

8 Remove the rail and lay it flat against a bench hook and then cut away the waste at the shoulder set-outs. Replace the rail vertically in the vice. Pencil gauge the width of the tenon 2 in. (50 mm) in, and cut down the tenon to make the haunch. Remove the waste by cutting across the top edge between the shoulders. Remember to cut both the haunches on the top edge. Test the fit and adjust as required. Repeat for the other top rails.

9 Cut a miter on the ends of the tenons to allow both rails to penetrate the full depth of the mortise. Measure the diagonals to check for square. Clamp the four legs and top rails together with sash clamps.

10 Prepare the two lower cross-rails. Lay each in turn across the diagonals and mark the shoulder lengths for the mortise-and-tenon joints with the legs from the dry assembled frame to ensure that the lengths are exact. Square the shoulder lines around each rail and mark the through tenons by scribing along the length with the already-set mortise gauge. Measure the distance between the shoulders and square a line around each rail ⅝ in. (15 mm) either side of the center for the half lap joint. Use the marking gauge to scribe the center of the face between all these squared lines. Remember to gauge from the face edge on both pieces.

11 Hold each cross-rail in a vice and cut the tenons. Lay flat and cross-cut the shoulders as for the top rails. Place vertically in the vice and cut the tenon to width to suit the mortise at the bottom of the leg.

12 Cut the half lap joint in the center of both rails. Secure horizontally in a vice and cut down the shoulder lines to the required depth with a tenon saw. Remove from vice and secure flat on the bench with a C-clamp. Remove the waste with a 1-in. (25 mm) chisel. Take out most of the waste in one or two cuts from one side, and then work back to the lines from both sides. Check the fit and adjust. Repeat on the other rail.

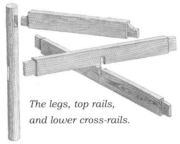

The legs, top rails, and lower cross-rails.

13 Assemble the whole underframe dry and check for square.

The dry assembled underframe.

Making the top cross-rails

14 Next, make the top cross-rails, which fit across the top of the top rails and form the main support for the tabletop planks. Prepare the cross-rails by marking them 36 in. (900 mm) long. Set out and cut the cross half lap joint in the center of this pair of rails in the same manner as the lower rails. The only difference is that these are 2 in. (50 mm) in width, and so the half lap will be 1 in. (25 mm). Assemble the two halves and check for square.

15 Next, measure and set out a 1³⁄₁₆ in. (30 mm) wide by 1 in. (25 mm) deep half lap in the center of each top rail. These should still be set up dry in the clamps. Position the two assembled cross-rails over these set-outs and make

Position the cross-rails over the assembled underframe and check for square.

sure they are square with an even overhang.

16 With a pencil, mark the top rail thickness on the underside of the assembled cross-rails. Square these marks up both faces at each end of the rails and use the marking gauge set at 1⁵⁄₁₆ in. (35 mm) to scribe the depth of the half laps from the top edge. The gauge can now scribe the depth of the half laps on the top rails ³⁄₈ in. (10 mm) deep. This will ensure the top of the cross-rails sits flush with the other planks of the tabletop. Cut the half laps as before.

Mark the thickness of the top rail on the assembled cross-rails.

17 Cut down ¾ in. (20 mm) at 45 degrees from the top at each end of the cross-rails using the radial-arm saw.

18 Next, make the stopped grooves along the top of the two cross-rails, which will accept the tongues when you fit the planks for the top. Set up a ⅜ x ³⁄₁₆-in. (10 x 5 mm) grooving bit in a router to run the groove ⅜ in. (10 mm) down from the top edge. Disassemble the cross-rails and secure on edge in a vice so that the groove can be run on half the rail.

19 Run the groove on the rail and stop 1³⁄₁₆ in. (30 mm) from the end. Turn around and repeat on the other end and then repeat on the other face and on the other cross-rail.

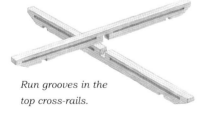

Run grooves in the top cross-rails.

20 Assemble the top cross-rails and place in position dry. Test all the work. If everything is satisfactory, disassemble, sand all the components with 120-grit sandpaper, and glue. Place in sash clamps and test for square and twist. Adjust the clamps as required to bring the frame true. Remove any excess adhesive with a damp cloth. When dry, remove any excess marks and apply a protective coat of finish.

Making the tabletop

21 Prepare the planks to the dimensions in the materials list. Take the four longest and rout grooves in the square ends and the sides from the face side to within 1³⁄₁₆ in. (30 mm) of the finished circular edge. Fit plywood tongues. Start to fit the planks into those rails as shown in the drawing on page 306.

Rout grooves in the tabletop planks and prepare plywood tongues.

22 Prepare and fit the other planks in order of descending length. The final segment over the top of the legs has the grain running parallel with the top edge, so cut four triangles and mark them up to fit. Rout the grooves, fit the tongues, and place in position.

Slot the final triangle into place.

23 Number each board for each quadrant. Remove them and apply adhesive to the groove, edge, and end of each board. Place back into position and tap each on the end to bring up tight. If required, use a sash clamp to pull up the joint. Remove excess adhesive and check for flatness with a straightedge. Allow to dry.

24 Mark the circular shape of the tabletop with a pencil by either making a compass from a thin strip of plywood, or by using a piece of cord with a small nail tacked in the center. Trim the planks to the mark with a jigsaw.

25 True the edge with a belt sander or spokeshave. Flush the top with a try plane or orbital sander. Sand the top and apply a finish of your choice.

Breakfast tray

This breakfast tray will enable you to practice a traditional method, veneering by hand. It is a tricky skill at first, but if you do make mistakes, you can put them right by reheating the adhesive and relaying the veneer.

MATERIALS

Part	Materials and dimensions	No.
	Manufactured board	
Base	20 x 15 x ¾ in. (500 x 370 x 20 mm)	1
	Solid wood	
Lips	20 x 1½ x 1 in. (500 x 40 x 25 mm)	2
	15 x 1½ x 1 in. (370 x 40 x 25 mm)	2
Handles	12 x 3 x 1 in. (300 x 75 x 25 mm)	2
Strips	16 x ⅝ x ⅜ in. (400 x 15 x 10 mm)	2
	Veneers	
Face	approximately 20 x 15 in. (500 x 400 mm)	1
Edge	the same species as the lips: 2½ in. (65 mm) wide	4
Underside	backing veneers required	1

Other materials: animal adhesive granules; glue pot and brush; adhesive (PVA); sandpaper; veneer tape; finish.

Tools

Smoothing plane
Miter square
Router with ¼-in. (6 mm) straight bit
Tenon saw
Sash clamps
Toothing plane
Veneer hammer
Veneer knife
Electric iron
Straightedge
C-clamp
Drill and 1-in. (25 mm) bit
Coping saw
1-in. (25 mm) bevel-edged chisel

1 First, prepare the lips for all four edges of the main tray section, which will give the final size of 19 x 14 in. (480 x 350 mm). Plane all the lips, but leave their width over the size of the base's thickness. Trim the base to size to allow for the lips. Using a miter square, mark miters on the ends of the lips so that they fit exactly.

2 The lips are joined to the base with tongues and grooves. Cut the grooves in lips and base to a depth of ¼ in. (6 mm) using a router with a ¼-in. (6 mm) straight bit. Cut the miters with a tenon saw and test the fit. Adjust the miters as required.

3 Glue the lips to the base, applying PVA adhesive to both surfaces, and placing the tongue in the groove. Position each lip carefully and hold it in place with sash clamps if required.

intermediate

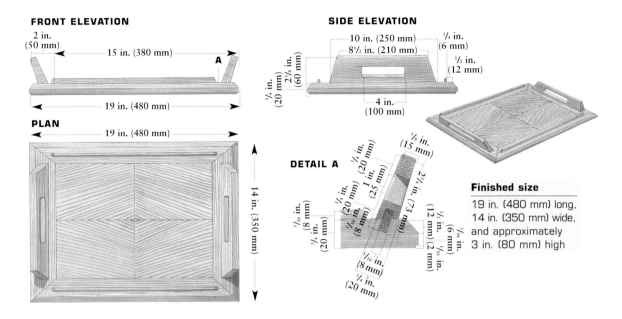

FRONT ELEVATION

2 in. (50 mm)

15 in. (380 mm)

A

19 in. (480 mm)

PLAN

19 in. (480 mm)

14 in. (350 mm)

SIDE ELEVATION

10 in. (250 mm)

8½ in. (210 mm)

¼ in. (6 mm)

½ in. (12 mm)

¾ in. (20 mm)

2⅜ in. (60 mm)

4 in. (100 mm)

DETAIL A

⅝ in. (15 mm)

¼ in. (20 mm)

1 in. (25 mm)

2¼ in. (73 mm)

⁵⁄₁₆ in. (8 mm)

¼ in. (20 mm)

¾ in. (20 mm)

¾ in. (8 mm)

½ in. (12 mm)

⁵⁄₁₆ in. (8 mm)

¹⁄₁₆ in. (2 mm)

¼ in. (20 mm)

Finished size

19 in. (480 mm) long,
14 in. (350 mm) wide,
and approximately
3 in. (80 mm) high

4 When the adhesive has cured, use a smoothing plane to plane the excess lip flush to the surface of both sides of the board, without rounding over. Key both surfaces with a toothing plane.

5 Since veneers can exert a pull on the face of a board, you must put a backing veneer on the underside. Cut one piece for the center and some strips for a border around the edge. Lay the pieces out, slightly overlapping each other and trim to fit, including the mitered corners where the borders meet.

6 Brush some slightly thinned animal adhesive onto the board's surface to act as a size, and then apply adhesive to the veneer. Lay the veneer in position, and using

Lay the backing veneer with the veneer hammer.

the veneer hammer, work from the center and squeeze out the excess adhesive and any air pockets.

7 If it is necessary to relay the veneer because of bubbles, the adhesive can be softened using an iron and damp cloth, and the veneer pushed down again with the veneer hammer. Tap the surface with a fingernail. You will hear if there are any areas that have not adhered.

8 Prepare the face veneers and board. Draw joint lines on the board where the pieces

of veneer will meet. Cut the four book-matched leaves the same size to give a total of 16 x 11 in. (400 x 280 mm). Set this out in place on the board over the joint lines.

9 Now lay the face veneers. Lay one of the four rectangles as described above. Then lay the second adjoining veneer with the edge to be joined overlapping the first. Using a sharp veneer knife and straightedge, cut through both veneers along the joint line. Soften the adhesive with the iron and remove the waste strips of veneer. Relay both so that the joint is perfect. Lay all four pieces in the same way. Slight movement is possible while the adhesive is wet.

Lay the first section of veneer with a veneer hammer.

10 The edge veneer can now be laid around the center. Trim the border and prepare the four edge veneers for application. Begin by laying one strip of veneer in position, trimming the corner to the lip but overlapping at the miter. Now lay the adjacent strip of veneer, overlap the corner, and using a sharp veneer knife and metal straightedge, cut the miter at the corner where they meet. Soften the adhesive using the method explained in step 7, remove the waste pieces and press down with the veneer hammer. Repeat on the other three corners and trim the veneers to the edge.

11 On the tray mark the position of the two long thin grooves for the side strips and the two angled grooves for the two handles. Cut these with a router. To run the angle grooves, use a C-clamp to clamp a ¾-in. (20 mm) thick block 1⅜ in. (40 mm) in from the end, parallel to the end. Use this fence to plunge cut the groove, and set the bit to protrude ⅞ in. (22 mm) from the baseplate. Steady the router and cut the groove 10 in. (250 mm) long and 2 in. (50 mm) in from each edge.

Use a router to cut the grooves.

12 Change the router bit and, using a fence, run the other two grooves ½ in. (12 mm) from the edge and ¼ in. (6 mm) wide to suit the side strips. These should be 11 in. (380 mm) long in the center and ¼ in. (6 mm) deep.

13 Plane the thin side strips to size, cut to length, and adjust them to fit the grooves.

Fit strips in the grooves.

14 Plane the material for the two handles, initially keeping the pieces square. Mark the handle hole

positions, drill a 1-in. (25 mm) hole in each end, and remove the waste from between the two holes with a coping saw. True up the edges with a chisel.

15 Mark and cut the tongues that will join the handles to the tray. Run a ⁵⁄₁₆-in. (8 mm) groove in the center bottom edge of each handle ⅝ in. (15 mm) deep.

16 To work the tapers, mark and plane the two angles on the faces, and then mark the ends; cut and plane. Plane the angle on the bottom ⁵⁄₁₆ in. (8 mm) on one side. Check the fit and adjust as required.

Mark and cut tongues and tapers on the handles.

17 Set up the router to run a small rabbet ¹⁄₁₆ x ¹⁄₁₆ in. (2 x 2 mm) on the bottom edge of the tray. There is also a bevel on the top of the tray. Mark this on all four sides and plane the rabbet.

18 Sand all components, glue the thin side strips in place and then the handles. Apply the required finish.

The handles and side strips are fixed to the tray with tongues and grooves.

Marquetry

This rich, decorative technique involves layering veneers in order to contrast light- and dark-colored woods to make a pictorial design. It was first developed in the 17th century in France, spread to the Low Countries, and from there to England by the 18th century. It was extremely popular until the 19th century and is still used today. Flowers and plants were popular subjects in marquetry in the late 17th century and the technique has often been combined with other forms of decoration, such as gilding. In the mid-18th century marquetry fans, shells, swags, pendant husks, and floral motifs were used on even the humblest pieces of furniture and panels of marquetry were put on more elaborate pieces. Engraved marquetry was introduced in the second half of the 18th century and consisted of cutting fine lines in the surface of veneers and filling them with a black composition.

advanced

Tools

Table saw

Router with ¼-in. (6 mm)
straight bit

C-clamps

Sash clamps

Electric iron (if applying veneer)

Second-cut file

Drill and ⅛-in. (3 mm) and
³⁄₁₆-in. (4.5 mm) bits

Screwdriver

Sanding block

Hacksaw

Additional tools for method two

Smoothing plane

Radial-arm saw

¼-in. (6 mm) dowel bit

Drill press or jig

Web clamps

Modular storage cubes

This storage system is flexible and expandable. Two alternative methods are outlined below: firstly, using preveneered MDF and secondly, using particleboard with lips. Be sure to check the sizes before you begin because you may need to alter them to suit your own storage needs.

MATERIALS

Part	Materials and dimensions	No.
Cube sides	**Manufactured board** – particleboard, plywood or MDF 8 x 4ft x ⅝ in. (2400 x 1200 x 16 mm)	1
Lips if required	**Solid wood** 71 x 1 x ⅝ in. (1800 x 25 x 16 mm)	1
Tongues for lips	**Plywood sheet** 18 x 18 x ¼ in. (450 x 450 x 6 mm)	1

Other materials: two 1³⁄₁₆-in. (30 mm) 8 gauge flat head screws per door; pegs; adhesive (PVA); masking tape; sandpaper (120-grit); ³⁄₁₆-in. (4.5 mm) diameter steel rod; finish (veneer, plastic, laminate, or paint).

The desired visual finish will affect the construction sequence. If you are using the first method, with preveneered board, then you do not need to use lips. If using the second method, with manufactured particleboard, you may need to attach lips to all four edges (unless you intend to use a painted finish).

The materials listed will make three basic cubes. The most common size for manufactured board is 8 x 4 ft. (2400 x 1200 mm), giving 18 squares, plus some extra for doors and

internal hardware, though more may be needed depending on your requirements.

If you use preveneered board, medium-density fiberboard (MDF) would be suitable. This can be bought cut-to-size. If all the edges are to be lipped, then you can use particleboard (chipboard), or plywood.

If you are cutting the board yourself, use a power saw and straight-edge, or a table saw. Cut the whole sheet to make three 16-in. (400 mm) wide strips. Cross-cut these to produce the squares.

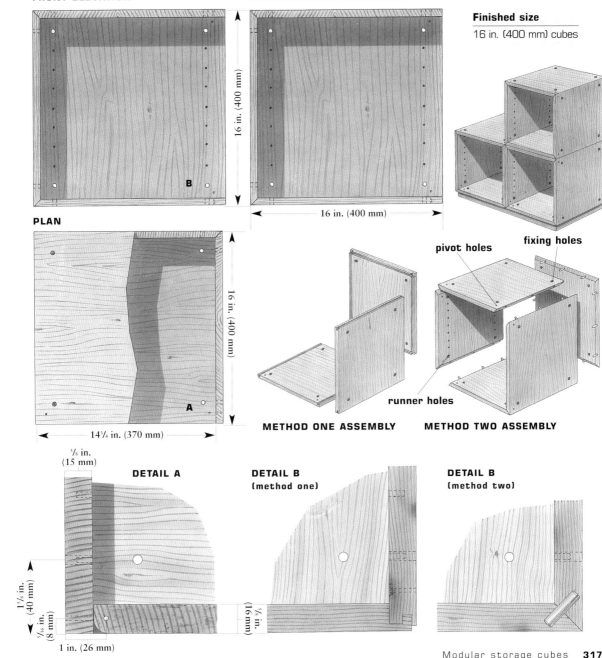

FRONT ELEVATION

SECTIONAL SIDE ELEVATION

Finished size

16 in. (400 mm) cubes

B

16 in. (400 mm)

16 in. (400 mm)

PLAN

16 in. (400 mm)

14¼ in. (370 mm)

A

fixing holes

pivot holes

runner holes

METHOD ONE ASSEMBLY

METHOD TWO ASSEMBLY

⅝ in. (15 mm)

DETAIL A

DETAIL B (method one)

DETAIL B (method two)

1⅝ in. (40 mm)

⅝ in. (16 mm)

⁵⁄₁₆ in. (8 mm)

1 in. (26 mm)

Method one: construction using preveneered MDF

This method uses a system of routed edges. Wear a face mask when working with MDF as the dust can be hazardous.

1 Cut the sheets precisely to size on a table saw. Ensure that all the parts for the four sides and the back of the cube are identical.

2 The edges of the panels are joined together with routed edges. There are two types of groove (shapes A and B), which fit together. All the edges of the back panel will be shape A. Each side panel will have two B edges and one A edge—remember to leave the front edges square.

3 To make shape A, remove the shaded area shown in the following diagram, either with a table saw or router. Then make the ¼-in. (6 mm) groove with a router—set this up so the base sits on the panel face and the fence runs along the edge. To make shape B, set the fence so that the groove is in the position shown—this time the router base needs to sit on the panel edge and the fence will run along the face.

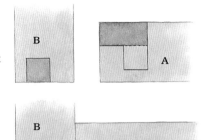

Cut grooves A and B to fit the edges together.

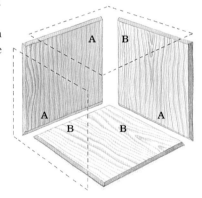

Cut the panels so that an A edge is always adjacent to a B edge—the back panel has four shape A grooves and each side panel has two shape B grooves and a shape A.

4 Before assembly, sand and finish all the internal faces of the panels. Glue the four side joints and place sash clamps along each side to pull the top and bottom up.

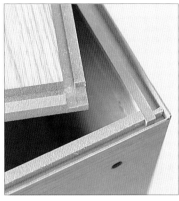

Glue the side joints together, before fitting the back panel.

5 Apply adhesive to the back panel and push it lightly down to close the joint. Additional clamps may be required if the joint does not close. Remove excess adhesive from around the joints and check the cube for square. Adjust as required.

Apply adhesive to the back panel and push lightly into place.

6 Since you are using preveneered board you will need to apply a matching veneer to the front surfaces. This is best done when the cube itself has been assembled. In this case, the veneers can be mitered at the corners. Use a preglued veneer and simply iron it on. This type of veneer has a heat-sensitive adhesive, which is similar to that used in hot glue guns. The preglued veneer has the adhesive on the back. Once the adhesive has been melted with the iron, apply an even pressure to the surface with a sanding block, rubbing over the veneer for a few seconds until the adhesive cools enough for it to fuse.

7 Clean off any overhang with a second-cut file, and sand smooth with 120-grit sandpaper.

8 Using this method, there will be a small rabbet on the four edges and around the back where a thin edge of veneer and MDF will show. You can apply a finish or, if you want, a small strip of wood can be glued into the rabbet. Alternatively, paint it black or another contrasting color. The first option is the method that

has been used to make the prototype as shown. The rabbet has been finished but left unfilled, since it creates a visual line between each cube when they are joined together.

Method two: construction using particleboard with lips

1 If using this method, attach lips to each of the edges that will make up the front face of the cube. Plane the solid wood lips perfectly square to a size just over the thickness of the board. It will be easier to leave these full length—71 in. (1800 mm)—or at least cut into two lengths of 35½ in. (900 mm) for planing.

2 When the lips are finished, cut the squares so that their dimension plus the width of the lip (where relevant) is slightly over the final measurement of 16 in. (400 mm) to allow for planing.

3 Hold each panel vertically in a vice and set up a router with a ¼-in. (6 mm) bit to a depth of ⅜ in. (10 mm). Use the fence as a guide and run the groove in the center of the front edge on four of the five pieces. Secure the edge lip onto the bench with a C-clamp and run a matching groove

along its length. Make a series of tongues by cutting plywood strips ⅝ in. (16 mm) wide and the same thickness as the groove—¼ in. (6 mm).

Make tongues to fit in the grooves in the lips and sides.

4 The lips will need to be mitered at the corners before they are glued to the sides. Cut these on a radial-arm saw for accuracy.

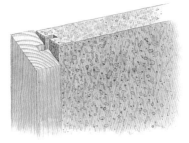

Miter the lips at the corners before fixing the joint.

5 Apply a little PVA to the face edge of the panel and edge lip, and carefully place a little into the groove. Insert the tongue into the groove and then position the lip. Align the long point of the miter with the end of the panel. Hold the lip in position with masking tape.

6 When completely dry, use a smoothing plane to plane the lip so that it is perfectly flat with the surface of the board. Take care not to roll the surface.

7 If you want a natural wood finish, a veneer can now be applied to both top and bottom surfaces. Use a veneer with a heat-sensitive adhesive. Simply iron it down to the surface and immediately follow the iron with a sanding block or roller to push the veneer down. Trim the edges with a second-cut file and sand the surface with 120-grit sandpaper.

Plane the lips flat and then apply veneer if required.

8 Five panels are needed for each cube. The front or open face edge of each cube will be the panels that have been lipped and left square. The other edges of each panel will need to be mitered to 45 degrees. The back will need to be mitered to 45 degrees on all four edges.

9 Hold each panel upright in a vice and gauge a line parallel to the short point of the already mitered lip (see step 4). Using a smoothing plane at a 45-degree angle, plane the edge down to the gauge line to produce the miter. Repeat on the opposite and back edges, leaving the lipped edge square. Plane the miter on all four edges of the back panel.

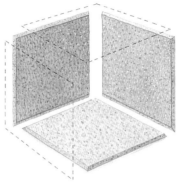

All the edges except the front four will be mitered to 45 degrees.

10 To aid in the assembly of the cubes, three locating dowels can be drilled into each miter. The dowels on the side miters need to be drilled at 90 degrees to the joint, while the dowels for the back are at 45 degrees to the joint. Position one dowel in the center and then two more dowels 2 in. (50 mm) in from each edge. Use a try square to mark these points along the edges. Mark the center of the dowel hole ¼ in. (6 mm) up from the inside face (the short side of the miter). Mark the holes on each miter face before you start to drill.

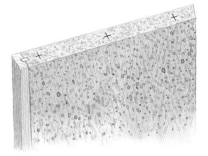

Mark the positions of the dowels.

11 Use a ¼-in. (6 mm) dowel bit to drill each hole ½ in. (12 mm) deep. Use a depth stop or masking tape to prevent drilling through the side. When the holes are drilled, place dowel centers in the holes. Position the corresponding panel in its correct alignment and push together. The dowel centers will mark the position of the holes on the other side of the joint.

12 Repeat this for all the joints around the side panels. The dowels in the back are set out the same. The only difference is the direction in which the holes are drilled; they must fit when the mitered edges are assembled.

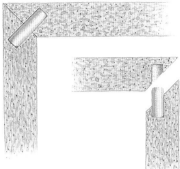

The corner joints.

13 Before assembly, sand all surfaces and apply finish to the internal faces. Cut the dowels to ¾-in. (20 mm) lengths. Dry test your work and adjust as required. Apply PVA to the miter joint and in the dowel holes, and insert the dowels in the side joints. Stand vertically on a flat surface and bring all four side panels together (see drawing on page 317). Position two web clamps around the work and apply just enough pressure to close the joints. Apply adhesive to the dowel holes and miters of the back panel. Lay the back panel in position on top of the cube and tap down lightly to close the joints. Roll the cube over to one side and close the back joint with the aid of sash clamps.

14 Remove excess adhesive and check the cube is square. Loosen or apply

pressure to the clamps to bring the work up true. If the back and sides were cut square and the job has no twist, it is true.

Whichever method you have followed, you should now have one completed cube. Make additional cubes as desired. The instructions for connecting the cubes together and fitting them out with doors, shelves, and drawers are the same.

Drilling the holes

Holes are needed to connect the cubes together, run drawers, or hold shelves. While you could just drill the holes needed for a particular application, here all the holes have been drilled so that the cubes are flexible and you can rearrange them at a later date.

1 Construct two jigs so that all the holes can be drilled in exactly the right position. On the first jig, there are four holes, one on each corner, which will hold the cubes together, and two small holes on each front edge, which can be used for door or flap pivots. Make the first jig out of a sheet of thin plywood exactly the size of the outer face of the cubes, marking up from the holes shown on the drawing on page 317.

Expert tip

Use blocks between the work and clamps to prevent any marking of the surface.

Making pivots with screws

The pivots are made from 1³⁄₁₆-in. (30 mm) 8 gauge screws. Mark a 45-degree line back from each corner where the pivots are required. Drill the ⅛-in. (3 mm) pilot holes and insert the two screws in the door or flap. Remove the screws, cut off the heads and cut another slot in the end in which a small screwdriver will fit. Place the door or flap in position with a washer in between. Use a screwdriver to insert the screws just below the surface of the cabinet.

2 The second jig is also made from a sheet of thin plywood, which will fit the inside face of the cube and has a line of smaller holes that will hold the shelves and drawer runners. These holes will be 1⅝ in. (40 mm) in and spaced to suit your requirements—for example, approximately 1³⁄₁₆ in. (30 mm) apart with a diameter of ³⁄₁₆ in. (4.5 mm).

3 Construct each jig and then position and drill the holes required.

Make two jigs for drilling the holes.

Making the doors/flaps, shelves, and drawers

4 Make the doors out of manufactured board, ensuring that they are lipped and finished to complement the cubes (see steps 1–7 on pages 319–20). Finish with a ¹⁄₁₆-in. (2 mm) clearance all around. The doors will fit the opening and be hinged on pivots (see page 321), which are inserted through two of the eight small holes near the front edge, so the doors can be left- or right-handed, and flaps to hinge down from the bottom or up from the top. Plane a small round on the pivot side so each door swings past the inside face.

5 Mini-wires—pieces of steel rod ³⁄₁₆ in. (4.5 mm) in diameter—hold the shelves in position. The legs are inserted into a pair of interior holes, while the projecting piece runs in a groove on the side edges of the shelf. Cut the rod to length with a hacksaw and bend each in a vice to fit the hole spacing. Cut the shelves with a table saw and edge the front. Hold with the side up in a vice. Set the router to run a groove for the rod in the center of the shelf. Stop the groove short of the front so it cannot be seen.

Fit pieces of steel wire to the inside of the cube to support the shelf.

Shelf components.

Insert rods in the holes and check the shelves for fit.

6 The drawer runners follow the same principle but are wood. They fit into grooves on the drawer sides and are held in place by the width of the drawer. The drawers are made from the same board, with dado joints in front and back, and the bottom grooved in. They have a barefaced tongue-and-groove joint on the sides. See pages 372–4 for more on making drawers.

The drawers are fixed with runners.

Folding chair

It is often useful to have extra chairs for unexpected visitors. This attractive chair takes up very little room when folded away and a set could even be mounted on a wall if you are short of space.

Tools

Miter square

Radial-arm saw

Drill and ⅛-in. (3 mm), ³⁄₁₆-in. (4.5 mm), ¼-in. (6 mm), ⅜-in. (10 mm) and countersink bits

Mortise gauge

C-clamp

½-in. (12 mm) and 1³⁄₁₆-in. (30 mm) chisel

Marking knife

Marking gauge

Tenon saw

Sash clamp

Wrench

Jigsaw

Smoothing plane

Second-cut file

Sanding block

Screwdriver

MATERIALS

Part	Materials and dimensions	No.
	Hardwood	
Legs	26 x 2 x ⅞ in. (650 x 50 x 22 mm)	4
Cross-rail	15 x 2⅜ x ⅞ in. (375 x 60 x 22 mm)	1
Hinge block	15 x 1½ x 1½ in. (375 x 40 x 40 mm)	1
Seat front rail	16½ x 2 x ⅞ in. (410 x 50 x 22 mm)	1
Grip rail	6 x ⅞ x ⅞ in. (150 x 20 x 22 mm)	2
	Plywood—⅜ in. (10 mm) thick	
Seat	16 in. (400 mm) square	1
Back	12½ x 14½ in. (316 x 370 mm)	1

Other materials: two ¼ x 2 in. (6 x 50 mm) domed nuts with bolts and washers; eight ½-in. (12 mm) 6 gauge nuts with countersunk bolts and washers; fourteen 1¼-in. (32 mm) 8 gauge flat head screws; four 1-in. (25 mm) 6 gauge flat head screws; two 2-in. (50 mm) 8 gauge round head screws; one 2-in. (50 mm) barrel bolt; two pairs of narrow butt hinges; adhesive (PVA); sandpaper (120-grit); finish.

Making the legs and cross-rail

1 Prepare the material for the four legs, face side, face edge, width, and thickness. There are two pairs of legs—the outside pair (A) and the inside pair (B). They need to be marked left- and right-handed (see drawing opposite).

2 Make the angles on the top and bottom of each leg. The first pair (A) are marked 24 in. (600 mm) long. Square a line around the leg at this length. Mark the center point across

the squared line at each end. From here, use a miter square and pencil to mark a 45-degree line back to the edge. Turn the miter square over and mark a second 45-degree line toward the opposite edge to create the point. Square this line around the edges. Repeat on both ends of the (A) legs. Cut these ends on the set-out lines (45 degrees) with a tenon saw. Set out the other pair of legs (B) 20½ in. (575 mm) long. Mark out the 45-degree points and cut as before.

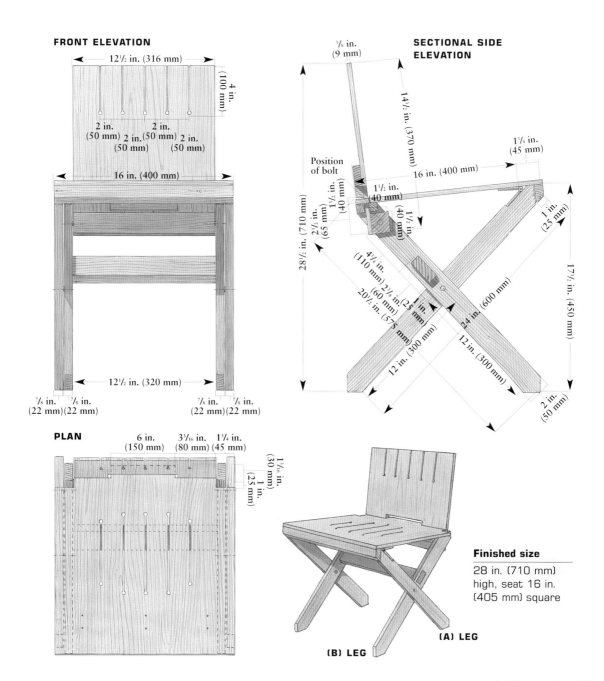

FRONT ELEVATION

12½ in. (316 mm)

4 in. (100 mm)

2 in. (50 mm) 2 in. (50 mm)

2 in. (50 mm) 2 in. (50 mm)

16 in. (400 mm)

12½ in. (320 mm)

⅞ in. (22 mm) ⅞ in. (22 mm)   ⅞ in. (22 mm) ⅞ in. (22 mm)

SECTIONAL SIDE ELEVATION

⅛ in. (9 mm)

14½ in. (370 mm)

1¾ in. (45 mm)

16 in. (400 mm)

Position of bolt

1½ in. (40 mm)

1½ in. (40 mm)

1 in. (25 mm)

28½ in. (710 mm)

2½ in. (65 mm)

4¼ in. (110 mm)

2⅜ in. (60 mm)

1 in. (25 mm)

20½ in. (575 mm)

12 in. (300 mm)

24 in. (600 mm)

17½ in. (450 mm)

12 in. (300 mm)

2 in. (50 mm)

PLAN

6 in. (150 mm) 3 1/16 in. (80 mm) 1¾ in. (45 mm)

1 3/16 in. (30 mm)

1 in. (25 mm)

Finished size

28 in. (710 mm) high, seat 16 in. (405 mm) square

(A) LEG

(B) LEG

3 Mark the positions toward the middle of the legs where they will cross and join. Measure up 12 in. (300 mm) from the bottom on all four legs. Square a line across the face and mark the center 1 in. (25 mm) in from the edge. Drill a ¼-in. (6 mm) hole through each leg at this location.

4 Mark the positions where the cross-rail will join the two (B) legs with through mortise-and-tenon joints. Lay the 20½-in. (575 mm) pair of legs side by side on a flat surface. Measure up 1 in. (25 mm) past the drilled hole, and then another 2⅜ in. (60 mm). Square a mortise line back in ⅛ in. (3 mm). Return this line around to the opposite side. Use a mortise gauge to scribe the width of the mortise ½ in. (12 mm) in the center face of each leg. Remember to gauge from the face side.

5 Secure the work on a firm, flat surface with a C-clamp. Take care to keep the sides of the mortise straight and square. Drill out the bulk of the waste in the mortise. Finish by working from both sides and paring back to the set-out lines at the ends with a ½-in. (12 mm) chisel, and a wider

1³⁄₁₆-in. (30 mm) chisel on the sides. Repeat on the other leg.

6 Next, cut the cross-rail to length—14¼ in. (360 mm). Measure in ¾ in. (20 mm) from each end. Square this around the wood with a marking knife. This is the shoulder line for the tenon. Set a marking gauge to ⅛ in. (3 mm) and scribe a line from the shoulder line on the face side back to the end, and then across the end and back down the other side to the opposite shoulder line. Repeat from face edge to face edge and then mark the tenon on the other end of the rail in the same way.

7 Stand the rail vertically in a vice and saw down on the waste side of the gauge lines to the shoulder line. Lay flat against a bench hook and cut the shoulders with a tenon saw. Clean the faces of the tenon with a sharp chisel. Test the fit and adjust as required.

8 Next, set out the pivot position where the (B) legs will be joined to the chair back. Set out a point in the center of each leg—another 4¼ in. (110 mm) up from the cross-rail. Drill a ³⁄₁₆-in. (4.5 mm) hole through each leg.

The two sets of legs and the cross-rail.

9 Apply adhesive to the tenons on the cross-rail and glue to the (B) legs. Place in a sash clamp and make sure that the frame is square. Wipe off the excess adhesive and allow to dry.

10 Join the legs together with the domed nuts and bolts. Tighten with a wrench, placing a washer each side and between the legs.

The completed underframe.

Making the seat

Make the seat initially as a separate component.

11 Cut the seat to the outside shape 16 x 16 in. (400 x 400 mm). In the two back corners mark the clearance cutouts 1¾ in. (45 mm) square across from the edges and 2³⁄₁₆ in. (55 mm) in from the back. Cut away the waste with a tenon saw or jigsaw. Mark a second cutout for the grip rail another 3³⁄₁₆ in. (80 mm) across and 1³⁄₁₆ in. (30 mm) wide. This will leave a 6 x 1³⁄₁₆-in. (150 x 30 mm) tongue on the underside of the seat. Mark the position of the front rail across the full width and the rear gripping rails 6 in. (150 mm) in the center of the back edge. Do not put the seat slits in yet.

12 Cut the front rail to match the width of the seat. Drill four holes of ³⁄₁₆ in. (4.5 mm) diameter across the front of the seat, making sure that they are evenly spaced and ³⁄₈ in. (10 mm) in from the edge. Countersink the top. Hold the rail in position and drill a ⅛-in. (3 mm) pilot hole through each clearance hole into the top edge of the rail. Apply the adhesive to the edge and fix in place

with 1¼-in. (32 mm) 8 gauge flat head screws. Turn the seat over and plane a 45-degree angle on the bottom edge of the front section to match the angle on the leg.

13 Cut two ⅞ x ⅞-in. (22 x 22 mm) grip rails 6 in. (150 mm) long. Fix the first rail 1¼ in. (32 mm) in, and the second rail should be flush with the back. Fix these in the same manner as for the front rail with three screws in each.

The components of the seat.

Making the back

Make the back initially as a separate component.

14 Cut the backboard 14½ in. (370 mm) high x 12½ in. (316 mm) wide. Use a try square and marking gauge to mark out the cutout for the tongue slot in the center 2½ in. (65 mm) up from the bottom edge, 1⁵⁄₁₆ in. (35 mm) high and

Ball and claw feet

These were widely used in European furniture in the late 17th and 18th centuries. The inspiration for them comes from China—the design is supposed to represent a three-clawed dragon holding a pearl but the Europeans replaced the dragon with an eagle. This type of chair foot is often found at the end of a cabriole leg and it is characteristic of early 18th-century furniture. The serpentine line found throughout this type of furniture runs through the chair back but is also seen in the legs right down to the feet. Ball and claw feet were extensively used by the French and English, who in turn influenced furniture makers from places such as Portugal and America. The latter created their own interpretation of the design, using more elongated feet. The foot design was not only used on chairs but can be seen on beds, cabinets, and desks from the period.

6 in. (150 mm) long. Hold firm on a flat surface with the set-out overhanging the surface. Drill a ⅜-in. (10 mm) hole through the back within the set-out. Place a jigsaw through the hole and cut around the set-out to remove the slot. Clean up all the edges with a second-cut file and then 120-grit sandpaper.

15 The back is fixed to the legs with a hinge block, 2½ x 1½ in. (65 x 40 mm). Fit it so it finishes flush with the outside edges and the bottom of the chair back. Glue and screw in place as you did with the front rail in step 12.

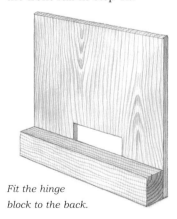

Fit the hinge block to the back.

16 Mark the diagonals on the ends of the hinge block and drill a ⅛-in. (3 mm) pilot hole in the middle where the lines meet. Hold the back

in position between the back legs with a washer separating them. Insert a 2-in. (50 mm) 8 gauge round-head screw with washer at each end of the assembly. Tighten with a screwdriver just enough to allow the hinging action to operate smoothly.

Fit the back to the legs.

Fitting the front hinges

17 The front hinges will be set in position as shown in the drawing on page 325: one half of the hinge will be screwed to the top of the (A) legs and the other leaf fitted to the bottom of the seat. Since there is not enough thickness for screws to be used through the seat, you will either need to rivet or bolt this section into place.

18 Chisel out the top of one leg to half the thickness of the hinge—approximately ⅛ in. (3 mm). Square a line across the edge of the leg 2³⁄₁₆ in. (55 mm) down from the end. Gauge back to the end of the leg ⅛ in. (3 mm) deep on both sides. Place several saw cuts with a tenon saw to the gauge line and carefully remove the waste with a chisel. Hold the leg in its upright position. Place the hinge in the recess and against the underneath of the seat. Mark through all the holes in the hinge leaf with a pencil. Fix one leaf to the leg with two 1-in. (25 mm) flat head screws. Drill the ³⁄₁₆-in. (4.5 mm) holes through the seat and fix the hinge with two ½-in. (12 mm) 6 gauge nuts and countersunk bolts with washers. Repeat the process on the other leg, once again fixing the hinge to both leg and seat.

Drill the hinge to the underside of the seat.

FOLDING SEQUENCE

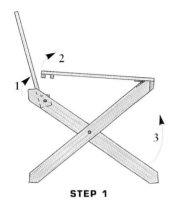

STEP 1

STEP 2

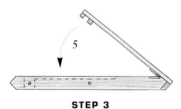

STEP 3

STEP 4

Assembly

19 Check that the whole chair system opens and closes as necessary.

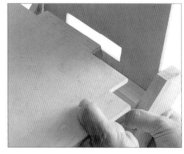

When the chair is up, the seat latches into the slot in the back.

Check that the chair folds and opens correctly.

20 Set up the chair in the open position. At this point there will be movement in the chair, so fix a barrel bolt to the underside of the seat in the center; the seat can then be bolted to the back when the chair is up. With the seat in the upright position, drill a hole through the inside grip rail, the plywood back, and into the outside grip rail. Extend the bolt and hold it in place; drill holes through the seat. Secure with nuts and bolt as for the hinges.

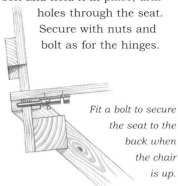

Fit a bolt to secure the seat to the back when the chair is up.

Finishing

21 Disassemble the chair. Sand the various components to remove any marks or sharp edges.

22 Cut the vertical slots in the back and the seat, if required. Drill a ⅜-in. (10 mm) hole, 4 in. (100 mm) down from the top, in the center of the back, then two more holes 2 in. (50 mm) apart toward each side. Cut a slot square down from the top to the center of each hole with a jigsaw. Clean up the edges with sandpaper. The slot in the seat can be cut in a similar manner. This will require a hole at each end of the slot, and a saw cut in between.

23 Apply a finish of your choice to the chair.

Single bed

This bed design offers an interesting use of wood in woven strips for the headboard and footboard. The dimensions given on the drawing on page 332 are to fit a standard, single-bed mattress, but since mattresses may vary slightly in size, you should double-check both the width and the length before you begin work to make sure that it will fit the bed properly.

MATERIALS

Part	Materials and dimensions	No.
	Solid wood: a light wood is preferable	
Headboard and footboard		
Legs	42 x 2⅜ in. (1050 x 60 mm) diameter	2
	34 x 2⅜ in. (850 x 60 mm) diameter	2
Cross-rails	36 x 1½ in. (900 x 40 mm) diameter	4
Dowels	32 x ½ in. (800 x 12 mm)	14
	2 x ⁵⁄₁₆ in. (50 x 8 mm)	8
Woven strips	34 x 2 x ⅛ in. (850 x 50 x 3 mm)	24
Head-to-foot components		
Bed rails	78¾ x 6 x 1³⁄₁₆ in. (2000 x 150 x 30 mm)	2
	or length to suit mattress	
Cleats	78¾ x 1½ in. (2000 x 40 mm) square	2
	or length to suit mattress	
Mattress support slats	35½ x 3 x ¾ in. (900 x 75 x 20 mm)	14

Other materials: four 4 x ⁵⁄₁₆-in. (100 x 8 mm) bolts with barrel nuts; twenty-eight 2-in. (50 mm) 8 gauge flat head screws; twenty-eight 1-in. (25 mm) 8 gauge flat head screws; adhesive (PVA); sandpaper (120-grit); finish.

Tools

Radial-arm saw

Brace and 1-in. (25 mm) auger drill bit

Lathe, if available

1-in. (25 mm) chisel

Router with ⅛-in. (3 mm) straight bit

C-clamp

Drill press and ½-in. (12 mm) bit

Drill and ⅛-in. (3 mm), ³⁄₁₆-in. (4.5 mm), and ½-in. (12 mm) bits, countersink bit, and ⁵⁄₁₆-in. (8 mm) dowel bit

Sash clamps

Box square

Tenon saw

Dowel centers

Screwdriver

Smoothing plane

Making the headboard and footboard frames

1 Prepare the cylindrical components (see box on page 335) for the head and footboard and then cut to length on a radial-arm saw. One pair of legs is 32 in. (800 mm) long and the second pair is 40 in. (1000 mm) long. The cross-rails joining the legs on the headboard and foot-board are 33 in. (840 mm) long.

2 Next, mark the positions of the holes in the legs, which will accommodate the cross-rails. The centers for the

Finished size
36 in. (900 mm) wide and
76 in. (1900 mm) long

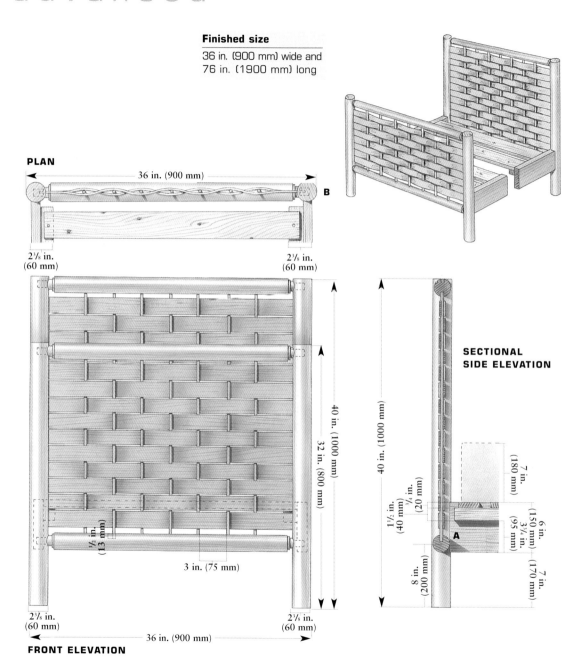

PLAN

36 in. (900 mm)

B

2³⁄₈ in.
(60 mm)

2³⁄₈ in.
(60 mm)

40 in. (1000 mm)

32 in. (800 mm)

**SECTIONAL
SIDE ELEVATION**

7 in.
(180 mm)

¼ in.
(20 mm)

6 in.
(150 mm)
3¾ in.
(95 mm)

1½ in.
(40 mm)

A

40 in. (1000 mm)

½ in.
(13 mm)

3 in. (75 mm)

8 in.
(200 mm)

7 in.
(170 mm)

2³⁄₈ in.
(60 mm)

2³⁄₈ in.
(60 mm)

36 in. (900 mm)

FRONT ELEVATION

PLAN AT B

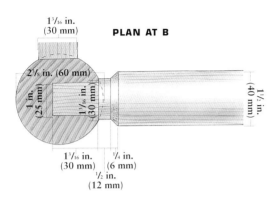

1³⁄₁₆ in.
(30 mm)

2³⁄₈ in. (60 mm)

1 in.
(25 mm)

1³⁄₁₆ in.
(30 mm)

1³⁄₁₆ in.
(30 mm)

¹⁄₄ in.
(6 mm)

¹⁄₂ in.
(12 mm)

1¹⁄₂ in.
(40 mm)

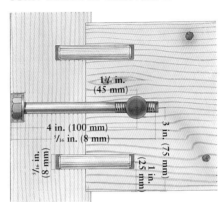

1³⁄₄ in.
(45 mm)

4 in. (100 mm)

⁵⁄₁₆ in. (8 mm)

3 in. (75 mm)

1 in.
(25 mm)

⁵⁄₁₆ in.
(8 mm)

bottom rails are 8 in. (200 mm) up from the bottom, and the centers for the top rail are 1³⁄₁₆ in. (20 mm) down from the top of each leg. Mark a line in the center of the legs so the holes will be in line. Hold each leg in a vice with the center line on top. Place a 1-in. (25 mm) auger drill bit in a hand brace. Position the drill bit on the set-out and drill the hole 1³⁄₁₆ in. (30 mm) deep. Care must be taken to drill the holes square. Check both ways as you drill. A depth stop or a piece of tape around the bit will help you to drill to the correct depth.

3 Next, turn the pegs at each end of the cross-rails. If you have a lathe, place each rail in the lathe and turn the ends down to 1 in. (25 mm) diameter and 1³⁄₁₆ in. (30 mm)

long. Shape the next ¹⁄₂ in. (12 mm) of the rail down to a 1³⁄₁₆ in. (30 mm) diameter and create a ¹⁄₄ in. (6 mm) chamfer back to the overall size (see detail B on drawing above). Follow all the safety procedures when operating a lathe. If you do not have a lathe, shape the ends by sawing around each shoulder line, then make the rounds with a chisel and smooth off with a file.

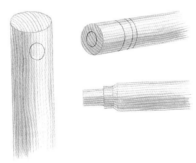

Mark and cut the joints in each leg and cross-rail.

4 Check each joint for fit and then dry assemble both end frames. Adjust as required.

5 Next, work the grooves on the inside faces of the legs, which will accept the woven wood strips. The groove is best cut with a plunge router. Make a jig from some scrap manufactured board for attaching to the router baseplate. Cut two guides for the jig—the same width as the diameter of the round leg. Fix the two guides to the baseboard so that the round section will fit neatly in between. Drill a hole through the top of the baseboard in the center, long enough for the bit to penetrate. Fix the router baseplate to the jig so that it lines up with the hole. Set a ¹⁄₈-in. (3 mm) straight bit to cut a groove ⁵⁄₈ in. (16 mm) deep.

6 Hold one leg down on a flat surface with a C-clamp. Make sure the previously drilled holes are directly on the top. The groove must run between these two holes. Position the router and jig over the leg so that the jig rests on the top edge. Following all the safety procedures for operation, start the router and plunge the cut to the correct depth. Move the router along the leg the required length between the holes. Continue routing until you achieve the required depth. Turn the router off and wait for the bit to stop before removing it. Repeat on the other three legs.

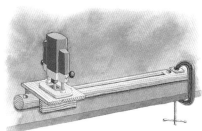

Make a jig to attach to the end of your router and then run a groove in each leg.

7 Next, mark the positions of the dowels in the cross-rails. Mark a straight line along their length with a pencil. Start with the center and measure out toward each end at 3-in. (75 mm) spacings along this line. There should be seven

holes in total. Place a ½-in. (12 mm) bit in a drill press and bore the holes at these set-outs to a depth of ½ in. (12 mm).

Rout grooves in the legs and holes in the cross-rails.

Weaving the wood strips

If you have your own machinery, you could saw the woven strips from larger pieces of wood and plane them on a combination plane. If you do not have the correct equipment, ask your lumberyard to see if they can do this for you. An alternative is to use ⅛-in. (3 mm) plywood as illustrated.

8 Dowels form the vertical lines of the cross-weave. Cut these to length to fit from the top to bottom cross-rail on each end frame, including the depth of the locating holes (1 in./25 mm each).

9 Insert the dowels into one of the cross-rails. Cut two strips of plywood to length

about 34 in. (850 mm) long and have a trial weaving of the strips. Remember to allow for the amount that will sit in the side grooves. Check the length and trim as required. Once the correct length is obtained, cut the remaining strips.

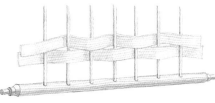

Try weaving the strips.

10 Glue the seven dowels in place between the two cross-rails and then place the rails into the legs, dry. When that adhesive has cured, glue and clamp one leg to the cross-rails with sash clamps. Put some adhesive in the groove and reweave the strips. Ensure they fit all the way into the groove.

Part assembly of the headboard.

11 Fit the second leg by placing the rails into the holes and the strips into the groove. Spread adhesive in the holes and groove in the second leg. Locate the pegs in the holes and the strips in the groove before final clamping. Repeat on the other end frame.

Fully assembled headboard with woven wood strips.

Making the bed rails and cleats

The main structural supports for the bed are the two large bed rails that connect the headboard and footboard. The bed rails are attached to the legs with two dowels and a bolt (see detail A on the drawing on page 333). On the inside of these are square cleats that support the mattress slats.

12 Prepare the two rails and mark the length. To be sure the holes connecting the bed rails and legs are the correct size, you will need to have the bolt and barrel nut at hand. On the inside face of each leg, cut a small flat to allow the end of the bed rail to sit flat. Measure up 6¾ in. (170 mm) and 12⅝ in. (320 mm) from the bottom. Square these lines across the leg with a box square and pencil. Mark two lines along the leg 1³⁄₁₆ in. (30 mm) apart, ensuring they are in the center of the leg. Cut across the top and bottom lines with a tenon saw to a depth of ³⁄₁₆ in. (4 mm), and pare away the surface with a 1-in. (25 mm) chisel to produce a flat surface.

13 In the end of the bed rails, set out the dowel location 1 in. (25 mm) from each edge on the center line. Drill the holes 1 in. (25 mm) deep with an ⁵⁄₁₆-in. (8 mm) dowel bit. Insert a pair of dowels and bring the joint together. The centers will mark the correct location for the matching holes in the leg. Bring the dowels to the leg and mark the positions. Drill the holes for the dowels 1 in. (25 mm) deep.

Making round shapes

The head and footboard both use round wood. You may be able to purchase this, but if it is not available you will need to make it. One option is to turn the wood on a lathe, but the components are quite long. Another way of producing cylindrical material is to plane from square.

To use the latter method, set out an octagon on the ends (see page 339) and mark a parallel line down each edge for the corners of the octagon. Plane the bevel edges, then shape to a round by removing the remaining corners. Finish with sandpaper to produce a smooth round.

14 On the outside of the leg 9 in. (225 mm) up, drill a ⁵⁄₁₆ in. (8 mm) diameter hole through the leg for the bolt. Hold the bed rail in place and place the drill back in the bolthole to mark the position on the end of the rail. Remove the leg and drill the hole in the rail to a depth of 2⅜ in. (60 mm). Mark the barrel nut hole on the inside face 3 in. (75 mm) up from the bottom edge and 1¾ in. (45 mm) in from the end. Drill a ½-in. (12 mm) hole ¾ in. (20 mm) deep to accept the nut. On the outside of the leg, counterbore the bolt head, if required.

Drill holes in the bed rails for the bolt and nut.

15 Next, mark the location of the cleats on the inside face of the bed rails. Scribe a line parallel to the top edge, ¾ in. (20 mm) down. Cut two 1½ x 1½ in. (40 x 40 mm) cleats ¾ in. (20 mm) shorter than the length of the bed rails. Fix in place—⅜ in. (10 mm) in from each end with 2-in. (50 mm) 8 gauge flat head

screws at 6-in. (150 mm) spacings. In the center of the cleat drill a ³⁄₁₆-in. (4.5 mm) countersunk hole. Apply adhesive, hold in position and drill ⅛-in. (3 mm) pilot holes. Insert the screws and tighten.

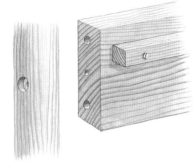

Fix the cleat in place on the inside face of the bed rail.

Assembly

16 Assemble the two bed rails on the head and footboards with locating dowels. Put the ⁵⁄₁₆-in. (8 mm)

Secure the barrel nut and screw.

bolt in its hole. Secure the barrel nut in its hole, and the screw, so that the joint is brought up tight. Repeat on the other three corners.

17 Cut 14 slats to length to fit between the bed rails on the cleats. Drill a ³⁄₁₆-in. (4.5 mm) hole, countersunk at each end of the slats. Remove any sharp edges by using a smoothing plane and then sandpaper.

18 Place each slat in position—space them evenly along the bed. Drill the ⅛-in. (3 mm) pilot holes through the slats into the cleats and fix with 1-in. (25 mm) 8 gauge screws.

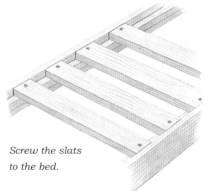

Screw the slats to the bed.

19 Disassemble the bed then and apply your chosen finish to it before final assembly.

Octagonal birdhouse

This design has been sized for small garden birds. It has individual compartments and stands on its own central support. The base is attached with dowels that can be removed for cleaning purposes.

Tools

Try plane

Pair of compasses

Marking gauge

1-in. (25 mm) chisel

Hand saw or power saw

Smoothing plane

Hammer

Nail punch

Pillar drill with ¼-in. (6 mm) and 1³⁄₁₆-in. (30 mm) drill bits

Hole saw

Jigsaw or coping saw

Sliding bevel

MATERIALS

Part	Materials and dimensions	No.
Support pole	**Softwood** or **hardwood** (exterior grade) 6 ft. x 1⅝ in. (1800 x 40 mm) or adjust to suit requirements	1
	Plywood (exterior grade)	
Roof	10 x 4 x ¼ in. (250 x 100 x 6 mm)	8
Walls	4³⁄₁₆ x 4 x ¼ in. (105 x 100 x 6 mm)	8
Internal partitions	10 x 4 x ⅜ in. (250 x 100 x 10 mm)	8
Base	8 x 8 x ½ in. (200 x 200 x 12 mm)	1

Other materials: eight 3 x ¼-in. (75 x 6 mm) diameter dowels; ¾-in. (20 mm) panel pins (exterior grade); adhesive (exterior grade); masking tape; sandpaper (120-grit); finish (exterior grade).

PLAN

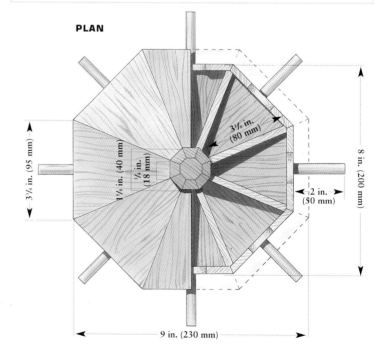

3¾ in. (95 mm)

1⅝ in. (40 mm)

¾ in. (18 mm)

3⅛ in. (80 mm)

8 in. (200 mm)

2 in. (50 mm)

9 in. (230 mm)

1 With the try plane, plane the upright support pole to 1⅝ in. (40 mm) square. Then, mark out an octagon on one end of the pole. Draw diagonals from corner to corner. To find the equal 45-degree lines across the corners, place the point of a pair of compasses on one of the corners, and rotate from the center point to the outside edge. Mark a line across the corner to the opposite edge. Repeat the measuring to mark 45-degree lines across the other corners. Set a marking gauge and scribe the points along the pole.

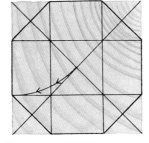

Setting out an octagon.

2 Secure the timber on a flat surface or in a vice and plane the octagon to shape with the try plane. At each point of the octagon, plane a ⅜-in. (10 mm) flat edge, along 12 in. (300 mm) from the top. Finish the bottom of this flat-edged length of pole with a chisel to give a square-stopped end.

Plane flat edges at each point of the octagon.

Finished size

11 in. (280 mm) high with 9-in. (230 mm) base, plus post height to suit

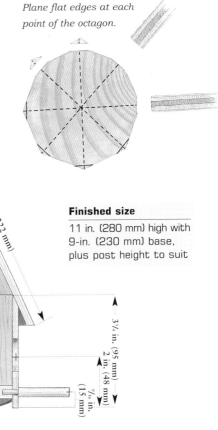

SIDE ELEVATION

1⅝ in. (40 mm)

1¼ in. (30 mm)

8 in. (200 mm)

8¾ in. (222 mm)

3 in. (75 mm)

½ in. (12 mm)

¼ in. (6 mm)

⁹⁄₁₆ in. (15 mm)

1³⁄₁₆ in. (30 mm)

3¾ in. (95 mm)

2 in. (48 mm)

⁷⁄₁₆ in. (15 mm)

3 Cut the internal partitions to 9⅝ in. (245 mm) long by 3⅛ in. (80 mm) wide. Taper the top by measuring up 3⅜ in. (85 mm) along the outside edge; draw a line up to the top of the opposite edge. Use a hand saw or power saw and true the edges with a smoothing plane.

4 Plane a bevel along the side and top edges and taper to 22.5 degrees off each face. This is best set out with a sliding bevel. Mark the bevel on the top edge and pencil gauge a line along the inside face to represent the amount to be removed. Hold on edge in a vice and plane to the line. Check with the bevel as you go.

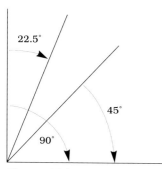

22.5°

45°

90°

Bisect a 45-degree angle to produce a 22.5-degree angle.

5 Use adhesive to position the partitions on the small flat edges of the support pole with the bottom of each resting

on the 12-in. (300 mm) stopped end. Secure them in place with ¾-in. (20 mm) panel pins. To prevent movement while the adhesive dries, wrap masking tape around the outside, ensuring the partitions are still evenly spaced.

Fix the internal partitions.

6 Cut the eight walls to 3⅜ in. (85 mm) wide and 4⅛ in. (105 mm) long. Measure the positions of the two holes in each wall at ⁹⁄₁₆ in. (15 mm) and 2 in. (48 mm) up from the middle of the bottom. Mark these and use a pillar drill to drill the ¼-in. (6 mm) bottom hole. Use a 1³⁄₁₆-in. (30 mm) hole saw to make the top hole.

7 Next, bevel the side edges of each wall to 22.5 degrees (see step 4). Plane one wall and then fit the rest individually by measuring them against the finished edge of the first.

8 In contrast, the bottom edge of each wall is slightly curved. Mark a pencil line along the length in the center of each wall. Measure up 2³⁄₁₆ in. (54.5 mm) from the bottom. Place the point of a pair of compasses on this spot and scribe the curve along the bottom edge. Cut this curve with a jigsaw or coping saw, and smooth with 120-grit abrasive paper.

Make the eight walls.

9 Next, mark and cut the base. Set out the octagon in the center of an 8-in. (200 mm) square board. Drill and chisel the octagonal hole for the upright from both sides. Slide this up the pole from the bottom and mark the point at which it meets the outside edge of the partitions. Remove from the upright. Adjust the shape with a hand or power saw. Test fit and adjust as required.

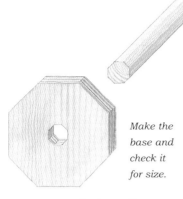

Make the base and check it for size.

10 Next, fit the walls to the partitions. Lay one wall piece on top of its two partitions so that the beveled edges of each match up. Plane to fit if necessary and fix in place with adhesive and pins.

Fit the walls to the partitions.

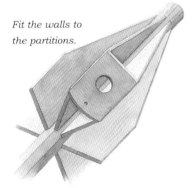

11 With the structure lying flat, plane the bevel at the top of each wall to match the bevel on top of the partition. Make the eight roof sections in the same way as the walls in step 6. Cut the basic pieces to 8⅞ x 3¾ in. (225 x 95 mm) and plane an angled bevel on the top of each section so that it will sit against the upright pole.

12 Position one of the roof sections on top of its wall and two partitions. Check the fit at the top and adjust the bevel as required. Mark the tapering sides on the underneath by tracing along the right-hand partition with a pencil. Cut and plane the bevel on this right-hand edge only. Repeat this on a second roof section but bevel the left-hand edge. Lay the two sections together in their adjacent locations and test their fit against one another. Plane and adjust as required.

13 Once a neat fit has been obtained, set the sliding bevel to the edge. Mark the width at the top and bottom of the first section. Hold the timber in the vice and plane it to match the sliding bevel. Fix that completed roof section in place with adhesive and pins.

14 Place the second section in position and mark it out. Plane to shape, but do not fix this yet as it will be used for a template for the remaining pieces.

15 Trace the shape of the second roof section onto the remaining pieces of timber. Cut these to shape, making

sure that they are slightly oversized. Plane the bevel on all the right-hand edges. Working counterclockwise, position each in turn, and check and mark the width, top and bottom. Plane the bevel along this edge to suit the sliding bevel and then fix as before. The last section may need a little extra fitting before you fix it in place.

Make and fit the roof sections.

16 The base of the birdhouse is held in position by dowels. Cut them to 3 x ¼ in. (75 x 6 mm). Put the base in position and drill through the ¼-in. (6 mm) hole in each wall. Drill 1 in. (25 mm) into the edge of each face of the base. Fix the base in place with the dowels. The dowels can be removed and the base taken away for cleaning.

Side view of the dowels.

Insert the dowels to hold the base in position.

17 Plane a ⅜-in. (10 mm) chamfer around the top of the upright support pole. Sand all the surfaces to remove any set-out lines and marks that may be left, and apply an exterior finish to all the outside faces. Leave the inside of the birdhouse in natural wood.

The finished birdhouse.

Easy chair

The attractive curves on this stylish chair are achieved in two ways: the curved seat is made by sawing from solid wood, while the curved back is made by laminating thin wood strips. Even though the design looks complex, it is relatively easy to make.

MATERIALS

Part	Materials and dimensions	No.
	Solid wood, species to suit—English ash was used here	
Rear legs	28 x 2 in. (700 x 50 mm) diameter	2
Front legs	21 x 2 in. (520 x 50 mm) diameter	2
Side rails	25 x 4 x 1¼ in. (640 x 100 x 30 mm)	2
Front rail	23 x 3 x 1 in. (580 x 75 x 25 mm)	1
Top back rail	22 x 3 x 2⅜ in. (550 x 75 x 60 mm)	1
Lower back rail	23 x 3 x 2⅜ in. (580 x 75 x 60 mm)	1
Button fixings	16 x 1 x ¾ in. (400 x 25 x 20 mm) to make 11	1
Seat slats	21 x 6 x 2⅜ in. (540 x 150 x 60 mm)	1
Dowel rod	24 x ¾ in. (600 x 20 mm) diameter	2
Dowel	12 x ¾ in. (300 x 20 mm) diameter	1
	12 x ¼ in. (300 x 6 mm) diameter	1
	Constructional veneer	
Curved back slats	30 x 3 x ⅛ in. (750 x 70 x 3 mm)	20
	Sawn softwood	
Jig for back slats	28 x 5 x 3 in. (700 x 120 x 70 mm)	1

Other materials: twenty 1³⁄₁₆-in. (30 mm) 8-gauge brass flat head screws; twelve 1³⁄₁₆-in. (30 mm) 8-gauge steel flat head screws; twelve 3½ in. (90 mm) with ¼-in. (6 mm) threaded studding; four ¼-in. (6 mm) thread T-nuts; four ¼-in. (6 mm) thread hex key head nuts; two 35½ x 2⅜-in. (900 x 60 mm) leather straps; four 36 x 2½ x ³⁄₁₆-in. (900 x 65 x 4 mm) belts or saddle leathers; adhesive (urea-formaldehyde and PVA); sandpaper (120-grit); finish of your choice (Danish oil was used here).

Tools

Pair of compasses

Box square

Mortise or marking gauge

Drill and ⅛-in. (3 mm), ³⁄₁₆-in. (4.5 mm), ¼-in. (6 mm), ⁵⁄₁₆-in. (8 mm) bits and ¾-in. (20 mm) clean-cut auger bits

⅜-in. (10 mm) mortise and 1-in. (25 mm) paring chisel

C-clamps

Tenon saw

39-in. (1 m) steel rule or straightedge

Bandsaw or jigsaw

Round-face spokeshave

Sanding block

Smoothing plane

Bradawl

Screwdriver

Sash clamps

Hex key

The project suggests using constructional veneer, which your lumber merchant may be able to supply. If you do decide to use it, you will need to use the same species for all the other components. If constructional veneer is not available, you can cut the strips from solid wood, but you will need a fairly powerful circular saw, or your local lumberyard may saw the strips for you. Whichever your source, you will need to plane the sawn strips on a machine thicknesser.

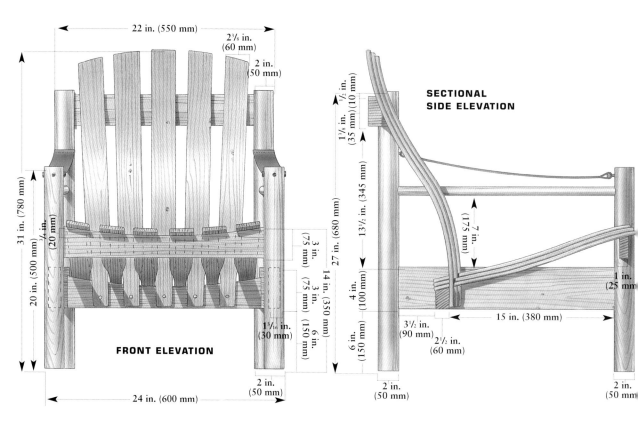

22 in. (550 mm)

2³⁄₈ in. (60 mm)

2 in. (50 mm)

½ in. (10 mm)

1³⁄₈ in. (35 mm)

13½ in. (345 mm)

SECTIONAL SIDE ELEVATION

31 in. (780 mm)

20 in. (500 mm)

¾ in. (20 mm)

3 in. (75 mm)

3 in. (75 mm)

27 in. (680 mm)

14 in. (350 mm)

4 in. (100 mm)

7 in. (175 mm)

1³⁄₁₆ in. (30 mm)

6 in. (150 mm)

FRONT ELEVATION

9 in. (150 mm)

3½ in. (90 mm)

2½ in. (60 mm)

15 in. (380 mm)

1 in. (25 mm)

2 in. (50 mm)

24 in. (600 mm)

2 in. (50 mm)

2 in. (50 mm)

When making the back laminations, a very strong adhesive, such as urea-formaldehyde, which resists creep between the laminate faces, is necessary. PVA can be used on the rest of the chair.

Making the basic frame

The legs are cylindrical in shape. First, plane the legs to an octagonal shape. It is best to leave them as octagons until final assembly as you will need to cramp the frame dry several times during the working process and you will avoid damaging the final surface by working with the flat octagonal edges.

1 Plane the wood for the four legs to an octagonal section by marking the octagon on the end of the legs and pencil gauging a line along each face (see page 339). Use a try plane to remove each corner to the gauged line and mark out the length of the legs.

2 Mark the final circular shape on both ends of each leg. Either draw the diagonals from the corners to give a center point and draw the circle with a pair of compasses, or use a domestic object such as a glass or a jar of the right size, around which you can draw.

PLAN

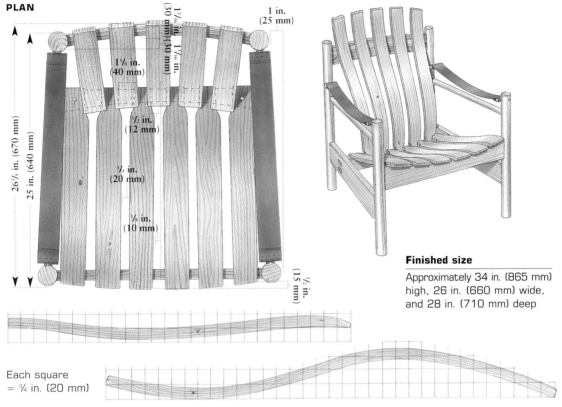

1 in.
(25 mm)

1³⁄₁₆ in.
(30 mm)

1¹⁄₁₆ in.
(30 mm)

1⅝ in.
(40 mm)

½ in.
(12 mm)

¾ in.
(20 mm)

⅜ in.
(10 mm)

½ in.
(15 mm)

26⅜ in. (670 mm)

25 in. (640 mm)

Finished size

Approximately 34 in. (865 mm)
high, 26 in. (660 mm) wide,
and 28 in. (710 mm) deep

Each square
= ¾ in. (20 mm)

3 Next, mark out the
positions of the mortises
for the side rails on the legs.
These rails sit 6 in. (150 mm)
up from the bottom and are
4 in. (100 mm) high. The tenon
will have a ⅜-in. (10 mm)
shoulder all around. Square
these across the face with a
box square and pencil. Set a
mortise or marking gauge to
mark the width in the center of
the leg—⅜ in. (10 mm). Set the

mortises on the other three legs
in the same way.

4 At the top of the back legs
set out the mortise for the
back rail—22 in. (560 mm)
from the bottom and 2³⁄₁₆ in.
(55 mm) long: remember to make
them a pair. On the inside face
of the front legs, set out a
mortise for the front rail 11¼ in.
(285 mm) up from the bottom
and 2³⁄₁₆ in. (55 mm) long.

Mark the
position of the
mortises.

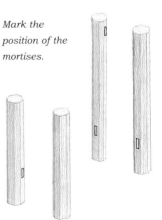

Marking a curve

When marking a simple curve from two end points to a given dimension at the center, mark the dimension of the required curve. Then, with a friend's help, bend a long steel rule between the end marks, springing it to the curve mark. Mark a line along this sprung curve.

5 Drill the center out of each mortise with a 5/16-in. (8 mm) bit to a depth of 1 3/16 in. (30 mm). Use a depth stop or wrap masking tape around the bit as a guide. Chisel the waste out with a 3/8-in. (10 mm) mortise chisel. Hold the leg down on a firm, flat surface with a C-clamp. Work toward each end, levering out the waste. True up the mortise with the mortise chisel at each end and a 1-in. (25 mm) paring chisel for the sides.

6 Prepare the side rails and mark out 24 in. (600 mm). Set out the tenon 1 3/16 in. (30 mm) long at each end, leaving 21 5/8 in. (540 mm) between the shoulders. Square this around the wood and gauge the tenons 3/8 in. (10 mm) thick in the center.

7 Mark the position of the double mortises in the side rails that will accept the double tenons on the ends of the curved lower back rail. Square a line around the side rail 4 in. (100 mm) along from the back shoulder line. Then square a second line 1 5/8 in. (40 mm) further along. Square these lines around to the opposite face. Gauge the width of each mortise—5/8 in. (15 mm) wide

with 5/8-in. (15 mm) spacings in between—on both sides of the rails. Drill a 3/8-in. (10 mm) hole through each mortise. Chisel out the waste from both sides using the 3/8-in. (10 mm) mortise chisel and cutting to the ends. Use the 1-in. (25 mm) paring chisel to finish the width. As always, use a C-clamp to ensure your work is secure.

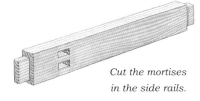

Cut the mortises in the side rails.

8 With the wood held vertically, cut all the marked tenons along the gauge lines on the waste side down to the shoulder line with a tenon saw. Test fit the components of the two side frames. Adjust as required.

9 Prepare the front curved rail by planing all around. Mark the length of the rail 22 in. (560 mm) long, and then the tenon shoulders 1 3/16 in. (30 mm) in from each end. Square the lines around the rail. Finish the lines for the tenons 3/8 in. (10 mm) thick and 2 3/16 in. (55 mm) wide. Cut the tenons as above.

10 Mark the curve from the top edge on the front rail ¾ in. (20 mm) down the center face (see far left).

11 To cut curves in thick wood, it is best to use a bandsaw. Cut the curve and finish with a spokeshave and sandpaper.

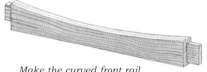

Make the curved front rail.

12 Cut and plane the top back rail with a smoothing plane. The rail is curved slightly both top and bottom. Mark the length of the rail 20 in. (510 mm) and tenons 1³⁄₁₆ in. (30 mm). Square the shoulder lines around the rail. Gauge the tenons ⅜ in. (10 mm) in from the face side and 4¾ in. (120 mm) thick at each end. Note that the back shoulder is 1³⁄₁₆ in. (30 mm) across. Cut the tenons in the usual manner.

13 Mark the curve from the center to the shoulders using the same method as for the curve on the front rail (see far left). From the inside face, measure 1³⁄₁₆ in.

(30 mm) across on the top edge in the center. Spring the straightedge or long steel rule from this center point to the outside shoulder line on the inside face. Repeat this for the back edge to create a parallel line on top.

Mark out the curve on the top back rail.

14 Using a bandsaw or a jigsaw, cut the curve and finish the surface with a spokeshave and sandpaper.

15 Prepare the curved lower back rail. Mark the length of the rail and tenons. Gauge the two tenons ⅝ in. (15 mm) with ⅝ in. (15 mm) between to suit the already-cut mortises. Cut the tenons. Test the fit in the side rail and adjust as required.

16 The back and bottom of this rail will remain flat and square. Mark the curve for the front face on top of the rail, referring to the curve shown in the plan on the drawing on page 345—across 1 in. (25 mm). Use the same method as for the curve on the front rail. Cut this curve.

17 Mark the curve for the top face on the front of the rail in the same way, referring to the curve shown in the front elevation on the drawing on page 344—down 1 in. (25 mm). Cut this curve as before.

18 Smooth the curved surfaces with a spokeshave. While smoothing the top curve, work the slight angle from front to back— approximately ¼ in. (6 mm) on the top edge.

The finished lower back rail.

19 Now cut the two ¾-in. (20 mm) dowels so that they are the same length as the side rails, plus ¾ in. (20 mm) at each end. These will be inserted between the front and rear legs to strengthen the underframe of the chair. Drill a ¾-in. (20 mm) hole, ¾ in. (20 mm) deep in the center of the inside face of each leg and 7 in. (175 mm) up from the side rail. Use a clean-cut auger bit in order to achieve a neat finish in the holes.

**Alternative for
making seat slats**

If you are unable to find
a piece of wood in the
same species as the
rest of the chair at this
size, it is possible to use
six lengths of timber 1 in.
(25 mm) thick. First, cut
the upper surface to
shape and then glue the
resulting piece of waste
to the underside of the
slats. Finish the shaping
as before.

20 Assemble the frame dry
and check that all
joints are tight. Adjust where
necessary. When working from
an octagon, the shoulders of
the tenons are flat on the
octagonal face. When the legs
are finally rounded most of this
flat is lost. Instead of trying to
round the shoulders to match
the curve, leave flats on the
round legs where the square
shoulders will connect.
Adjusting these joints will
mean a slight loss in overall
length of about ⅛ in. (3 mm) on
each face. Adjust as required to
compensate for the loss.

Assemble the seat frame dry.

Making the seat slats
When curves are only slight,
as on the seat slats, there is
unlikely to be a problem with
breakage on short grain. These
components can therefore be
sawn from solid wood. Even

though this could be done by
hand, the task is made much
easier and quicker if you can
use a bandsaw.

21 Mark out the six slats
on the main face of the
solid wood. Using a pattern in
card or thick paper made from
the grid in the drawing on
page 345, mark the six slats,
ensuring that you leave enough
space in between each to
account for the saw cut.

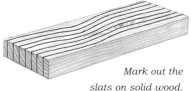

*Mark out the
slats on solid wood.*

22 Carefully saw the slats
just to the waste side of
the line using the bandsaw.
Smooth the sawn surfaces with a
spokeshave and sandpaper.

23 Mark the lengths of the
slats, which vary
depending on the width across
the lower back rail. Mark the
center line across the top edge
of the front and back rails.
Mark two more lines ⅜ in.
(10 mm) each side of the first
on each rail. Position one of the
two center slats against the two
right-hand marks and mark the
position of the front and back

edges of the back rail on the slat. Repeat with the other center slat. To find the lengths of the other four slats, mark their positions in a similar way, remembering to allow 1½ in. (40 mm) between each seat slat to accommodate the back slats. Mark the center line lengthways along each slat and then the rest. They narrow at the back of the seat—starting at 2⅜ in. (60 mm) wide at the front with a cut-out to 1½ in. (40 mm) across the back rail. Cut to length; smooth to shape.

24 Mark the positions of the screws on the center line of the slats, 1³⁄₁₆ in. (30 mm) from the back edge. Drill the holes using a ³⁄₁₆-in. (4.5 mm) bit and countersink the tops of the holes.

25 Place the slats in position on the two rails. Mark the screw hole centers on the back rail with a bradawl. Start from the center two and work outward, adjusting the end of each slat to allow the back slats to fit between them when they are inserted—a 1⅝-in. (40 mm) space is needed for the back slats. Remember, as you are fitting these you need to dry clamp the main frame joints.

26 Drill ⅛-in. (3 mm) pilot holes in the back rails and screw the slats in place one by one, using steel 1³⁄₁₆-in. (30 mm) 8-gauge screws. When all the slats are in position, mark the front curve as shown on the drawing on page 345.

Fix the seat slats into place.

27 Remove the screws and cut and shape the front ends of each slat. Sand the slats and apply the first coat of finish.

Making the back slats

The back slats are laminated in a jig to achieve more of a curve.

28 On one face of a piece of softwood, scale up the grid on the drawing on page 345 of the shape of the back slats and plot the two curved lines of a slat.

29 Using a bandsaw, very carefully saw down on

the waste or slat area sides of both lines.

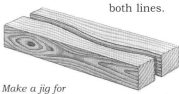

Make a jig for laminating the back pieces.

30 Prepare the thin strips of constructional veneer ready for laminating. Cut them about ⅜ in. (10 mm) wider than the final slat, since you will need to plane the edges after laminating. There will be four strips per slat. Make sure that you have some thick sheets of paper or polythene to line the faces of the jig and set up some sash clamps to apply pressure while the adhesive cures.

31 Make a package of four strips for one slat— sandwiched between the two pieces of sheet polythene. Put it into the jig dry. Tighten up the clamps to check that the strips are fully under pressure and then remove from the jig.

Dry assemble the package.

32 Apply adhesive to the inside faces of the strips. Replace the glued bundle between the polythene, return to the jig and clamp tightly. Leave the jig in the clamps overnight so that the glue cures. Make four more slats.

33 Plane one edge of a slat straight. Mark its width with a marking gauge set at 2⅜ in. (60 mm). Plane the edge to the correct width. Hold in the jig, with the marked edge above the surface of the jig. Place in a vice; plane length.

Shape the slat at the bottom.

35 Mark screw positions on the center line at the bottom of each slat and 1 in. (25 mm) from the end. Place the first slat between the two seat rails; adjust length of the shaping to fit flush on the bottom of the back rail. Mark hole centers with a bradawl, drill pilot holes and screw in place. Repeat with each slat.

adding the buttons and the leather arms.

37 Sand all components to remove any marks. Glue up the two side frames first by applying the adhesive to the tenons on each end of the side rails and in the holes for the ¾-in. (20 mm) dowels. Place each side frame in sash clamps and tighten. Check for square and ensure that it is free of wind. Remove excess adhesive, and leave to dry.

38 Remove from the clamps and complete the assembly by applying the adhesive to the tenons on the other rails. Position each rail and clamp up the whole frame. Check for square and wind. Remove excess adhesive and leave to dry.

Place the jig in a vice and plane.

Screw the back slats into place.

34 Mark the length and the narrowing shape at the bottom of the back slats (1⅝ in./40 mm wide and 4 in./100 mm long with round corners). Cut the shape, plane, and sand the edges. Shape the other slats in the same way.

36 Mark out the curve across the top of the slats. Disassemble and cut on the bandsaw.

Final assembly

Sand and apply first finish coat. Assemble the chair before

39 Remove from the clamps and sand off any marks. Apply the final finish to the frame, seat, and back slats.

40 Refit the seat and back slats with the brass screws on the lower back rail. The other ends will be "floating" over the front and top back rails. It would be possible to screw through the outside face

into these rails—however this would show so make "buttons" to hold the slats in place. They are made with a flat face so they can be screwed under or behind the slats and will locate in holes drilled into the rail (see main photograph, page 351).

41 Take the 1 x ¾ in. (25 x 20 mm) strip and mark the eleven buttons, each 1³⁄₁₆ in. (30 mm) long. Mark the position of the screw holes in the center and then drill and countersink using a ³⁄₁₆-in. (4.5 mm) bit and a countersink bit. Cut the buttons to length and drill the holes to accept ¼-in. (6 mm) dowels in the end, ⅜ in. (10 mm) down.

42 Cut the dowels to length and glue into the holes. Either shape the top round, or chamfer the edge and end on the face.

Make the buttons and cut the dowels to length.

43 Using one button as a pattern, mark where the dowel will enter the rails on the bottom edge of the top rail for the back and behind the front rail for the seat. Fix the slats with the buttons by inserting the dowel into the hole. Mark with a bradawl where the screw will be positioned. Drill a pilot hole and fix into place with 1³⁄₁₆-in. (30 mm) 8-gauge steel screws.

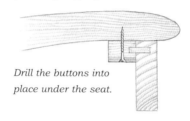

Drill the buttons into place under the seat.

Making the leather strap arms

The chair is very comfortable without any upholstery but, rather than using solid arms, use leather straps as a contrast to what is otherwise an all-wooden piece.

44 Make the strap supports/tensioners by cutting four pieces of ¾-in. (20 mm) dowel to the same length as the width of the straps. Mark and drill a ⁵⁄₁₆-in. (8 mm) clearance hole at right angles in the center of each rod for the threaded studding. Drill the same size holes in the four

legs at heights to suit. T-nuts are used to hold the threaded studding to the dowel. A hexagonal (hex key) nut that shows on the outside of the legs is used to tighten and stretch the straps. For the screw or bolt, use four short lengths of ¼-in. (6 mm) threaded studding.

45 Mark the leather straps to length and ensure they are long enough to fold over to make the "eye" for the dowel and be secured beneath.

46 Determine the length between the eyes and fold the strap over, marking the end of the overlaps. Take the straps to your local upholsterer to have the overlaps sewn. Cut a slot in the end of the eye so bolt can be screwed through the dowel and T-nut. Fit the straps and tension as required.

Fit the leather straps in place.

Garden bench

The design for this garden bench provides a strong basic frame with a comfortably shaped seat. There are three different options given for the back of the seat: a back with curved top rails, three cross-rail panels, and a cross-weave effect. This bench is a two-seater, but it is possible to modify the dimensions and extend the length slightly if you wish.

MATERIALS

Part	Materials and dimensions	No.
	Any hardwood with resistance to weathering, such as oak, elm, or teak; if you use a softwood, make sure that it is treated	
Legs	25 x 2½ x 2½ in. (620 x 60 x 60 mm)	4
Side rails	28 x 4 x 1 in. (700 x 100 x 25 mm)	2
Longitudinal rails	56 x 4 x 1 in. (1425 x 100 x 25 mm)	2
Arms	31 x 4 x 1 in. (770 x 100 x 25 mm)	2
Back rail	57 x 4 x 1 in. (1450 x 100 x 25 mm)	1
Seat bearers	19⅝ x 4 x 1¼ in. (500 x 100 x 32 mm)	2
Seat slats	49 x 4 x 1 in. (1250 x 100 x 25 mm)	

Option 1: back with curved top rails

Curved	17¾ x 6 x 1 in. (450 x 150 x 25 mm)	2
back rails	29½ x 6 x 1 in. (750 x 150 x 25 mm)	1
Vertical uprights	29½ x 6 x 1 in. (450 x 45 x 25 mm)	2
Angled uprights	15¾ x 1¾ x 1 in. (400 x 45 x 25 mm)	2
Back rail	47 x 2¾ x 1⅛ in. (1200 x 70 x 30 mm)	1
Dowels	17¾ x ⅝ in. (450 x 15 mm)	5
	12 x ⅝ in. (300 x 15 mm)	6

Sheet of plywood or particleboard for set-out

Option 2: back with three cross-rail panels

Horizontal rails	47 x 2¾ x 2¾ in. (1200 x 70 x 70 mm)	2
External vertical stiles	23½ x 2 x 2 in. (600 x 50 x 50 mm)	2
Internal vertical stiles	15 x 1⅞ x 1⅞ in. (380 x 47 x 47 mm)	2
Cross-rails	18 x 2½ x 2½ in. (460 x 60 x 60 mm)	6

Option 3: back with cross-weave effect

Horizontal rails	147 x 2 x 2 in. (1200 x 50 x 50 mm)	2
External vertical stiles	23½ x 1¾ x 1¾ in. (600 x 45 x 45 mm)	2
Internal vertical stile	16 x 1³⁄₁₆ x 1³⁄₁₆ in. (400 x 30 x 30 mm)	1
Vertical strips	16 x ⅝ x ⅝ in. (400 x 15 x 15 mm)	14
Horizontal strips	45 x ⅝ x ⅝ in. (1145 x 15 x 15 mm)	5

Tools

Jack plane
Marking gauge
Try plane
Mortise gauge
C-clamp
Drill and ⅜-in. (10 mm), ⅝-in. (15 mm), and ¾-in. (20 mm) bits
½-in. (12 mm) mortise and 1-in. (25 mm) bevel-edge firmer chisel
Marking knife
Tenon saw
Ripsaw
Sliding bevel
Brace and ¾-in. (18 mm) auger bit
Hand saw
Sanding block
Sash clamps
Hammer
Nail set

Other materials: 2 x ⅛-in. (50 x 3 mm) 500-gauge galvanized finish nails; adhesive (exterior grade); sandpaper (120-grit); finish (exterior grade).

FRONT ELEVATION

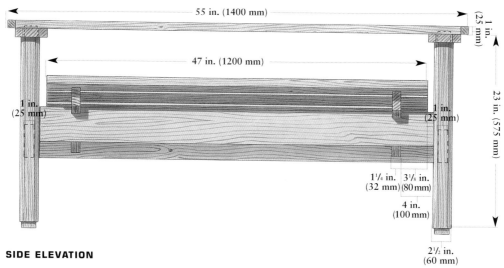

55 in. (1400 mm)

1 in. (25 mm)

23 in. (575 mm)

47 in. (1200 mm)

1 in. (25 mm)

1 in. (25 mm)

1¼ in. (32 mm) 3⅛ in. (80 mm)

4 in. (100 mm)

2½ in. (60 mm)

SIDE ELEVATION

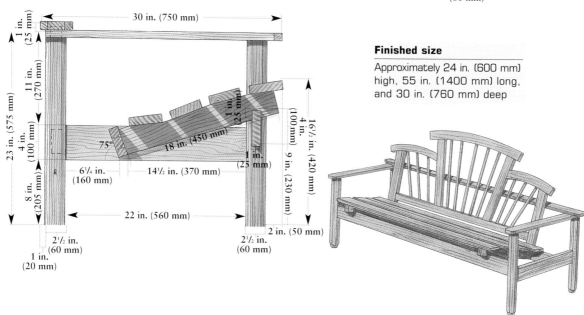

1 in. (25 mm)

30 in. (750 mm)

11 in. (270 mm)

23 in. (575 mm)

4 in. (100 mm)

8 in. (205 mm)

75°

6¼ in. (160 mm)

14½ in. (370 mm)

18 in. (450 mm)

1 in. (25 mm)

1 in. (25 mm)

16½ in. (420 mm)

4 in. (100 mm)

9 in. (230 mm)

2 in. (50 mm)

22 in. (560 mm)

2½ in. (60 mm)

2½ in. (60 mm)

1 in. (20 mm)

Finished size

Approximately 24 in. (600 mm)
high, 55 in. (1400 mm) long,
and 30 in. (760 mm) deep

Making the main frame

1 Plane all the components with a jack plane to the finished size. Your lumber merchant may do this for you, which will save time and effort.

2 Make the legs. Mark the height of the legs 23½ in. (595 mm) for the front and 24¼ in. (615 mm) for the back. Square a line around and cut to length with a tenon saw. Mark out an octagon on one end of one leg (see page 339) and set a pencil gauge to scribe the points along the leg length. Secure the wood and plane the octagon to shape with the try plane. Repeat for the other legs.

3 Make the two end frames—the two side rails are fixed to the legs with stopped mortise and tenon joints. First, make the mortises in the legs. Square two lines across the face edge 8½ in. (205 mm) and 12½ in. (285 mm) up from the bottom. Use a mortise gauge to scribe the width of the mortise ½ in. (12 mm) in the center of the leg between the squared lines.

4 Lay flat and secure with a C-clamp on a firm surface. Use a drill with a ⅜-in. (10 mm) bit to drill the bulk of the waste out of the set-out mortise to a

depth of 1⅝ in. (40 mm). Use a depth stop or place masking tape around the bit to maintain the correct depth. Remove the waste from the mortise with a ½-in. (12 mm) mortise chisel to the squared lines.

5 Finish the width with a 1 in. (25 mm) bevel-edged firmer chisel, paring back to the gauged lines. Ensure you chisel straight to keep the mortise true.

6 Next, cut the side rails 25¼ in. (640 mm) long. Set out the shoulder lines 1⅝ in. (40 mm) in from each end. Square these around the rails with a marking knife. Scribe the tenons ½ in. (12 mm) thick. Place vertically in a vice and cut down to the shoulder lines with a tenon saw. Remove and lay flat against a bench hook. Cut on the waste side of the shoulder line to remove the waste on both sides. Stand upright again and cut ¼ in. (6 mm) off the

width on each edge. Cut across the shoulder lines to reveal the tenon. Test for fit and adjust.

7 Mark the mortise and tenon joints for the front longitudinal rail. The rail is 9 in. (230 mm) up and 4 in. (100 mm) high. Set out and cut the mortises in the front legs, 1⅝ in. (40 mm) deep. Cut the rail 53½ in. (1356 mm) long and set out and cut the tenons.

8 Cut the bottom long rail 52⅜ in. (1330 mm) long. Square a shoulder line 1⅛ in. (28 mm) in from each end. Set the marking gauge to 1 in. (25 mm) and mark the double tenon on each end. Scribe a line off each edge from the shoulder line to the end, across the end and back down to the shoulder line. Hold flat on a sawhorse and cut on the waste side to the shoulders with a ripsaw. Remove the center with a 1-in. (25 mm) chisel from both sides—use a square cut so the rail fits against the side rail.

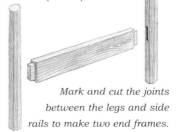

Mark and cut the joints between the legs and side rails to make two end frames.

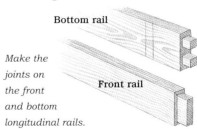

Bottom rail

Front rail

Make the joints on the front and bottom longitudinal rails.

OPTION 1: BACK WITH CURVED TOP RAILS

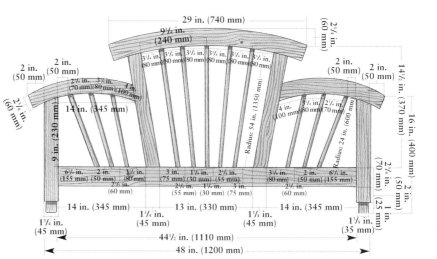

OPTION 2: BACK WITH THREE CROSS-RAIL PANELS

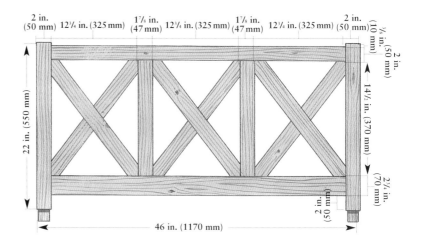

OPTION 3: BACK WITH CROSS-WEAVE EFFECT

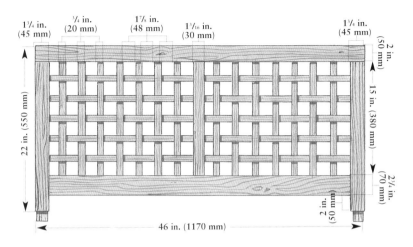

1¾ in. (45 mm)   ¾ in. (20 mm)   1⅞ in. (48 mm)   1³/₁₆ in. (30 mm)   1¾ in. (45 mm)

2 in. (50 mm)

15 in. (380 mm)

22 in. (550 mm)

2¾ in. (70 mm)

2 in. (50 mm)

46 in. (1170 mm)

9 Mark and cut the through mortises on the side rails, to accommodate the bottom longitudinal rail. Cut these at an angle so the rail sits in the correct position. Measure 6⅜ in. (160 mm) across from the back leg on the bottom edge. Square this across the bottom edge, sloping up to the back. Mark a 75-degree bevel up each face with a sliding bevel and pencil. Mark a second line 1 in. (25 mm) parallel. Lay the side rail on a flat surface and stand the back rail on end between these beveled lines. Keep the bottom corner flush with the bottom of the side rail. Trace the tenon

width onto the rail to mark the mortise sizes. Mark the mortises on both sides of the side rails. Bore a hole in the center of each mortise with a ¾-in. (20 mm) auger bit in a brace. Chisel the mortises square from both sides with a 1-in. (25 mm) chisel. Test the fit and adjust as required.

10 Set out a square stub tenon on top of both front and back legs. From the bottom of each leg measure 22½ in. (575 mm), giving a larger tenon on the two longer back legs. Set a marking gauge to ½ in. (12 mm) and scribe the width of the tenon. Lay flat and

cut on the waste side of the shoulder line down to the gauge line on all four sides. Hold the leg vertically in a vice and cut with the tenon saw.

11 Make the bench arms. Cut them to 28¾ in. (730 mm) long. Set out the stopped mortises to match the stub tenons on top of the front legs—1⁷/₁₆ in. (36 mm) square and ¾ in. (20 mm) deep. Square the first line across at 2½ in. (62 mm) from one end. Square the second line a further 1⁷/₁₆ in. (36 mm) along. Gauge the width with a marking gauge set at 1¼ in. (32 mm) from both edges.

12 Cut the front stopped mortise with a 1-in. (25 mm) chisel. First cut a small mortise the size of the chisel down to the required depth of ¾-in. (20 mm), then work back to the set-out lines.

13 Set out the through mortises of the same size for the back legs in the underside of the arms—½ in. (12 mm) in from the end. Transfer the mortise set-out on the bottom to the top. Drill this mortise through the arm and chisel square to the set-out.

14 The front end of the bench arm can be shaped: in this case, a beveled 45-degree corner has been cut, which echoes the angles in the octagonal legs.

Cut a mortise in the shaped arm and fit it to the tenon on the leg.

15 Assemble the end frames dry. If all is well, use 120-grit sandpaper to sand off all marks. Glue up with exterior grade adhesive. Check the frame for square and twist. Apply pressure with sash clamps until the adhesive has set. Remember to remove any excess with a damp cloth before it dries.

The completed end frame.

16 Next, cut the upper back rail square and to a length of 55 in. (1400 mm). Set out a stopped mortise on each end to fit over the tenon that protrudes through the arm. The mortise is 1¼ in. (32 mm) in from each end and only ⁵⁄₁₆ in. (8 mm) deep. Cut this in the same way as you did before. The ends of the back rail can also be shaped with a 45-degree corner.

17 Cut the mortises in the bottom longitudinal rail. Set out a mortise ½ in. (12 mm) wide and 4⅞ in. (123 mm) on the face side along from the shoulder line at each end. Scribe lines ⅜ in. (10 mm) and 3³⁄₁₆ in. (80 mm) down from the top edge to give a 2¾-in. (70 mm) long mortise. Cut these mortises ¾ in. (20 mm) deep as before. On the top of this rail, set out a mortise 1½ in. (37 mm) in from each shoulder line, 1⁵⁄₁₆ in. (35 mm) long and ½ in. (12 mm) wide. Hold the rail securely in a vice, and drill and chisel the mortise out in a similar manner to the other mortises.

Cut two mortises in either end of the back rail to fit onto each arm.

18 Assemble the glued end frames, two longitudinal rails and back rail dry. Keep them clamped and check for fit and square. Adjust the joints as required.

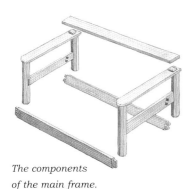

*The components
of the main frame.*

19 Disassemble and glue the main frame together. Place in clamps again and ensure the frame is square and true. When dry, remove from clamps and clean all surfaces with sandpaper. You now have a strong frame to which you will add the seat and back.

Making the seat

20 Mark out the two seat bearers 18½ in. (475 mm) long. Set out and cut

*Fit each seat bearer into the
back longitudinal rail.*

the 2¾ in. (70 mm) wide x ½ in. (12 mm) thick tenons at one end to fit the ¾-in. (20 mm) deep mortises in the face of the back rail.

21 Mark the position of the bearer on the front rail. Square these marks down the inside face of the front rail. Scribe a line across this squared line 1 in. (25 mm) down. Measure the distance between this scribed line and the inside of the bottom edge of the back rail. Square a line across the bottom of the bearer this distance from the shoulder. Mark the beveled line on the face side at a 75° angle. Mark a second parallel line 1 in. (25 mm) further forward. Measure up 1 in. (25 mm) on the inside bevel. Square a line off the bevel between the two. Remove the center by cutting down to the line and chiseling away the waste to create the dado.

22 The top edge of the bearer has a shape cut for the seat slats to sit on, which makes it more comfortable. Square lines across the top edge from the front at 3³⁄₁₆ in. (80 mm), 7 in. (180 mm), 11½ in. (290 mm), and 15¾ in. (400 mm). At the

front end, measure down ½ in. (12 mm) from the 11½-in. (290 mm) mark to create the shape. Cut to shape with a hand saw and clean up with sandpaper. Position the bearers in the mortises and over the front rail.

23 Check the fit; adjust as required. Apply adhesive and fix in place with a 2-in. (50 mm) galvanized nail through the back of the front rail to hold the bearer in place.

*The shaped bearers in position
on the end frame.*

24 Mark and cut the four seat slats 47 in. (1200 mm) long. After giving the slats a light sand, apply a little adhesive to the back of each slat and hold in place, ensuring the overhang at each end is equal. Nail through the top of the slats with two

advanced

Using a trammel

A trammel is used to draw large circles. It works like a protractor, enabling you to mark out accurate curves.
A trammel has a pair of points that are attached to a timber arm. Each point is adjustable along the arm to provide varying centers. One point can usually be replaced with a pencil.

Additional tools for back option 1

Trammel

Jigsaw

2 x ⅛ in. (50 x 3 mm) finish nails into each bearer. Angle each nail to increase the holding power. Punch the nails below the surface.

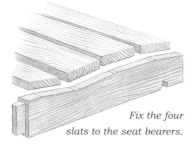

Fix the four slats to the seat bearers.

The drawings on pages 356–7 show the seat with three alternative backs.

Option 1: back with curved top rails

The curved effect of the top rails is marked out with a tool called a trammel (see far left).

1 First, mark and cut the tenons on the lower end of the vertical uprights 1 in. (25 mm) long, 1⅜ in. (35 mm) wide, and ½ in. (12 mm) thick. Test the fit in the top of the back longitudinal rail.

2 Next, cut the back rail 46 in. (1170 mm) long. Set out a 1-in. (25 mm) tenon at each end—½ in. (12 mm) thick and 2 in. (50 mm) wide. Cut these in the usual manner.

3 Mark out and cut a matching mortise in each upright 2½ in. (60 mm) up from the shoulder line of the tenon, for the bottom rail. Cut these in the usual manner.

Cut the joints between the back and the bottom rail.

4 Next, set out and draw a full scale drawing (set-out) of the back on a sheet of plywood or particleboard (see drawings on pages 354 and 356 for measurements). This will help you when you are setting out the curved rails and angled uprights.

5 Lay the bottom rail over the set-out and mark the position of the two angled uprights on the top edge. Be careful to keep the shoulder lines at each end in the correct location and set out the mortises on the top of the rail. Chisel the two mortises 1 in. (25 mm) deep, ½ in. (12 mm) wide, and 1⅜ in. (35 mm) long. Chisel out and check for fit.

6 Next, prepare the pieces from which you are going

to cut the curved rails. Position one of the lower curved rail pieces over the top of the set-out. Set a trammel to a 24-in. (600 mm) radius. Place the base of the trammel arm on the top edge of the bottom rail position on the set-out and use the trammel to trace the curve of the lower edge of the rail on the timber piece.

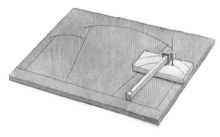

Mark the curve on the timber with a trammel.

7 Fix the rail over the sawhorse and hold it firmly with a C-clamp. Carefully cut the curve with a jigsaw. Sand the cut edge with sandpaper to true it up. Lay over the set-out and check the shape. If all is right, change the radius on the trammel to 26 in. (660 mm) and scribe the top curve. Cut as before. Repeat this for all three curved back rails, using the measurements given on the drawing on page 356. Clean up the curves with sandpaper.

8 Next, mark and cut the mortises and tenons on the curved rails. Position each of the three curved rails in its correct location over the set-out and transfer the shoulder lines from all the upright pieces onto the edge of the rails. The two lower curved rails have a tenon on the inside end while the other end is cut at an angle. A mortise is also cut in from the outside end to match the tenon on the vertical upright. The top curved rail has a mortise cut in at each end and the ends cut at a bevel.

9 Set a sliding bevel to the angles the mortises are to be cut and mark the bevels down the face. Gauge the width of the mortises on the edges and at the ends for the tenons. Hold each curved rail in a vice and drill out and cut the mortises as before. Note all these mortises are at an angle.

10 Stand each of the lower rails in the vice and cut the tenons in the ends. Clamp the rails horizontally to a flat surface and cut the shoulder lines. Cut the tenon 1 in. (25 mm) long and parallel to the

shoulder. Cut it 2 in. (50 mm) wide and trim the waste.

11 Next, mark the shoulders for the tenons on the uprights from the set-out—there should be one at the top of each vertical upright and one at the top of each angled upright. Note the shoulders are at an angle. Cut these tenons as before. Test each for accuracy.

12 Fit the angled uprights to the back rail and to the top curved back. Check each joint for an accurate fit over the set-out and mark the mortises in the outside edges. Cut as before.

13 Dry assemble the whole frame in clamps and check for fit. Adjust as required. Mark the position of the centers of the splayed dowels on the inside edges of the back rail, top curved rail and lower curved rails. Lay the dowel across from top to bottom to find the splay. Mark each angle on the face. Mark the length of each dowel to fit ⅝ in. (15 mm) into each rail (see the drawing on page 356). Number each dowel as the lengths vary, and cut to length with a tenon saw.

14 You are now ready to disassemble the frame. Drill each dowel hole ¾ in. (20 mm) deep in the center of each edge. Hold the drill with the lead screw of the auger on the center line. Tilt the drill and carefully bore the hole at the angle marked on the face. Test that each of the dowels fits and is leaning at the angle required.

Splay out the dowels and fix to the curved rails.

15 At this stage carry out a dry assembly of the complete back frame and, if all is well, disassemble, apply adhesive and clamp. Ensure the frame is square and free of wind. Remove all excess adhesive and leave to dry.

16 After a final sand, the back frame can now be fitted to the main frame. Apply

the adhesive to the tenons at the bottom of the uprights. Insert the frame and push it onto the back rail. Fix each upright to the rail with two nails.

Finished bench with back in place.

Option 2: back with three cross-rail panels

1 Start by making a back frame of two horizontal rails, two external vertical stiles and two internal vertical rails. First, make the two external vertical stiles: cut them 22 in. (550 mm) long and set out the tenons at one end of each, to fit into the back longitudinal rail (see step 1, option 1). Set out two mortises on each stile 2 in. (50 mm) up from the shoulder line and ¾ in. (20 mm) down from the top—to suit each horizontal rail. The mortises are 1 in. (25 mm) deep, 2 in. (50 mm) long, and ½ in. (12 mm) wide in the center of the edge.

2 Make the two horizontal rails by cutting to 46 in. (1170 mm) in length, and at each end set out and cut the tenons 1 in. (25 mm) long, 2 in. (50 mm) wide, and ½ in. (12 mm) thick. Test the fit and adjust as required.

3 Set out the mortises, which will accommodate the internal vertical stiles. Square a line across the edge of each rail 13⅜ in. (340 mm) along from each shoulder. Square a second line the width of the internal stiles—1¾ in. (45 mm). As with the other mortises, gauge a line ½ in. (12 mm) wide in the center. Cut each mortise as before, 1 in. (25 mm) deep.

4 Cut the two internal vertical stiles 16½ in. (420 mm) long, and set out 1-in. (25 mm) tenons at each end to suit the mortises.

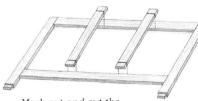

Mark out and cut the joints on the stiles.

5 Test the frame dry. Adjust and glue up. Ensure it is square and free of wind.

6 Make the cross-rails to fit into the back frame. Set out a half lap joint on each pair of cross-rails 17¾ in. (450 mm) long. The half laps are in the center of each rail. Mark the width of the wood and square it around the rail. Set a marking gauge to half the thickness and then scribe a line in between the set-out lines.

7 Lay flat against a bench hook and hold with a C-clamp. Cut with a tenon saw to the line. Place several other cuts across the wood between the set-out lines. Remove the waste with a chisel. Check the bottom for flatness. Repeat on the other rails. Test the fit of the three pairs and adjust the components as required.

8 Mark a center line down the length on the face of each end with a pencil. Hold the assembled cross-rail under the back frame so that the pencil lines align with the intersections of the vertical and horizontal rails. Trace the shapes onto the face of the cross-rail.

9 Cut the cross-rails to length. Square the corner marks down each edge of the rails. Hold flat and cut the ends of the rails to produce pointed ends. Cut, test the fit and adjust as required. Repeat for all three crosses.

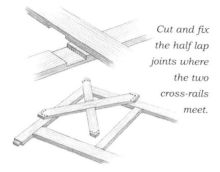

Cut and fix the half lap joints where the two cross-rails meet.

10 Apply a little adhesive to the half lap and the pointed ends. Insert the crosses into the back frame so that the faces are flush. Tap a 2-in. (50 mm) nail at each end of the cross-rails into the back frame. Leave to dry. Sand all surfaces flat. Remove any sharp edges and fit the back to the seat and main frame.

Option 3: Back with cross-weave effect

This third option is made up of three vertical stiles and two horizontal rails. Plywood strips are interwoven within this frame to create the cross-weave effect.

1 Follow the step instructions given for option 2 to cut

three vertical stiles and the horizontal rails to length. Fix stiles and rails together to make the basic frame as before with mortise and tenon joints.

2 Next, rout a ⅛-in. (3 mm) groove along the inside edge of each of the frame members to accommodate the cross-weave strips.

3 Cut two vertical and two horizontal beech strips to length about 15¼ in. (385 mm) long and 45¼ in. (1150 mm) long respectively and have a trial weaving of the strips. Remember to allow for the amount that will sit in the grooves. Check the length and trim as required. Once the correct length is obtained, cut the remaining strips.

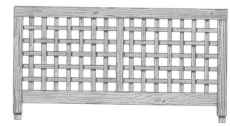

Weave the strips into the frame.

4 Put some adhesive in the grooves of the frame and reweave the plywood strips. Ensure they fit all the way into the grooves.

Additional tools for back option 3

Router

Linen cupboard

This linen cupboard is very versatile, and features two different cupboard doors and two drawers. If necessary, the dimensions of the linen cupboard can be adjusted to suit your own particular storage requirements. It could, of course, be used for storing other items if desired.

Tools

Smoothing plane

Radial-arm saw

C-clamp

Sanding block

Router with ¼-in. (6 mm) straight cutter

Sash clamps

Sliding bevel

Dovetail saw

Coping saw

¼-in. (6 mm) bevel-edged and ½-in. (12 mm) paring chisels

Marking knife

Marking gauge

Tenon saw

Bradawl

Drill and ⅛-in. (3 mm), ⁵⁄₃₂-in. (4 mm), ³⁄₁₆-in. (4.5 mm), and countersink bits

Screwdriver

Hand saw

Drill press and 1⅝-in. (40 mm) Forstner bit or hole saw

MATERIALS

Part	Materials and dimensions	No.
	Solid wood, hardwood to suit (light-colored advised):	
Legs	40 x 2 x ¾ in. (1000 x 50 x 20 mm)	4
Sides	30 x 12½ x ¾ in. (750 x 310 x 20 mm)	2
Top	21 x 16 x 1 in. (520 x 400 x 25 mm)	1
Top cross-rails	16 x 3⅜ x 1 in. (400 x 85 x 25 mm)	2
Bottom rails	16 x 2 x 1 in. (400 x 50 x 25 mm)	1
	16 x 1¾ x 1 in. (400 x 44 x 25 mm)	1
Inside cross-rails	16 x 2 x ¾ in. (400 x 50 x 20 mm)	4
Door fronts	13 x 6 x ¾ in. (330 x 150 x 20 mm)	1
Cupboard fall	13 x 12 x ¾ in. (330 x 300 x 20 mm)	1
False top drawer front	13 x 5 x ¾ in. (330 x 100 x 20 mm)	1
Top drawer front	13 x 3½ x ½ in. (330 x 85 x 12 mm)	1
Top drawer sides	13 x 3½ x ½ in. (330 x 85 x 12 mm)	2
Top drawer back	13 x 3 x ⅜ in. (330 x 75 x 10 mm)	1
False bottom drawer front	13 x 6 x ¾ in. (330 x 150 x 20 mm)	1
Bottom drawer front	13 x 5 x ½ in. (330 x 100 x 12 mm)	1
Bottom drawer sides	13 x 5 x ½ in. (330 x 100 x 12 mm)	2
Bottom drawer back	13 x 3¾ x ⅜ in. (330 x 95 x 10 mm)	1
Drawer runners	12½ x 1½ x ⅝ in. (320 x 40 x 15 mm)	4
	Plywood	
Cabinet back	28½ x 12½ x ¼ in. (710 x 320 x 6 mm)	1
Drawer bottoms	12¼ x 11½ x ¼ in. (310 x 290 x 6 mm)	2
Shelves	14½ x 9½ x ¼ in. (360 x 240 x 6 mm)	2
Tongues	30 x ⅜ x ¼ in. (750 x 10 x 6 mm)	4

Other materials: fourteen ½-in. (12 mm) 5 gauge flat head screws; three ¾-in. (20 mm) 6 gauge flat head screws; twelve 1¼-in. (30 mm) 8 gauge flat head screws; one pair of 2-in. (50 mm) broad butt hinges with screws; two pairs of 2-in. (50 mm) butt hinges with screws; double-sided tape (thin); adhesive (PVA); sandpaper (120-grit); finish.

FRONT ELEVATION

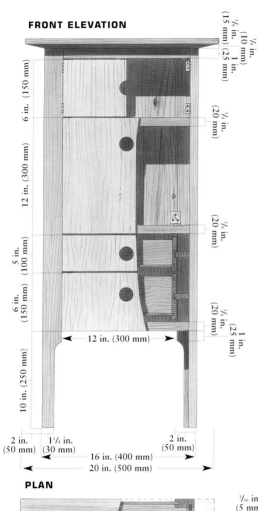

⅜ in. (15 mm)
⅜ in. (10 mm)
1 in. (25 mm)

6 in. (150 mm)

12 in. (300 mm)

¾ in. (20 mm)

5 in. (100 mm)

¾ in. (20 mm)

6 in. (150 mm)

¾ in. (20 mm)
1 in. (25 mm)

12 in. (300 mm)

10 in. (250 mm)

2 in. (50 mm)
1¼ in. (30 mm)
2 in. (50 mm)
16 in. (400 mm)
20 in. (500 mm)

PLAN

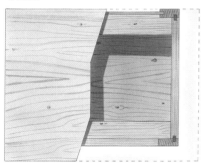

15½ in. (390 mm)
2½ in. (65 mm)
2½ in. (65 mm)

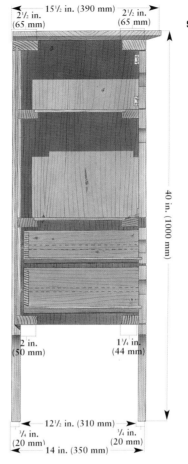

40 in. (1000 mm)

2 in. (50 mm)
1¾ in. (44 mm)

12½ in. (310 mm)
¾ in. (20 mm)
¾ in. (20 mm)
14 in. (350 mm)

SIDE ELEVATION

Finished size

40 in. (1000 mm) high, 20 in. (500 mm) wide, and 15½ in. (390 mm) deep

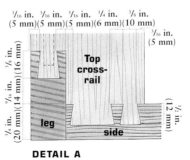

1/16 in. (5 mm) 1/16 in. (5 mm) 1/16 in. (5 mm) ¼ in. (6 mm) ⅜ in. (10 mm)

3/16 in. (5 mm)

3/16 in. (5 mm)

Top cross-rail

6 in. (152 mm)
1¼ in. (30 mm)
20 in. (500 mm)

½ in. (12 mm)

leg

side

½ in. (12 mm)

DETAIL A

DETAIL B

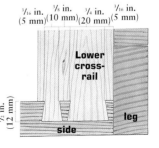

1/16 in. (5 mm)
⅜ in. (10 mm)
¾ in. (20 mm)
1/16 in. (5 mm)

Lower cross-rail

½ in. (12 mm)

side

leg

Linen cupboard   **367**

advanced

Making the cabinet

1 The cabinet sides may need to be made from two or more pieces of wood in order to obtain the required width (see box, page 283). Cut and plane the sides to 2 x ¾-in. (50 x 20 mm). Cut and plane the four legs to size—28½ x 12½-in. (725 x 310 mm). Cut them to a length of 38¾ in. (984 mm) on a radial-arm saw.

2 The bottom of each leg is shaped. Square a line around each leg at 8⅞ in. (225 mm) up from the bottom to represent the top of the cut-out shape. Pencil gauge a line ¾ in. (20 mm) in from the face edge, from the bottom to this line. Set out a curve between the set-out lines by tracing around a can or jar. Repeat the shaping on each leg. Clamp each leg down on a flat surface with a C-clamp and cut along the set-out on the waste side. Clean up the sawed edge with 120-grit sandpaper.

Cut the curved legs to shape.

3 Make the grooves that will accept the sides on the inside face of each leg (set out in pairs). Square a line 1 in. (25 mm) up from the curve on the inside face of each leg. Set up the router with a ¼-in. (6 mm) straight cutter and the fence to run a groove ¼ in. (6 mm) deep and ⁵⁄₁₆ in. (7 mm) in from the face. Hold the leg on a firm, flat surface with a C-clamp, and run the router from the top along the length to the squared set-out lines.

4 A second groove is required in the inside face edge of the back legs to accept the plywood backing. This groove is routed with the same set-up. Hold each leg on edge in the vice and run the groove. The same grooves can be run along both edges of the side panels to match. Repeat on the other legs.

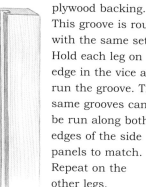

Cut a groove in the inside face of each leg for the panel sides.

5 Cut a ⅜ in. (10 mm) wide plywood tongue for each side panel joint. Glue the legs onto the sides, applying PVA adhesive to each groove, and insert the tongue. Make sure that the outsides are flush and each leg is flush on the top edge. Place in a pair of sash clamps and remove any excess adhesive with a damp cloth. Check the panel unit is flat and flush across the surface. Let dry. Make the second panel unit in the same way.

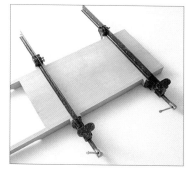

Clamp the frames together and allow to dry.

6 Make the top cross-rails, which will dovetail into the top of the legs and sides. Cut the rails 15⅛ in. (384 mm) long. Square a line around each end for the shoulders. Mark the dovetails on the rails, as shown in detail A on page 367, at a pitch of 1:6. Note the top rails are 3⅜ in. (85 mm) wide and have two shoulder lines. Mark the dovetails with a sliding bevel down the face to the shoulder lines. Square them across the end and return the set-out bevels to the opposite side.

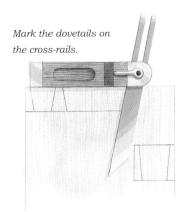

Mark the dovetails on the cross-rails.

7 Hold vertically in a vice and cut the sides of the dovetails on the waste side to the shoulders with a dovetail saw. Turn the piece in the vice horizontally and accurately cut the half pin sockets to the line with the dovetail saw. Remove the bulk of the waste from the full pin sockets using a coping saw and cutting approximately ⅛ in. (3 mm) on the waste side of the line. Hold the wood firmly on a flat surface and trim the socket back to the

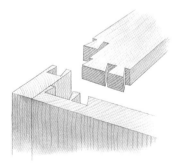

Dovetail the top rails into the sides and legs.

shoulder line with a sharp ¼-in. (6 mm) bevel-edged paring chisel. Cut half way through and then turn the piece over and pare the remaining waste to the shoulder line.

8 The two bottom cross-rails are similar, but are only dovetailed in the sides, not the legs (see detail B on page 367).

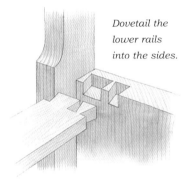

Dovetail the lower rails into the sides.

9 Place each completed rail in position on the appropriate end of the cabinet sides. Number the end of each rail and side panel for ease of matching later. Accurately align the shoulders and edges. Carefully cut around the shape of the tails to set out the sockets, using a sharp marking knife. Square the set-out back down the inside face. Set a marking gauge to the thickness of the rail and then scribe the depth on the inside face.

Linenfold panels

These are stylized representations of linen arranged in vertical folds, and were first made in the late 15th century, probably by Flemish carvers. Regional variations appeared in France, England, and Germany by the end of that century. Linenfold was used on chests, presses, wall paneling, and chimneypieces and was the commonest form of furniture decoration in the late 15th and 16th centuries, although it lost favor after about 1570. Some authorities have suggested that the panels were originally intended to indicate the storing place of bed linen, but there is no evidence for this. The term linenfold was given to the decoration much later, probably in the 19th century. Despite its origin, linenfold is now regarded as the trademark of the English carver.

10 Hold the side firmly and cut at an angle with the dovetail saw on the waste side of the sockets. The cut will extend from the depth line on the end grain down to the shoulder line on the face. Lay flat and remove the waste from the socket with a sharp chisel. Use the chisel to remove the bulk of the waste by cutting straight down—in from the shoulder line and then along the grain—splitting out the waste to approximately ⅛ in. (3 mm) from each set-out line. Trim the shoulder and depth lines with a sharp paring chisel. Assemble the parts and adjust as necessary by carefully paring with a chisel.

11 With the top and bottom rails in position, the cabinet should now stand. The four inside cross-rails will be stub-tenoned into the sides, and so these joints need to be marked and cut. The shoulder lengths are the same as for the top and bottom rails. The tenons are also the same length as the dovetails—½ in. (12 mm) at each end. Cut the four rails to length and square the shoulder lines around each end. The tenon is 1 in. (25 mm) wide. Set a marking gauge to ½ in. (12 mm)

and scribe the tenon from each edge. Cut the tenons with a tenon or dovetail saw down the gauge line and then across the shoulder line. The two back rails will require the same cutout at each end as the bottom rail—⁵⁄₁₆ x 1³⁄₁₆ in. (7 x 30 mm). Check the fit of the cross-rails in the carcass and adjust as required.

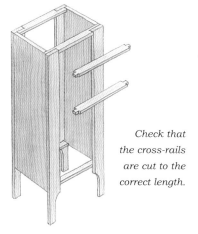

Check that the cross-rails are cut to the correct length.

12 Set out the mortises on the inside face of the side panels. The first rail is 6 in. (150 mm) down from under the top rail. Measure down another 12 in. (300 mm) for the second. Mark the thickness of each rail below these points. Hold the rails in position between the set-outs and mark the tenon width with a pencil. Hold firmly on a flat surface and chisel the mortise

to a depth of ½ in. (12 mm). Cut down the required depth, and work back to the shoulder lines. Check the fit and adjust as required.

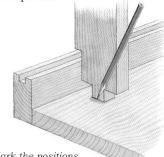

Mark the positions of the mortises on the inside face of the carcass.

13 With the router set as before, run a groove on the underside of the back top rail to accept the plywood backing. Move the fence on the router and run a ¼ x ¼-in. (6 x 6 mm) rabbet along the top inside edge of each inside cross-rail.

14 Assemble the cabinet dry to check all is correct. When you are satisfied, sand all the components to remove the set-out lines and marks with 120-grit sandpaper. Apply the first finish coat on the inside faces. Assemble the carcass using PVA glue and sash clamps. Check the cabinet is square and free of twist.

Any correction may be made by moving the clamps a little. Clean off excess adhesive. Let to dry.

15 Cut the plywood to size. Check that it will fit in the grooves in the back legs, and will slide up from the bottom to the top groove. Finish both sides of this panel, slide it in position and fix to the bottom rear rail with three ¾-in. (20 mm) screws.

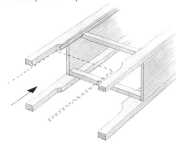

Slide the back panel into position.

The completed carcass.

Making the top

16 Plane the top all round to 20 x 15½ in. (500 x 390 mm). Be sure the surface is flat and the edges true.

17 Mark the bevel with a pencil. Gauge one line ⅝ in. (15 mm) down from the top and another 2 in. (50 mm) inside the three edges on the bottom. This will be the bevel that needs to be planed off on the two ends and front while the back is left square. Hold upright in a vice or clamp down on a flat surface, and plane the bevels on the end grain first. Plane at a slight angle to prevent breakout. Plane with the grain along the front edge.

Plane the underside bevel on the cabinet top.

18 The cabinet top will be fastened with screws inserted from underneath the top rails. Drill and countersink four ³⁄₁₆ in. (4.5 mm) clearance holes in these rails. Position the top and mark the holes with a bradawl.

19 The top can be removed and ⅛-in. (3 mm) pilot holes drilled, and then secured temporarily with 1¼-in. (30 mm) 8 gauge screws.

Screw the top in place.

Fitting out the cabinet

20 Take the two plywood shelves and cut to fit neatly in place between the rabbets on the inside rails. Cut slightly oversize with a hand saw and trim to fit with a smoothing plane. Secure with a little adhesive in each rabbet.

Fit the plywood shelves.

Fitting doors

There are two ways of fastening doors to the linen cupboard. Here, the top doors are held in place with two hinges in each side. The bottom door is a fall, which is held secure with a pivot hinge in the bottom.

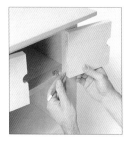

Door on side hinges.

Door as a fall.

21 Now gather the pieces that will make the two top doors, the fall, and the two bottom drawer fronts. The grain should run horizontally through all of these. Each piece can be cut approximately to its vertical size and planed to fit between the front legs with a ⅛-in. (3 mm) clearance. Now mark the positions of the centers of the handle cutouts and drill with a Forstner bit or a hole saw using a drill press.

22 The top two doors are cut from the one piece already fitted. Crosscut this through the center vertically and plane to fit. Fasten the top doors to the cabinet with hinges on the sides and the bottom one as a fall (see left).

23 Because the legs form a recess within the cabinet sides, normal drawer-running methods cannot be used. Here the drawer runners are fixed to the inside of the cabinet, projecting from the line of the legs as shown in the drawing on page 367. Prepare, mark, and cut the runners. Fit each with two 1³⁄₁₆-in. (30 mm) 8 gauge flat head screws through the side panel. Be sure that the screw heads are well below the surface.

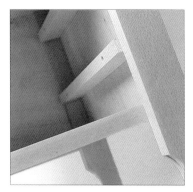

Fit the drawer runners.

Making the drawers

24 The two drawers are joined at the corners with dovetail joints. Cut the wood to length. The sides are 12 in. (300 mm) long, and the back and front are cut to the distance between the runners, plus ½ in. (12 mm) for the side grooves. Note the width of the material for the back is smaller than that of the sides and front to fit the plywood bottom.

25 Mark the thickness of material on the ends of all the pieces. Square this around each. Determine the number of dovetails required. The side pieces will have the tails cut on each end. Measure ½ in. (12 mm) across from the left-hand edge on the squared line. Divide the remaining width up into even parts equal to the number of tails required.

26 Mark the width of each tail—½ in. (12 mm)—to the left of each division. Set a sliding bevel to a pitch of 1:6 as before. Mark the sides of each dovetail using the sliding bevel. Square the tails across the end and bevel down the other side to match. Clearly mark the waste in the pin sockets.

27 Cut the sides of the dovetails with a dovetail saw and remove the waste using a coping saw. Then pare back to the shoulder lines with a chisel. Cut the pins as shown on pages 267–8.

28 With the router, run a ¼ in. (6 mm) wide groove ¼ in. (6 mm) deep. Run the top edge of the groove to line up with the bottom edge of the back, but set inside the bottom edge on the side pieces and front. Apply adhesive to the contact surfaces and assemble the drawer. Clamp if required and allow to dry, ensuring the drawer is square and free of twist.

29 Remove the drawer from the clamps and clean up the joints. Cut the drawer bottom and slide it into the groove. Check for square and fix in place through the bottom of the drawer into the edge of the back with three ½-in. (12 mm) 5 gauge flat head screws. Make the other drawer.

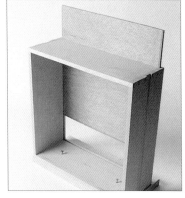

Fit the drawer together.

30 The drawers require a groove along each side of the drawer. Adjust the router to cut a groove wide enough for the runner in the center of the side. The depth is already set to ¼ in. (6 mm). Adjust the fence to run the groove. Make several passes along the drawer, adjusting each time until you have a width of ¾ in. (20 mm). Clean the groove with a chisel and sandpaper.

31 False decorative fronts are attached to the drawers. Place each drawer in the cabinet and apply two small pieces of thin double-sided tape on the front. Push all the way in. Hold the false front in position and bring the drawer forward to meet the back of the false front. The tape will hold the two together. Remove and place face down on a flat, smooth surface. Drill four ½-in. (12 mm) screws through the inside of the drawer into the decorative front. Replace drawer to check alignment and adjust. Repeat for the other drawer, leaving enough room for the fall above to operate.

Finishing

32 Sand and apply the required finish. A strap or flap stay can be added to the fall to prevent straining the hinges.

The finished drawers in place.

Dining chair

This chair has simple classic but modern lines. Dining chairs are normally made without arms, but there are often two chairs in a set called carving chairs, which are versions with arms. Instructions and measurements are given for both.

MATERIALS

Part	Materials and dimensions	No.
Hardwood		
Front legs	18 x 1⅜ in. (450 x 35 mm) diameter	2
Back legs	33½ x 1⅜ in. (850 x 35 mm) diameter	2
Front rail	16 x 2½ x ¾ in. (400 x 65 x 20 mm)	1
Back rail	16 x 2½ x ¾ in. (400 x 65 x 20 mm)	1
Top rail	13 x 1½ x ¾ in. (320 x 35 x 20 mm)	1
Cross-rails	16½ x 3¾ x ¾ in. (420 x 95 x 20 mm)	2
Arms for carver	16 x 3½ x ⅞ in. (400 x 90 x 22 mm)	4
Bending plywood		
Chair seat	18 x 16 x ¹⁄₁₆ in. (450 x 400 x 1.5 mm)	5
Chair back	22 x 18 x ¹⁄₁₆ in. (560 x 450 x 1.5 mm)	5
Manufactured board		
Two preform	17¾ x 2 x ¾ in. (450 x 50 x 20 mm)	28
molds	23⅝ x 4 x ¾ in. (600 x 100 x 20 mm)	16

Other materials: six 1-in. (25 mm) 8 gauge brass flat head screws; adhesive (PVA); sandpaper (120-grit); finish.

Tools

Radial-arm saw

Smoothing plane

Box square

Marking gauge

C-clamps

Drill press and 1-in. (25 mm) Forstner bit

⅜-in. (10 mm) mortise

½-in. (12 mm) and 1-in. (25 mm) paring chisels

Drill and ⁵⁄₁₆-in. (8 mm) and ⅜-in. (10 mm) bits

Sliding bevel

Tenon saw

Jigsaw

Coping saw

Router with ⁵⁄₁₆-in. (8 mm) straight bit

Smoothing plane

Screwdriver

Making the underframe

The underframe is made up of four legs, a front rail, a back rail, two cross-rails, and a backrest top rail.

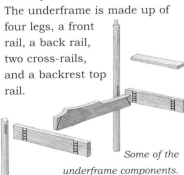

Some of the underframe components.

1 Prepare the two back and two front legs. Saw these four pieces square with a radial-arm saw, leaving a little extra on the length. You will make these pieces round later either by turning or planing. Plane each to an octagonal shape in order to make marking and cutting the joints easier (see page 339). Mark the length and the position of the

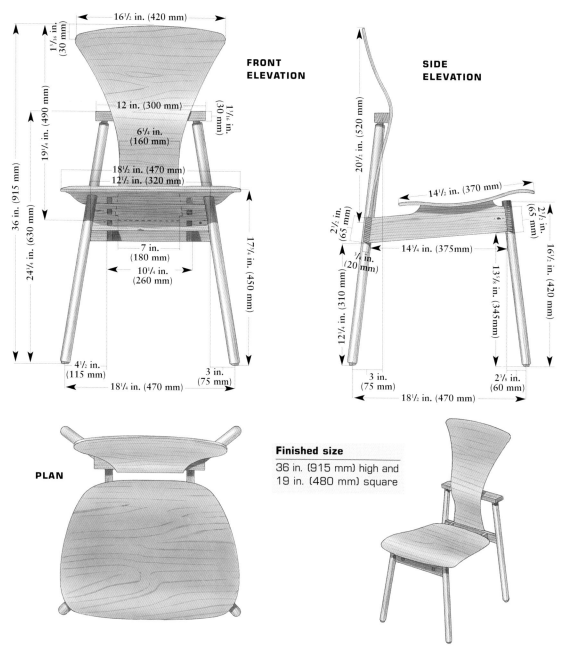

FRONT ELEVATION

16½ in. (420 mm)

1³⁄₁₆ in. (30 mm)

12 in. (300 mm)

1³⁄₁₆ in. (30 mm)

6¼ in. (160 mm)

19¼ in. (490 mm)

18½ in. (470 mm)

12½ in. (320 mm)

36 in. (915 mm)

24¼ in. (630 mm)

7 in. (180 mm)

10¼ in. (260 mm)

17¾ in. (450 mm)

4½ in. (115 mm)

3 in. (75 mm)

18¼ in. (470 mm)

SIDE ELEVATION

20½ in. (520 mm)

14½ in. (370 mm)

2½ in. (65 mm)

2½ in. (65 mm)

2½ in. (65 mm)

¾ in. (20 mm)

14¾ in. (375mm)

16½ in. (420 mm)

12¼ in. (310 mm)

13⅝ in. (345mm)

3 in. (75 mm)

2⅜ in. (60 mm)

18½ in. (470 mm)

PLAN

Finished size

36 in. (915 mm) high and 19 in. (480 mm) square

rail joints on each piece using a box square. Measure up 12¼ in. (310 mm) on the back legs and 13⅜ in. (345 mm) on the front legs.

2 Then mark a mortise on each leg 2³⁄₁₆ in. (55 mm) farther up. Set a marking gauge and mark the mortise between the lines. Hold the leg

on a solid surface with a C-clamp and drill out the bulk of the waste from the mortise to a depth of 1 in. (25 mm). Use a depth stop or masking tape to prevent drilling all the way through. Chisel the mortise to the set-out lines with a ⅜-in. (10 mm) mortise chisel. Clean up the sides of the mortise with a 1-in. (25 mm) paring chisel.

Take care that you chisel true to the set-out.

3 Next, prepare the front rail. Cut to 14⅝ in. (370 mm) long on a radial-arm saw. Square a line across the bottom edge at both ends—1 in. (25 mm) in from each end, leaving 12⅝ in. (320 mm) in between. Set a sliding bevel to a pitch of 1:6 and mark the shoulder across both faces. Return the squared line across the top edge.

4 Cut the tenons on the ends of the rail to match the mortises in the front legs. Hold vertically in a vice and cut down to the shoulder line on the waste side of the line with a tenon saw.

5 Remove from the vice and lay flat on the bench. Hold in place with a C-clamp and cut the shoulder line to remove the waste. With the marking gauge already set, scribe a line down each side of the tenon and then saw away the sides so that the tenon is 2³⁄₁₆ in. (55 mm) wide. The end of the tenon will also be beveled parallel to the shoulders. Cut this with the tenon saw and check the fit. Adjust the components as required.

CARVING CHAIR

3¼ in. (95 mm)

6 The back rail is set out the same as the front with one exception—it needs to be slightly longer as it is lower down the legs. To find the length, assemble the front rail and legs. Lay the back legs on top of the front ones with the bottoms flush. Mark the back legs at the top and bottom edge of the rail ³⁄₁₆ in. (5 mm) below these points, giving the shoulder lines. Set this out on the bottom edge of the back rail. Mark the bevels on the face and complete the set-out. Cut the tenon in the same manner as for the front rail.

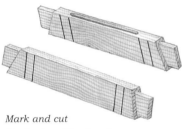

Mark and cut the front and back rails.

7 Set out the two cross-rails of the seat frame by marking the bevel across the face at one end at a pitch of 1:85. Mark the shoulder line—parallel to the bevel 1³⁄₁₆ in. (30 mm) along. Measure up this line 1³⁄₈ in. (35 mm) from the bottom edge. This represents the distance that the back rail is lower than the front rail.

Measure a 14¾-in. (375 mm) line perpendicular to the bevel from this point to the bottom edge—this indicates the length between the shoulders on the bottom edge. Mark the other shoulder line at a pitch of 1:7, and then the tenon length of ¾ in. (20 mm).

Carefully mark out all the cut lines on the cross-rails.

8 Set out the cutouts for the cross-rails. Measure up the front of each shoulder line 2⅝ in. (65 mm), and mark a line along the length from shoulder to shoulder. From the front shoulder, measure back 2 in. (50 mm), and then another 8 in. (200 mm) on the top edge. Make a curve from this point back toward each end down to the previous line along the length. Cut these with a jigsaw, and clean up with a plane or chisel.

9 Cut the cross-rails slightly over length. They will be cleaned up when assembled.

10 The width of the double tenons on the cross-rails is ½ in. (12 mm). Divide

the 2⅝-in. (65 mm) shoulder line into five equal spaces. Cut these down on the waste side to the shoulder lines and crosscut away the waste on the outside. Remove the waste between the tenons with a coping saw, and pare back to the shoulder line with a chisel.

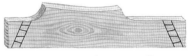

Cut the tenons on the cross-rail.

11 To set out the double mortises in the front and back rails, find the center of the bottom edge of both rails and measure 4³⁄₈ in. (110 mm) on each side, plus the thickness of the wood. Square a line across the faces of both rails. Measure up five spaces of ½ in. (12 mm) from the bottom edge. The second and fourth are the through mortises. Set these out on all four faces. Cut the mortises with a ³⁄₈-in. (10 mm) drill bit and then a chisel. Check the fit and adjust as necessary.

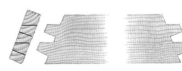

Mark and cut the double mortises for the front and back rails.

12 Dry-assemble the chair frame and check the shoulders of the rails. It will be necessary to adjust the shoulders with a chisel in order to achieve neat fitting joints.

The main seat frame assembled dry.

13 The octagonal legs should now be planed or turned to a round shape. At the top of the back legs, turn a 1-in. (25 mm) diameter dowel ⁵⁄₁₆ in. (35 mm) long.

14 Mark out the top rail. Here the tops of the back legs are rounded to fit the holes in the rail. Mark the rail and these angled holes by holding the rail behind the legs and marking the positions of the dowel tops. Square the lines across the face and mark the centers for the holes. Drill the holes in the center on this set-out. These holes will also be at an angle in order to match

the marks on the edge. This is best achieved on a drill press with a Forstner bit. Cut the rail to approximately 12 in. (300 mm) on a radial-arm saw.

Fit the legs to the top rail.

15 Set up a router with a ⁵⁄₁₆-in. (8 mm) straight bit and cut a groove 6⅜ in. (160 mm) long and ⁵⁄₁₆ in. (8 mm) deep in the center of the top edge of the lower back rail.

Assembling the underframe

You should now assemble the whole underframe dry.

16 The cross-rail joints are wedged through mortise and tenons, so disassemble and cut the slots for the wedges. Cut the wedges from any piece of scrap. Sand off any set-out marks.

17 Assemble the seat frame, cross, front, and back rails by gluing and clamping the joints. Insert the wedges. Be sure the frame is completely square and free of twist.

18 When the adhesive has cured, plane off the excess tenons and wedges on the outside face.

19 Fix the four legs to this frame by gluing the tenons and clamping. Pull the joints tight with the clamps. Check that each pair of legs is in line with the other and that there is no twist in the frame.

20 Finally, fit the top rail over the dowels and wedge these joints into place. Skim any projection with a smoothing plane and sand as necessary.

Fit the legs and cross-rails together.

Using preforms to mold the seat and back to shape

The interesting feature of this chair is the preformed seat and back. If produced in a factory these would be made from sheets of constructional veneer,

advanced

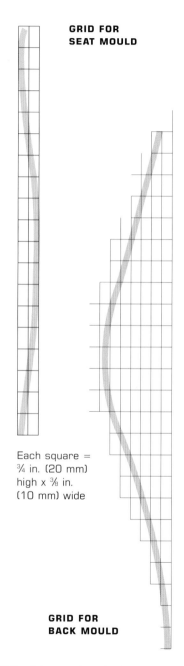

Each square =
¾ in. (20 mm)
high x ⅜ in.
(10 mm) wide

**GRID FOR
BACK MOULD**

but for our purposes it is better to make them from thin plywood. First, it is necessary to make the molds that will form these individual sheets of plywood into the required shape. The seat is a single curvature, while the back has a single curve but also wings that are slightly curved at the top of the central shape. Very precise work is necessary to make these molds.

21 First, determine the availability of suitable thicknesses of plywood. The final form does not need to be any thicker than ⅜ in. (10 mm), and so if you use ⅛-in. (3 mm) plywood you will need three layers. If you use ¹⁄₁₆-in. (1.5 mm) plywood, you would get a thinner form using five layers, resulting in a thickness of ⁵⁄₁₆ in. (7.5 mm). Since it is desirable for the grain direction on both outside faces to run the same way, particularly on the back preform, you will need to use an uneven number of layers.

22 Now, make the seat mold. First, make the sides of the mold by setting out a curve on the piece of manufactured board to suit the grid shape on the right. Set out

another line parallel, equal to the thickness of the form. Cut both lines with a jigsaw. This will give two matching sides (top and bottom) with a space for the form to go between.

23 Next, cut the lateral strips to length and fix them into the sides as shown below. Make sure that the top edges are flush. Check fit and finish by shaping or sanding to the correct curvature.

24 Cut and fix the two end pieces, which stabilize the mold when pressure is applied. Finally, cut the top of the mold and glue in place.

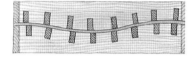

Make the seat mold.

Fix the top of the seat mold.

25 Try the mold dry with the pieces you have cut for one seat form. Clamp the jig together.

26 If all is well, apply adhesive to the faces to be glued and clamp the mold, leaving it clamped long enough for the adhesive to cure. Remove from the mold, mark the shape of the seat on it, trim to shape with a jigsaw, and sand the edges.

Clamp the plywood in the mold.

27 The back mold is made in a similar way as the seat, except that at the top there is a slight curve on each side (see drawing on page 376). Make the center of the mold in the same way as you made the seat mold (see opposite for grid). In addition, make a second mold for the wings of the back—this takes in the curve

Make the back mold.

of the first mold along its side edges. Cut and fit into the first mold as shown below.

28 When this mold is finished, follow the above procedure to produce the preform, and when it is complete, cut the correct shape and finish the edges.

Final assembly

29 Sand and apply the required finish to all components and then set the preforms in position. The bottom of the back will need to be trimmed to fit into the groove on the top edge of the back rail. A ⅜ in. (10 mm) wide x ⁵⁄₁₆ in. (8 mm) high cutout in each corner is required.

30 The back will be glued at the bottom into the groove and held in position

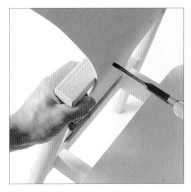

Screw the back in position.

Expert tip

Place paper or polyethylene sheets between the mold and the work to keep any adhesive that may seep out between the laminated pieces from gluing the work to the form.

Windsor chairs

Windsor chair is now the generic term for chairs and seats that are made with a stick construction: they have turned spindles socketed into solid wooden seats to form the back and legs. The place of origin of these chairs is unknown but by the early 19th century one locality in particular was identified with the production of Windsor chairs—Chepping Wycombe (now High Wycombe) in Buckinghamshire, England. The name Windsor has been traced to 1724 and a sale in 1728 included in its catalogue a Windsor chair, which refutes the romantic legend associated with how the chair got its name. It is popularly believed that George III, who in fact was not born until 1738, discovered the chair type in a cottage near Windsor while he was sheltering from a storm. He found the chair so comfortable that he ordered some to be made for Windsor Castle and the chair was called Windsor in his honor.

with two 1-in. (25 mm) 8 gauge brass flat head screws into the top rail. Drill the two ³⁄₁₆-in. (4.5 mm) holes through the back, followed by ⅛-in. (3 mm) pilot holes. Countersink the top of the holes so the screw heads sit just below the surface.

31 The seat will be held on the cross-rails with four screws. Check the fit of the seat on the cross-rails. Plane the top edge of these for a neat fit. Drill holes through the seat, as for the back. Apply adhesive to the cross-rails and screw in place. Sand and apply required finish.

Making the carving chair

The carving chair is based on the standard chair described above, with just a few changes.

1 The seat frame is the same except that the front legs are straight and extend up past the seat to support the arms. The front rail is longer and the tenons are square.

The front rail is longer.

2 The front legs are also longer—mark and cut to length. Cut a dowel top in the front legs as you did for the back legs in step 14. Fit the back legs and top rail as before, and then fit the longer front legs in position. The back will be the same, as will the seat, except for slight shaping around the legs.

3 Make and fit the arms. They are made in pairs with ⅞-in. (22 mm) wood. The arms are made from two pieces joined together with half lap joints on the sharp back curve. Join the two pieces together. Mark and cut the shape.

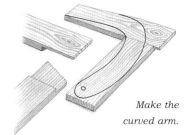

Make the curved arm.

4 When the arms are ready, drill the hole that will accept the top of the leg. Place in position and check that each fits on the top of the top rail. Mark and cut so that they join in the center of the back. Glue in place. The top of the leg can be wedged, while the back parts can be glued to the top of the top rail. Sand and finish.

Display shelves

These display shelves look both modern and attractive. The back piece (inserted as six separate panels of plywood) is optional—if you want to add it, follow the instructions on pages 389–90.

Tools

Smoothing plane

Sliding bevel

Marking knife

Tenon saw

Panel saw

C-clamps

Router with ¼-in. (6 mm) and ½-in. (12 mm) straight bit and ½-in. (12 mm) rabbet cutter with a ball race

Marking gauge

1-in. (25 mm) paring chisel

Drill and ⅛-in. (3 mm), ³⁄₁₆-in., (4.5 mm) countersink, and ⅜-in. (10 mm) dowel bits

Screwdriver

Sash clamps

Dovetail saw

MATERIALS

Part	Materials and dimensions	No.
	Solid wood—hardwood	
Triangle		
Long sides	82 x 12½ x 1 in. (2100 x 310 x 25 mm)	2
Bottom short side	60 x 12½ x 1 in. (1520 x 310 x 25 mm)	1
Plinth	59 x 2 x 1 in. (1500 x 50 x 25 mm)	2
	12 x 2 x 1 in. (300 x 50 x 25 mm)	2
Shelves		
Top	86 x 8 x 1 in. (2200 x 200 x 25 mm)	1
Second	81 x 8¾ x 1 in. (2050 x 220 x 25 mm)	1
Third	75 x 9½ x 1 in. (1900 x 240 x 25 mm)	1
Fifth	63 x 10¼ x 1 in. (1600 x 260 x 25 mm)	1
Shelf/drawer	71 x 10½ x 1 in. (1800 x 270 x 25 mm)	1
Build-up	71 x 6 x 1 in. (1800 x 150 x 25 mm)	1
Thickness	71 x 3 x 1 in. (1800 x 75 x 25 mm)	1
battens	16¾ x 2 x 1 in. (420 x 50 x 25 mm)	4
Dowels	2 in. x ⅜ in. (50 x 10 mm) diameter	30
Support battens	71 x 3 x ¾ in. (1800 x 75 x 20 mm)	2
	82 x 3 x ¾ in. (2100 x 75 x 20 mm)	2
	94½ x 3 x ¾ in. (2400 x 75 x 20 mm)	1
Drawer		
Sides	16 x 2 x ⅝ in. (400 x 50 x 15 mm)	2
Back	32 x 2 x ⅝ in. (800 x 50 x 15 mm)	1
Drawer runner	16 x ⁵⁄₁₆ x ⁵⁄₁₆ in. (400 x 8 x 8 mm)	2
	Plywood—the approximate sized triangles will be base x height x ¼ in. (6 mm) thick; do not cut these until the carcass is assembled	
Top back	14½ x 12 in. (370 x 300 mm)	1
Second back	21 x 9 in. (530 x 230 mm)	1
Third back	29 x 8¼ in. (740 x 210 mm)	1
Fourth back	37½ x 8¼ in. (950 x 210 mm)	1
Fifth back	47 x 10¼ in. (1200 x 260 mm)	1
Sixth back	56 x 12½ in. (1440 x 320 mm)	1
Drawer bottom	32 x 16 x ¼ in. (800 x 400 x 6 mm)	1

Other materials: forty 1³⁄₁₆-in. (30 mm) 8 gauge flat head screws; fifty ½-in. (12 mm) 6 gauge flat head screws; six 2-in. (50 mm) 8 gauge flat head screws; adhesive (PVA); sandpaper; finish.

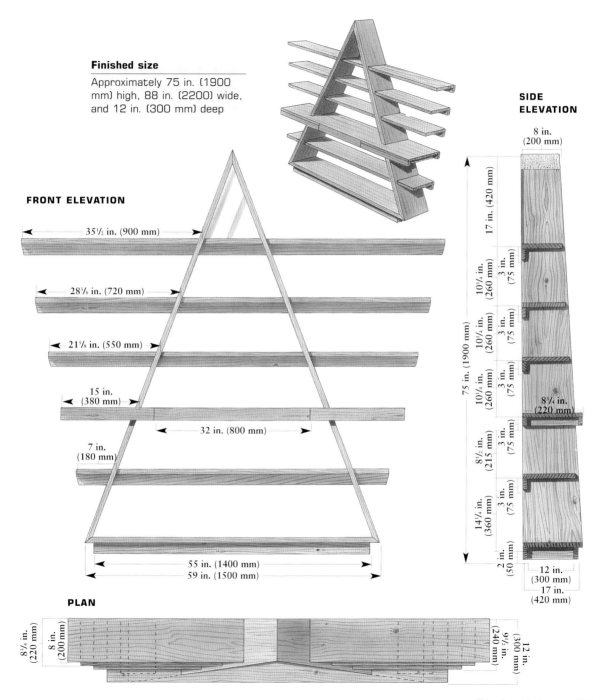

Finished size

Approximately 75 in. (1900 mm) high, 88 in. (2200) wide, and 12 in. (300 mm) deep

SIDE ELEVATION

8 in. (200 mm)

17 in. (420 mm)

10¼ in. (260 mm)

3 in. (75 mm)

10¼ in. (260 mm)

3 in. (75 mm)

10¼ in. (260 mm)

3 in. (75 mm)

8¾ in. (220 mm)

8½ in. (215 mm)

3 in. (75 mm)

14¼ in. (360 mm)

3 in. (75 mm)

2 in. (50 mm)

75 in. (1900 mm)

12 in. (300 mm)

17 in. (420 mm)

FRONT ELEVATION

35½ in. (900 mm)

28⅛ in. (720 mm)

21⅝ in. (550 mm)

15 in. (380 mm)

32 in. (800 mm)

7 in. (180 mm)

55 in. (1400 mm)

59 in. (1500 mm)

PLAN

8¾ in. (220 mm)

8 in. (200 mm)

9½ in. (240 mm)

12 in. (300 mm)

Making the triangular carcass

1 Make the slanting front face of the two long sides of the triangle (see drawing on page 385, side elevation)—the

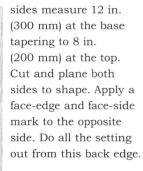

sides measure 12 in. (300 mm) at the base tapering to 8 in. (200 mm) at the top. Cut and plane both sides to shape. Apply a face-edge and face-side mark to the opposite side. Do all the setting out from this back edge.

Taper the front edge of the sides.

2 On a piece of manufactured board, make a set-out, either full-sized or scaled, for the miters on each corner. Remember that the top one is a more acute angle than the two at the bottom. Set up a sliding bevel to the miter joint.

3 The overall measurements of the two sides are 80½ in. (2043 mm) long and the bottom is 59 in. (1500 mm) long. Mark these lengths with the miter joints on the side faces. Mark the joints across each face.

4 These miters should be cut first with a marking knife and then sawed on the waste side with a tenon saw—a power saw will not tilt over the required angle. Hold each side on edge in a vice and cut the miter down the waste side of the line, stopping periodically to check the cut. Remove from the vice and lay flat on a firm surface. Hold with a C-clamp.

5 Plane the miter true with a finely set, sharp smoothing plane. Hold the plane at an angle and plane across the miter from side to side. Test the surface with the sliding bevel and then place a metal straightedge on the planed surface to check that it is flat. Plane off any highs down to the knife lines. Repeat on all the miter joints.

Cut and plane the miters to make the triangular corners.

6 Next, cut a bevel on the edge of six softwood clamping blocks, which give parallel faces to the miter surface so that the clamps will pull the miter joint together securely and precisely as well as protecting the surface of the project during clamping. When a block is cut along its length on the bevel, the scrap will form the clamping block for the opposite side of that miter. The beveled edge must be carefully cut to produce a 90-degree surface off the face of the joint, and with the outside edge parallel to that of the joint.

7 Glue the blocks to the outside faces at the three miters. Apply PVA adhesive to all the surfaces, align the top edge of the block to the end of the miter and allow to dry completely.

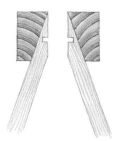

Glue softwood clamping blocks to each miter.

8 Set up a router with a ¼-in. (6 mm) straight bit to run a ¼-in. (6 mm) deep groove in the face of each miter for a loose tongue. Run the router fence off the block. The groove must be set across the face of the joint, taking care not to cut through to the outside of the work. Run the groove on all six faces. Cut three ½ x 12¼ in. (12 x 310 mm) tongues from ¼ in. (6 mm) thick plywood. Test the fit of each joint and dry-assemble the three pieces in clamps. Adjust as required.

9 Do not glue these mitered corners together yet. Leave them in the clamps face down on a flat surface.

10 On the edge of the sides of the triangular carcass, mark the position of the shelves, ensuring that they will be parallel with the base. Use a scrap piece of wood as a sample—the same thickness as the shelf material. Lay this on top of the assembled carcass and measure the spacing required at each end from the bottom to ensure that they are parallel. Mark both ends of the sample on the carcass with a pencil and square across each face. Repeat for all the shelves.

11 Now, mark the positions of the support battens that go under the rear edge of the shelves. The battens are 3 in. (75 mm) high x ¾ in. (20 mm) thick. Measure 3 in. (75 mm) below each shelf mark on the carcass. Mark this across the back edge parallel to the shelf and square down each face. Set a marking gauge to the thickness of ¾ in. (20 mm), and scribe the line back to the shelf. These slots will be cut later in step 17. Take the carcass out of the clamps.

12 Cut the dado joints in the sides of the carcass to accommodate the shelves. Mark the depth of the dado ¼ in. (6 mm) between the set-out shelf lines on the back edge. Square a line from the top of the shelf across to the depth line. Repeat this on the bottom inside shelf line.

13 Construct a router jig to cut the dado. Note that one shoulder is square to the face while the other is angled. The router needs to cut the dado to the width at the bottom ¼ in. (6 mm) line. Use a ½ in. (12 mm) straight bit and a template collar fixed to the baseplate. Make the jig and test on a piece of scrap wood before

cutting the work. Make a stop to fit to the jig that can be adjusted for each different shelf width. Set up the jig and machine each dado.

Set up a router jig, ready to pare away the waste.

14 Use a sharp chisel to cut the angled shoulder on one side of each housing. Pare away the waste and square up the ends with a chisel. Reassemble dry in the clamps.

Chisel the angled edge of the housing.

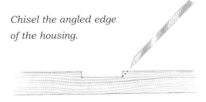

Making the shelves

Prepare the materials for the five shelves to their full lengths (see drawing on page 385). The instructions are virtually the same for each shelf but, of course, each is a different length. The center portions of these shelves will be fitted to the inside of the carcass on the rear battens first and the outside extensions will be fitted later. The ends of the shelves will fit into dadoes on both the inside and outside faces of the triangle sides and they will have dowels fitted within for added strength.

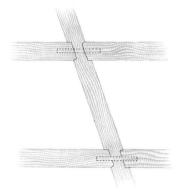

The shelves are held in place with dado joints and dowels.

15 When preparing the shelves, mark each to the final length so that the grain will match. First, mark the part of the shelf that will fit inside the carcass and the outside parts to match up later. Cut the center part of each shelf to length with a panel saw, shaping a bevel in each end to match the angle of the triangle side. Plane this true. Note that the bottom edge of the bevel will require a matching angle planed on it to

fit the dado. Fit the three top shelves and the bottom shelf. Be sure that they will fit into the dadoes. It is always best to work on one shelf at a time.

16 Next, construct drilling jigs to match the angles of the shelf and the sides. Use the jigs to drill the holes in the ends of the shelves and in the sides, right through to a depth of ¾ in. (20 mm) for the dowels.

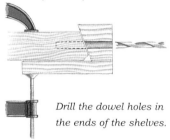

Drill the dowel holes in the ends of the shelves.

Drill the dowel holes in the sides.

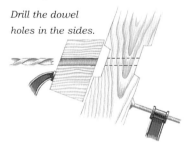

17 Next, check the positions of the slots for the rear battens, which you marked out in step 11. Ensure that they are all level with each other and the back. Then cut these slots into the carcass sides with a tenon saw.

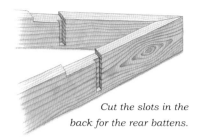

Cut the slots in the back for the rear battens.

18 Prepare to assemble the three top shelves and the bottom shelf. Assemble the triangle and shelves dry to check fit and then apply adhesive to the joints on the inside faces of the shelves. Insert dowels through the sides into the ends of the shelves, leaving them protruding on the outside of the carcass.

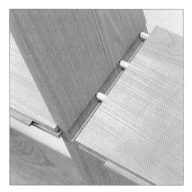

Glue the shelves into place. The grooves will be cut in step 28.

19 Next, apply adhesive to the mitered corners and insert the tongues at the joints. C-clamp the miters and check the work for true.

Clamp the mitered bottom corners of the triangular carcass.

Check the rear battens are parallel.

Cut rabbets for the back panels.

Clamp the top miters together.

Fixing the rear battens

20 Next, prepare the five rear battens that support the shelves. Check that they all fit into the slots already cut in step 17, that they are the correct length and that when positioned they are all parallel with each other and the base.

21 Glue and screw the rear battens into place through the back using 1³⁄₁₆ in. (30 mm) 8 gauge flat head screws. You will now have a triangular cabinet with four inside shelves in place and with five battens extending out the sides to support the outside shelves.

Making the back and plinth

22 Prepare the plywood backs for fitting. Since the back will not be one whole piece, rabbets need to be made around each opening in the sides and in the rear battens into which the plywood backs will fit. Use a ½ in. (12 mm) rabbet cutter with a ball race, and carefully cut the rabbets ¼ in. (6 mm) deep and ½ in. (12 mm) wide.

23 Now mark each of the six back pieces of wood—because of the angled ends you will be able to cut economically from a single sheet of plywood. Cut and fit each back into the rabbets and fix with ½ in. (12 mm) 6 gauge flat head screws.

Screw the back panels in position.

24 Now fit the bottom plinth. Prepare the wood and mark and cut the dovetails in the corners. Glue the four sections of the plinth together. When dry, sand the surface.

25 Fix the plinth in place by pocket screwing through the bottom edge, using three 2 in. (50 mm) 8 gauge flat head screws along each long edge.

Screw the plinth into place on the bottom of the unit.

26 Now, prepare the outer shelf extensions. You will already have these pieces from when you measured them before step 15. Using the jig as shown in step 16, drill the holes for the dowels and offer up to the unit so that you can ensure that the shelf ends fit into the dadoes.

27 When the outside ends are finished, place the shelves into position. The rear battens and the shelves can be pocket screwed together. Drill pocket holes ⁵⁄₁₆ in. (8 mm) in diameter and a clearance hole of ³⁄₁₆ in. (4.5 mm). Check that all fits well, apply the adhesive, and clamp and screw the shelves into place.

Check the fit and then fix the outer shelves into position.

Making the shelf with a drawer

Now make the fourth shelf with the drawer. This shelf is made in a similar way to the others but is deeper and comes to the front of the carcass. It has a groove worked on the front to accept a full-length piece, which will be attached to it with tongues. This buildup is designed to house the drawer.

28 Rout a groove along the front edge of the extended shelf section ¼ in. (6 mm) wide and ⅜ in. (10 mm) deep. Hold in a vice and cut the groove. Prepare the buildup wood to size and then run the groove along the length of it. Fit the shelf ends to the carcass in the same way as before. Keep the front edge vertical, not slanting like the carcass. When dry, glue the strip to the front edge with tongues in the grooves, extending the depth of the shelf. Wipe away any excess adhesive with a damp cloth before it dries. Hold in place with sash clamps until dry.

29 The visual thickness of the shelf is increased by applying extra strips beneath the shelf. Cut a 3 x 1 in. (75 x 25 mm) front the same length as the shelf. Plane a 45-degree angle along the edge. Plane a matching angle on the front edge of the shelf. Cut a drawer front 31½ in. (800 mm) long from the center so the grain will match. Glue the two outside pieces to the edge of the shelf. Screw the end strips beneath the ends of the shelf. Cut two guides 2 x 1 in. (50 x 25 mm) to fit behind the front across to the back edge. These will support the drawer

runners. Screw these from beneath and be sure that they are square to the front and parallel to each other.

Increase the visual thickness by adding extra strips to each edge.

30 Now, make the drawer to go in the middle section of the shelf. The drawer front has already been cut from the center of the front strip. Prepare the components to make the sides, back, and bottom.

Prepare the materials for the sides, back and bottom of the drawer.

31 Prepare the 2 x ⅝ in. (50 x 15 mm) wood for the sides and back. Construct

a drawer with lapped dovetails at the front and through dovetails at the back. Keep the mitered edge at the top edge for the front. Cut the dovetails in the usual way using a dovetail saw.

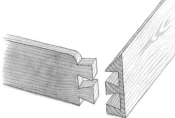

Fit the drawer together with dovetail joints.

32 Assemble the drawer and check its fit. Adjust the components as required.

33 Next, measure and cut the ⁵⁄₁₆ x ⁵⁄₁₆ in. (8 x 8 mm) strips on which the drawer will run.

34 Fix the runners to the drawer guides, ⅞ in. (21 mm) down from the top and stopping 1¹³⁄₁₆ in. (20 mm) from the front edge.

Side view

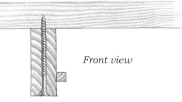

Front view

Make runners and guides for the drawer.

35 Next, set the router to run a matching groove along each side of the drawer. Make sure that you stop ¾ in. (20 mm) short of the front edge. Check the fit of the drawer and adjust the components as necessary.

The finished drawer.

36 Remove the blocks from the mitered corners of the carcass. Sand all the surfaces carefully and then apply the finish of your choice to your lovely new display shelves.

Home office

The home office has an interesting and unusual structure, which forms a neat visual unit that unfolds to give working and storage space. The top part of the front, when lowered, slides into the structure to form the projecting working surface.

MATERIALS

Part	Materials and dimensions	No.
	Solid wood, hardwood or softwood	
Main frame		
Upright posts	60 x 4 x 4 in. (1525 x 100 x 100 mm)	2
Feet	28 x 6 x 2¾ in. (725 x 150 x 45 mm)	2
Cross-rails	39⅜ x 3 x 2¾ in. (1000 x 75 x 45 mm)	1
	39⅜ x 4 x 2¾ in. (1000 x 100 x 45 mm)	2
Support rails	18 x 4 x 2¾ in. (450 x 100 x 45 mm)	2
	Assorted solid wood and manufactured board	
Fall/work surface		
Fixed working surface	¾-in. (20 mm) plywood, 36¼ x 21¼ in. (920 x 540 mm)	1
Fall writing surface	½-in. (12 mm) plywood, 36 x 26¾ in. (900 x 680 mm)	1
Frame ribs	softwood: 36 x 2 x 1 in. (900 x 50 x 25 mm)	7
Fall front	3/16-in. (4 mm) plywood, 36 x 36 in. (900 x 900 mm)	1
Frame uprights	softwood: 36 x 2 x 1 in. (900 x 50 x 25 mm)	3
Top storage area		
Top	½-in. (12 mm) plywood, 36 x 22 in. (900 x 560 mm)	1
Fixed work surface	¾-in. (20 mm) plywood, 36¼ x 21⅝ in. (920 x 548 mm)	1
Side panels	½-in. (12 mm) plywood, 32 x 16 in. (800 x 400 mm)	2
Back panels	½-in. (12 mm) plywood, 32 x 10 in. (800 x 250 mm)	3
Corner batten	softwood: 16 x ¾ x ¾ in. (400 x 20 x 20 mm)	2
	23⅝ x ¾ x ¾ in. (600 x 20 x 20 mm)	1
Bottom storage area		
Top and base	½-in. (12 mm) plywood, 36 x 18 in. (900 x 450 mm)	2
Side panels	½-in. (12 mm) plywood, 22 x 18 in. (550 x 450 mm)	2
Back panels	½-in. (12 mm) plywood, 36 x 22 in. (900 x 550 mm)	1
Corner batten	softwood: 16 x 3¾ x ¾ in. (400 x 20 x 20 mm)	2
	23⅝ x ¾ x ¾ in. (600 x 20 x 20 mm)	1
Doors		
Backboards	½-in. (12 mm) plywood, 36 x 24 in. (900 x 600 mm)	1
Framed ribs	softwood: 36 x 2 x 1 in. (900 x 50 x 25 mm)	5
Frame uprights	softwood: 22 x 19¾ x 1 in. (550 x 500 x 25 mm)	4
Door fronts	3/16-in. (4 mm) plywood, 36 x 24 in. (900 x 600 mm)	1

Tools

- Smoothing plane
- Router with ¼-in. (6 mm) and ½-in. (12 mm) straight bits
- Power plane
- Try plane
- Radial-arm saw
- Tenon saw
- 1-in. (25 mm) firmer and ¾-in. (20 mm) mortise chisels
- C-clamps
- Drill press and ⅛-in. (3 mm), 3/16-in.(4.5 mm), 5/16-in. (8 mm), ¾-in. (20 mm), and 1-in. (25 mm) bits
- Jigsaw or bandsaw
- Marking gauge
- Mortise gauge
- Screwdriver
- Power saw

Other materials: six 1⅝-in. (40 mm) 8 gauge flat head screws; twenty-four 1-in. (25 mm) 6 gauge flat head screws; ten 6 x 5/16-in. (150 x 8 mm) furniture bolts, plus barrel nuts to fit; two ½ x ¼-in. (12 x 6 mm) pins for the slides, plus bearings; two 18-in. (450 mm) metal channels plus rollers; two pairs of 2-in. (50 mm) butt hinges; four magnetic cupboard catches; adhesive (PVA); sandpaper (100-grit); finish.

PART FRONT ELEVATION

SIDE ELEVATION

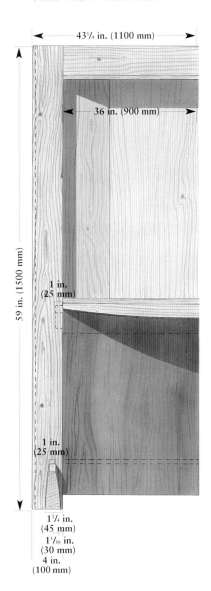

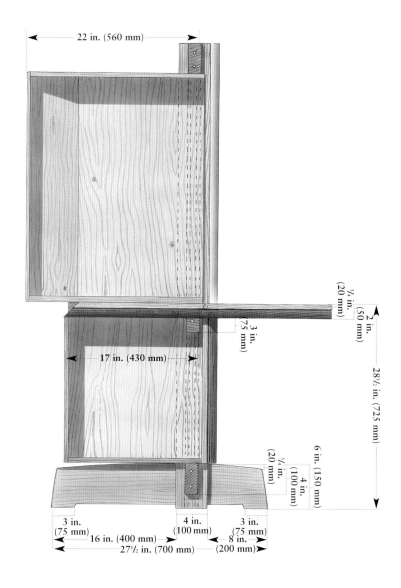

PART PLAN

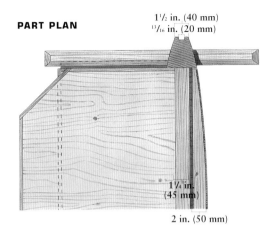

1½ in. (40 mm)
13/16 in. (20 mm)

1¼ in. (45 mm)

2 in. (50 mm)

Finished size

Approximately 59 in. (1500 mm) high, 43¼ in. (1100 mm) wide, and 31 in. (683 mm) deep

The design of this home office can be adapted to a size that fits your needs. It consists of two main units: the main frame, fall and working surface, and the storage areas.

Making the main frame

1 Begin by making the two inverted T-frames—there are two upright posts and two feet. Mark and cut the components for the wood frame as shown in the drawing opposite.

2 First, cut a groove along the outside edge of each upright post, 1⅜ in. (40 mm) in from each edge. Place one of the uprights in a vice and set up a router to cut the groove ⅜ in. (10 mm) deep x ¾ in. (20 mm) wide. Repeat to cut a groove on the other upright post.

3 Next, shape the upright posts, which taper from 4 in. (100 mm) on the inside to 1¹⁄₁₆ in. (27.5 mm) on the outside. Pencil gauge a line along the post to mark this taper. Remove the bulk of the waste with a power plane and then finish off the shape with a try plane.

4 Next, shape the feet, which taper from bottom to top. Pencil gauge to a depth of ⅜ in. (10 mm) along the top edge from both sides. Use the power plane and try plane to shape these. Make a taper along the top edge, starting ¾ in. (20 mm) along from each end of the dado that will be cut in step 7. Shape with a smoothing plane. Recut each end on the radial-arm saw at a slight bevel.

5 The feet are also shaped at the bottom to prevent them rocking on the floor. Remove ⅜ in. (10 mm) from the center with a jigsaw or bandsaw. Mark a line parallel to the bottom edge ⅜ in. (10 mm) up. Square the ends 3 in. (75 mm) in from each end. Cut this out, rounding the corners as you go.

6 Now, mark out the half-lap joints between the bottom of the upright posts and feet—note that these are made with dadoes where the shaped sections meet.

Mark the positions of the half-lap joints.

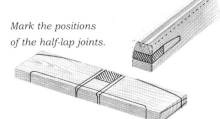

7 Cut the joint in one of the upright posts using a tenon saw and then trace the shape of the post onto the top of one foot to mark the position of the joint. Carefully cut it to shape. Use a tenon saw and chisel to cut the dadoes. Repeat to cut the joints in the other post and foot.

8 Fit each foot onto its post to check the fit and square of the joint. Apply adhesive to the joint once the fitting is complete, and allow the adhesive to dry.

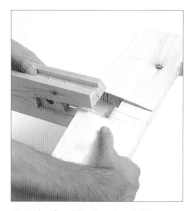

Test the fit of the half-lap joint.

Making the horizontal fall/support rails

These front-to-back rails have grooves in them, along which the pins on the bottom of the fall/work surface run. In order to reduce wear, let in some metal channel sections and give the pins bearings. These rails are halved, glued, and screwed to finish flush with the inside of the main column. They are further reinforced by the inclusion of the top and bottom storage section sides.

9 Mark and cut the two horizontal support rails to a length of 17 in. (430 mm). Work two grooves, one for the fall pins (preferably inserting a metal channel) and another for the fixed work surface inside the cabinet. The pin groove is ¼ x ¼ in. (6 x 6 mm), and matches the width of the pin and bearing (if used). Set up the router as before and run this groove 1¾ in. (45 mm) down from the top edge. The groove for the work surface is ¾ in. (20 mm) wide x ⅜ in. (10 mm) deep. Set up and run this groove from the same edge, ½ in. (12 mm) down.

10 Set out the half-lap joint at one end, which will be fixed to the upright posts. Set these out as a pair 2¾ in. (70 mm) long, and square around the outside face and both edges. Scribe the depth with a marking gauge, ¾ in. (20 mm) from the outside face. Hold vertically in a vice and cut down to the squared lines on the waste side. Lay flat against a bench hook and cut the shoulders.

11 Set out the stopped dado on the inside of each post to match, positioning the top of the rail 29 in. (737 mm) from the bottom of the post. Lay each post flat and hold firm. Cut the shoulders with a tenon saw and remove the waste with a chisel, ensuring that the stopped dado is square. Test the fit to check the face of the rail ends flush with the post and is square.

12 Screw and glue the rails in place. Use three 1⅜ in. (40 mm) 8 gauge flat head screws on each end. Drill the holes for the screws, taking care that the holes do not interfere with the grooves.

Fit the support rails into place.

Making the three cross-rails

The top and bottom are simple straight rails, but the center rail is shaped so that it supports the work surface when it is open and in use.

13 Set out the mortises in the posts to locate the cross-rails. The bottom mortise is 2⅜ in. (60 mm) up from the bottom of the post and 3½ in. (90 mm) long. Mark the center mortise 23⅞ in. (605 mm) up and 3⅛ in. (55 mm) long, and the top mortise ⅜ in. (10 mm) down and 3³⁄₁₆ in. (80 mm) long. Square all the mortises across the inside face of both posts.

14 Set the mortise gauge to scribe the mortises 1 in. (25 mm) wide between the squared lines. Secure posts on a firm surface with a C-clamp. Remove the bulk of the waste by drilling several holes ¾ in. (20 mm) in diameter and 1 in. (25 mm) deep in the center of the set-out. Cut the mortise to length with a mortise chisel. Straighten the sides with a 1 in. (25 mm) firmer chisel.

15 Cut the three cross-rails to 37½ in. (950 mm) long and cut a 1 in. (25 mm) long tenon on each end. Square a shoulder line around each end, set a marking gauge to ⅜ in. (10 mm) and scribe the tenon from the shoulder line out across the end and back to the opposite shoulder from both faces. Hold each rail vertical in a vice and cut down each side of the tenon on the waste side to the shoulder line. Secure each rail on a flat, firm surface, and cut along the squared shoulder lines on the waste side with a tenon saw. Cut the tenon to width by removing ⅜ in. (10 mm) from each side. Test the fit of each joint and adjust as required until you achieve a neat fit.

16 Shape the top edge of the middle cross-rail to accommodate the slide in the fall or work surface. Square a line across the center on the face side. Mark a curve on this face 1³⁄₁₆ in. (30 mm) down at the center, to finish the full width at each end. To do this, bend a thin piece of wood to shape, and mark with a pencil. Cut this shape on the bandsaw or jigsaw on the waste side, and smooth out with 100-grit sandpaper.

17 To enable the whole unit to be assembled and disassembled, it is best to use barrel nuts and bolts instead of adhesives to hold the mortise-and-tenons tight.

18 From the outside, drill the holes central to the post and into the mortise for the ⁵⁄₁₆ in. (8 mm) bolts. Drill two in the bottom and top rails 1 in. (25 mm) in from each edge, and one in the middle of the center rail. Remember that the middle rail will be fitted over the end of the horizontal support rail. Hold the middle rail in the mortise and drill through the hole again into the end of the tenon. Remove the rail and drill the hole in the end 3⅜ in. (85 mm) deep.

19 Square a line 1¾ in. (45 mm) along from each shoulder. Measure 1 in. (25 mm) in from each edge for the top and bottom and the center of the middle rail. Drill holes into each face at this set-out to match the barrel nuts.

Use barrel nuts and bolts to secure the mortise-and-tenon joints.

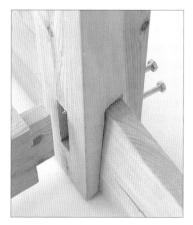

Fit the bottom rail in place, insert the bolts and nuts, and tighten.

Assemble the whole frame.

(50 mm) in the center. Bend a thin piece of wood between these points and trace the curve. Cut to shape on a bandsaw or jigsaw. True the curve with sandpaper. Use this as the template for all the other ribs, including those for the lower doors. There are 12 in all.

23 Fit the curved fillets to the back of the work surface. Start by fixing the top and bottom ribs between the two uprights. Cut and fit a center upright in between. Fix with adhesive so that the top edges are flush. Cut and fix five more ribs with PVA between the uprights, dividing them to accommodate the center upright. Test the fit in the opening of the main frame. Plane until you obtain a ⅛ in. (3 mm) clearance on each side.

Fit the middle rail into place after the support rail has been fitted.

Making the fall/work surface

The work surface is made from flat board while the shaped front is constructed by using curved fillets. These support a thin sheet of veneer plywood that is glued to them to give the curved surface.

20 Fit this whole frame together, placing the middle rail over the horizontal support rail. Insert the bolts and nuts, and tighten. Check the frame for size, twist, and square. Adjust as required.

21 Cut the ply board to 35¼ x 26⅝ in. (895 x 675 mm). Cut two frame uprights 26⅝ in. (675 mm). Fix along the two side edges of the plywood on the back with PVA.

22 Next, cut the curved fillets. You will need to construct each rib so that its centerpoint is 1¼ in. (30 mm) higher than the ends. Cut and set out one rib 31¼ in. (795 mm) long. Mark ¾ in. (20 mm) on each end and 2 in.

24 Drill a ⅛ in. (3 mm) hole ⅜ in. (10 mm) up from the bottom and ⅜ in. (10 mm) from the back edge of the frame uprights for the pins. Insert the pins into these holes. If required, the pins can be made by cutting the heads off some screws and placing a slit in the end for a screwdriver. The pins should not protrude more than ¼ in. (6 mm) from the edge of the fall.

Make the fall/work surface.

Check the hinge system of the fall.

25 Remove one side of the frame and place a washer on the pin before placing it into the frame. Check the fall fits the grooves in the horizontal support rails and then make any necessary adjustments. Once you are satisfied, remove the fall from the frame so that you can fit the top.

Check the fit and adjust if necessary.

26 Clamp the thin veneered plywood sheet to the curve and fix with adhesive onto all the curved ribs and uprights. Use a C-clamp to secure a scrap block over the full length of each upright until dry.

27 Trim the face ply so that it finishes flush on the edges.

Making the top storage area

28 Next, make the fixed work surface by cutting to the shape on the drawing on page 394—21½ in. (548 mm) wide and 36¼ in. (920 mm) long. Fit into the top grooves in the horizontal support rails. The back corners are cut off at 45 degrees from the ends of the support rails.

29 Cut the side panels to fit from the fixed work surface up to the bottom edge of the top cross-rail, plus ¾ in. (20 mm) for the corner battens. The back edge will need to be beveled at an angle to match the work surface. The front top corner will need a section cut around the cross-rail. Fix the side upright panels in position, screwing to the main uprights and the work surface.

30 Cut and fit the top. This will also need the back corners cut off at an angle to match the work surface. Screw this to the underside of the top frame rail. Cut and fit the corner battens to go around the side and back edges of the top. Then screw the side panels to the corner battens.

Complete the back of the top storage section.

31 Fit the two angled panels to the back of the work surface, the top and side panels. Finally, fit the back panel in place and screw to the work surface and the angled panels. Cut each in turn to fit, with angled edges. Add shelves to suit your needs.

Making the bottom storage area

32 Fit the sides to the main frame and the horizontal support rails, fixing them with 1 in. (25 mm) 6 gauge flat head screws. Leave enough clearance at the top and front edge for the doors to operate.

33 Fit the base to the lower cross-rail and screw into a corner batten fitted to the sides in a similar way to those fitted in the top storage area.

34 Cut and fit the back over the base and side pieces with screws.

35 Make and fit the two doors, using the same method as that used for the fall front. This time, however, cut two backboards. Cut the uprights to the same height as the backboards. Glue flush on each vertical edge. The upright

on the hinge side is 1 in. (25 mm) wide; that on the opening side is wider to match the curves. Trim the curved ribs, which have already been cut, to fit between the uprights, maintaining the curve surfaces. Once dry, test-fit the doors and plane for 1/8 in. (3 mm) clearance. On each door cut in two 2 in. (50 mm) butt hinges.

Test the fit of the lower doors before fastening in place.

36 Remove the doors of the home office and clamp the thin plywood to the curves, fixing it with adhesive onto all the curved ribs and uprights.

Final finishing

37 Dismantle the whole office unit and sand all surfaces in order to remove any marks that may be left.

38 Apply the finish of your choice to all the components of the home office.

39 Reassemble the unit and check that all the doors and the fall function properly. Adjust the components as necessary to obtain a perfect fit. Finally, fit a pair of catches to the fall and one on each door in order to keep the unit secure when shut.

Apply the required finish and reassemble the unit.

The home office doors closed.

Useful
information

Glossary

A

abrasive paper

Another name for sandpaper; *see* page 414.

air drying

A method of seasoning lumber by stacking it so that the circulation of dry air slowly dries the wood.

aluminum-oxide paper

A very hard abrasive paper, used mainly for sanding hardwoods and in power sanders as a sheet or belt.

animal glue

Adhesive made from the skin and bones of animals, available as powder or small dry globules or pearls; largely superseded by PVA and UF adhesives.

arc

Any part of an unbroken curved line.

arris

A sharp edge produced where two surfaces meet at an angle.

awl

A small pointed tool; makes holes or pilot holes for nails.

axis

An imaginary straight line around which a solid piece of material or object appears to be symmetrical.

B

backing-grade veneer

Inexpensive, low-grade veneers that are glued to the back of a piece of wood, in contrast to the best-grade ones, which are glued to the face edge or front; *see also* face quality.

backsaw

A small saw with a strip of brass or steel set over the top of the blade, both to keep it straight and inflexible and to add weight when cutting.

balk

A groove or ridge in lumber.

barefaced joint

A joint that has one shoulder.

batten

A strip of wood; often used as an unseen support to hold workpieces to walls, etc.

bead

A narrow strip of semicircular molding used for decoration; or a convex, rounded shape produced by turning.

belt sander

A power sander in which a continuous belt of sandpaper is rotated around rollers to remove the finish from large areas of wood; sometimes clamped to a bench.

bench dog

Removable wooden or metal stop that is placed into premade holes in a bench and acts as a stop for a workpiece.

bench hook

A square or rectangular piece of wood with a batten attached to the top at one end and to the bottom at another; used for holding wood when cutting with a backsaw.

bending

Three methods are generally used to bend wood. These are steam-bending, applying pressure to steamed wood around a form; kerfing, using equally spaced saw cuts; and laminating, building up layers of wood around a shaped form.

bevel

An angle that slopes at more than 90 degrees; to cut such an angle.

biscuit jointer

A power tool that cuts matching shaped grooves in two pieces of wood, into which an oval wooden shape, or biscuit, is glued like a dowel.

bit

The end of a tool used for cutting, biting, or boring; bits used in drills are removable and interchangeable.

blank

A plain piece of wood cut to an approximate size for mounting in a lathe and turning.

blister

An area or patch of veneer that has come away from its mounting surface, usually because the glue has failed.

blockboard

A strong, rigid laminate board made from strips of solid wood laid edge to edge and sandwiched between two sheets of plywood; *see also* laminboard.

book-matched veneer

Leaves of off-centered veneer laid out and glued in place to produce a symmetrical design.

bore

To cut, drill, or pierce a hole in wood.

bowed

A term for a twisted length of wood; *see also* winding.

burl

A growth on a tree trunk, cut off and sliced to produce burl or speckled veneer.

burr

The thin, rough edge of metal left after sharpening or honing.

C

cabinet scraper

A thin piece of steel, either rectangular, convex at one end, or goose-neck shape, used for a final smoothing of wood before applying finish.

calibrated

A tool with at least one scale of measurement, such as a ruler.

carborundum

A powder made from silicon carbide, mixed with water as a paste for extremely fine sharpening, and removal of rust spots on metal tools.

caul

Flat or curved stiff board, used to press and shape groundwork and veneer sheets.

C-clamp

An open clamp with one fixed and one screw-adjustable head, used for holding workpieces in position on benches, etc.

chamfer

A flat surface planed on the edge of a piece of wood, usually at 45 degrees, either to soften a sharp edge or for decoration; to plane such a surface.

checks

Cracks, splits, or flaws in lumber, brought about by uneven seasoning; in veneer sheets, knife checks are splits made by badly adjusted blades.

chipboard

A man-made board manufactured by compressing small chips of wood and glue; difficult to screw and not very strong, but used for inexpensive furniture and other units.

chisel, bevel-edged

A chisel with a tapered-profile blade; used for cleaning up the corners of joints or recesses, either by hand pressure or with a mallet.

chisel, firmer

A chisel with a rectangular-profile blade; used with a mallet to chop out large mortises and lock recesses.

chisel, mortise

A small chisel similar to a firmer chisel, used for the same tasks in smaller section.

chuck

In a drill, the part that holds a bit, adjusted either by a chuck key or opposing rotation; in a lathe, a piece of wood attached to the faceplate and used to hold a blank or workpiece.

clamp

An adjustable device used to hold work to a bench or to apply pressure and hold pieces of wood being glued together; see also C- and sash clamp.

coarse-textured

Used to describe the surface quality of open grain lumber.

collet

A slit sleeve with an external taper, made in two or more segments, which tightens to hold a bit or cutter when it is pushed into an internally tapered socket.

combination or universal machine

A machine that combines a number of different operations into one unit, such as table saw, planer, slot mortiser, spindle router, etc.

compound miter

A miter angled in more than one plane.

concave

A surface that curves inward.

contact glue

An adhesive that, when applied to two surfaces and brought

together, creates an instant bond without the need for clamping or supporting the pieces.

convex

A surface that curves outward.

coping saw

A small curve-cutting saw with a blade held in tension by a sprung metal frame; the blades, being thin, are disposable.

core

In manufactured boards, the central strips of wood or layers of board that are held in place by the two outermost surfaces.

counterbore

A hole that enables the head of a bolt or screw to lie below the surface of a workpiece; to cut such a hole.

countersink

A tapered hole that enables the head of a flat-topped bolt or screw to lie flush with the surface of a workpiece; to cut such a hole.

cove

A concave surface; or a concave edge molding.

cross grain

Wood grain that does not follow the direction of the axis.

cross-banding

Thin strips of veneer cut across the grain and used for decorative bordering or inlay.

crosscut saw

A general-purpose saw used for cutting wood to length.

crosscutting

Sawing against or across the grain of a piece of wood.

crown-cut

Veneer produced by flat-slicing, with curved patterns of grain.

cure

In adhesives or finishes, to set or fix by a chemical reaction.

curly figure

Alternating bands of dark and light grain across a veneer sheet sliced from curly grain wood.

curly grain

Grain with a random, irregular wavy pattern.

D

dado

A flat groove, cut across the grain of one piece of wood, that holds the end of another piece.

DAR lumber

Dressed all round lumber; another name for planed all round lumber (PAR).

detail sander

Also known as a delta sander, this tool is a small power sander with a triangular plate used for sanding into corners.

disk sander

A flat faceplate designed to fit into a power drill chuck and be fitted with an abrasive disk;

can be used with a bench-clamped support table for sanding pieces.

dovetail joint

An interlocking joint in which wedge-shaped pins and tails are cut to fit tightly, producing a strong and decorative joint.

dovetail saw

A small backsaw, often with a straight handle, used for cutting precise joints.

dowel

A short length of round-profile wood used to join two pieces of wood by being glued into a precut hole in each piece; often with small grooves or flutes along the length.

dowel bit

A cylindrical drill bit with a central point, two side spurs, and spiral grooves or flutes, used to drill dowel holes; *see also* twist drill.

dowel pin

A small brass or metal pin with a sharp point on the upper edge, used for marking dowel positions.

drill press

A machine for using interchangeable drill bits for cutting holes through wood.

E

earlywood

The pale wood that develops as wide tree rings in the earlier part of the growing season.

edge

The sharpened side of a cutting tool; a right angle where two surfaces of a piece of wood meet.

edge grain

The quality of grain of wood produced by quarter-sawing; *see also* quarter sawn.

end grain

The exposed wood fibers at the end of a piece of wood that has been cut across the grain direction; *see also* crosscutting.

ergonomics

The study of the relationship between people and their working environment; used of furniture specially designed to suit the human body.

escutcheon

A metal plate around a keyhole, which protects the surrounding surface; or the metal lining of the keyhole itself.

F

face edge

The surface of a piece of wood that is adjacent at a right angle to the face side, and that takes its measurements next after it.

face mask

A disposable mask that covers the nose and mouth when working with dust-producing or toxic substances.

face quality

The best grade of veneers, used for covering the visible or front surfaces of wood; *see also* backing-grade veneer.

face side

The surface of a flat, planed piece of wood that is used for the first marks and measurements, and from which all other measurements are taken.

faceplate

A flat-faced metal disk that is rotated by a lathe's drive spindle, and that holds blanks for woodturning.

feed on a machine

To move a workpiece along the table and into the cutting or shaping area.

fence

An adjustable length of metal or wood that is fixed or clamped in position to guide a workpiece in a straight line as it is being cut.

ferrule

A metal ring or cap fitted on a tool handle to strengthen it where it meets the tang.

fettling

General term for sharpening, cleaning and keeping tools in good order.

fiberboards

Boards manufactured from reconstituted wood fibers, particularly hardboards, low-density boards, and medium-density fiberboard (MDF).

fielded panel

A panel of wood with tongues cut around the edges to fit into grooves in a frame.

figure

The grain pattern in a piece of wood.

file

A carving tool used to smooth wood after it has been worked with a rasp; *see also* rasp and riffler.

fillet

Another name for batten.

flat grain

The quality of grain of wood produced by plain-sawing.

flat-sawn

Another name for plain-sawn.

flat-sliced

Veneer tangentially cut from a log; *see also* crown-cut.

flitch

A bundle of leaves of veneer, selected for sale.

Forstner bit

A drill bit used for cutting flat-bottomed holes or for drilling clean holes through pieces of wood.

fox wedging

A stopped mortise-and-tenon joint where small wedges are hammered into the spread tenon.

French polish

A traditional wood finish made from a solution of shellac in alcohol, sometimes tinted; produces a mirror-like smooth finish, but is easily scratched or damaged by heat or liquid.

fretsaw

A thin, narrow blade stretched vertically in a frame, used for cutting thin wood to ornamental, often scrolled, designs and patterns.

frog

The support, usually of steel, for a blade in a hand plane.

front elevation

The front view of a workpiece in a scale or working drawing.

G

garnet paper

A good general-purpose abrasive paper, suitable for use on both hardwoods and softwoods.

gauge

Also called a marking gauge, a length of half-curved-profile hardwood with a steel pin protruding from one end and a movable stock or fence that is locked in place to scribe lines at a fixed distance along wood; *see also* mortise gauge.

gents saw

A small tenon saw, used for cutting small joints or delicate angles; *see also* backsaw.

glasspaper

Coarse abrasive paper with glass as the abrasive, mainly for rough-sanding softwoods.

grain

The arrangement, direction, and size of the fibers and particles in a length of wood.

grind

To make smooth or sharpen a surface by friction.

grit

The minute particles used in making up sandpaper; also various gradings of roughness and smoothness of the abrasive surface.

groove

A channel cut along a piece of wood; to cut such a channel.

groundwork

The piece of wood to which a sheet of veneer is glued.

guide hole

Another name for pilot hole.

gullet

The spaces between the teeth of a saw; a smaller gullet makes a finer cut; *see also* kerf.

H

half-lap joint

Joint where both overlapping halves of wood joined together are of equal thickness, used for framing.

hand saw

Any saw powered by hand.

hardwood

Wood that comes from deciduous or broad-leaved trees of the family Angiospermae; not always harder than softwoods.

haunch

On a tenon, the part nearest the corner of the full-width wood that prevents the tenon from twisting or snapping off; *see also* sloping haunch.

headstock

The part of a lathe that contains the motor and gearing.

headstock spindle

The rotating drive cylinder protruding from a lathe headstock; used to mount a faceplate or drive center for turning.

heartwood

The hard, dense cells at the center of a tree; the most stable wood; *see also* sapwood.

hollow

A concave shape produced in woodturning.

hone

To produce the final, sharpest edge on a blade by sharpening on a stone such as an oilstone or diamond stone.

HSS

High-speed steel, standard material used manufacturing bits and blades; *see also* TCT.

I

infeed

The part of the table of a cutting or shaping machine that holds the wood before and as it is cut.

inlay

A piece of wood, metal, or other material glued into a precut groove or hollow and smoothed flush with the surrounding surface; to insert such a piece.

J

jig

A proprietary or homemade machine or device that holds a workpiece or tool so that identical operations can be repeated.

jigsaw

A portable power saw with a small, narrow blade, which is used to cut curves and intricate shapes.

K

kerf

The groove or cut made by saw teeth in wood.

kickback

The sharp violent motion made by a power tool when its cutter or blade jams; or the violent reaction made by a workpiece when thrown by a machine cutter or blade.

kiln drying

A method of seasoning wood in a kiln, which speeds up the removal of moisture.

knots or knotting

Hard outgrowths of branches in lumber, sometimes kept for decoration, but usually regarded as flaws; seal resinous knots with knot sealer before applying a finish.

L

laminate

A board made from thin strips of wood glued together tightly; to make such a board.

laminboard

A board that is made by gluing thin strips of wood together and sandwiching them between two sheets of plywood; it is similar to blockboard.

latewood

The dense, often dark wood that develops as narrow tree rings in the later part of the growing season.

lathe

A machine consisting of a headstock containing a motor, tailstock, lathe bed, and tool rest; used for turning.

lip

A strip of thin wood, used to protect the edges of manu-factured boards or tabletops.

long grain

Grain that is in the same direction as the axis on a piece of lumber; *see also* axis and short grain.

M

machine

A power tool fixed in one place in a workshop.

marking

Used to describe the process of measuring, making pencil marks, and scoring wood for cutting to length and cutting joints.

marking knife

A sharp knife with its blade beveled on one side, used to mark wood for cutting.

glossary

marquetry

The decorative art of cutting out and laying pieces of veneer to make pictures or patterns; *see also* parquetry.

MDF

Medium-density fiberboard, a close-textured, heavy manufactured board made by gluing fine wood particles together with resin; a substitute material for solid wood.

miter

A corner joint where the meeting pieces of wood are cut to the same angle, usually 45 degrees, though this need not always be the case.

miter square

A marking tool similar to a try square, but with a 45-degree angle between the blade and the stock, used to check the accuracy of miter joints; *see also* try square.

mock-up

A trial version of a construction piece, which is made from scrap materials and used to test the measurements and design before starting the piece itself.

mortise

A square or rectangular hole or recess cut into wood to accept a matching tenon.

mortise gauge

A marking gauge with two steel pins for marking the edges of a mortise.

N

nail set

Also known as a nail or center punch, a length of steel tapered to a thin end, used with a hammer to punch small nail heads beneath a surface.

O

oil

Transparent liquid finish for wood, can be tinted; usually made from natural ingredients, or blended with polyurethane for a tougher finish.

oilstone

A flat-surfaced manufactured stone, lubricated with light oil and used to sharpen and hone blades of chisels, planes, etc.

open grain

Wood with large pores, known as ring-porous.

orbital sander

A power sander where a pad of sandpaper is clamped to a baseplate that rotates in small elliptical movements.

outfeed

The part of the table of a cutting or shaping machine that holds the wood after it has been cut.

P

panel saw

Smaller than a ripsaw or crosscut saw, a general-purpose saw used for cutting manufactured boards to length

PAR lumber

Planed all round lumber—lumber that has been planed on all sides and is thus likely to be smaller than its nominal size.

pare

To remove fine shavings with a chisel, using hand pressure only.

parquetry

The decorative art of cutting out and laying geometrical pieces of veneer to make patterns; *see also* marquetry.

particleboard

A range of boards made by gluing together wood chips or particles; *see also* chipboard.

pilaster

A thin wooden column attached to the front of a cabinet or dresser for decoration.

pilot hole

A small hole drilled into wood that allows the threads of a larger screw to bite into the wood without splitting it.

plain-sawn

A way of cutting a log so that the growth rings meet the face of each board at an angle of less than 45 degrees.

plan

The top view of a workpiece, drawn to scale; also called plan elevation.

plane, block

A small general-purpose plane, often used for planing end grain.

plane, combination

Used in conjunction with a surface planer, a machine used to plane smooth the two remaining faces of a workpiece.

plane, jack

A medium-length general-purpose plane, used for most planing tasks.

plane, jointer

Also known as a try plane, a long plane used for smoothing long pieces of timber and planing for butt joints.

plane, shoulder

A thin plane used for planing rebates or trimming square shoulders on large joints.

plane, smoothing

A small plane with a fine blade, used to give a smooth finish to wood.

plane blade

The removable cutting part of a plane; sharpened on an oilstone.

planer, surface

A machine that is used to plane smooth the face side and face edge of a workpiece.

plywood

A board made by gluing together wafers of wood in a sandwich; often faced with veneer.

power tool

Any portable electric tool.

push stick

A stick cut with a notch in it, used to push wood into a machine cutter or blade.

PVA glue

A general-purpose woodworking adhesive, also known as white glue, made from an emulsion of polyvinyl-acetate in water, which sets as the water evaporates; a water-resistant version is available.

relief carving

A carving in which the subject or decorative motif is set above the background surface.

riffler

A small double-ended carving file, used for intricate smoothing; *see also* file.

rift-sawn

A way of cutting a log so that the growth rings meet the face of each board at an angle of 30–60 degrees.

ripping

Cutting wood with a ripsaw.

ripsaw

A large handsaw, used for cutting wood in the direction of the grain.

rotary-cut

A method of cutting veneer by slicing a continuous sheet from a log; used mainly to produce veneers for manufactured boards.

rotary sander

A power sander where a disk of sandpaper is clamped to a faceplate that rotates in circular movements.

rottenstone

A finely ground abrasive, which is used to rub down finishes between coats.

router

A versatile power tool, used for molding wood, cutting grooves and rabbets, cutting dadoes and shaping wood for joints or decoration; can also be used as a fixed tool.

rubbing pad

A cloth pad used for applying finishes and stains to wood; in French polishing, a cloth folded around an inner pad of batting or cotton.

runner

A strip of wood along which a drawer runs and which supports it.

Q–R

quarter-sawn

A way of cutting a log so that the growth rings meet the face of each board at an angle of more than 45 degrees.

rabbet

A recess, step, or groove, usually with a rectangular section, cut into wood for a slotted-in matching piece.

rail

Horizontal member of a window or door frame; or a supporting member in a table or chair.

rasp

Carving tool used to rough out shapes; *see also* file and riffler

S

sandpaper

A paper backing sheet with particles of abrasive material glued to one surface, used for smoothing and rounding wood.

sapwood

The light, soft cells farthest from the center of a tree; the least stable wood; *see also* heartwood.

sash clamp

A straight length of metal with one screw-adjustable head and a movable head that can be positioned in different places; used to hold large or long pieces of wood together.

scraper plane

A small, two-handled metal body that holds a scraper blade; used for taking tiny shavings of wood.

screwdriver, ratchet

An elongated screwdriver fitted with a ratchet device that drives the head in one direction only when the handle is pushed in.

scribe

To mark or score wood with a pointed marking tool, to indicate where it should be cut or shaped; or to shape the edge of a workpiece so that it fits the profile of another piece or of a shaped or uneven surface.

seasoning

The various methods used to reduce the moisture content of wood; *see also* air drying and kiln drying.

section

A representation of a workpiece as it would appear when cut across, along a vertical or horizontal plane.

set

To adjust the teeth of a saw alternately in opposite directions, thus regulating the width of the kerf; or to adjust a plane blade relative to the sole, thus regulating the depth of cut.

shakes

Splits in wood caused by shrinkage or defects in growth.

shellac

A natural product exuded by the lac insect, used in manufacturing French polish.

short grain

Grain that is in the opposing direction to the axis on a piece of wood; *see also* axis and long grain.

shoulder

A squared end on one or both sides of a tongue or tenon.

side elevation

On a scale drawing, the side view of a workpiece.

silicon-carbide paper

Used wet and dry with water, a fine abrasive for hardwoods; a dry, self-lubricating version is used for sanding between coats of French polish.

skew

Of a nail or screw, inserted at an angle other than a right angle; to insert a nail or screw at such an angle.

sliding bevel

A marking tool similar to a miter square, but with an adjustable blade that can be placed and locked at any angle; *see also* miter square.

sloping haunch

On a tenon, a haunch cut on a slope, invisible when the joint is assembled; *see also* haunch.

glossary

softwood

Wood that comes from coniferous trees of the family Gymnospermae; not always softer than hardwoods.

sole

A flat metal or wooden base of a tool such as a plane, that allows it to slide smoothly over wood surfaces.

sole plate

A smooth, flat-bottomed metal surface attached to the bottom of a plane or power saw, with the blade protruding through and held at a constant angle and depth.

splitting out

The splits and hole created when a cutter or drill breaks through a face of wood.

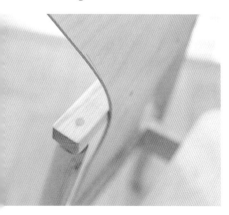

springwood

Another name for earlywood.

square

To use a try square to measure or set out a right angle; or, when checking a workpiece for accuracy, a precise right angle.

stile

A vertical member in a window or door frame.

stop

A piece of wood fixed to the frame of a door on which the door shuts.

stopped dado

A dado that does not run across the full width of a panel or workpiece; *see also* dado.

stopped mortise

A mortise that is not cut through the wood; *see also* mortise and through mortise.

straight grain

Another name for long grain.

strike plate

A metal plate fixed onto the recess that accepts a latch.

stringing

Thin inlaid line of wood, in furniture decoration or veneer.

strop

A strip of leather on which a sharp edge can be given to a blade by rubbing back and forth; to produce such an edge.

stub mortise

See stopped mortise.

stub tenon

A tenon that does not fit through a workpiece.

summerwood

Another name for latewood.

T

tack cloth

A resin-impregnated cloth used to pick up dust from a surface before applying a finish.

TCT

Tungsten-carbide-tipped bits or blades that stay sharp longer than HSS ones; used especially on chipboard and MDF; *see also* HSS.

template

A pattern or shape cut out of thin rigid material, used for

marking wood and guiding tools, particularly when making more than one identical piece.

tenon

A square or rectangular tongue or projecting piece, cut on the end of a piece of wood to fit into a matching mortise.

tenon saw

A large backsaw used for cutting joints and battens; *see also* backsaw, gents saw.

throat

In a drill press, the distance from the center of the worktable to the column.

through and through

A way of cutting a log using parallel cuts through its length; this produces various types of board; *see also* plain-sawn, quarter-sawn, and rift-sawn.

through mortise

A mortise that is cut through a piece of wood; *see also* mortise and stopped mortise.

tongue

A narrow strip cut along the edge of a board or panel that fits into a groove cut into a matching piece of wood; the term is also used in tongue-and-groove joints.

try square

A marking tool with a parallel-sided blade fixed at right angles to a stock, used to check and mark the accuracy of right angles.

twist drill

A cylindrical drill bit with a pointed tip and spiral grooves or flutes, used to drill holes and clear waste from the holes; *see also* dowel bit.

U–V

UF adhesive

Urea-formaldehyde adhesive, available in powder form and then mixed with water before application; some UF adhesives require a catalyst to be mixed in as well.

veneer

A thin sheet or layer of sliced wood, glued or bonded to a surface, usually wood or manu-factured board; or a layer used in manufacturing plywood; to apply such a sheet to a surface.

veneer hammer

A wooden or metal hammer with one thin flat face on its head, used to apply pressure to veneer and remove blisters and air pockets.

vertical grain

The quality of grain of wood produced by plain-sawing.

viscosity

The measurable glutinous or viscous nature of a fluid.

W

warping

A twist or swelling in a piece of lumber, caused by the wood absorbing moisture or drying out.

wavy grain

A regular, wave-like pattern in the same direction as straight grain in a piece of wood.

wild grain

An irregular, random pattern of grain; wild-grain wood is hard to work, and blunts tools quickly.

winding

A term used for warped or twisted wood.

Author's acknowledgments

I have been involved with the woodworking and furniture trades for over 30 years, and have also been involved as a lecturer and course planner in many colleges and university departments of Design and Manufacture. I remember many colleagues and friends. The world of furniture designers and craftsmen is full of lively and interesting people, who gain pleasure from designing and making fine and individual pieces that in themselves give pleasure to recipients. I recognize and thank them for their advice and help.

I have lectured in many design education institutions and I wish to thank my many colleagues for their interest and support. I have also been fortunate to have known many students on these design and craftsmanship courses and have gained much enjoyment from seeing them develop and utilize their professional skills in their chosen careers, in particular those from Rycotewood College, the School of Architecture at Oxford Brookes University and The Furniture College at Letterfrack, Co. Galway.

Other contributors

Michael Bradley who made the plant stand (see pages 295–9) is a woodturner from Farringdon, Oxfordshire, where he lives with his wife and son. He started woodturning with a local furniture maker after graduating in 1969. His continued love for his craft encouraged him to branch out on his own in 1981. He currently has a small workshop in Farringdon, specializing in commissioned pieces.

Having served a four-year apprenticeship in cabinet and chair making, **Roland Gadsdon** who made the circular dining table (see pages 305–10) and the single bed (see pages 331–7) then went into research and development before opening his own workshop making and repairing furniture. For the last eight years he has worked as a lecturer, from which he gains a great deal of satisfaction. Periodically he enjoys making one-of-a-kind pieces of furniture.

Ian Heseltine originally studied at Parnham House in Dorset and then set up his partnership with **Declan O'Donoghue**. Their workshop and studios, SF Furniture in Acton Turville, Gloucestershire, have developed an enviable reputation in the field of furniture design and making with an impressive list of clients. Ian designed and made the glass-topped feature table (see pages 281–6) and it is recognized

that his making abilities are at the forefront of his profession.

Andrew Humphries was apprenticed to his father's furniture making and restoration company, and is now recognized as one of the foremost craftsmen in these trades, having a wide clientele and restoring valuable pieces for many influential owners and lovers of quality classic furniture. For many years he taught these skills at Rycotewood College, and contributed to the education of fine craftsmen and restorers when the college's reputation was at its height; a fact recognized by past students who have successfully developed their own businesses. He made the chessboard (see pages 244–7), the mirror/picture frame (see pages 251–3) and the breakfast tray (see pages 311–15).

After a grammar school education, **Jack Lazenby** D.L.C. (Hons) who designed and made the small box (see pages 265–9) and the all-purpose workbench (see pages 270–6) apprenticed as an Engineering Patternmaker from 1942–7, going on to train at Loughborough College (now University) where he developed a passionate interest in the Arts and Crafts Movement and was influenced, helped, and encouraged by Edward Barnsley CBE. He first became a lecturer in Furniture Making and Design at Rycotewood

College from 1950 and was Chief Examiner in Fine Craft and Design for GCSE and A-Level with the University of Oxford Delegate of Local Examinations. Jack rejoined Rycotewood in the mid-1970s, and was an inspiration to many students between then and his retirement in the late 1990s. His craftsmanship skills and teaching ability helped students to reach the highest standards, while assisting the college to attain and maintain its premier position as one of the country's leading institutions. Many past students recognize the contribution that he made to their personal and professional development. Now retired, he continues to pursue his love of furniture making.

David Ramsey who made the pergola (see pages 277–80) and the curved back garden bench (see pages 353–65) is a furniture and interior designer with 30 years experience in commercial and private work. He studied at the Royal College of Art to obtain a Master of Design. His work has included designing furniture and interiors for hotels, in particular for bedrooms and bathrooms, and he has undertaken the complete design of the structure and interior of a 4-star hotel in Saudi Arabia. He has also taught arts and crafts in a grammar school and in several colleges. New ventures include the restoration of antique furniture.

Chris Smith who made the modular storage cubes (see pages 316–23) trained at Rycotewood College, and then set up a workshop in his home village of Tackley in Oxfordshire. Working mainly by himself, at first making only small items on speculation or to order, he now works with a wide range of architects, interior designers, shops, and furniture manufacturers.

One of the most original and capable furniture designers who graduated from the Royal College of Art in the late 1950s, **Alan Tilbury** has had an outstanding career as both a teacher and practitioner. He has lectured in the Furniture School at the RCA for over 30 years and has designed furniture for many top British and European companies, as well as making special pieces for individual and corporate clients. He contributed to the section on "Design and construction" (see pages 48–65).

Publisher's acknowledgments

The Publishers would like to thank the following for their help with this book:

Mrs K. Medlock, Chandlers Ford (for permission to photograph her workbench and in her home)

Mr Ian White, Princes Risborough (for permission to photograph in his workshop)

For providing props for photography:

Peacock Blue, 201 King's Road London SW6. Tel: + 44 (0)20 7384 3400 for Boston checked bedlinen (single bed project)

Holding Company, 243–245 King's Road London SW3 Tel: + 44 (0)20 7352 1600 for six-drawer wicker chest (home office project)

Isaac Lord, Desborough Road High Wycombe HP11 2QN. Tel. +44 (0) 1494 462 121 (for tools)

Marilyn Phipps, The Battery Admiralty Walk Seasalter Kent CT5 4ET. Tel: + 44 (0)1227 277 994 for cut-out birds (birdhouse project)

Metabo UK Ltd, 25 Majestic Road Nursling Industrial Estate Southampton SO16 0YT (for machinery)

Purves & Purves, 80–81 Tottenham Court Road London W1T 9QE. Tel: + 44 (0)20 7580 8223 for suede square footstools (chessboard project), ivory Phoenix chairs (dining table project) and Zen rug (home office project)

Record Power Ltd, Parkway Works Sheffield S9 3BL

Smee Timber Ltd, Smokehall Lane Winsford Cheshire (for timber)

Index

Page numbers in *italics* indicate an illustration.

A

index

index

H

hacksaws, 81, 221
half-lap joints, 149–52, 410
half-round spokeshave, 136
hammers, 187–8
hand drills, 140, *141*, 144–5
hand power routers, 129–31, *130*, 132–5
hand router plane, *102*, 103
hand saws, 410
hand sledge, 188, *188*
handles, 195
hardboard, 35–6
hardware, 191–5
hardwood, 13, 15–20, 410
  buying, 29–30
  storage, 31
haunch, 410
headstock, 410
headstock spindle, 410
health and safety, 74–5
heartwood, 13, 410
hemlock, 21
hinges, 191–2
home office, 393–400, *401*
honeycombing, 27, *28*
honing, 98–9, 410
hook scraper, 177, *177*
hot glue, 182
hot-dish stand, 237–9, *239*
HSS (high-speed steel), 410

I

in-cannel gouge, 122, *124*
infeed, 410
inlay, 410
interlocked grain, 26, *26*
internal pin chuck, 217
iroko, 18

J

jack plane, *80*, 81, 100, *101*, 413
Japanese chisels, 124–5, *125*
Japanese dovetail joints, 169
Japanese saws, 118
Japanese waterstone, *98*, 99
jarrah, 18
jelutong, 18
jig work, 184
jigs, 411
jigsaws, 81, 92–4, 117, 411
joint stay, 193
jointer plane, 100, *101*, 413
joints, 56
  biscuit, 131
  butt, 131, 135
  dado, 163–6
  decorative, 64–5
  dovetail, 56, 167–71
  half-lap, 149–52
  mortise-and-tenon, 56, 153–62

K

kerf, 89, 411
keyhole saw, *116*, 117, 120
kickback, 411
kiln drying, lumber, 25, 411
kingwood, 18
knives
  craft/veneer, 206, *207*
  filler, 196, *197*
  marking, 79, 84, *84*, 411
  putty, 196, *197*
knobs, 195
knock-down hardware, 194
knots, 28, *28*, 411

L

lacewood, 19
lacquers, 203, 204–5
laminating, 64, 411
laminboard, 34, 411
larch, 21
latewood, *14*, 411
lathes, 215–16, *215*, 217–20, 297, 411
leather, 45, 65
leather strop, 99, *214*, 416
lignum vitae, 19
lime (tree), 19
liming, 63
linen cupboard, *9*, *192*, 366–74, *373*

index

index

index

First published in 2004 by Bay Books, an imprint of Murdoch Magazines Pty Ltd

Reprinted in 2004

Copyright© 2004 Murdoch Books®

ISBN 1 74045 279 8

All rights reserved. No part of this publication may be reproduced, stored in a retrieval system, or transmitted in any form or by any means, electronic, mechanical, photocopying, recording or otherwise, without the prior permission of the copyright owner.

Senior Commissioning Editor: **Karen Hemingway**

Managing Editor: **Anna Osborn**

Design Manager: **Helen Taylor**

Editors: **Dawn Henderson, Alastair Laing, Ruth Matheson,**

Claire Musters, Angela Newton

Consultants: **John Bowler, Greg Cheetham, Ian Kearey, Mark Ramuz**

Styled and location photography: **David Brittain**

Studio and location photography: **Dominic Blackmore, Alan Holtham**

Additional photography: Lorna Rose (pp. 16, 18), Murdoch Books Picture Library (p. 22), Andre Martin (p. 52), Tony Lyon (p. 59), Joe Filshie (p. 60), Valerie Martin (p. 193 bottom left)

Photography art direction: **Marylouise Brammer**

Design concept: **Tracy Loughlin**

Material in this book was originally published in *The Essential Guide to Woodwork*

Murdoch Books® is a trademark of Murdoch Magazines Pty Ltd

Colour separation by Colourscan, Singapore

Printed by Sing Cheong Printing Co. Ltd.

PRINTED IN HONG KONG